Kamisama Kiss

uzuki

CHARACTERS

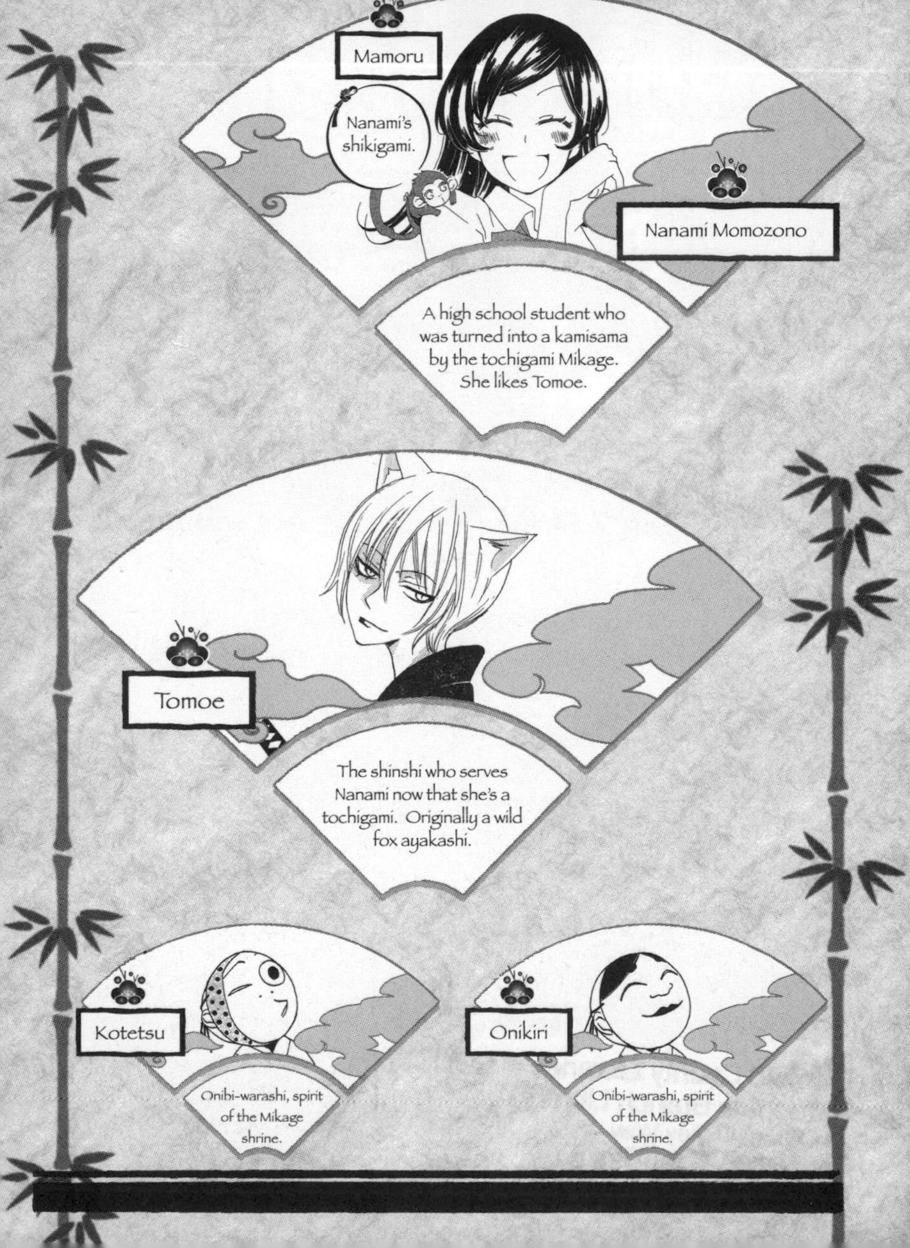
Mamoru
Nanami's shikigami.
Nanami Momozono
A high school student who was turned into a kamisama by the tochigami Mikage. She likes Tomoe.
Tomoe
The shinshi who serves Nanami now that she's a tochigami. Originally a wild fox ayakashi.
Onikiri
Onibi-warashi, spirit of the Mikage shrine.
Kotetsu
Onibi-warashi, spirit of the Mikage shrine.

Mizuki

Nanami's second shinshi. The incarnation of a white snake.

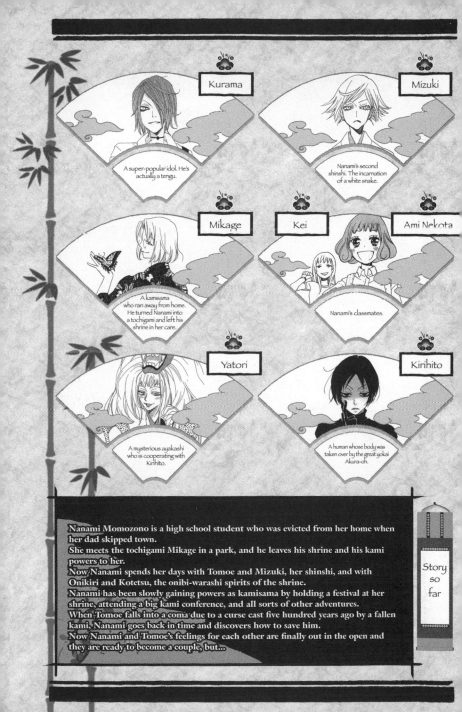

Kurama

A super-popular idol. He's actually a tengu.

Kei

Ami Nekota

Nanami's classmates.

Mikage

A kamisama who ran away from home. He turned Nanami into a tochigami and left his shrine in her care.

Kirihito

A human whose body was taken over by the great yokai Akura-oh.

Yatori

A mysterious ayakashi who is cooperating with Kirihito.

Story so far

Nanami Momozono is a high school student who was evicted from her home when her dad skipped town.
She meets the tochigami Mikage in a park, and he leaves his shrine and his kami powers to her.
Now Nanami spends her days with Tomoe and Mizuki, her shinshi, and with Onikiri and Kotetsu, the onibi-warashi spirits of the shrine.
Nanami has been slowly gaining powers as kamisama by holding a festival at her shrine, attending a big kami conference, and all sorts of other adventures.
When Tomoe falls into a coma due to a curse cast five hundred years ago by a fallen kami, Nanami goes back in time and discovers how to save him.
Now Nanami and Tomoe's feelings for each other are finally out in the open and they are ready to become a couple, but...

Kamisama Kiss

Volume 18
CONTENTS

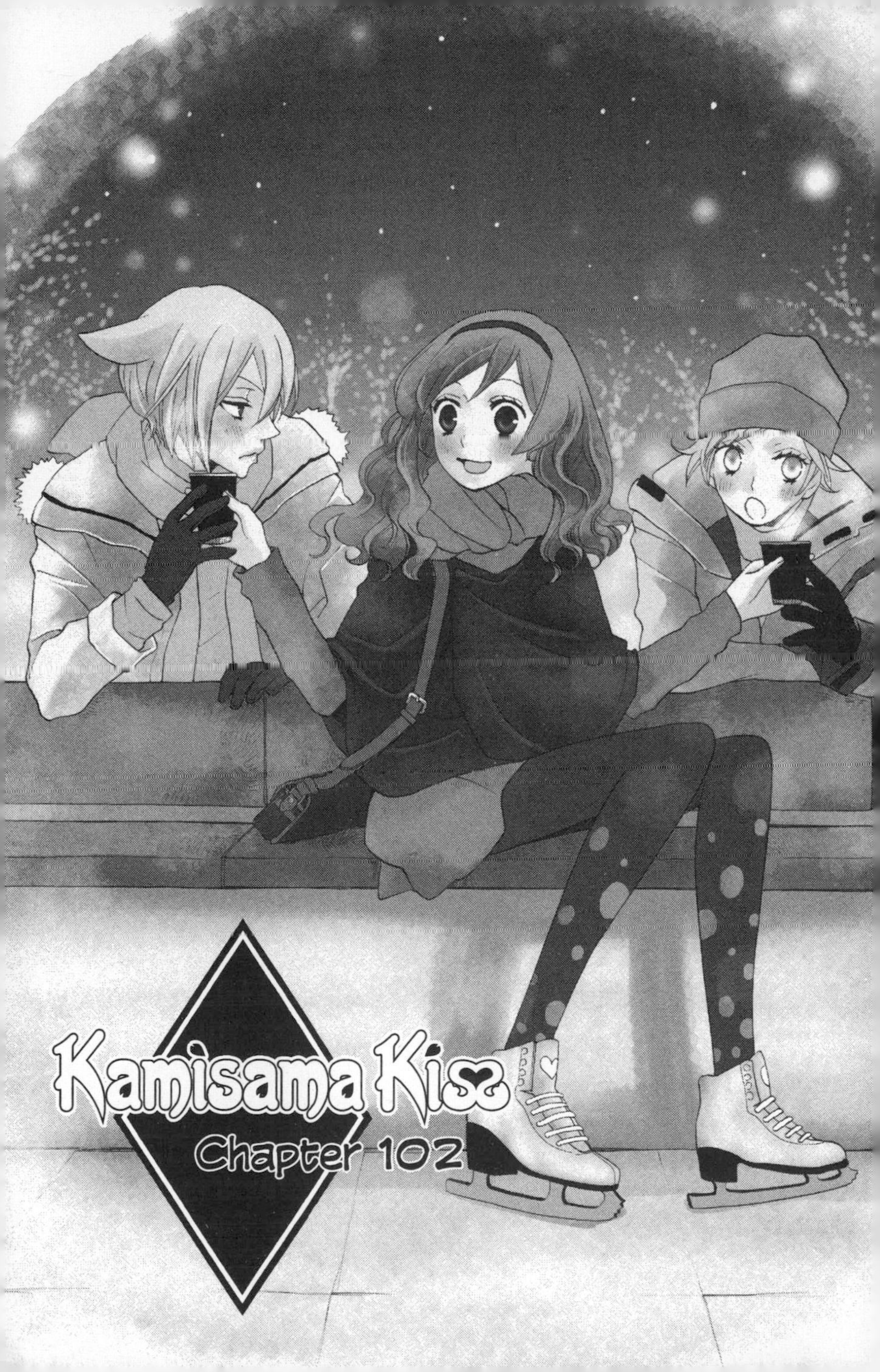
Kamisama Kiss
Chapter 102

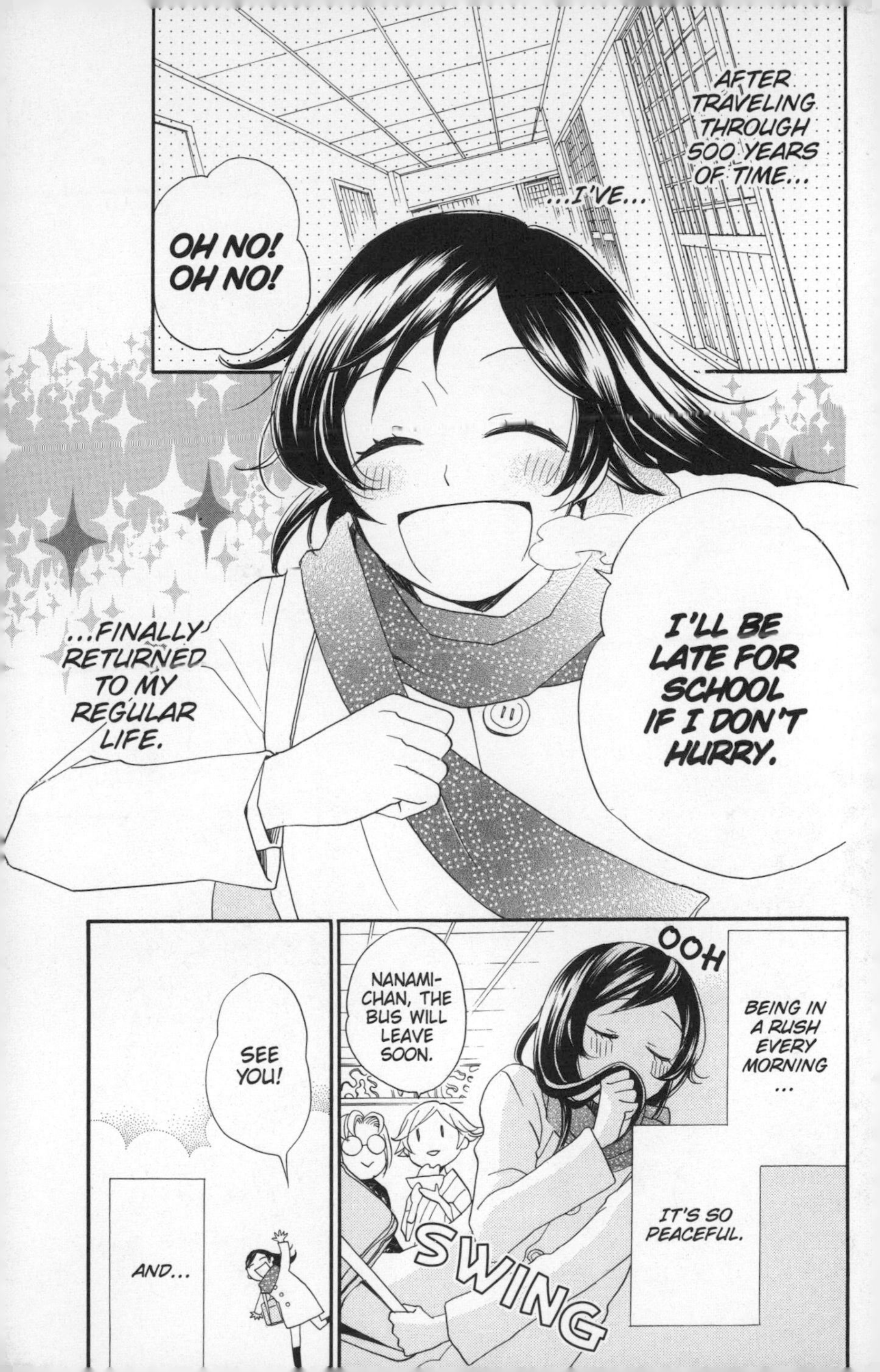
AFTER TRAVELING THROUGH 500 YEARS OF TIME...
...I'VE...
OH NO! OH NO!
I'LL BE LATE FOR SCHOOL IF I DON'T HURRY.
...FINALLY RETURNED TO MY REGULAR LIFE.
OOH
BEING IN A RUSH EVERY MORNING ...
NANAMI-CHAN, THE BUS WILL LEAVE SOON.
IT'S SO PEACEFUL.
SWING
SEE YOU!
AND...

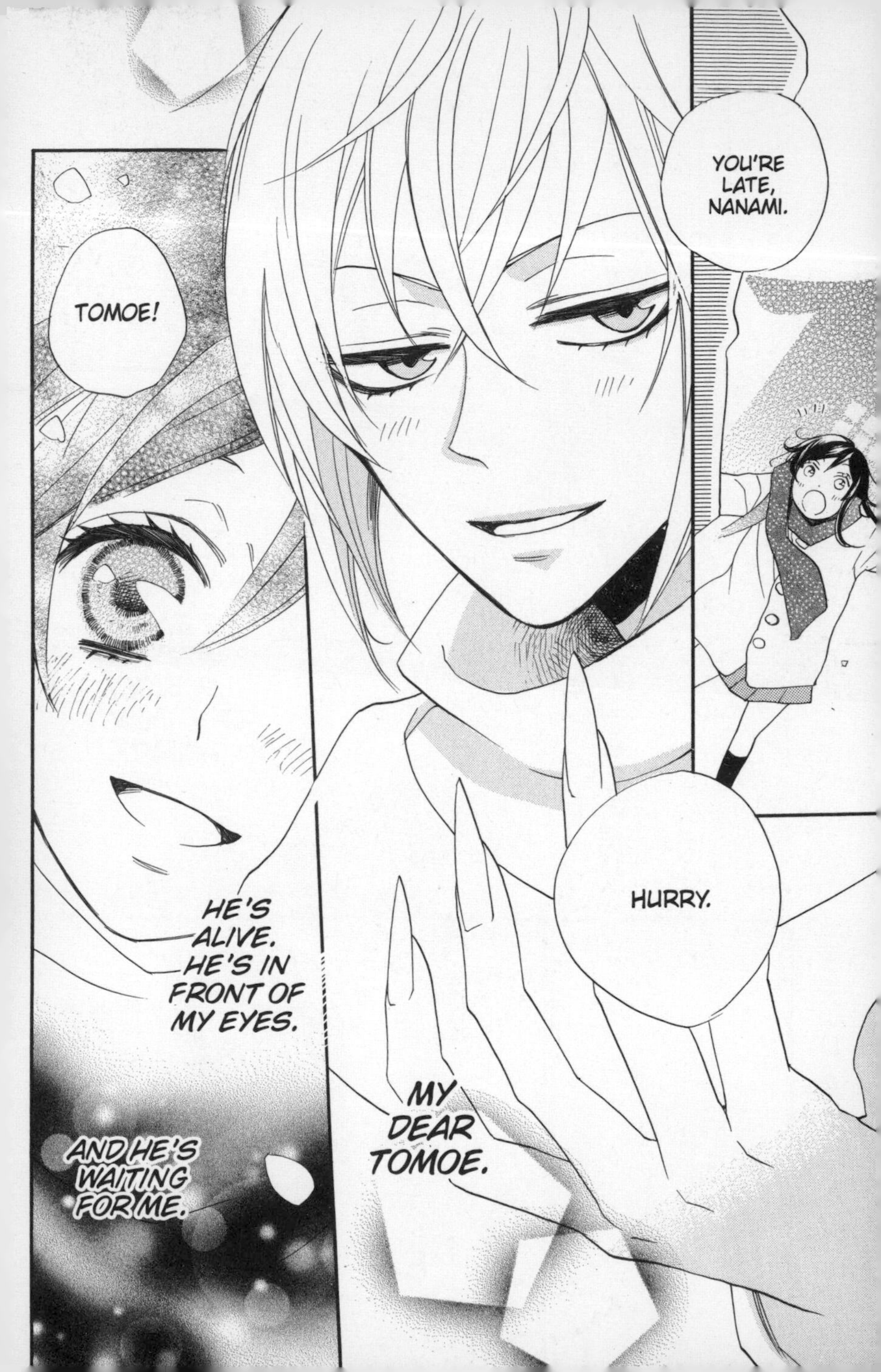
YOU'RE LATE, NANAMI.
HURRY.
MY DEAR TOMOE.
TOMOE!
HE'S ALIVE. HE'S IN FRONT OF MY EYES.
AND HE'S WAITING FOR ME.

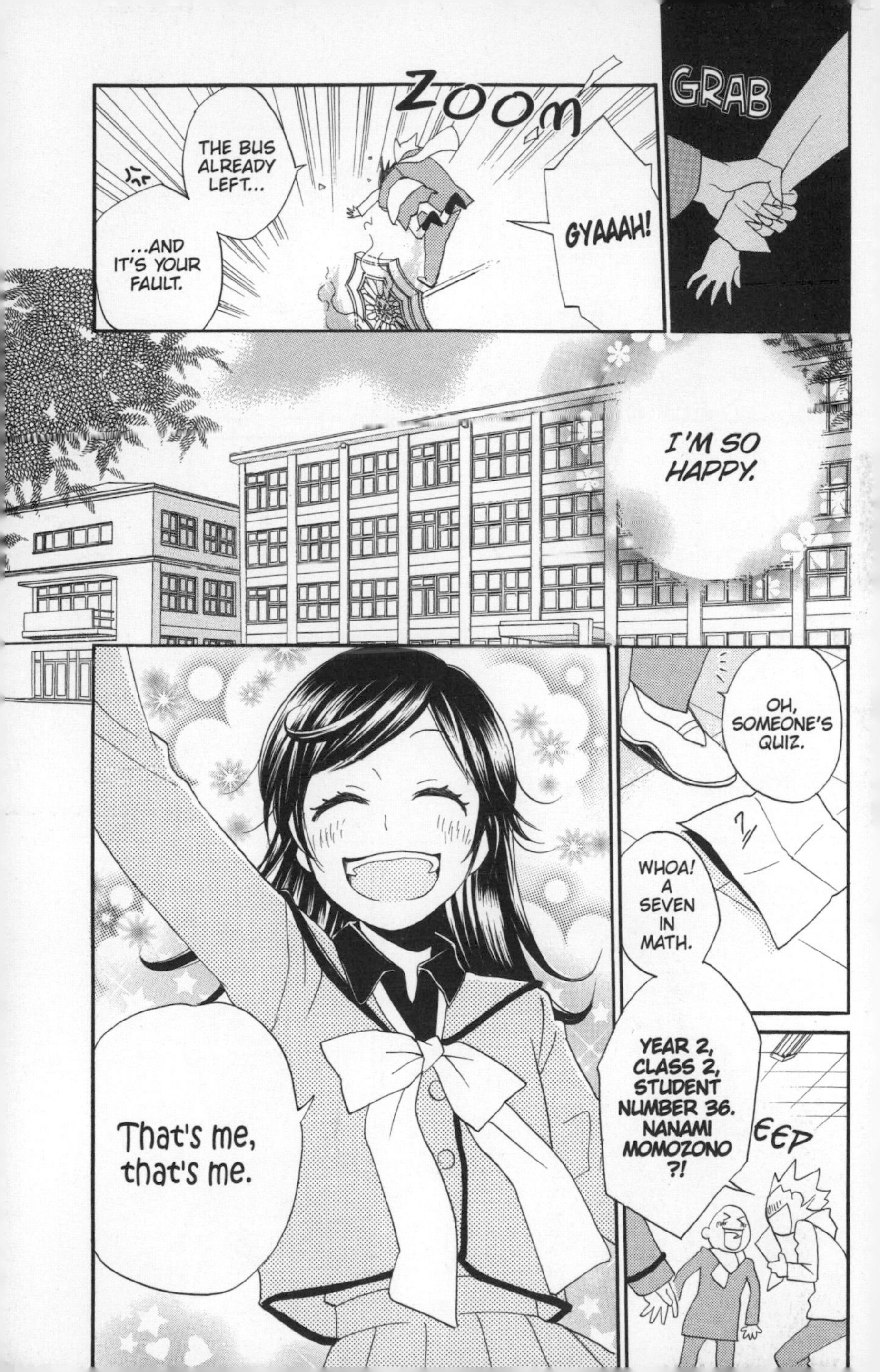
GRAB
ZOOM
GYAAAH!
THE BUS ALREADY LEFT...
...AND IT'S YOUR FAULT.
I'M SO HAPPY.
OH, SOMEONE'S QUIZ.
WHOA! A SEVEN IN MATH.
YEAR 2, CLASS 2, STUDENT NUMBER 36. NANAMI MOMOZONO ?!
EEP
That's me, that's me.

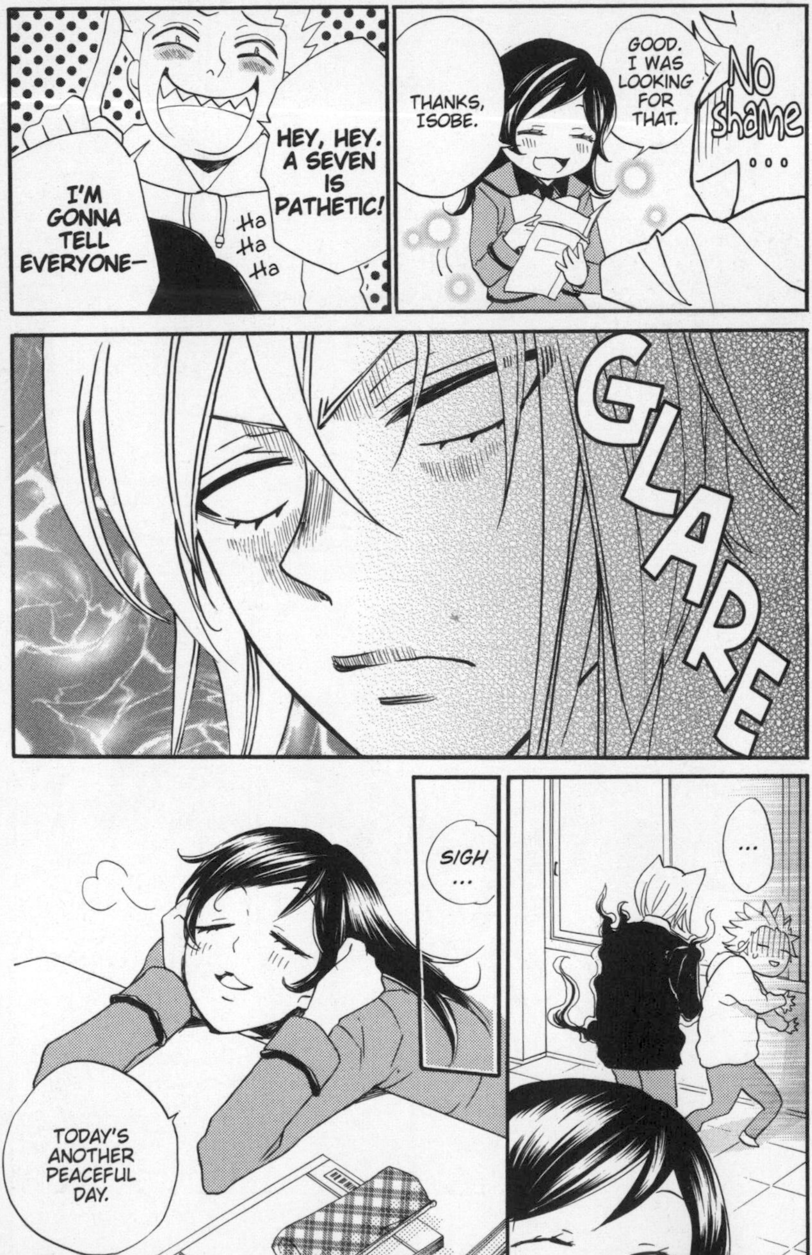
No shame ...
GOOD. I WAS LOOKING FOR THAT.
THANKS, ISOBE.
HEY, HEY. A SEVEN IS PATHETIC!
Ha Ha Ha
I'M GONNA TELL EVERYONE—
GLARE
...
SIGH ...
TODAY'S ANOTHER PEACEFUL DAY.

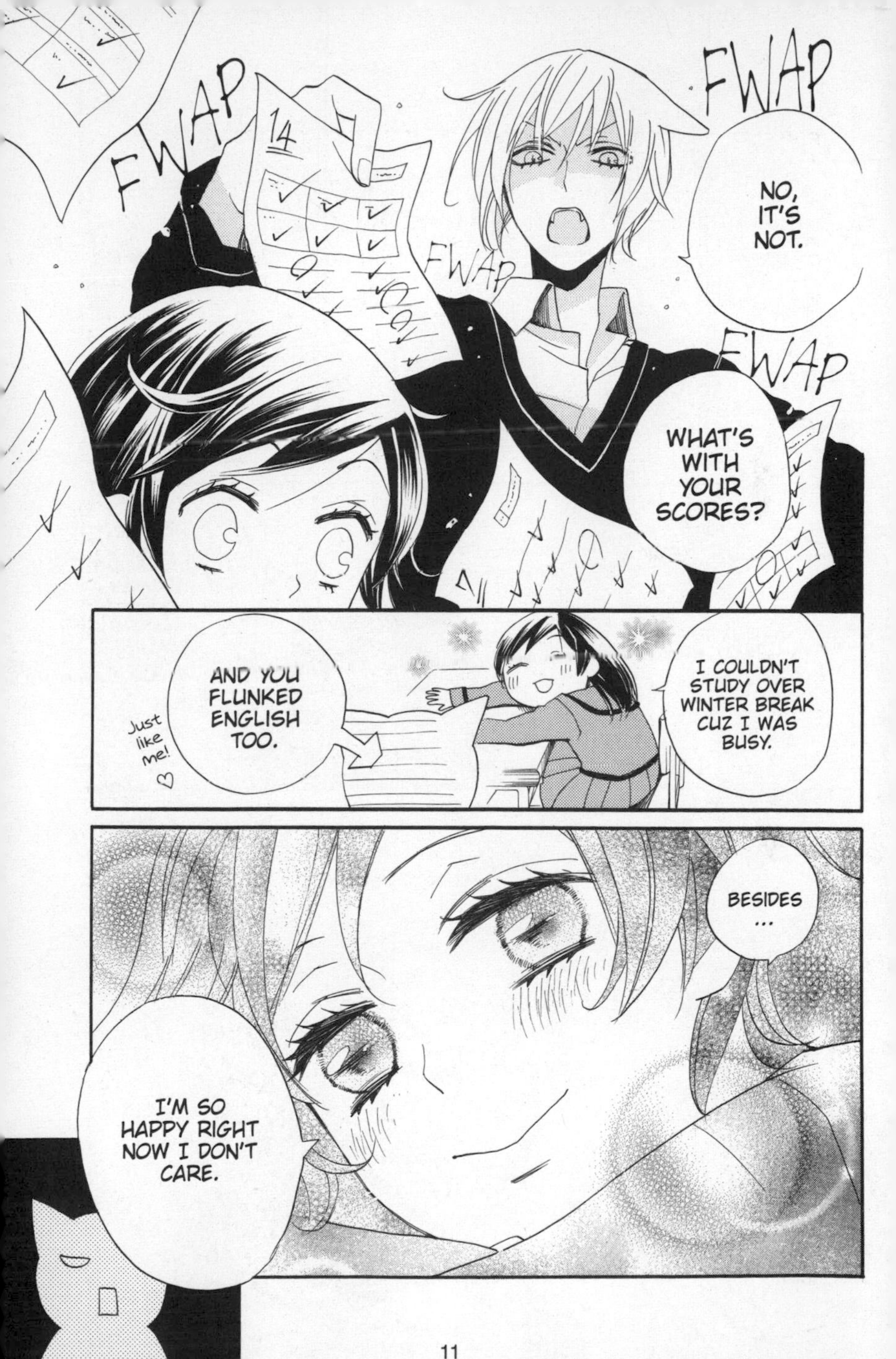
FWAP
NO, IT'S NOT.
FWAP
FWAP
FWAP
WHAT'S WITH YOUR SCORES?
I COULDN'T STUDY OVER WINTER BREAK CUZ I WAS BUSY.
AND YOU FLUNKED ENGLISH TOO.
Just like me! ♡
BESIDES ...
I'M SO HAPPY RIGHT NOW I DON'T CARE.

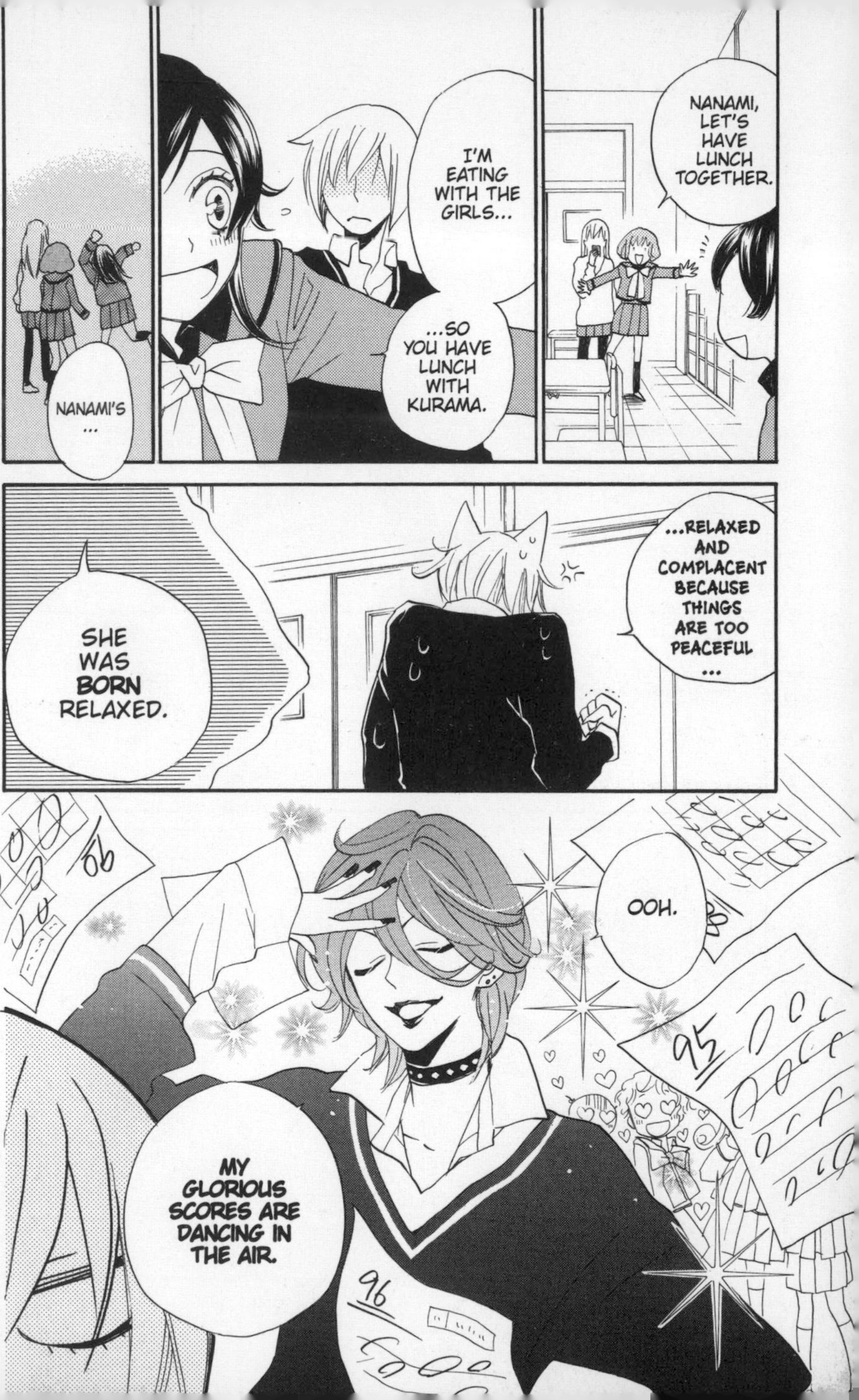
NANAMI, LET'S HAVE LUNCH TOGETHER.
I'M EATING WITH THE GIRLS...
...SO YOU HAVE LUNCH WITH KURAMA.
NANAMI'S ...
...RELAXED AND COMPLACENT BECAUSE THINGS ARE TOO PEACEFUL ...
SHE WAS BORN RELAXED.
OOH.
MY GLORIOUS SCORES ARE DANCING IN THE AIR.

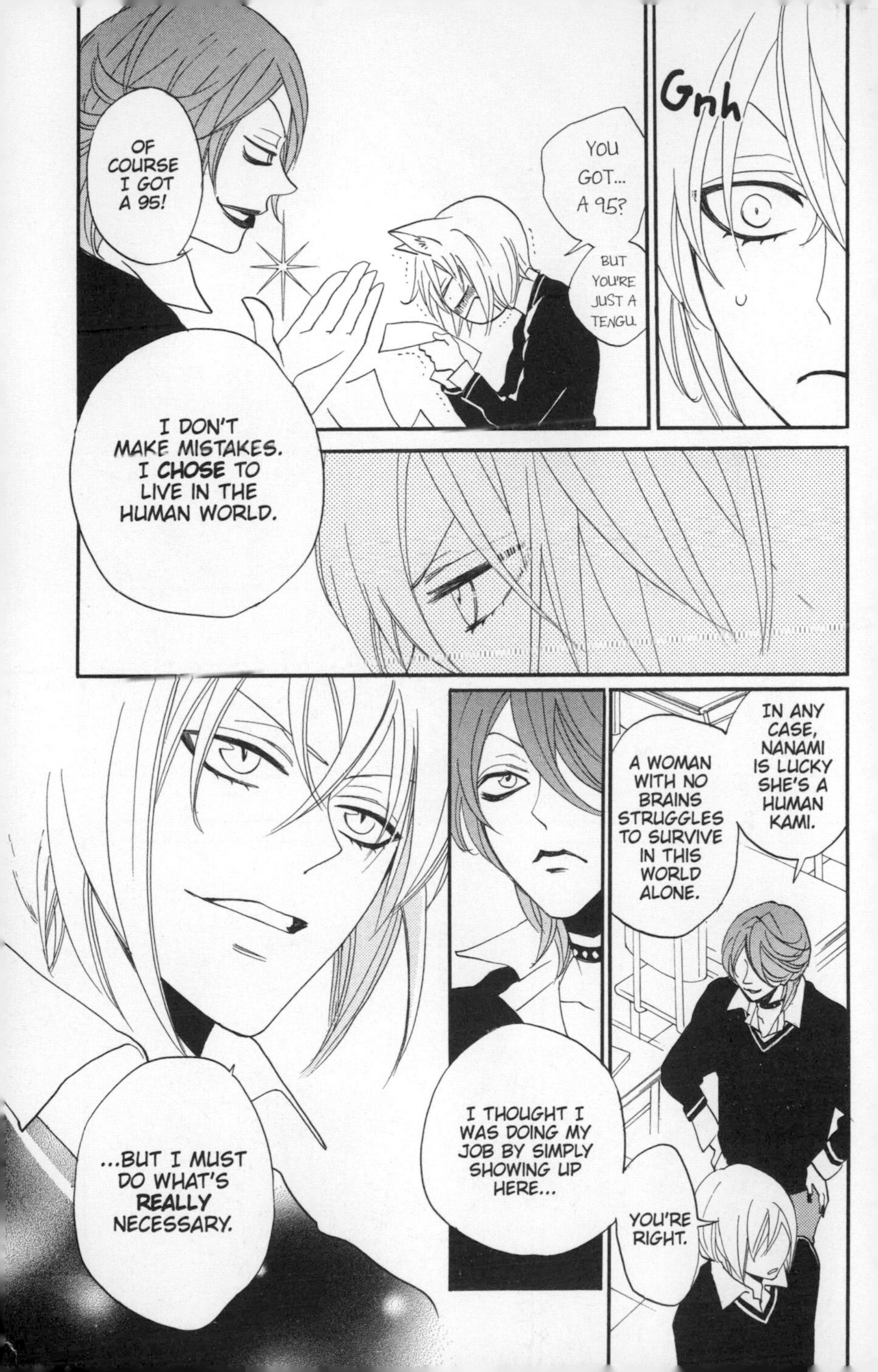
Gnh
YOU GOT... A 95?
BUT YOU'RE JUST A TENGU.
OF COURSE I GOT A 95!
I DON'T MAKE MISTAKES. I CHOSE TO LIVE IN THE HUMAN WORLD.
IN ANY CASE, NANAMI IS LUCKY SHE'S A HUMAN KAMI.
A WOMAN WITH NO BRAINS STRUGGLES TO SURVIVE IN THIS WORLD ALONE.
YOU'RE RIGHT.
I THOUGHT I WAS DOING MY JOB BY SIMPLY SHOWING UP HERE...
...BUT I MUST DO WHAT'S REALLY NECESSARY.

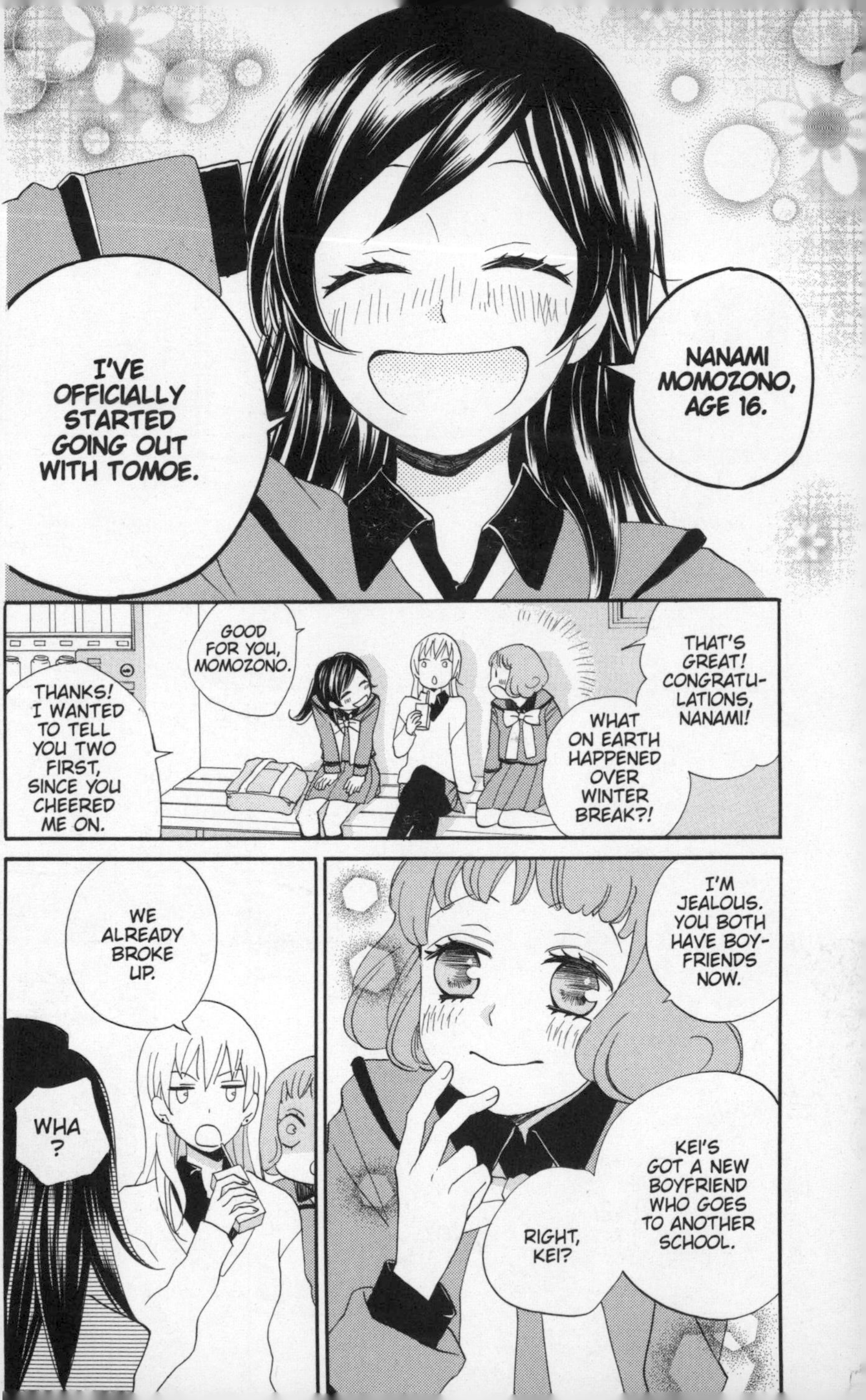
NANAMI MOMOZONO, AGE 16.
I'VE OFFICIALLY STARTED GOING OUT WITH TOMOE.
THAT'S GREAT! CONGRATULATIONS, NANAMI!
WHAT ON EARTH HAPPENED OVER WINTER BREAK?!
GOOD FOR YOU, MOMOZONO.
THANKS! I WANTED TO TELL YOU TWO FIRST, SINCE YOU CHEERED ME ON.
I'M JEALOUS. YOU BOTH HAVE BOYFRIENDS NOW.
KEI'S GOT A NEW BOYFRIEND WHO GOES TO ANOTHER SCHOOL.
RIGHT, KEI?
WE ALREADY BROKE UP.
WHA?

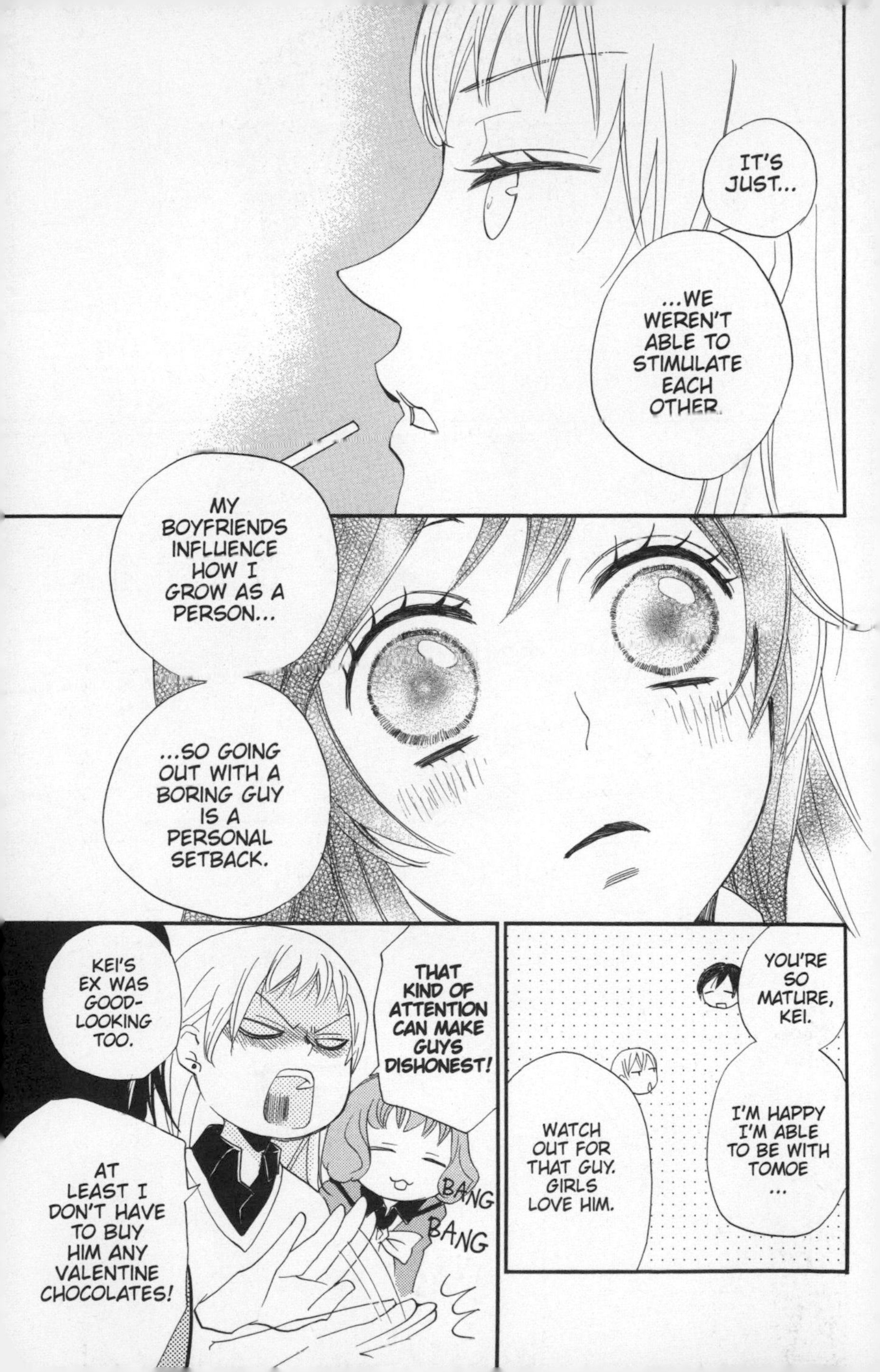
IT'S JUST...
...WE WEREN'T ABLE TO STIMULATE EACH OTHER.
MY BOYFRIENDS INFLUENCE HOW I GROW AS A PERSON...
...SO GOING OUT WITH A BORING GUY IS A PERSONAL SETBACK.
YOU'RE SO MATURE, KEI.
I'M HAPPY I'M ABLE TO BE WITH TOMOE ...
WATCH OUT FOR THAT GUY. GIRLS LOVE HIM.
THAT KIND OF ATTENTION CAN MAKE GUYS DISHONEST!
KEI'S EX WAS GOOD-LOOKING TOO.
AT LEAST I DON'T HAVE TO BUY HIM ANY VALENTINE CHOCOLATES!
BANG
BANG

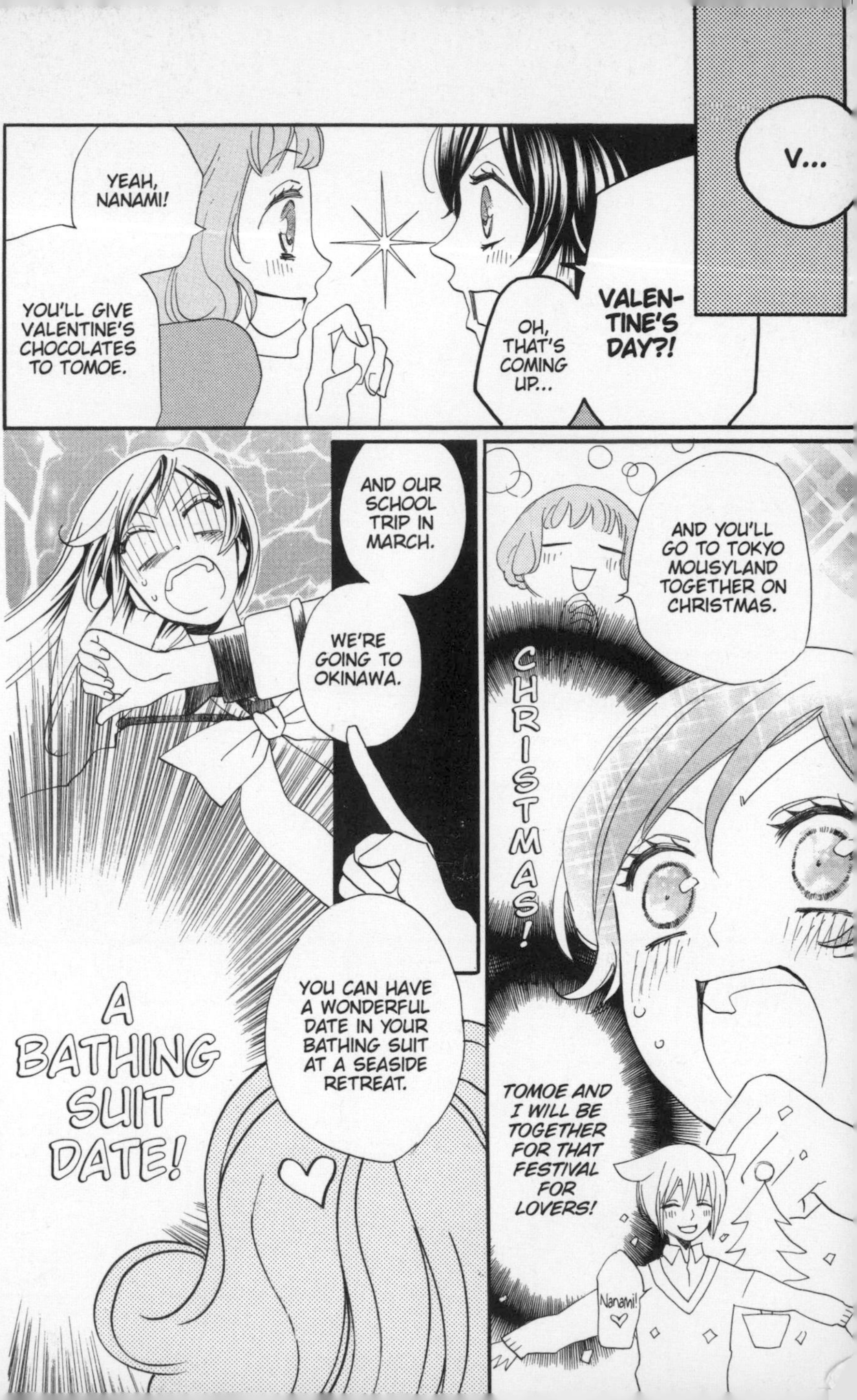
V...
VALENTINE'S DAY?!
OH, THAT'S COMING UP...
YEAH, NANAMI!
YOU'LL GIVE VALENTINE'S CHOCOLATES TO TOMOE.
AND YOU'LL GO TO TOKYO MOUSYLAND TOGETHER ON CHRISTMAS.
CHRISTMAS!
TOMOE AND I WILL BE TOGETHER FOR THAT FESTIVAL FOR LOVERS!
Nanami!
AND OUR SCHOOL TRIP IN MARCH.
WE'RE GOING TO OKINAWA.
YOU CAN HAVE A WONDERFUL DATE IN YOUR BATHING SUIT AT A SEASIDE RETREAT.
A BATHING SUIT DATE!

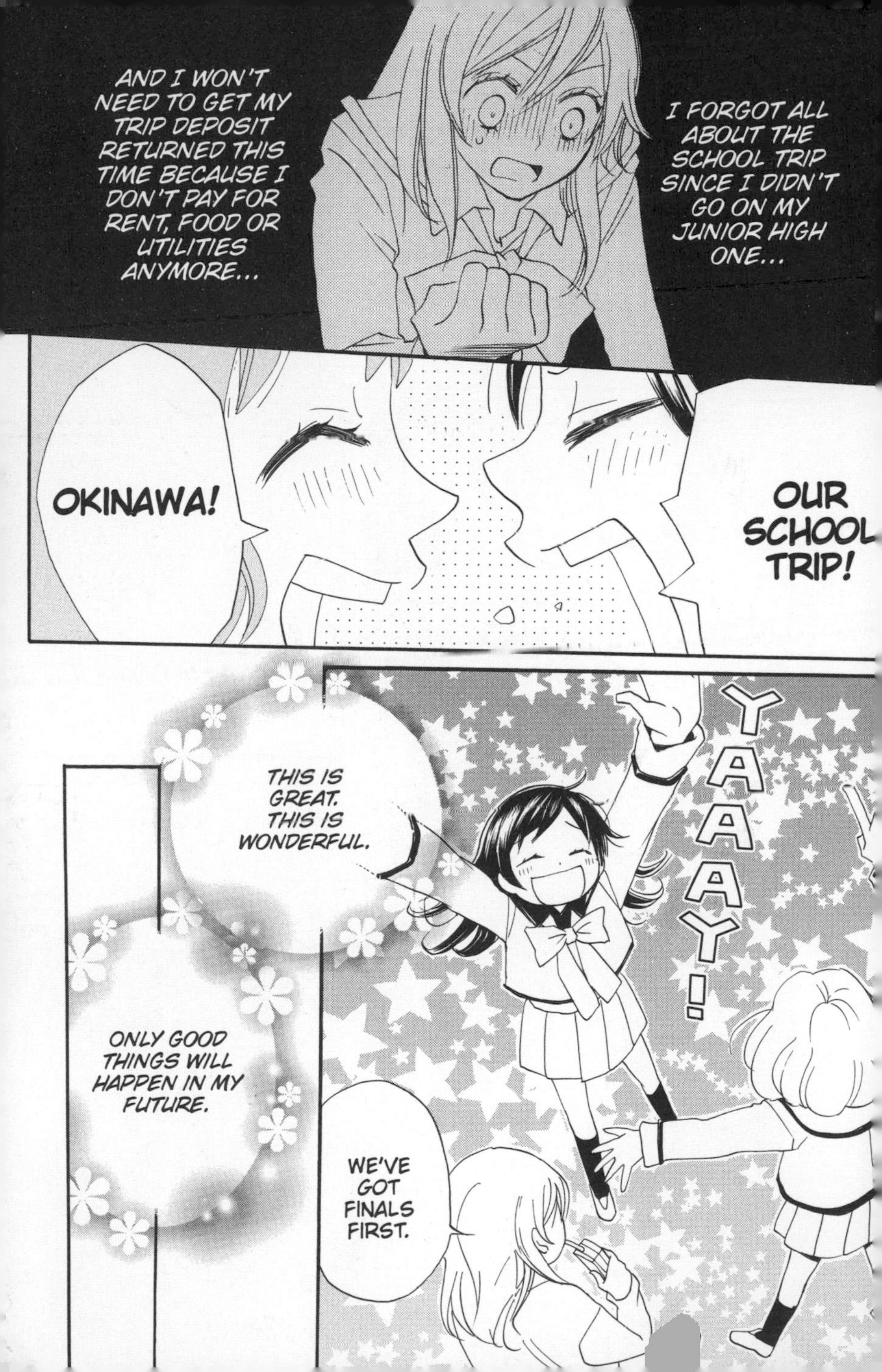
I FORGOT ALL ABOUT THE SCHOOL TRIP SINCE I DIDN'T GO ON MY JUNIOR HIGH ONE...
AND I WON'T NEED TO GET MY TRIP DEPOSIT RETURNED THIS TIME BECAUSE I DON'T PAY FOR RENT, FOOD OR UTILITIES ANYMORE...
OUR SCHOOL TRIP!
OKINAWA!
YAAAAY!
THIS IS GREAT. THIS IS WONDERFUL.
WE'VE GOT FINALS FIRST.
ONLY GOOD THINGS WILL HAPPEN IN MY FUTURE.

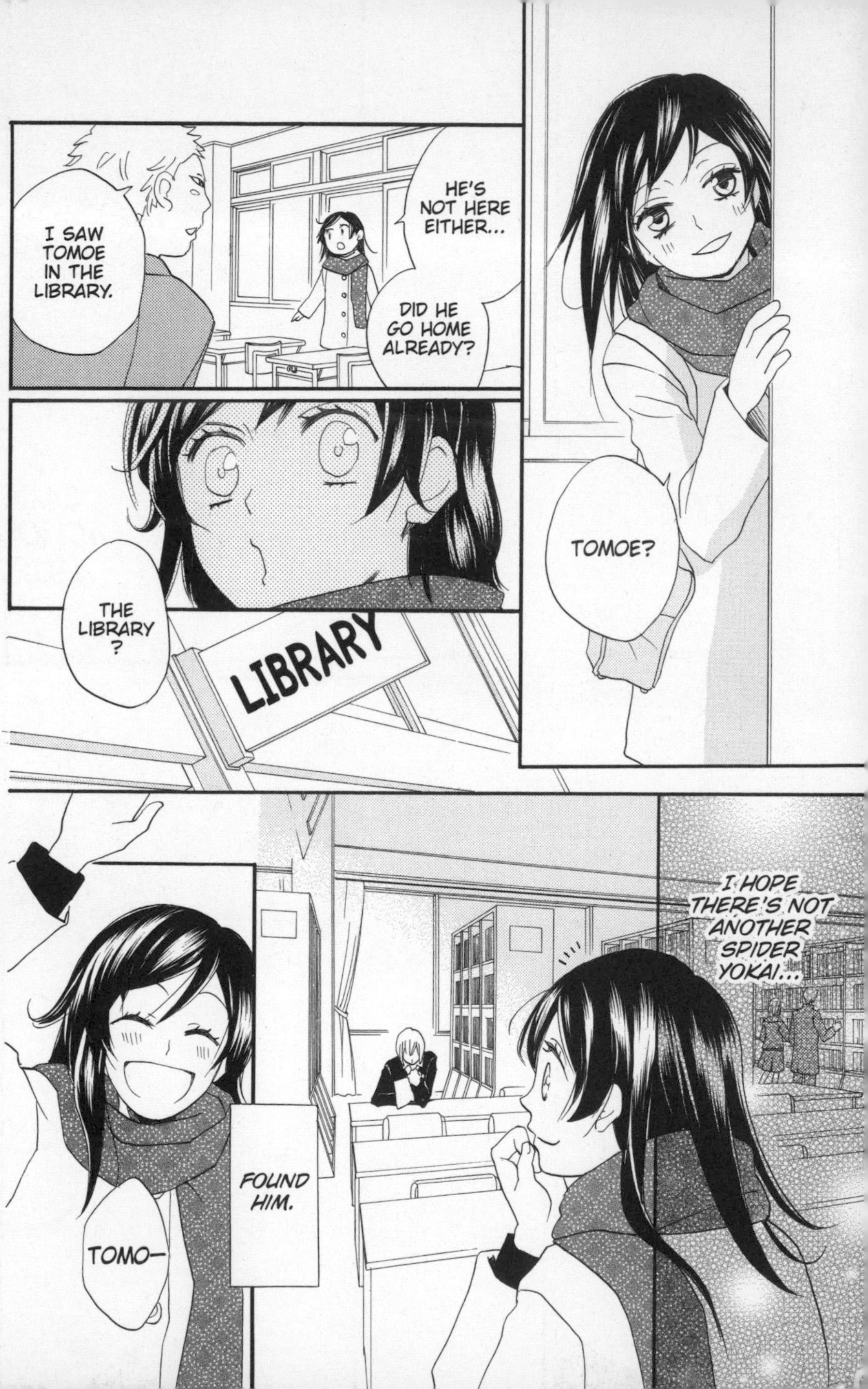
TOMOE?
HE'S NOT HERE EITHER...
DID HE GO HOME ALREADY?
I SAW TOMOE IN THE LIBRARY.
THE LIBRARY?
LIBRARY
I HOPE THERE'S NOT ANOTHER SPIDER YOKAI...
FOUND HIM.
TOMO—

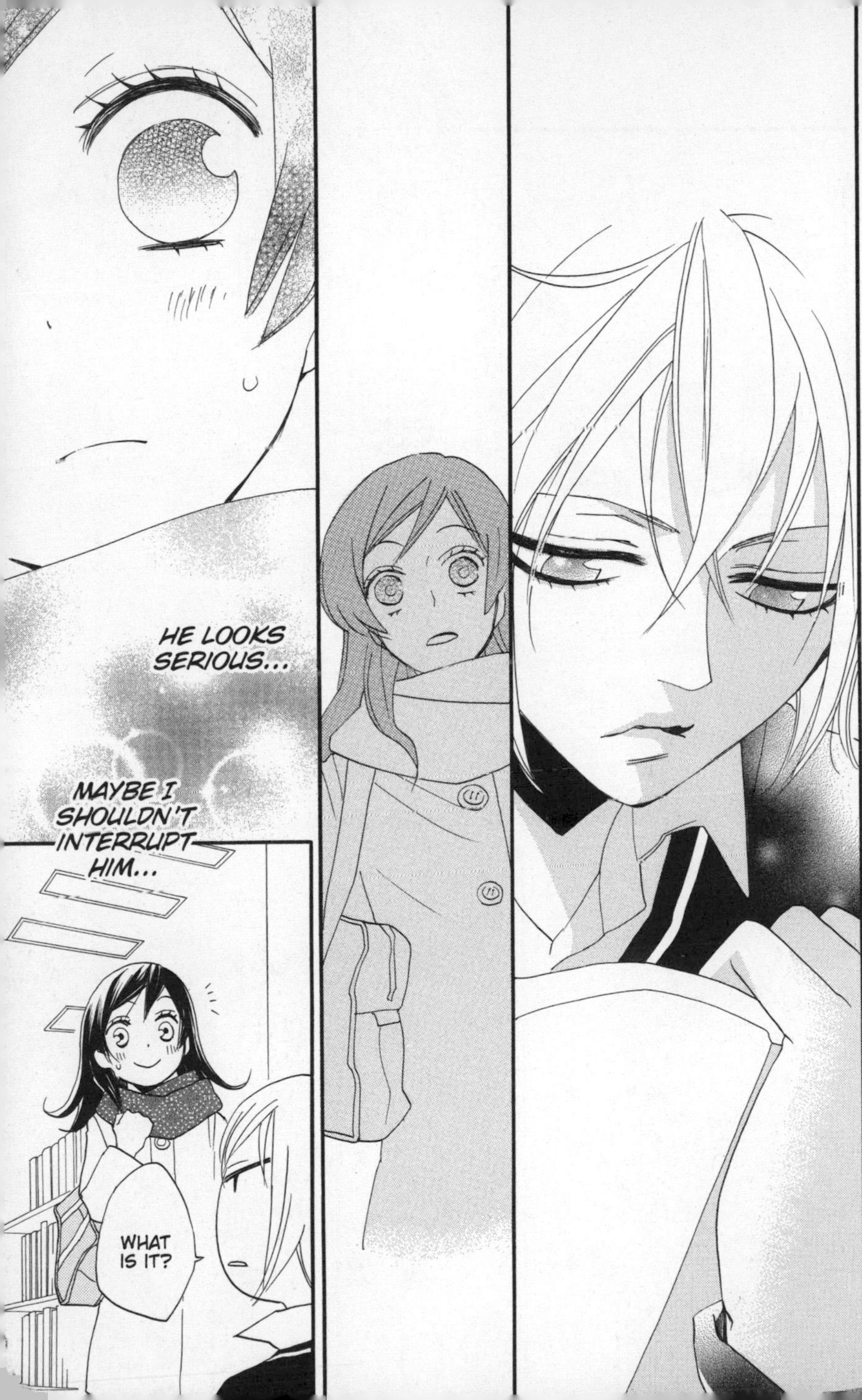
HE LOOKS SERIOUS...
MAYBE I SHOULDN'T INTERRUPT HIM...
WHAT IS IT?

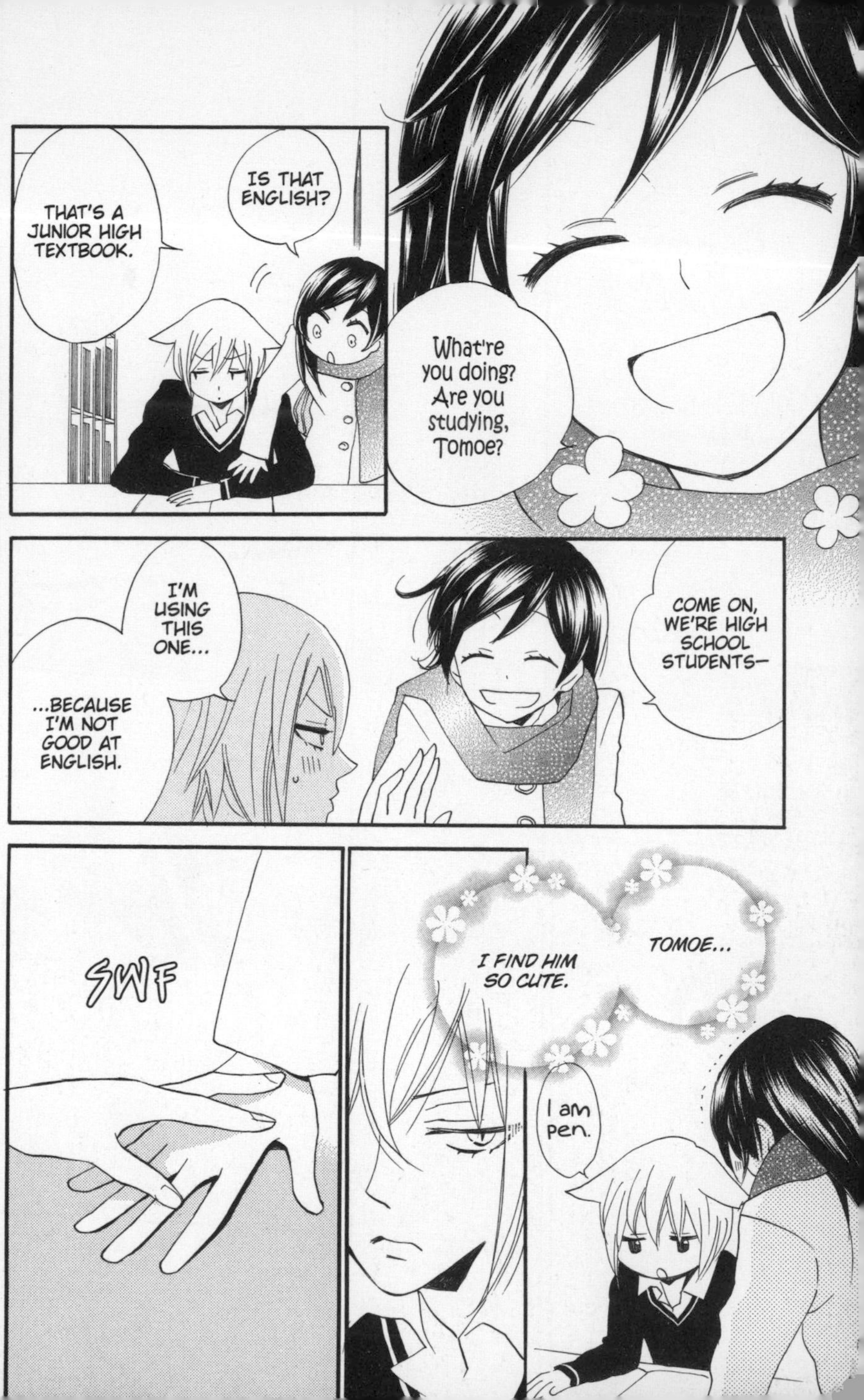
What're you doing? Are you studying, Tomoe?
IS THAT ENGLISH?
THAT'S A JUNIOR HIGH TEXTBOOK.
COME ON, WE'RE HIGH SCHOOL STUDENTS—
I'M USING THIS ONE...
...BECAUSE I'M NOT GOOD AT ENGLISH.
TOMOE...
I FIND HIM SO CUTE.
I am pen.
SWF

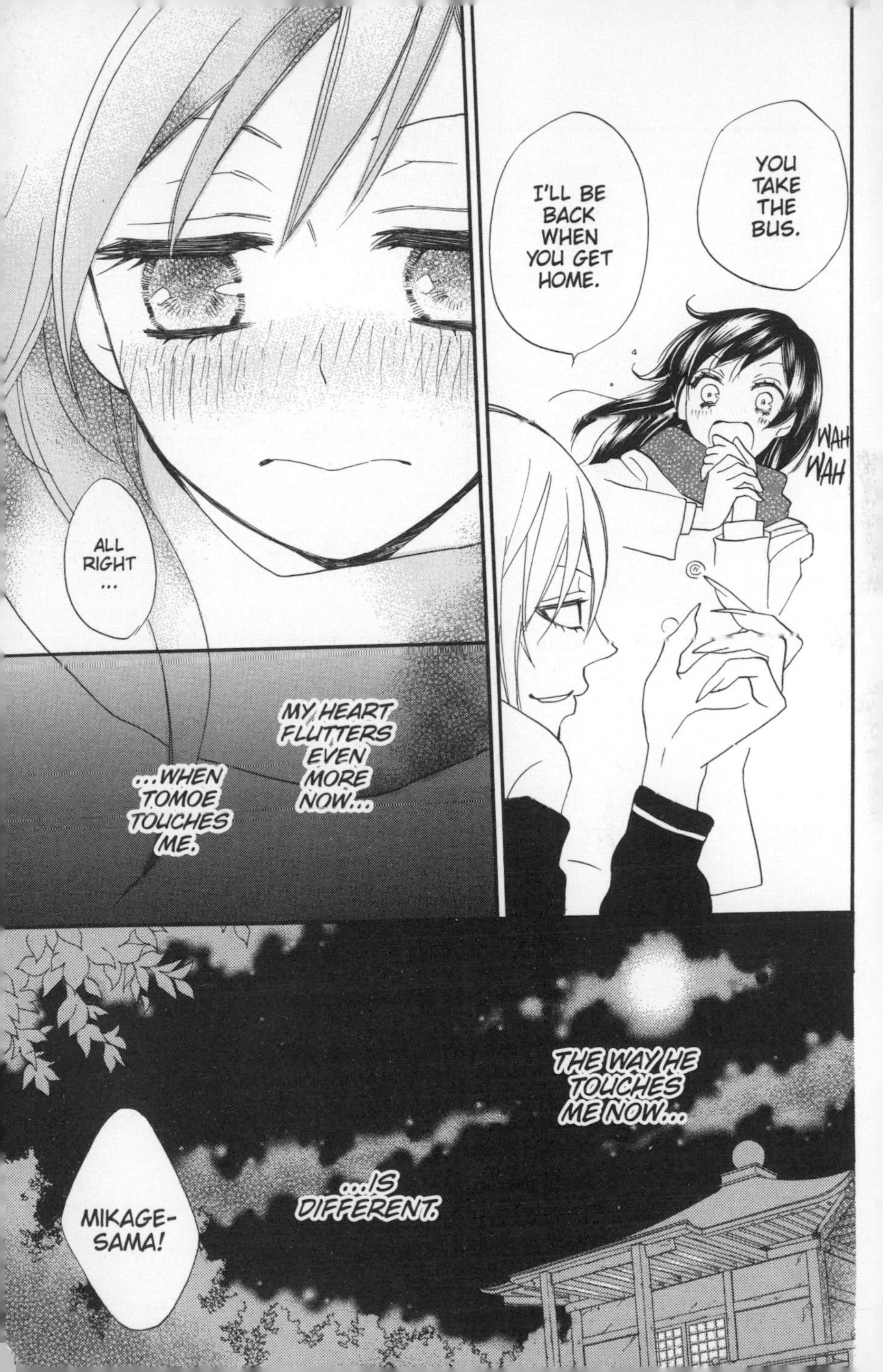
YOU TAKE THE BUS.
I'LL BE BACK WHEN YOU GET HOME.
WAH WAH
ALL RIGHT...
MY HEART FLUTTERS EVEN MORE NOW...
...WHEN TOMOE TOUCHES ME.
THE WAY HE TOUCHES ME NOW...
...IS DIFFERENT.
MIKAGE-SAMA!

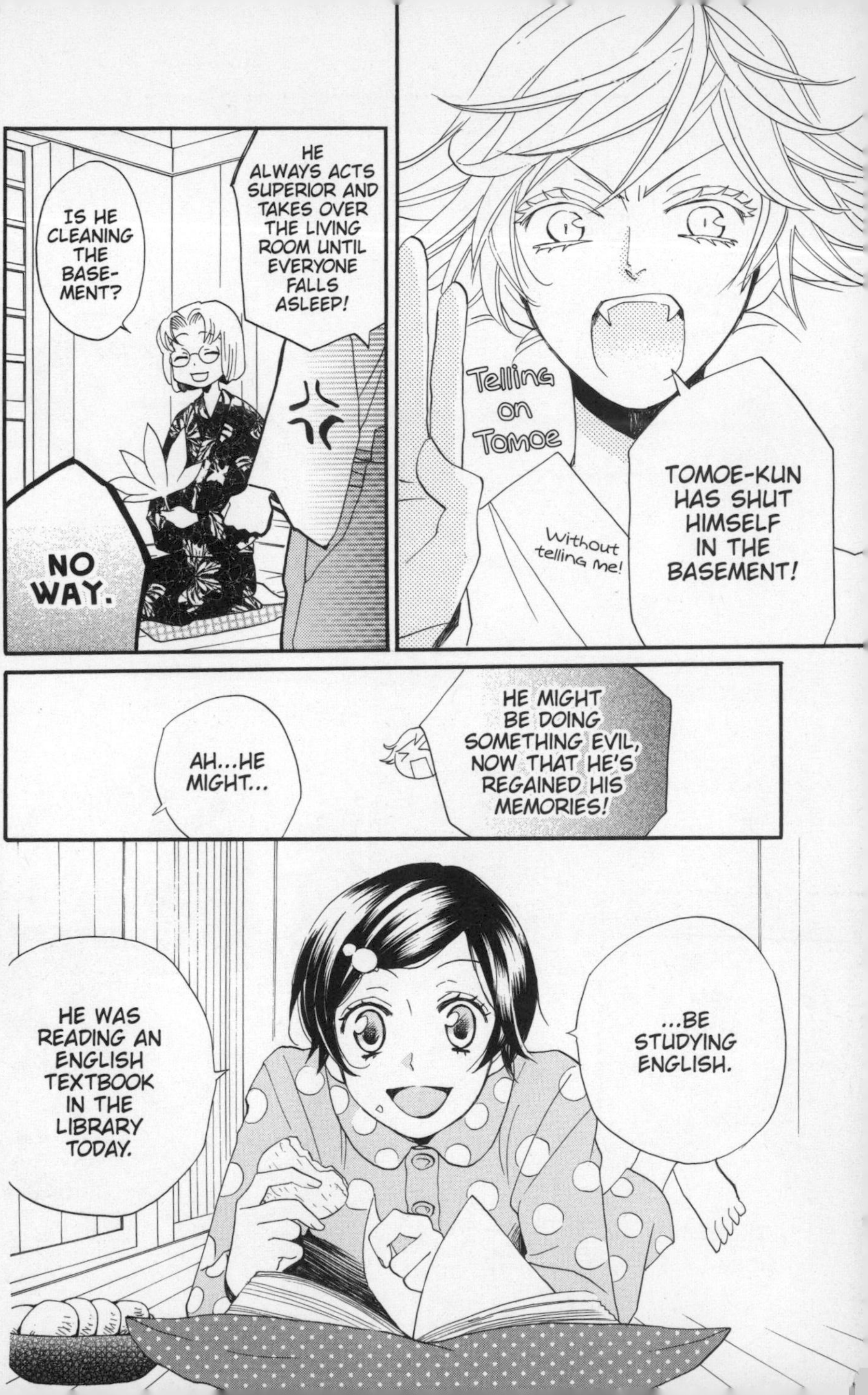
TOMOE-KUN HAS SHUT HIMSELF IN THE BASEMENT!
Telling on Tomoe
Without telling me!
HE ALWAYS ACTS SUPERIOR AND TAKES OVER THE LIVING ROOM UNTIL EVERYONE FALLS ASLEEP!
IS HE CLEANING THE BASEMENT?
NO WAY.
HE MIGHT BE DOING SOMETHING EVIL, NOW THAT HE'S REGAINED HIS MEMORIES!
AH...HE MIGHT...
...BE STUDYING ENGLISH.
HE WAS READING AN ENGLISH TEXTBOOK IN THE LIBRARY TODAY.

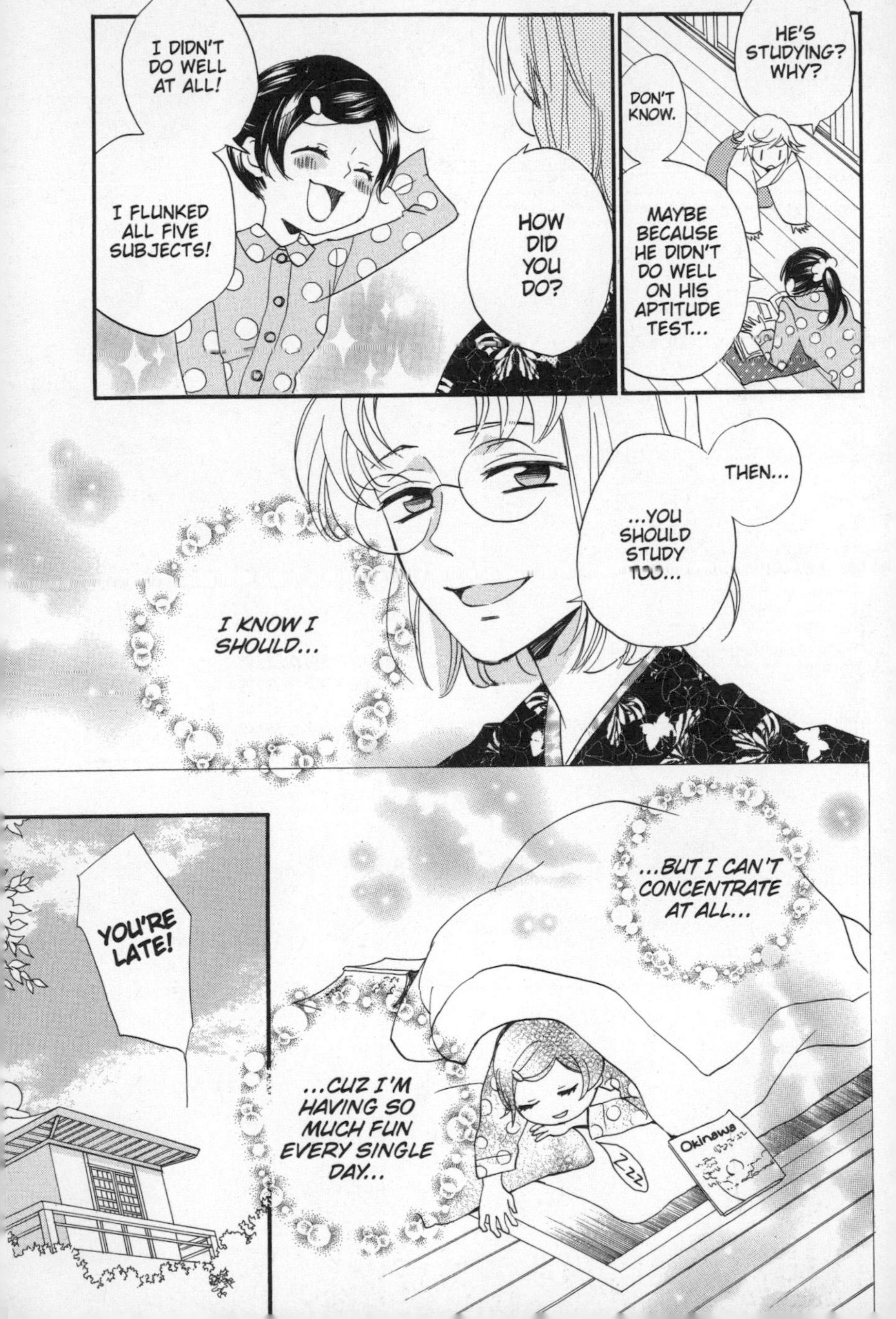
HE'S STUDYING? WHY?
DON'T KNOW.
MAYBE BECAUSE HE DIDN'T DO WELL ON HIS APTITUDE TEST...
HOW DID YOU DO?
I DIDN'T DO WELL AT ALL!
I FLUNKED ALL FIVE SUBJECTS!
THEN...
...YOU SHOULD STUDY TOO...
I KNOW I SHOULD...
...BUT I CAN'T CONCENTRATE AT ALL...
...CUZ I'M HAVING SO MUCH FUN EVERY SINGLE DAY...
ZZZ
Okinawa
YOU'RE LATE!

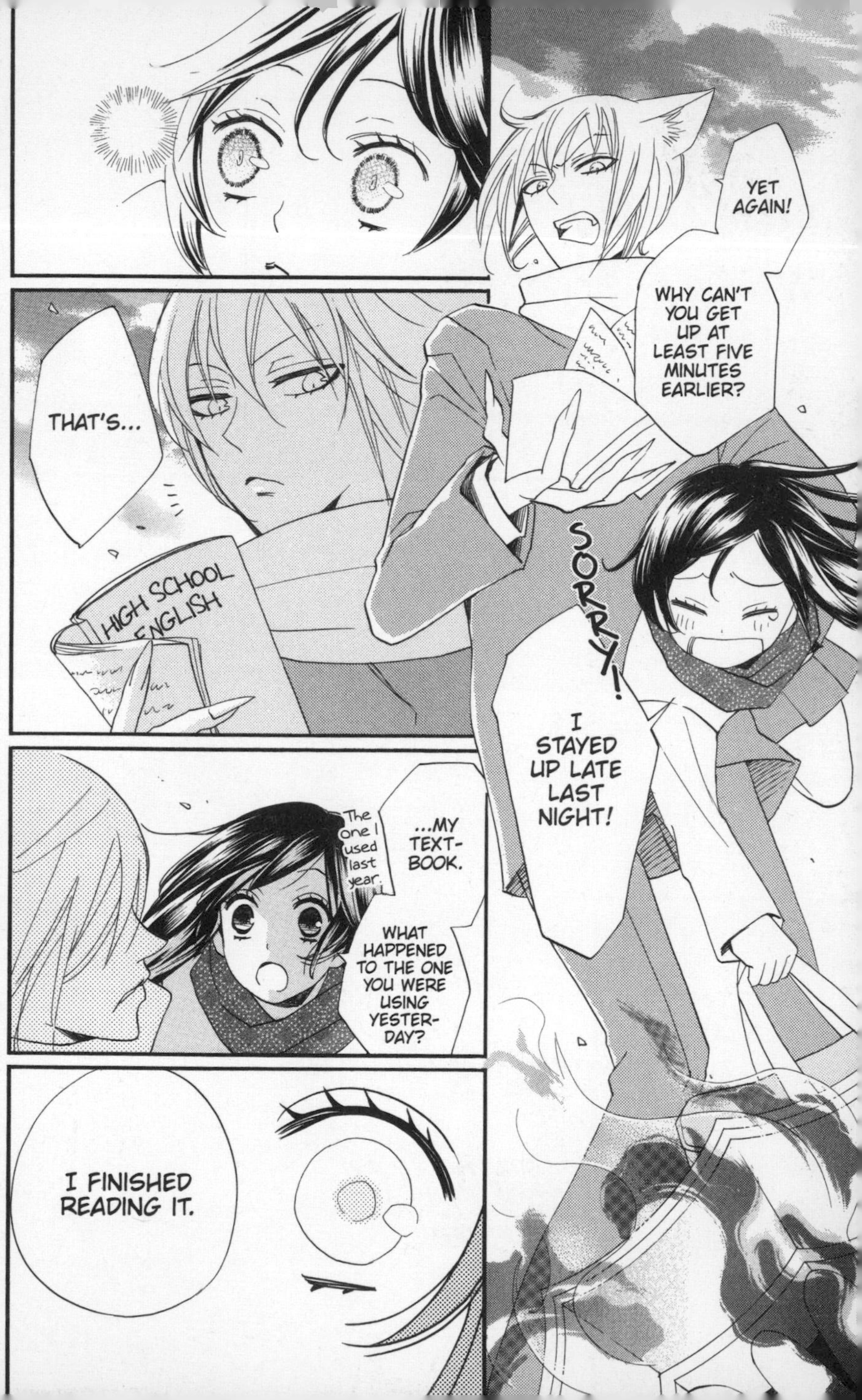
YET AGAIN!
WHY CAN'T YOU GET UP AT LEAST FIVE MINUTES EARLIER?
SORRY!
I STAYED UP LATE LAST NIGHT!
THAT'S...
HIGH SCHOOL ENGLISH
...MY TEXT-BOOK.
The one I used last year.
WHAT HAPPENED TO THE ONE YOU WERE USING YESTER-DAY?
I FINISHED READING IT.

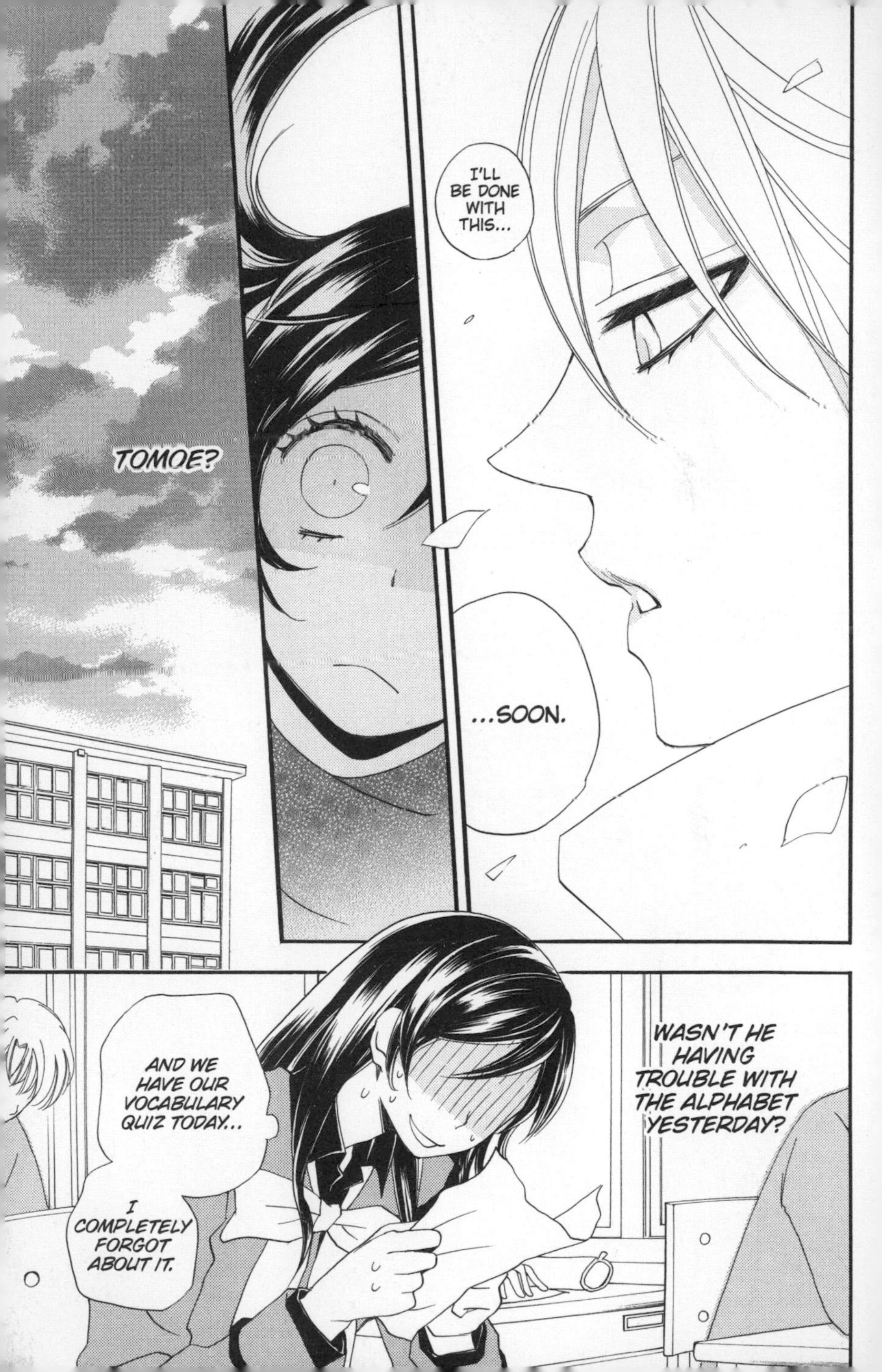
I'LL BE DONE WITH THIS...
...SOON.
TOMOE?
WASN'T HE HAVING TROUBLE WITH THE ALPHABET YESTERDAY?
AND WE HAVE OUR VOCABULARY QUIZ TODAY...
I COMPLETELY FORGOT ABOUT IT.

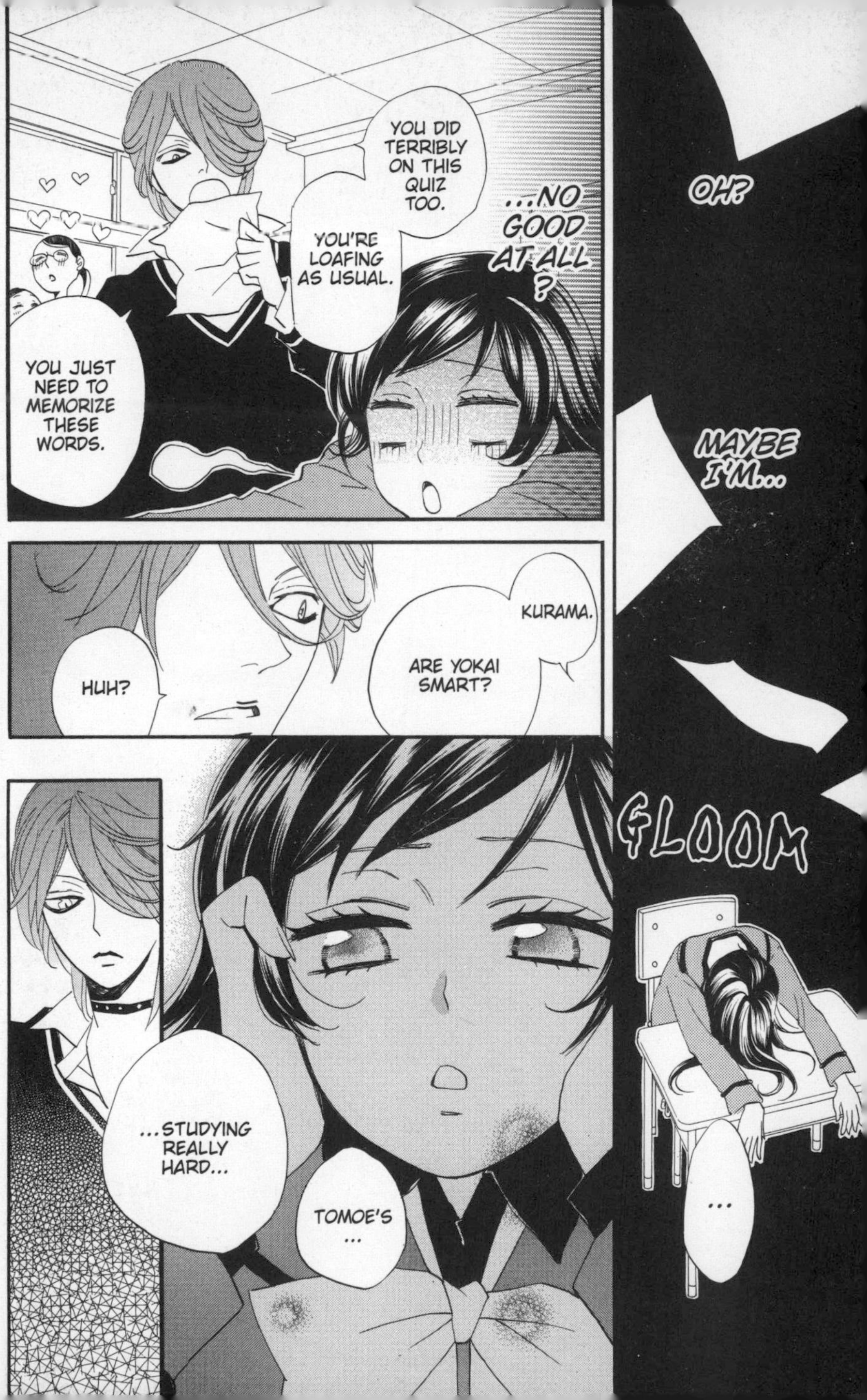
OH?
MAYBE I'M...
GLOOM
...
...NO GOOD AT ALL?
YOU DID TERRIBLY ON THIS QUIZ TOO.
YOU'RE LOAFING AS USUAL.
YOU JUST NEED TO MEMORIZE THESE WORDS.
KURAMA.
ARE YOKAI SMART?
HUH?
TOMOE'S ...
...STUDYING REALLY HARD...

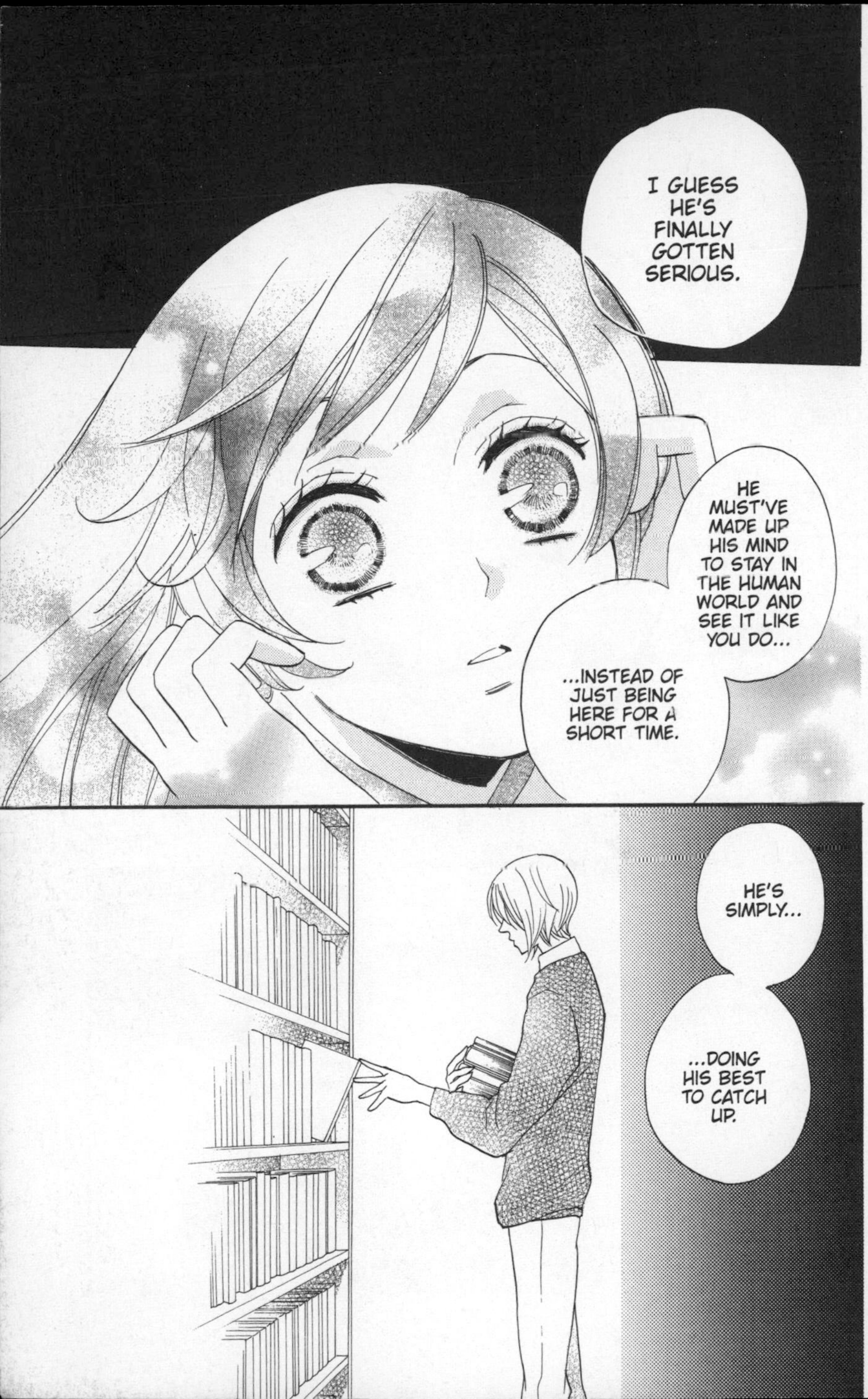
I GUESS HE'S FINALLY GOTTEN SERIOUS.
HE MUST'VE MADE UP HIS MIND TO STAY IN THE HUMAN WORLD AND SEE IT LIKE YOU DO...
...INSTEAD OF JUST BEING HERE FOR A SHORT TIME.
HE'S SIMPLY...
...DOING HIS BEST TO CATCH UP.

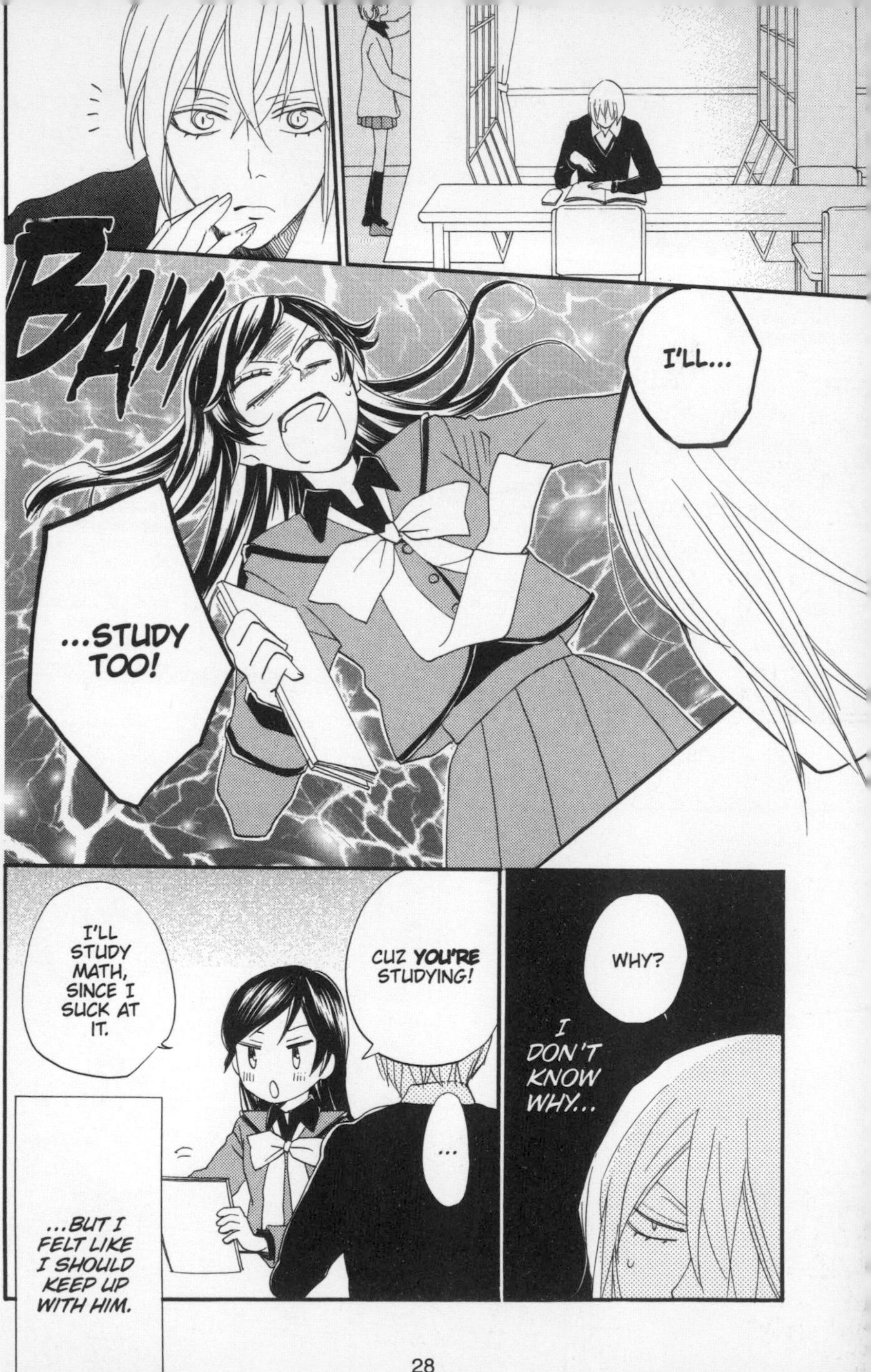
BAM
I'LL...
...STUDY TOO!
WHY?
I DON'T KNOW WHY...
CUZ YOU'RE STUDYING!
...
I'LL STUDY MATH, SINCE I SUCK AT IT.
...BUT I FELT LIKE I SHOULD KEEP UP WITH HIM.

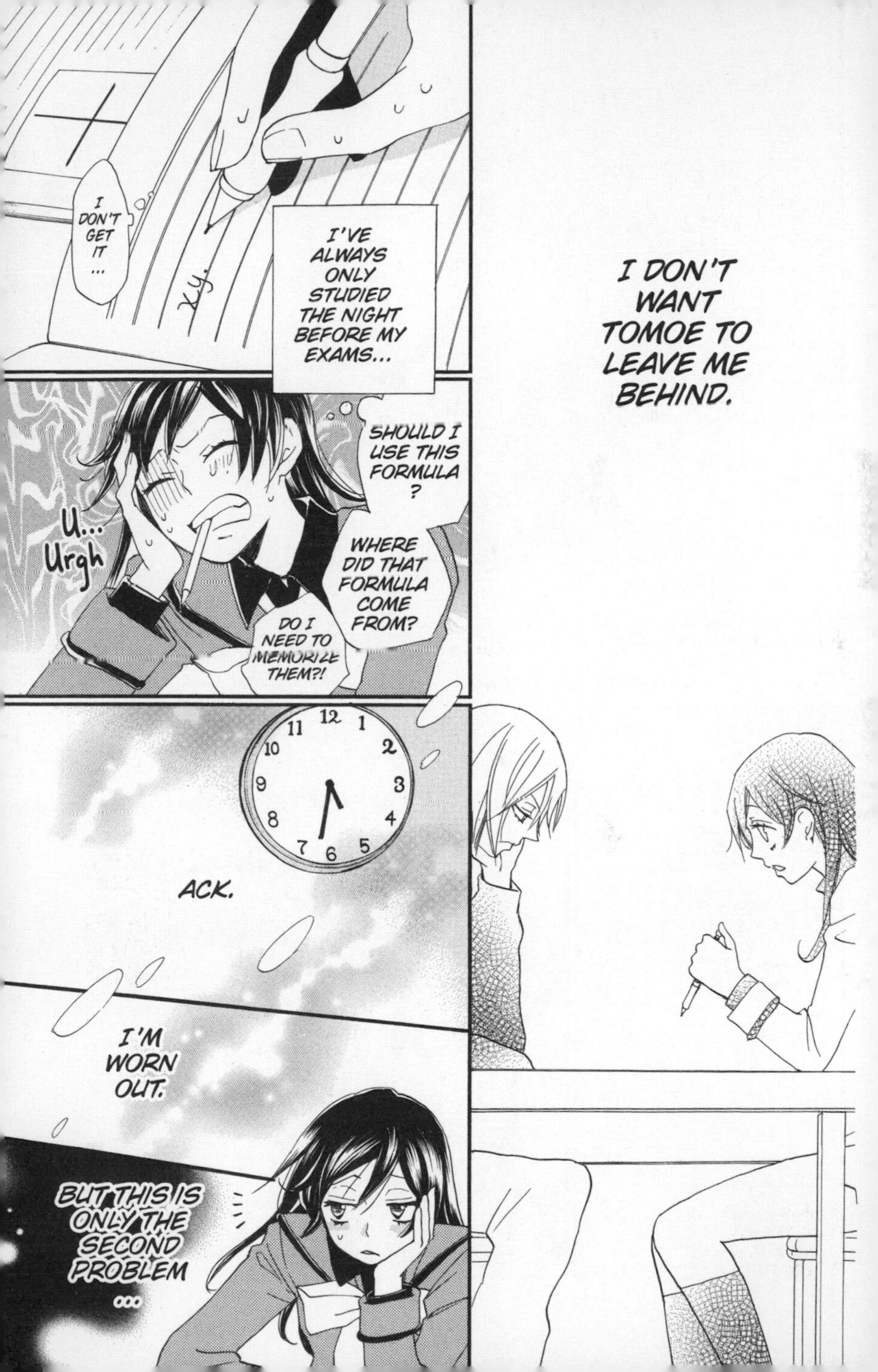
I DON'T WANT TOMOE TO LEAVE ME BEHIND.
I DON'T GET IT ...
I'VE ALWAYS ONLY STUDIED THE NIGHT BEFORE MY EXAMS...
SHOULD I USE THIS FORMULA ?
WHERE DID THAT FORMULA COME FROM?
DO I NEED TO MEMORIZE THEM?!
U... Urgh
ACK.
I'M WORN OUT.
BUT THIS IS ONLY THE SECOND PROBLEM ...

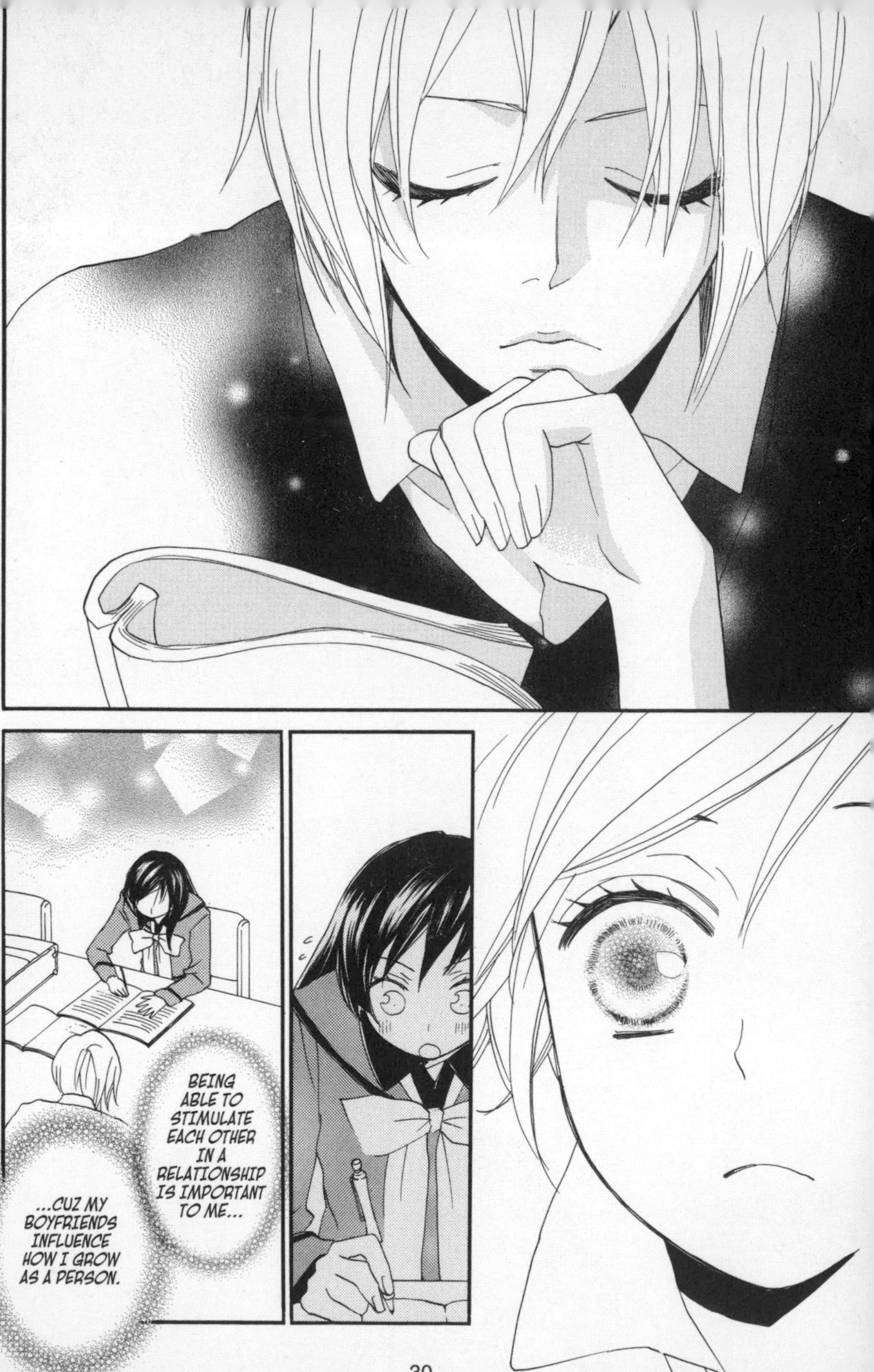
BEING ABLE TO STIMULATE EACH OTHER IN A RELATIONSHIP IS IMPORTANT TO ME...
...CUZ MY BOYFRIENDS INFLUENCE HOW I GROW AS A PERSON.

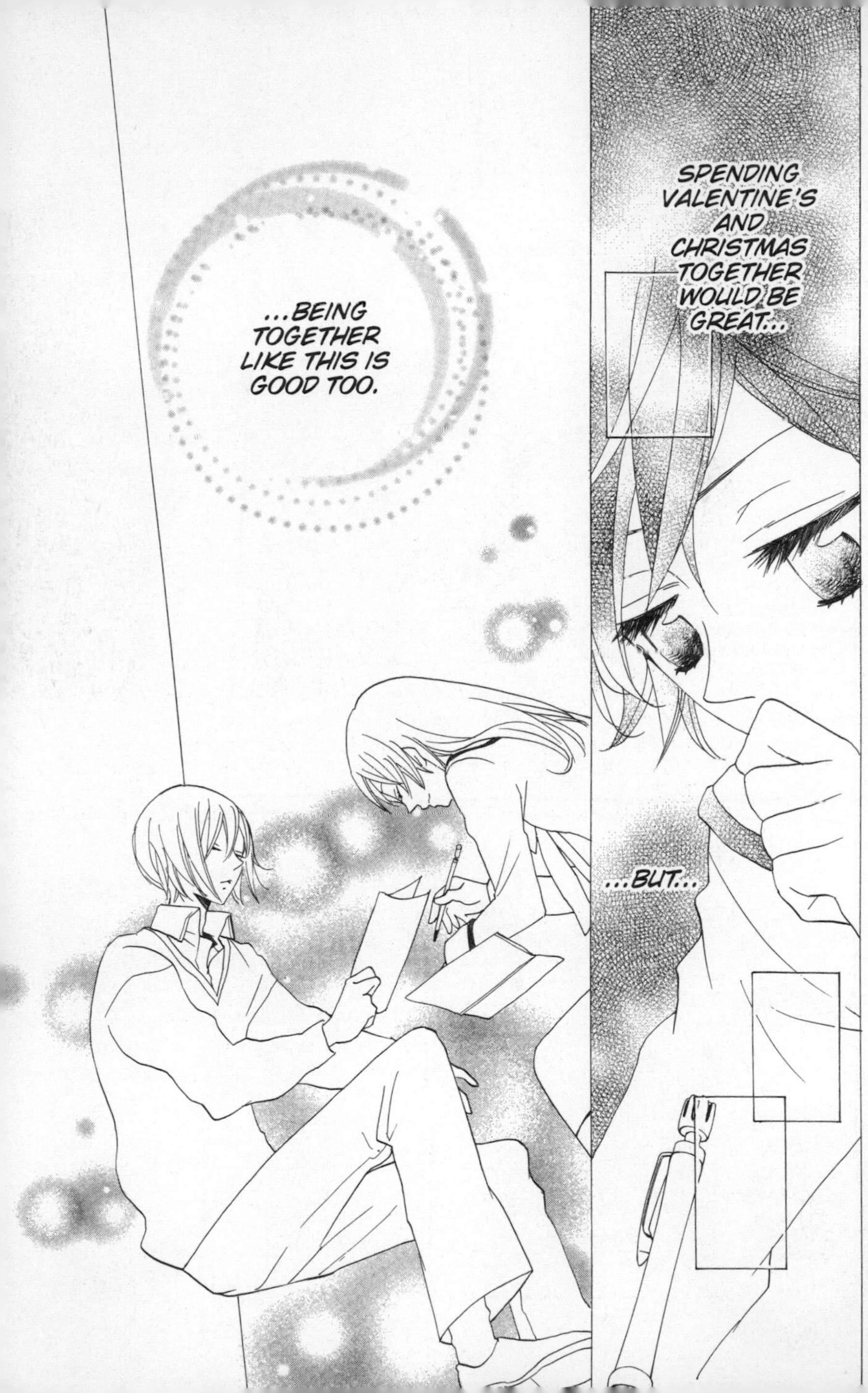
SPENDING VALENTINE'S AND CHRISTMAS TOGETHER WOULD BE GREAT...
...BUT...
...BEING TOGETHER LIKE THIS IS GOOD TOO.

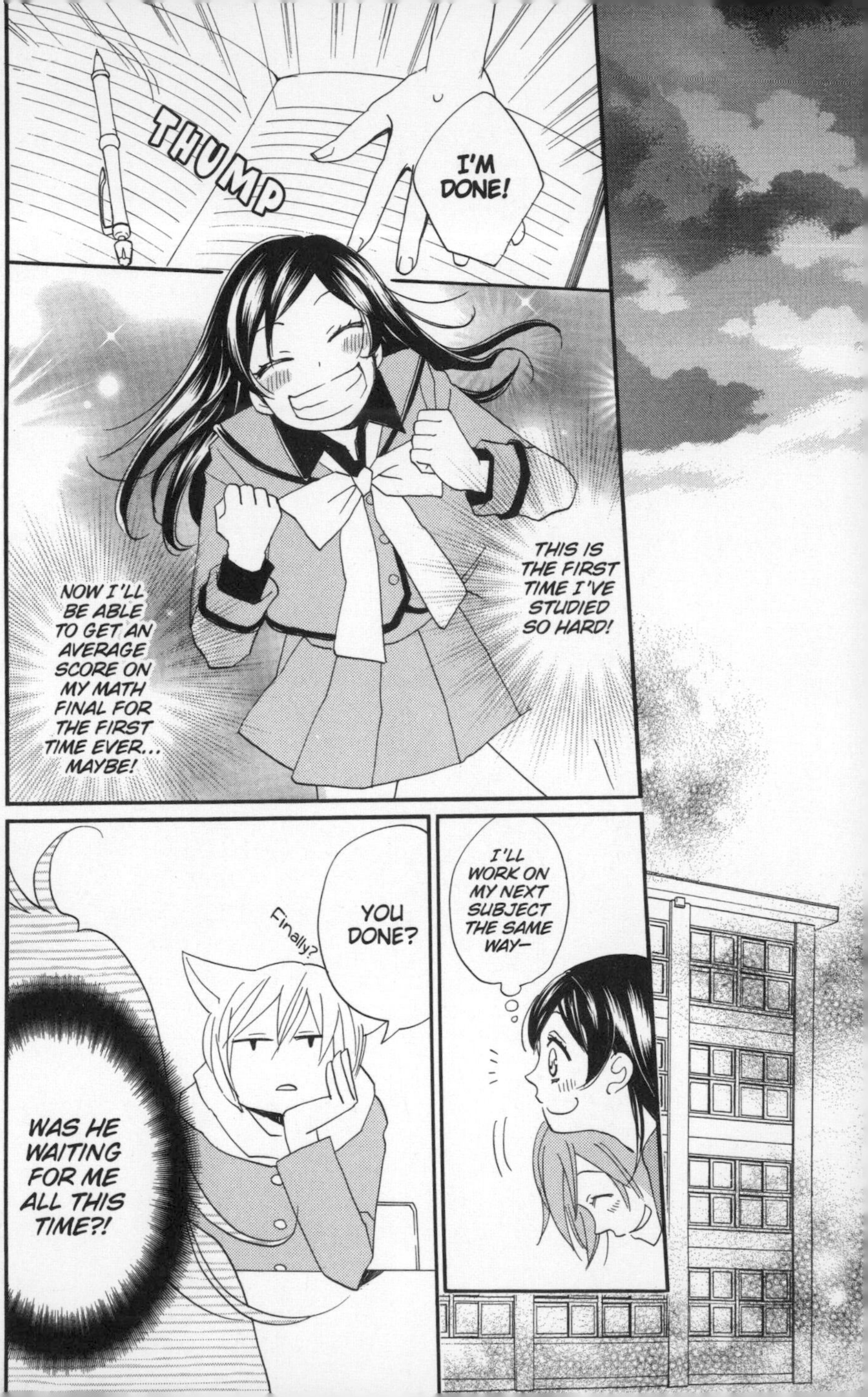
THUMP
I'M DONE!
THIS IS THE FIRST TIME I'VE STUDIED SO HARD!
NOW I'LL BE ABLE TO GET AN AVERAGE SCORE ON MY MATH FINAL FOR THE FIRST TIME EVER... MAYBE!
I'LL WORK ON MY NEXT SUBJECT THE SAME WAY—
YOU DONE?
Finally?
WAS HE WAITING FOR ME ALL THIS TIME?!

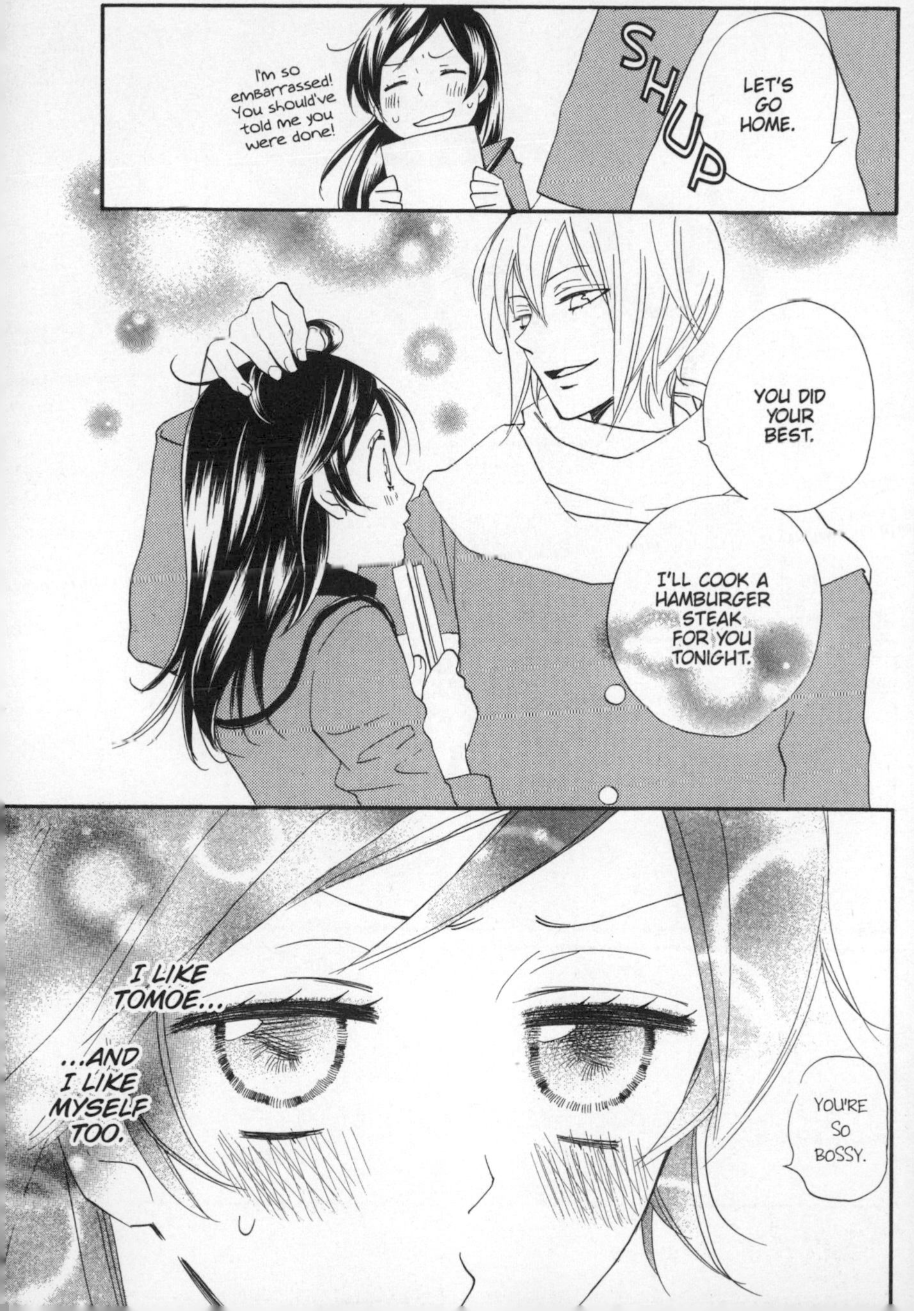
SHUP
LET'S GO HOME.
I'm so embarrassed! You should've told me you were done!
YOU DID YOUR BEST.
I'LL COOK A HAMBURGER STEAK FOR YOU TONIGHT.
YOU'RE SO BOSSY.
I LIKE TOMOE...
...AND I LIKE MYSELF TOO.

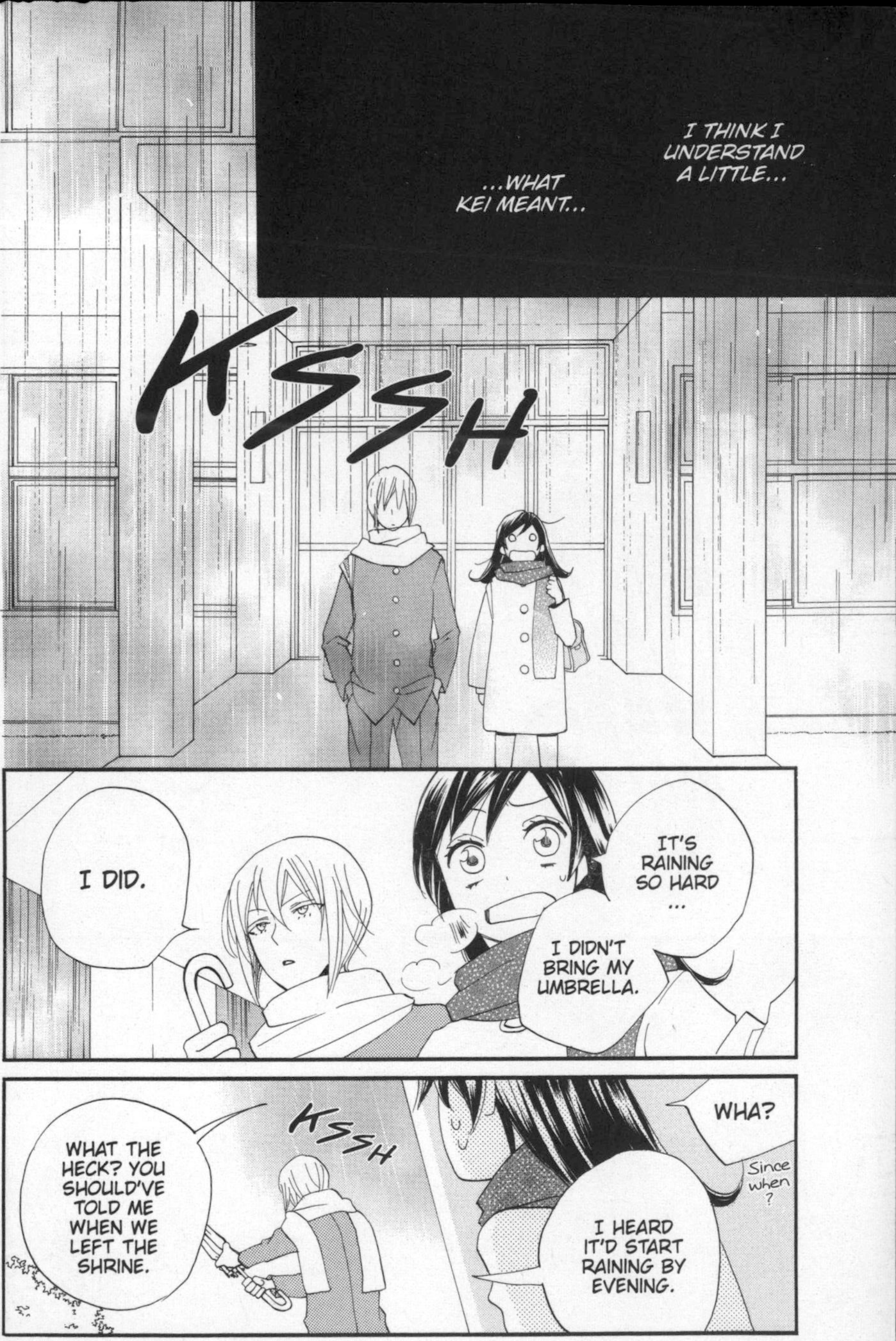
I THINK I UNDERSTAND A LITTLE...
...WHAT KEI MEANT...
KSSH
IT'S RAINING SO HARD ...
I DIDN'T BRING MY UMBRELLA.
I DID.
WHA?
Since when ?
I HEARD IT'D START RAINING BY EVENING.
KSSH
WHAT THE HECK? YOU SHOULD'VE TOLD ME WHEN WE LEFT THE SHRINE.

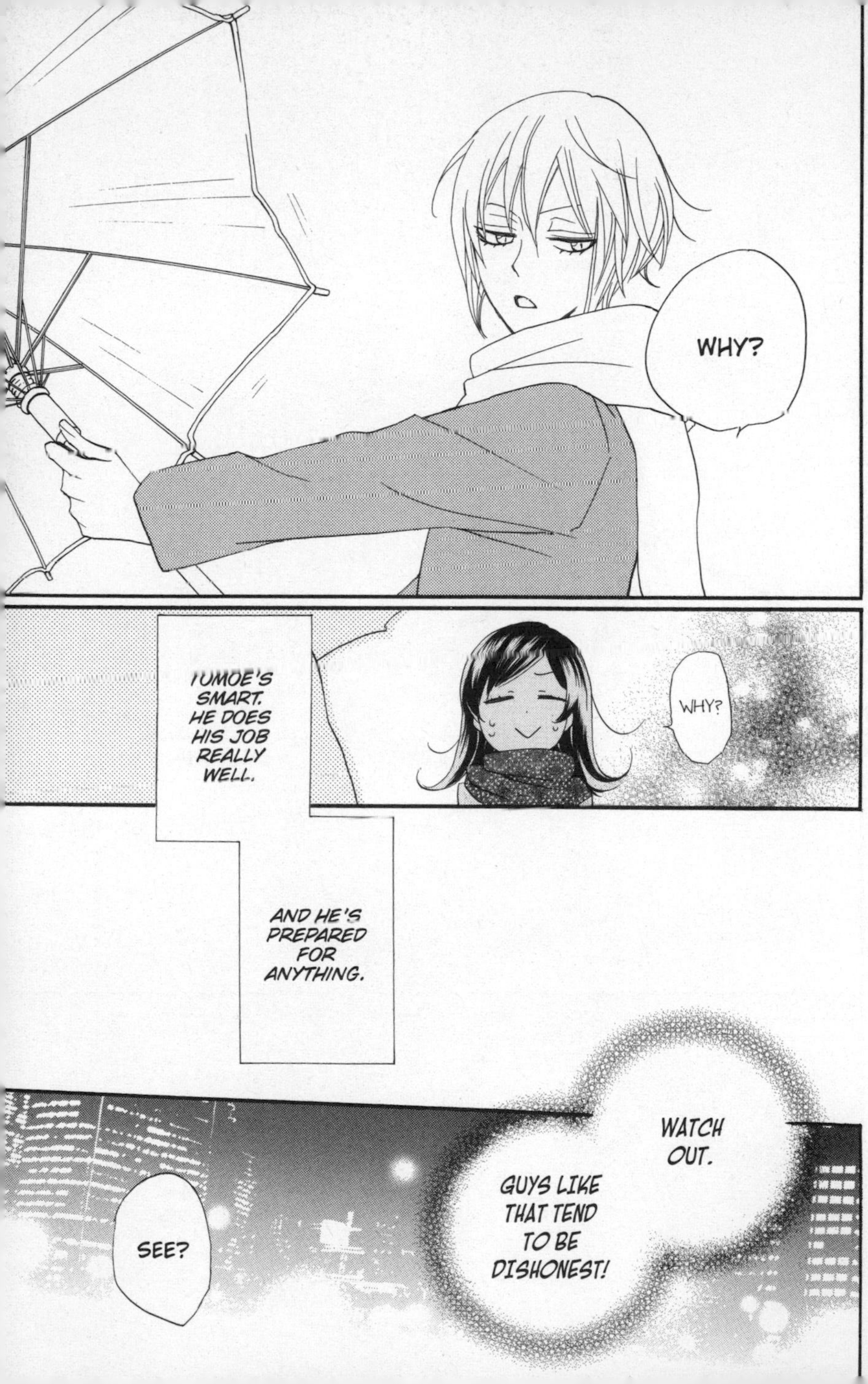
WHY?
WHY?
TOMOE'S SMART. HE DOES HIS JOB REALLY WELL.
AND HE'S PREPARED FOR ANYTHING.
WATCH OUT.
GUYS LIKE THAT TEND TO BE DISHONEST!
SEE?

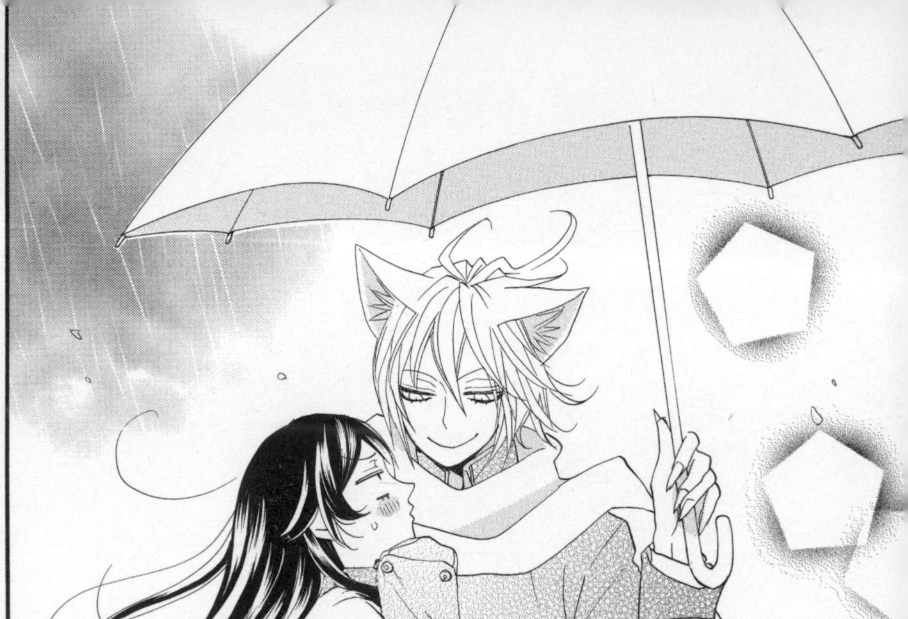
ONE UMBRELLA IS ENOUGH.
...

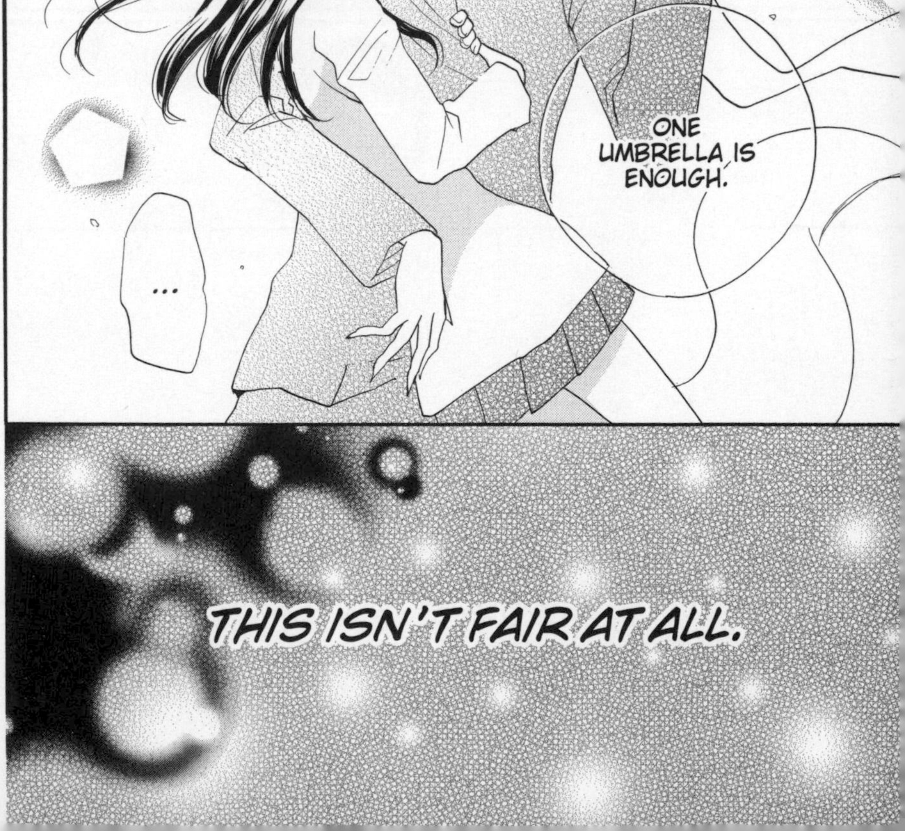
THIS ISN'T FAIR AT ALL.

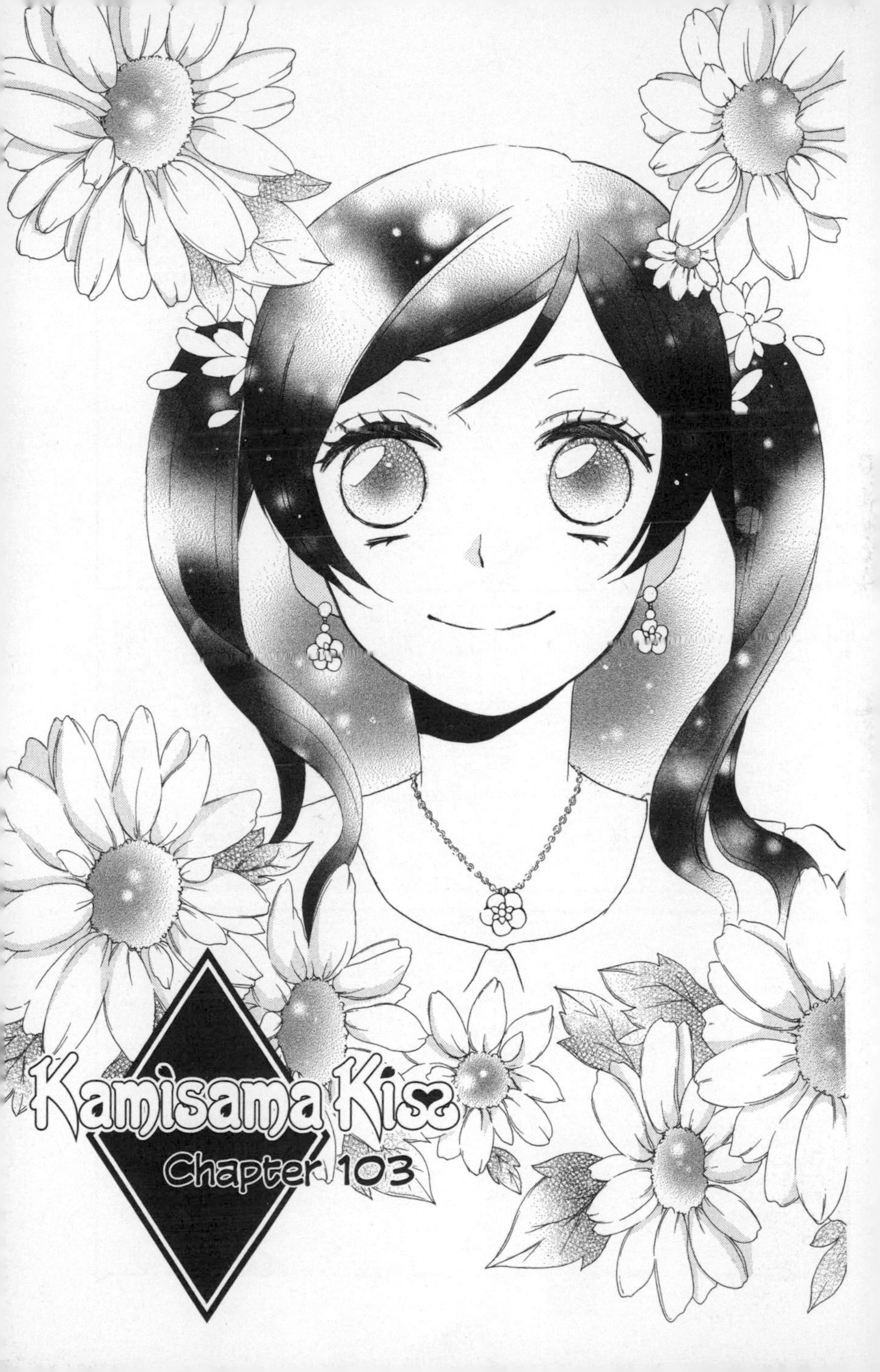
Kamisama Kiss
Chapter 103

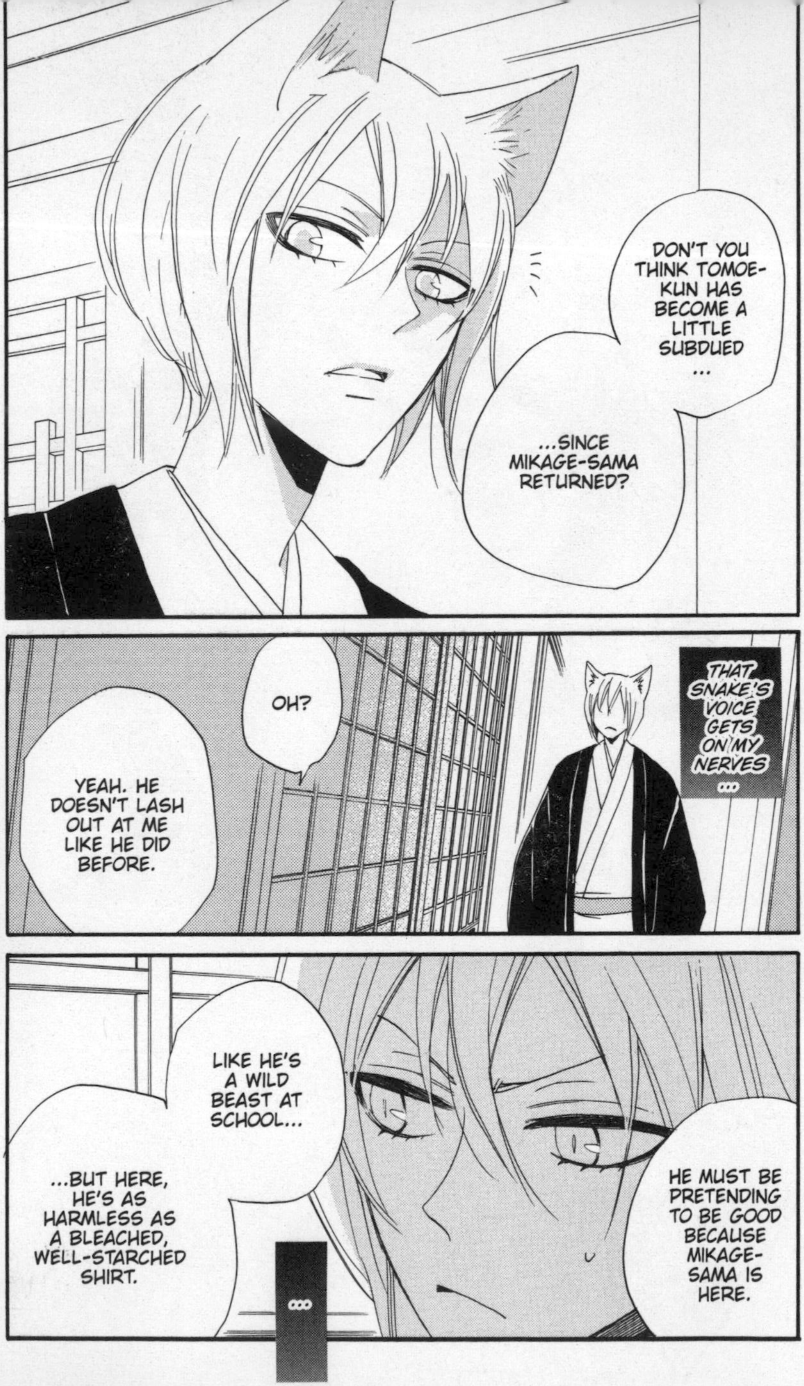
DON'T YOU THINK TOMOE-KUN HAS BECOME A LITTLE SUBDUED...
...SINCE MIKAGE-SAMA RETURNED?
THAT SNAKE'S VOICE GETS ON MY NERVES...
OH?
YEAH. HE DOESN'T LASH OUT AT ME LIKE HE DID BEFORE.
LIKE HE'S A WILD BEAST AT SCHOOL...
...BUT HERE, HE'S AS HARMLESS AS A BLEACHED, WELL-STARCHED SHIRT.
HE MUST BE PRETENDING TO BE GOOD BECAUSE MIKAGE-SAMA IS HERE.
...

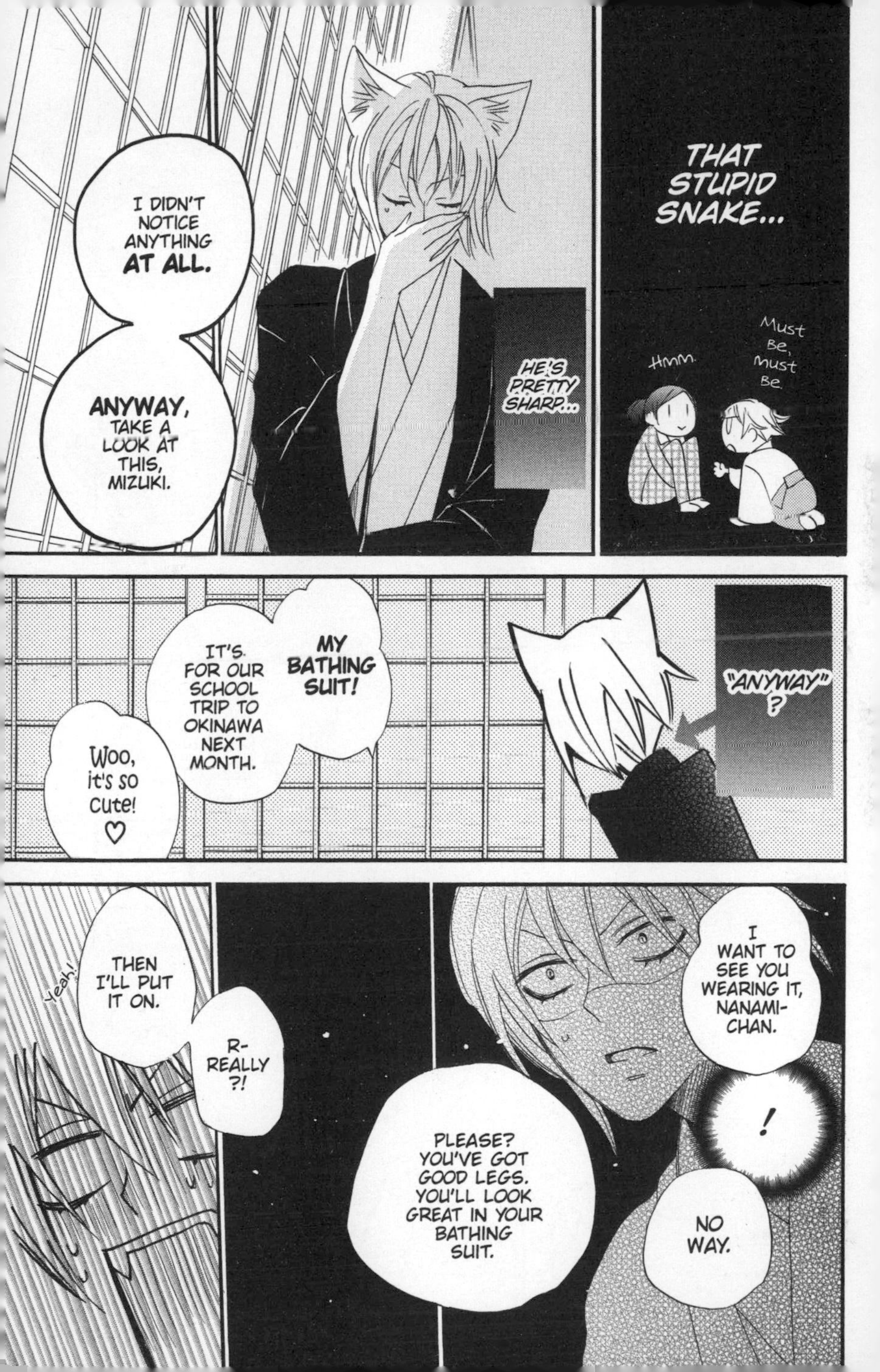
THAT STUPID SNAKE...
Must be, must be.
Hmm.
HE'S PRETTY SHARP...
I DIDN'T NOTICE ANYTHING AT ALL.
ANYWAY, TAKE A LOOK AT THIS, MIZUKI.
"ANYWAY"?
MY BATHING SUIT!
IT'S FOR OUR SCHOOL TRIP TO OKINAWA NEXT MONTH.
Woo, it's so cute! ♡
I WANT TO SEE YOU WEARING IT, NANAMI-CHAN.
!
NO WAY.
PLEASE? YOU'VE GOT GOOD LEGS. YOU'LL LOOK GREAT IN YOUR BATHING SUIT.
THEN I'LL PUT IT ON.
R-REALLY?!
Yeah!

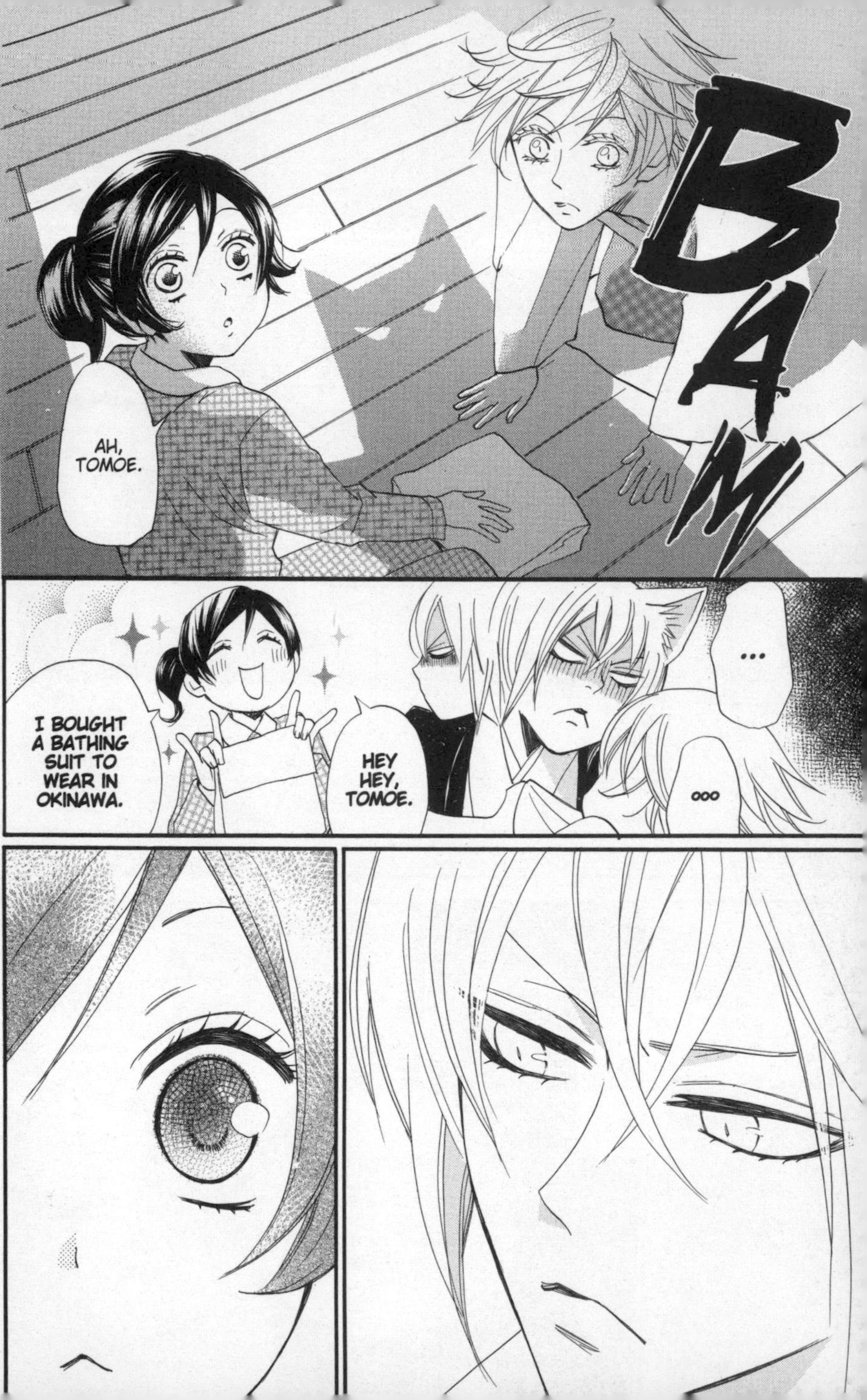
BAM
AH, TOMOE.
...
ooo
HEY HEY, TOMOE.
I BOUGHT A BATHING SUIT TO WEAR IN OKINAWA.

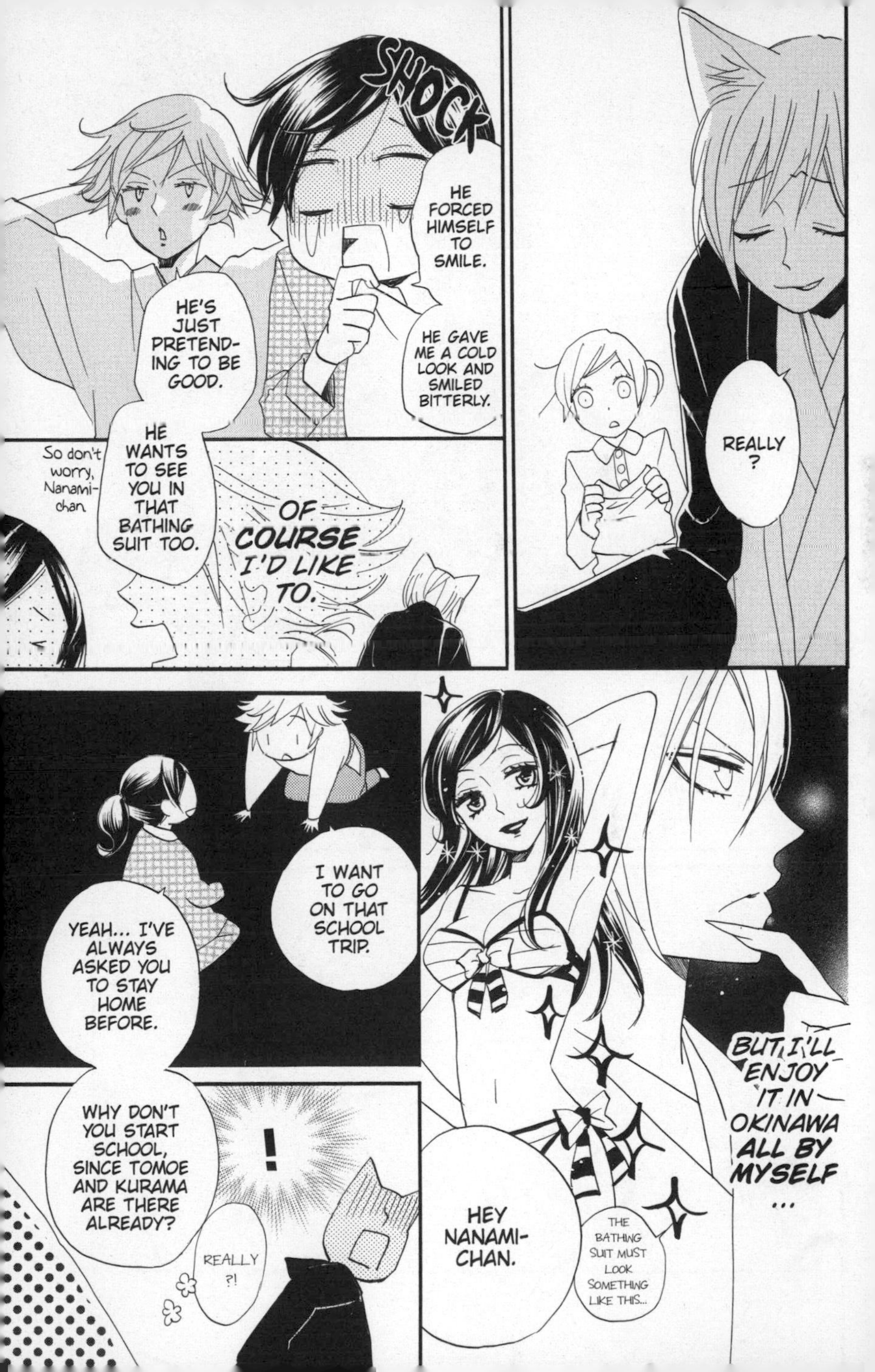
REALLY?
SHOCK
HE FORCED HIMSELF TO SMILE.
HE GAVE ME A COLD LOOK AND SMILED BITTERLY.
HE'S JUST PRETENDING TO BE GOOD.
OF COURSE I'D LIKE TO.
HE WANTS TO SEE YOU IN THAT BATHING SUIT TOO.
So don't worry, Nanami-chan.
BUT I'LL ENJOY IT IN OKINAWA ALL BY MYSELF...
THE BATHING SUIT MUST LOOK SOMETHING LIKE THIS...
HEY NANAMI-CHAN.
I WANT TO GO ON THAT SCHOOL TRIP.
YEAH... I'VE ALWAYS ASKED YOU TO STAY HOME BEFORE.
WHY DON'T YOU START SCHOOL, SINCE TOMOE AND KURAMA ARE THERE ALREADY?
!
REALLY?!

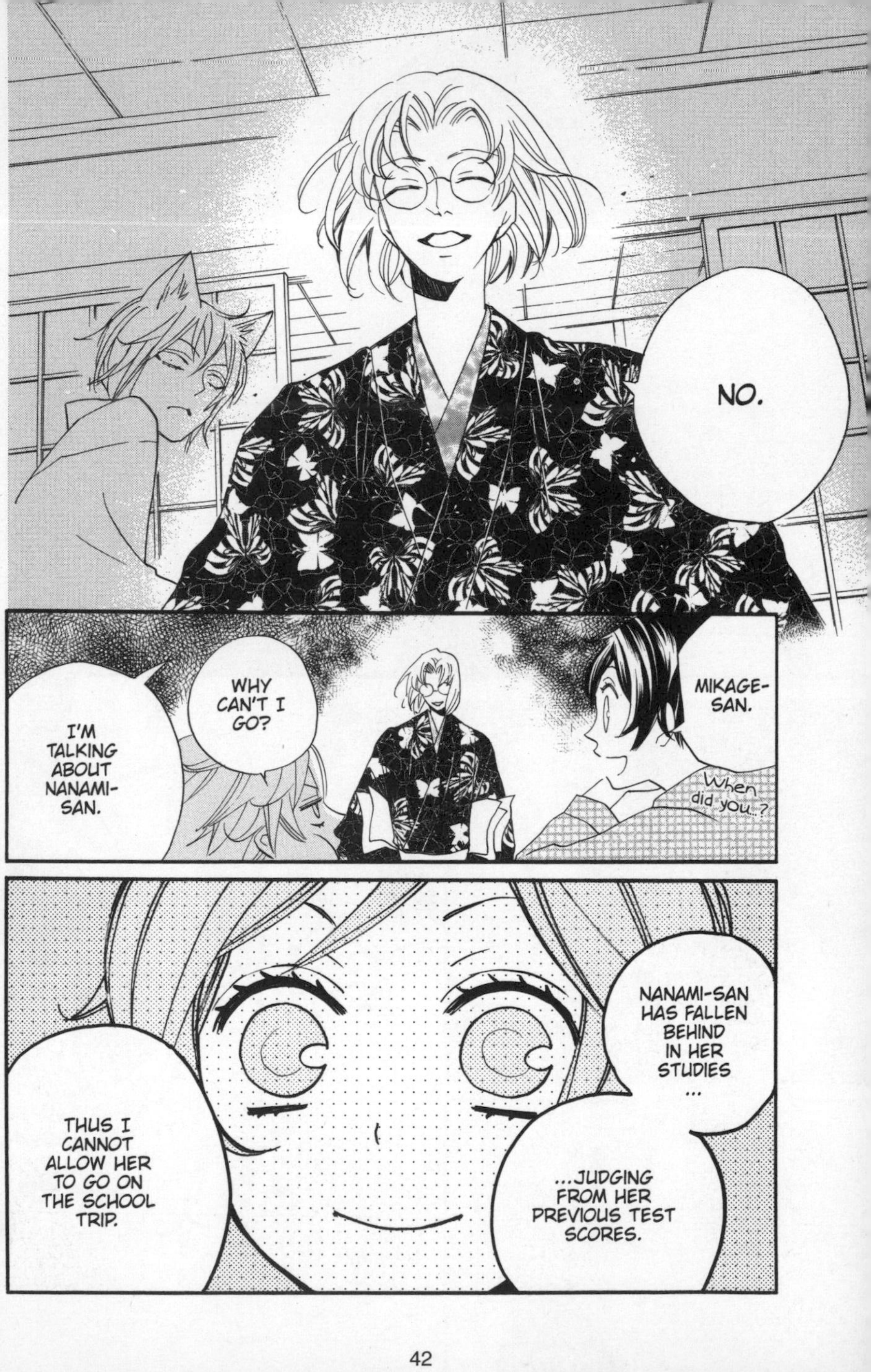
NO.
MIKAGE-SAN.
When did you...?
WHY CAN'T I GO?
I'M TALKING ABOUT NANAMI-SAN.
NANAMI-SAN HAS FALLEN BEHIND IN HER STUDIES ...
...JUDGING FROM HER PREVIOUS TEST SCORES.
THUS I CANNOT ALLOW HER TO GO ON THE SCHOOL TRIP.

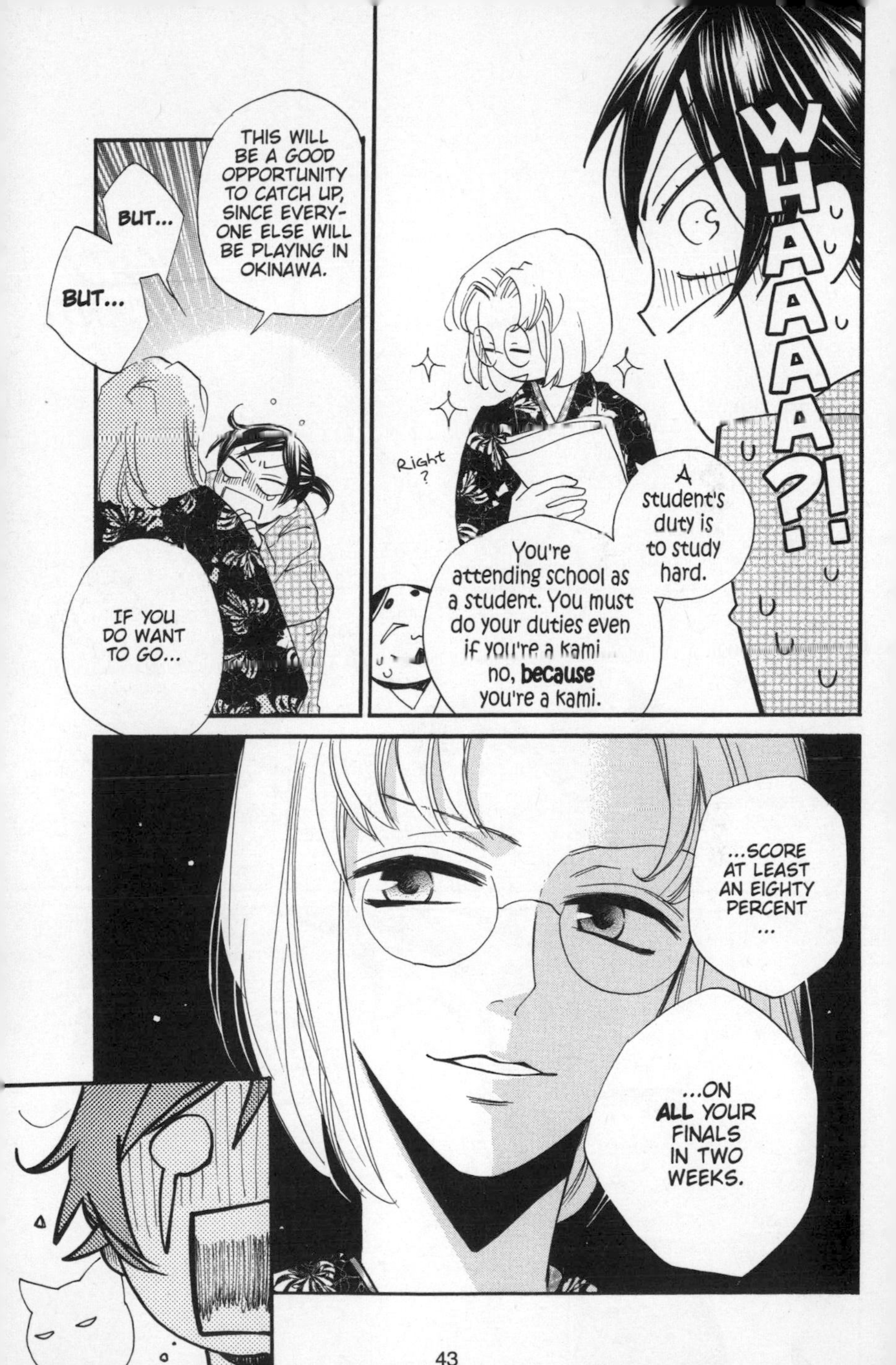
WHAAAA?!
A student's duty is to study hard.
Right?
You're attending school as a student. You must do your duties even if you're a kami... no, **because** you're a kami.
THIS WILL BE A GOOD OPPORTUNITY TO CATCH UP, SINCE EVERYONE ELSE WILL BE PLAYING IN OKINAWA.
BUT...
BUT...
IF YOU DO WANT TO GO...
...SCORE AT LEAST AN EIGHTY PERCENT...
...ON **ALL** YOUR FINALS IN TWO WEEKS.

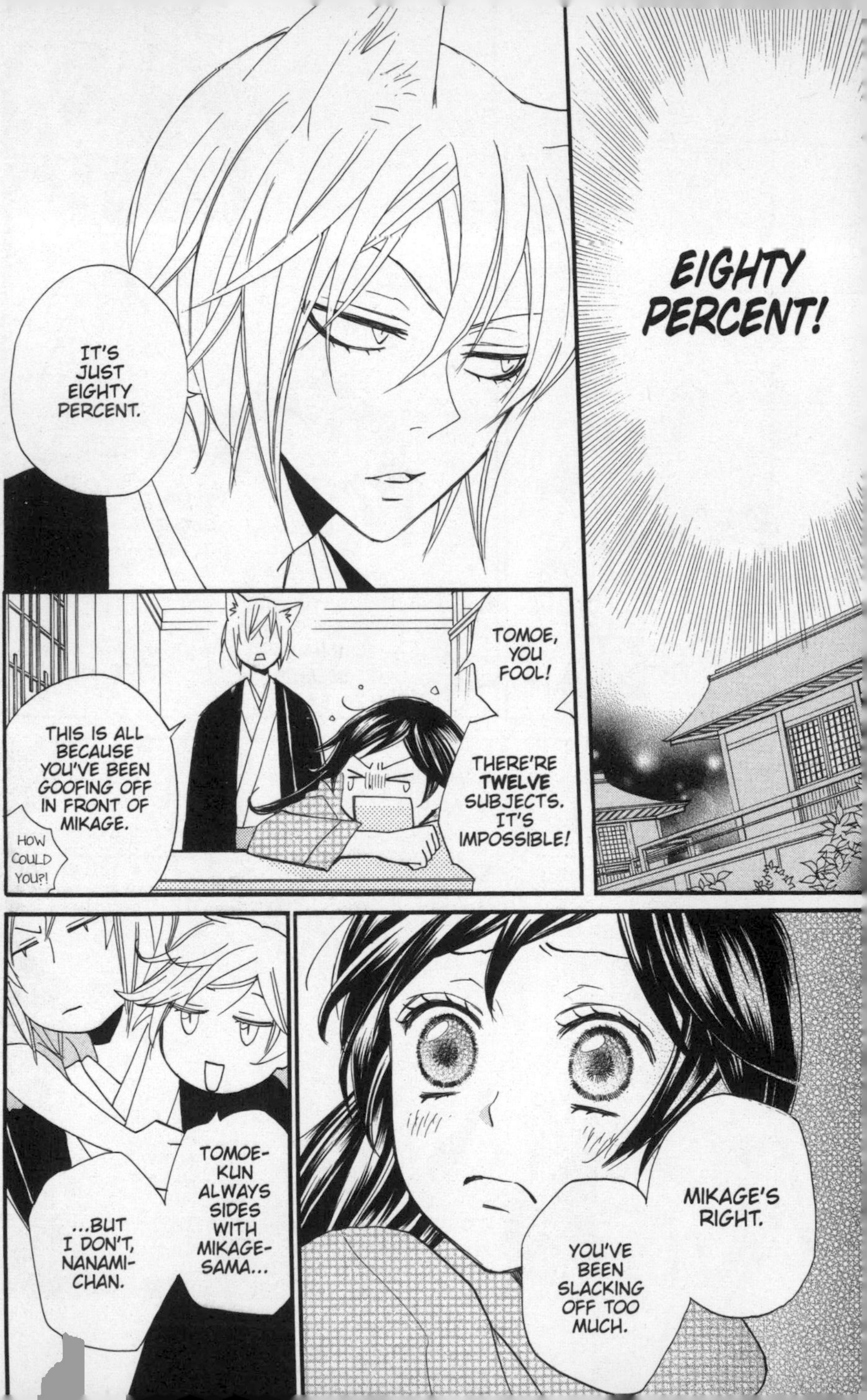
EIGHTY PERCENT!
IT'S JUST EIGHTY PERCENT.
TOMOE, YOU FOOL!
THERE'RE **TWELVE** SUBJECTS. IT'S IMPOSSIBLE!
THIS IS ALL BECAUSE YOU'VE BEEN GOOFING OFF IN FRONT OF MIKAGE.
HOW COULD YOU?!
MIKAGE'S RIGHT.
YOU'VE BEEN SLACKING OFF TOO MUCH.
TOMOE-KUN ALWAYS SIDES WITH MIKAGE-SAMA...
...BUT I DON'T, NANAMI-CHAN.

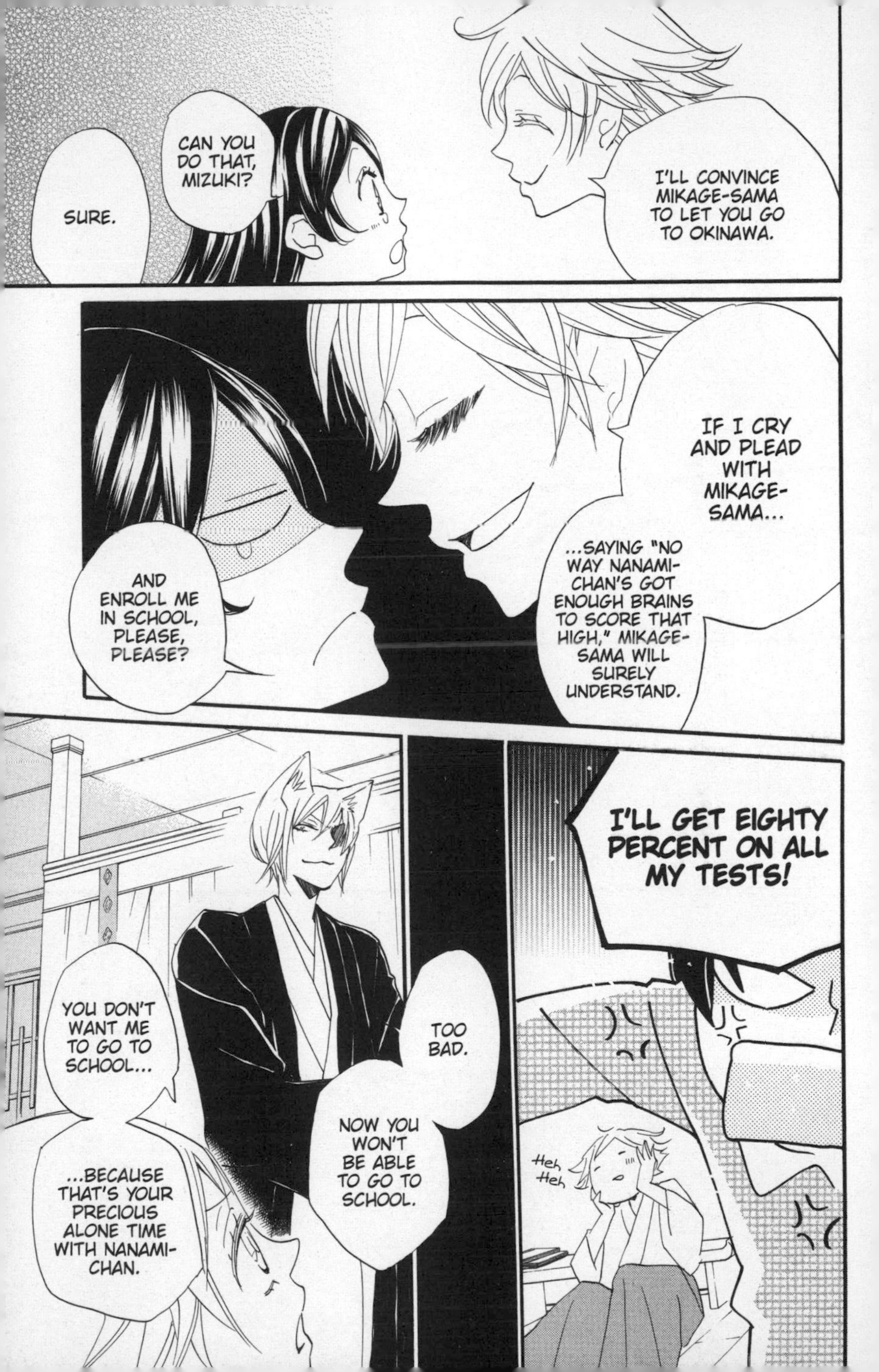
I'LL CONVINCE MIKAGE-SAMA TO LET YOU GO TO OKINAWA.
CAN YOU DO THAT, MIZUKI?
SURE.
IF I CRY AND PLEAD WITH MIKAGE-SAMA...
...SAYING "NO WAY NANAMI-CHAN'S GOT ENOUGH BRAINS TO SCORE THAT HIGH," MIKAGE-SAMA WILL SURELY UNDERSTAND.
AND ENROLL ME IN SCHOOL, PLEASE, PLEASE?
I'LL GET EIGHTY PERCENT ON ALL MY TESTS!
Heh, Heh
TOO BAD.
NOW YOU WON'T BE ABLE TO GO TO SCHOOL.
YOU DON'T WANT ME TO GO TO SCHOOL...
...BECAUSE THAT'S YOUR PRECIOUS ALONE TIME WITH NANAMI-CHAN.

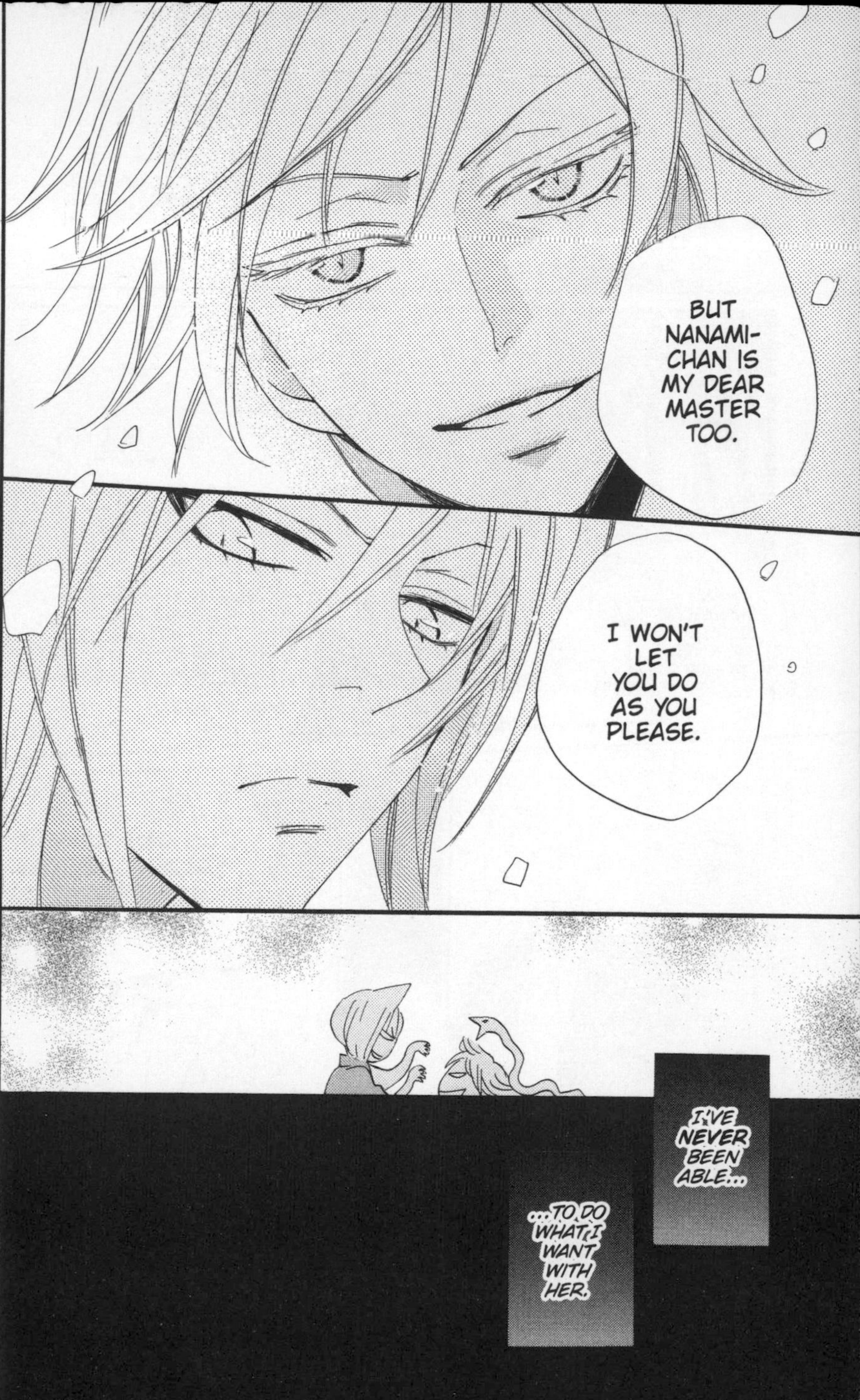
BUT NANAMI-CHAN IS MY DEAR MASTER TOO.
I WON'T LET YOU DO AS YOU PLEASE.
I'VE NEVER BEEN ABLE...
...TO DO WHAT I WANT WITH HER.

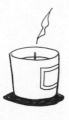

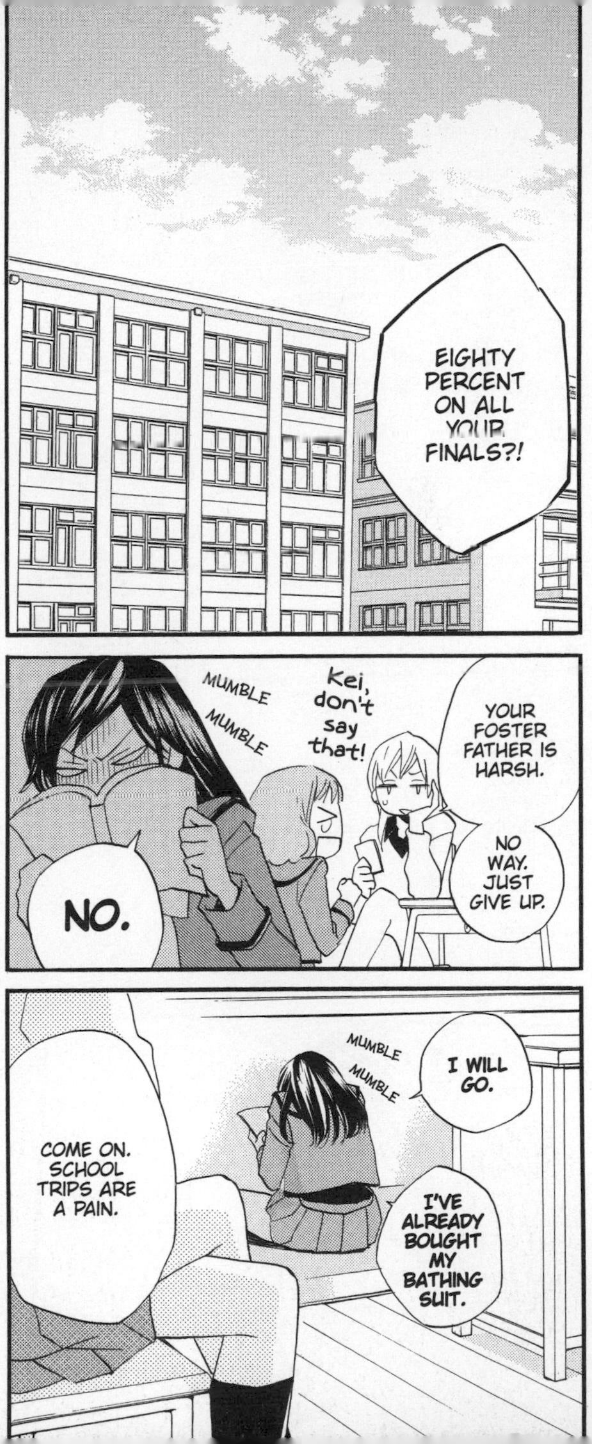
EIGHTY PERCENT ON ALL YOUR FINALS?!
YOUR FOSTER FATHER IS HARSH.
Kei, don't say that!
MUMBLE MUMBLE
NO WAY. JUST GIVE UP.
NO.
I WILL GO.
MUMBLE MUMBLE
I'VE ALREADY BOUGHT MY BATHING SUIT.
COME ON. SCHOOL TRIPS ARE A PAIN.

Hello!

Thank you for picking up volume 18 of Kamisama Kiss!

I hope you enjoy reading it.

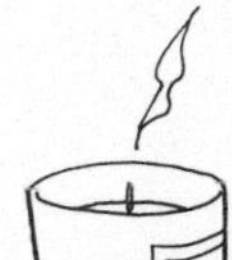

I've recently fallen in love with scented candles.

I really feel good when the wonderful fragrance fills the room. ☺

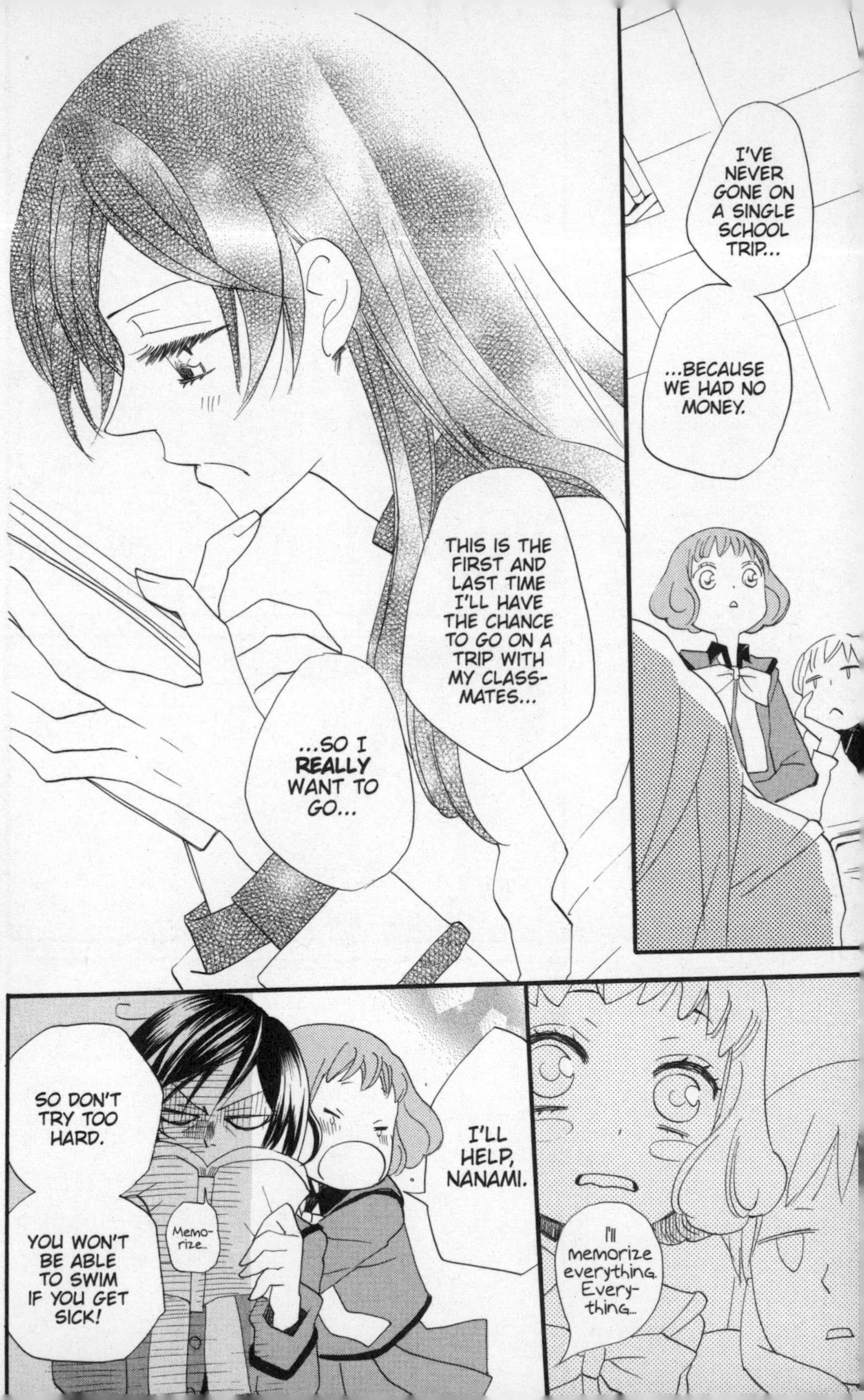
I'VE NEVER GONE ON A SINGLE SCHOOL TRIP...
...BECAUSE WE HAD NO MONEY.
THIS IS THE FIRST AND LAST TIME I'LL HAVE THE CHANCE TO GO ON A TRIP WITH MY CLASS-MATES...
...SO I **REALLY** WANT TO GO...
I'll memorize everything. Every-thing...
I'LL HELP, NANAMI.
SO DON'T TRY TOO HARD.
Memo-rize...
YOU WON'T BE ABLE TO SWIM IF YOU GET SICK!

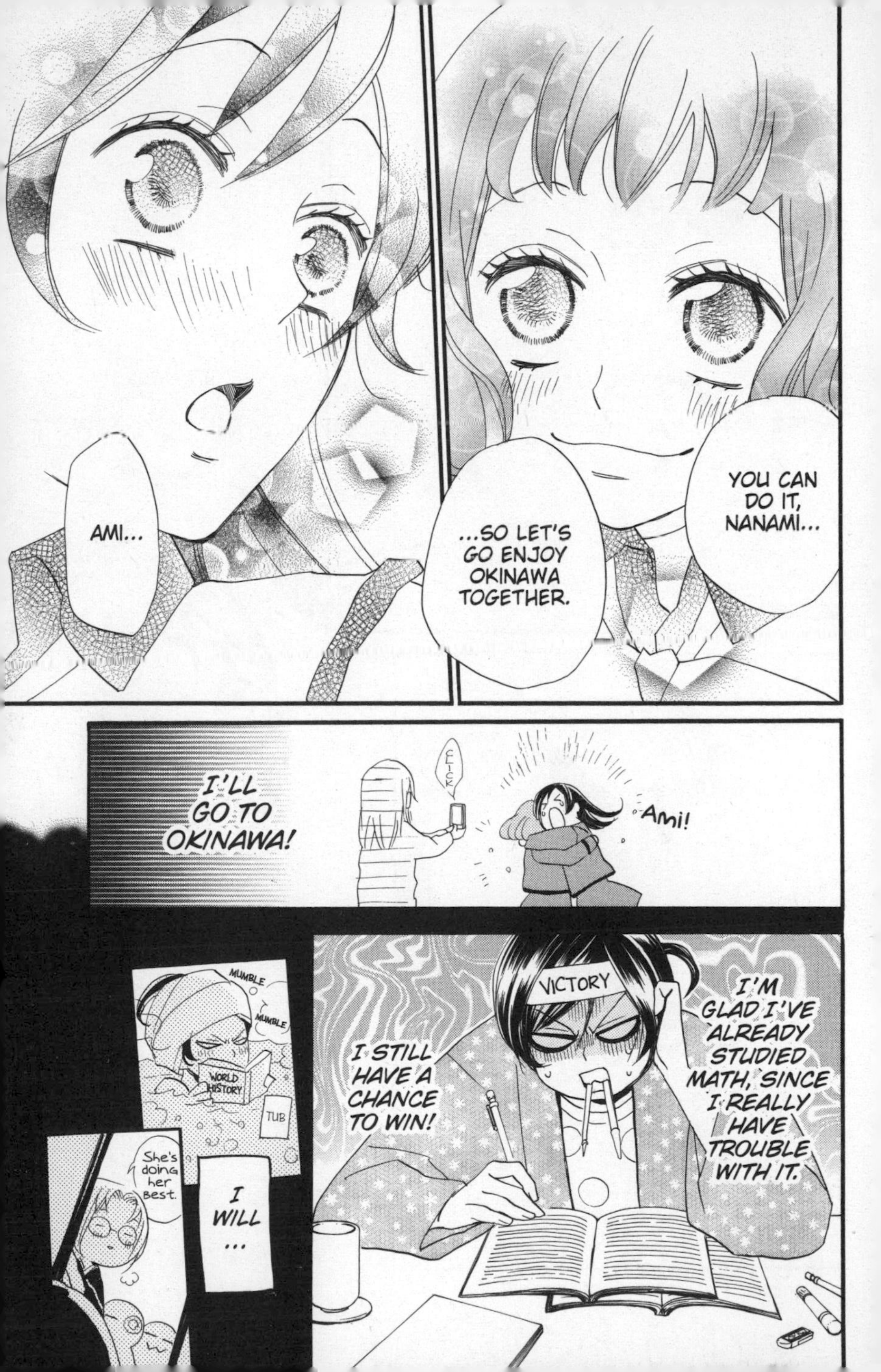
YOU CAN DO IT, NANAMI...
...SO LET'S GO ENJOY OKINAWA TOGETHER.
AMI...
FLICK
Ami!
I'LL GO TO OKINAWA!
VICTORY
I'M GLAD I'VE ALREADY STUDIED MATH, SINCE I REALLY HAVE TROUBLE WITH IT.
I STILL HAVE A CHANCE TO WIN!
MUMBLE
MUMBLE
WORLD HISTORY
TUB
I WILL ...
She's doing her best.

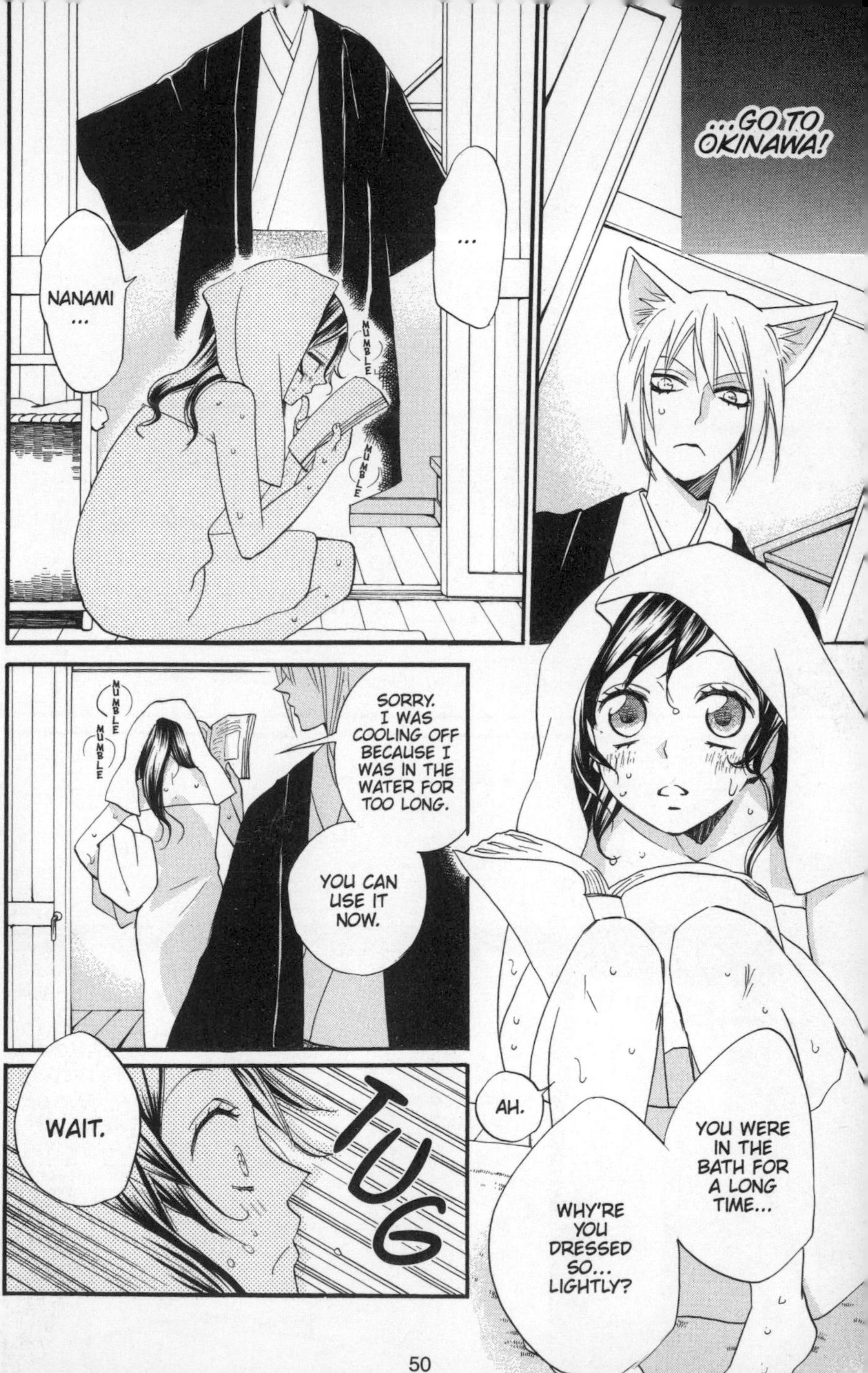
...GO TO OKINAWA!
...
NANAMI ...
MUMBLE
MUMBLE
AH.
YOU WERE IN THE BATH FOR A LONG TIME...
WHY'RE YOU DRESSED SO... LIGHTLY?
SORRY. I WAS COOLING OFF BECAUSE I WAS IN THE WATER FOR TOO LONG.
MUMBLE
MUMBLE
YOU CAN USE IT NOW.
TUG
WAIT.

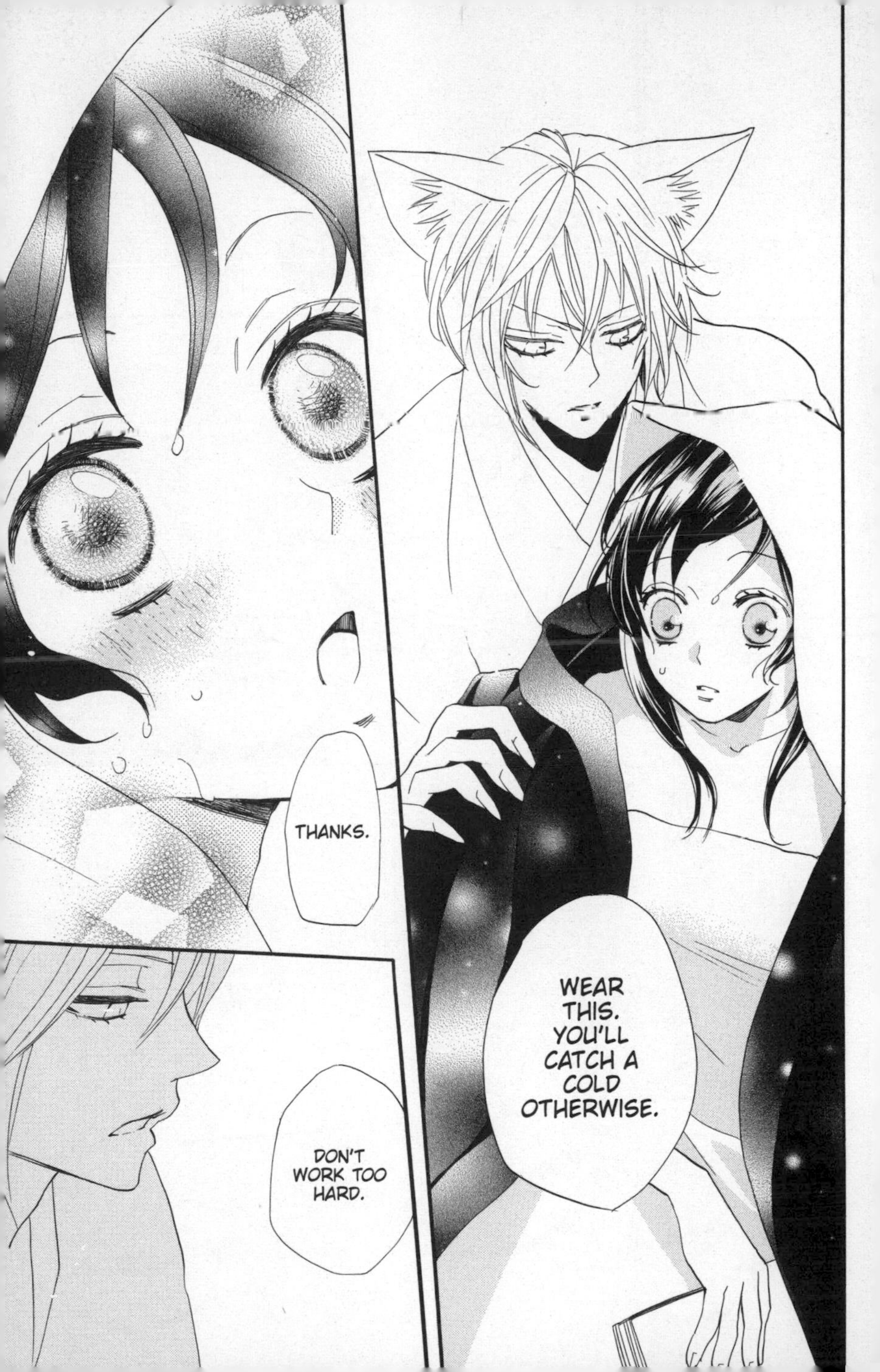
WEAR THIS. YOU'LL CATCH A COLD OTHERWISE.
THANKS.
DON'T WORK TOO HARD.

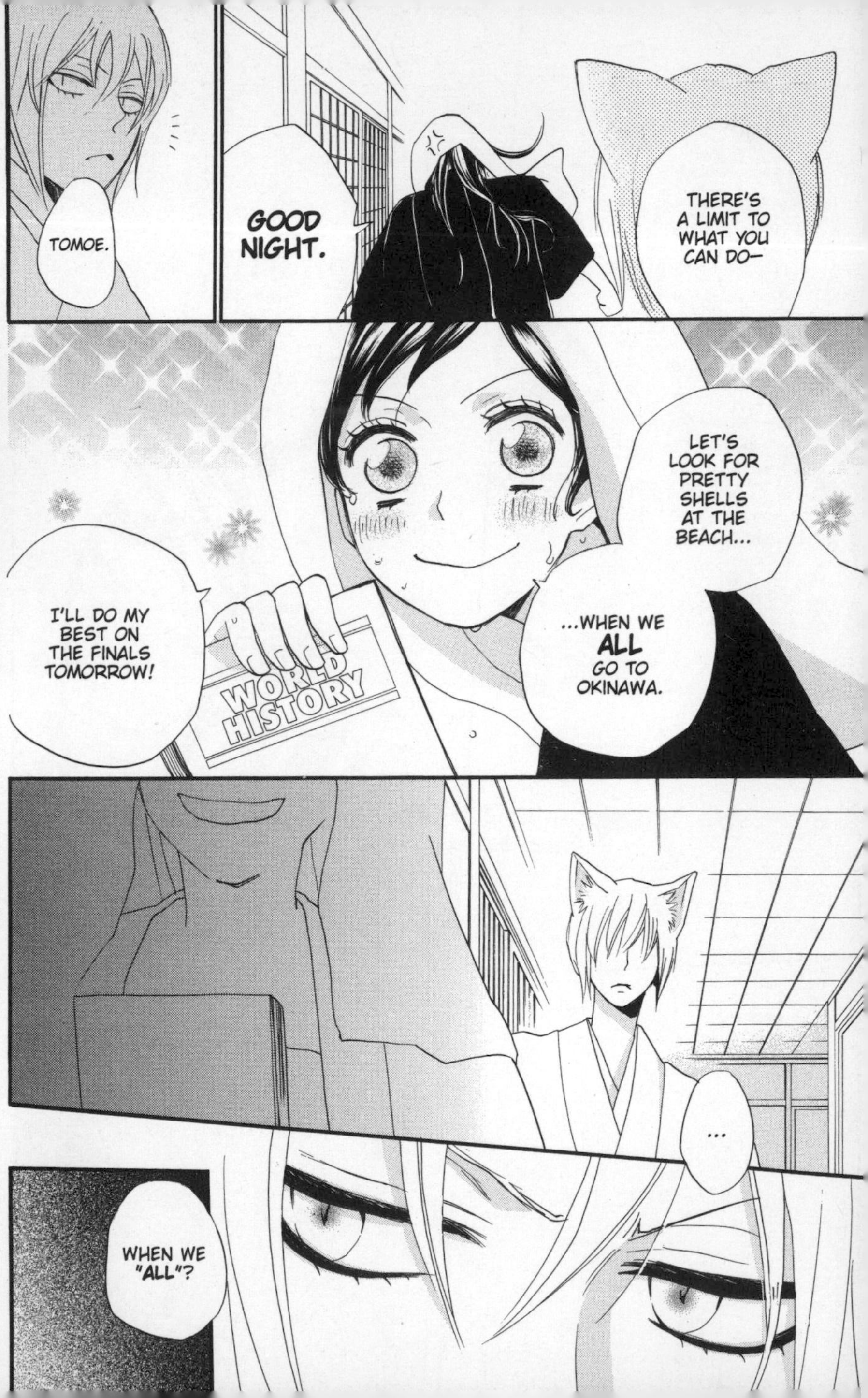
THERE'S A LIMIT TO WHAT YOU CAN DO—
GOOD NIGHT.
TOMOE.
LET'S LOOK FOR PRETTY SHELLS AT THE BEACH...
...WHEN WE ALL GO TO OKINAWA.
I'LL DO MY BEST ON THE FINALS TOMORROW!
WORLD HISTORY
...
WHEN WE "ALL"?

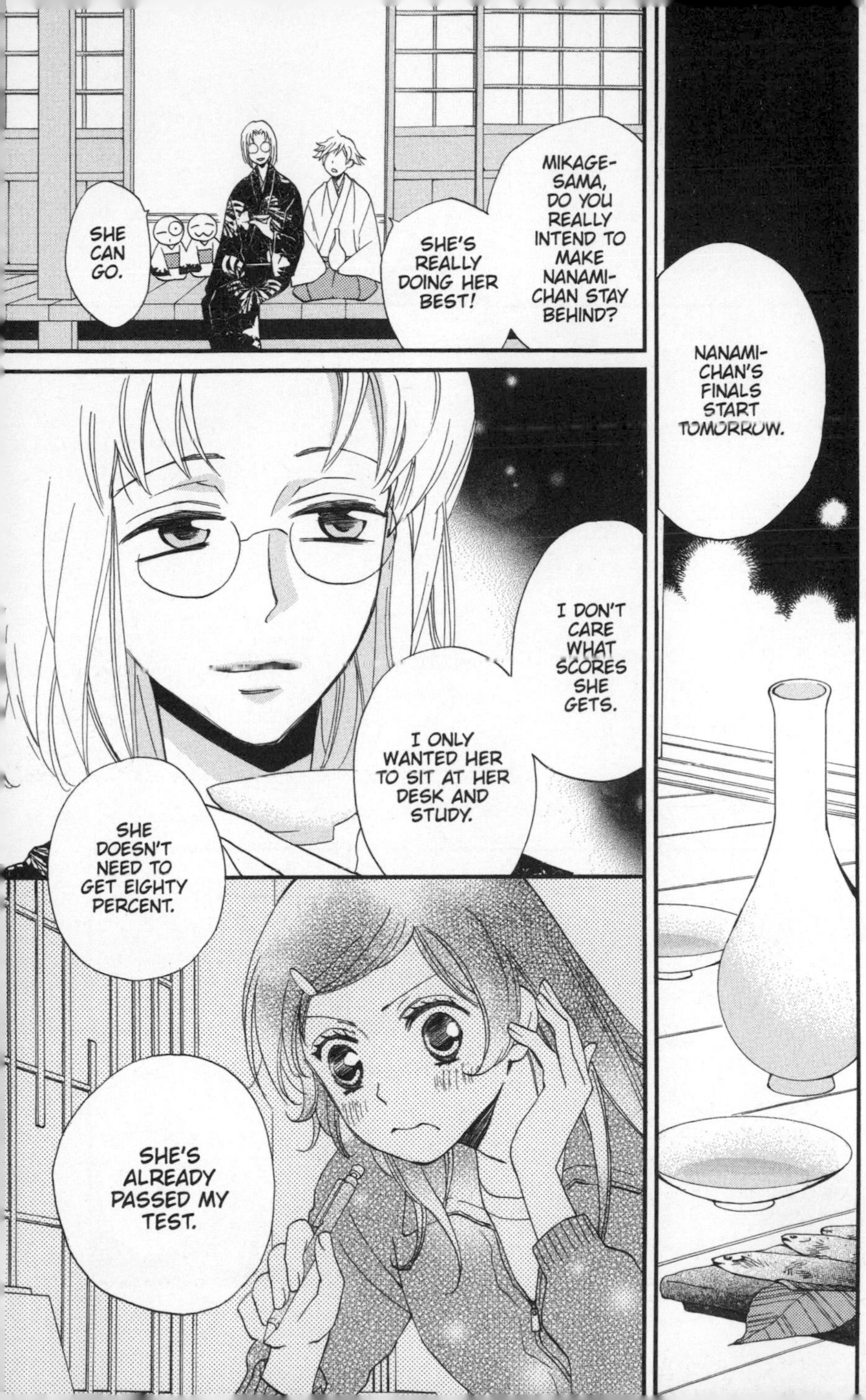
NANAMI-CHAN'S FINALS START TOMORROW.
MIKAGE-SAMA, DO YOU REALLY INTEND TO MAKE NANAMI-CHAN STAY BEHIND?
SHE'S REALLY DOING HER BEST!
SHE CAN GO.
I DON'T CARE WHAT SCORES SHE GETS.
I ONLY WANTED HER TO SIT AT HER DESK AND STUDY.
SHE DOESN'T NEED TO GET EIGHTY PERCENT.
SHE'S ALREADY PASSED MY TEST.

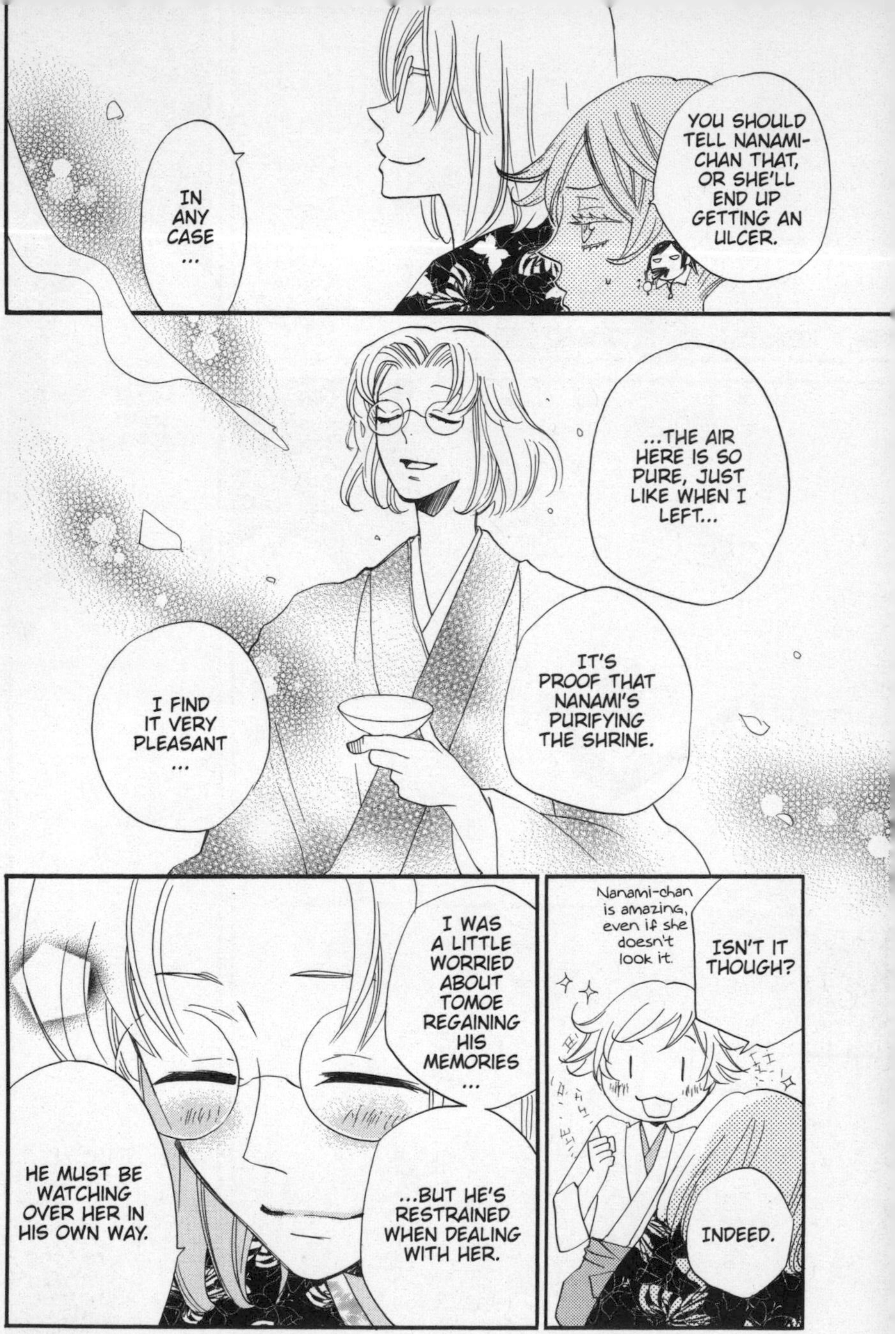
YOU SHOULD TELL NANAMI-CHAN THAT, OR SHE'LL END UP GETTING AN ULCER.
IN ANY CASE...
...THE AIR HERE IS SO PURE, JUST LIKE WHEN I LEFT...
IT'S PROOF THAT NANAMI'S PURIFYING THE SHRINE.
I FIND IT VERY PLEASANT...
Nanami-chan is amazing, even if she doesn't look it.
ISN'T IT THOUGH?
INDEED.
I WAS A LITTLE WORRIED ABOUT TOMOE REGAINING HIS MEMORIES...
...BUT HE'S RESTRAINED WHEN DEALING WITH HER.
HE MUST BE WATCHING OVER HER IN HIS OWN WAY.

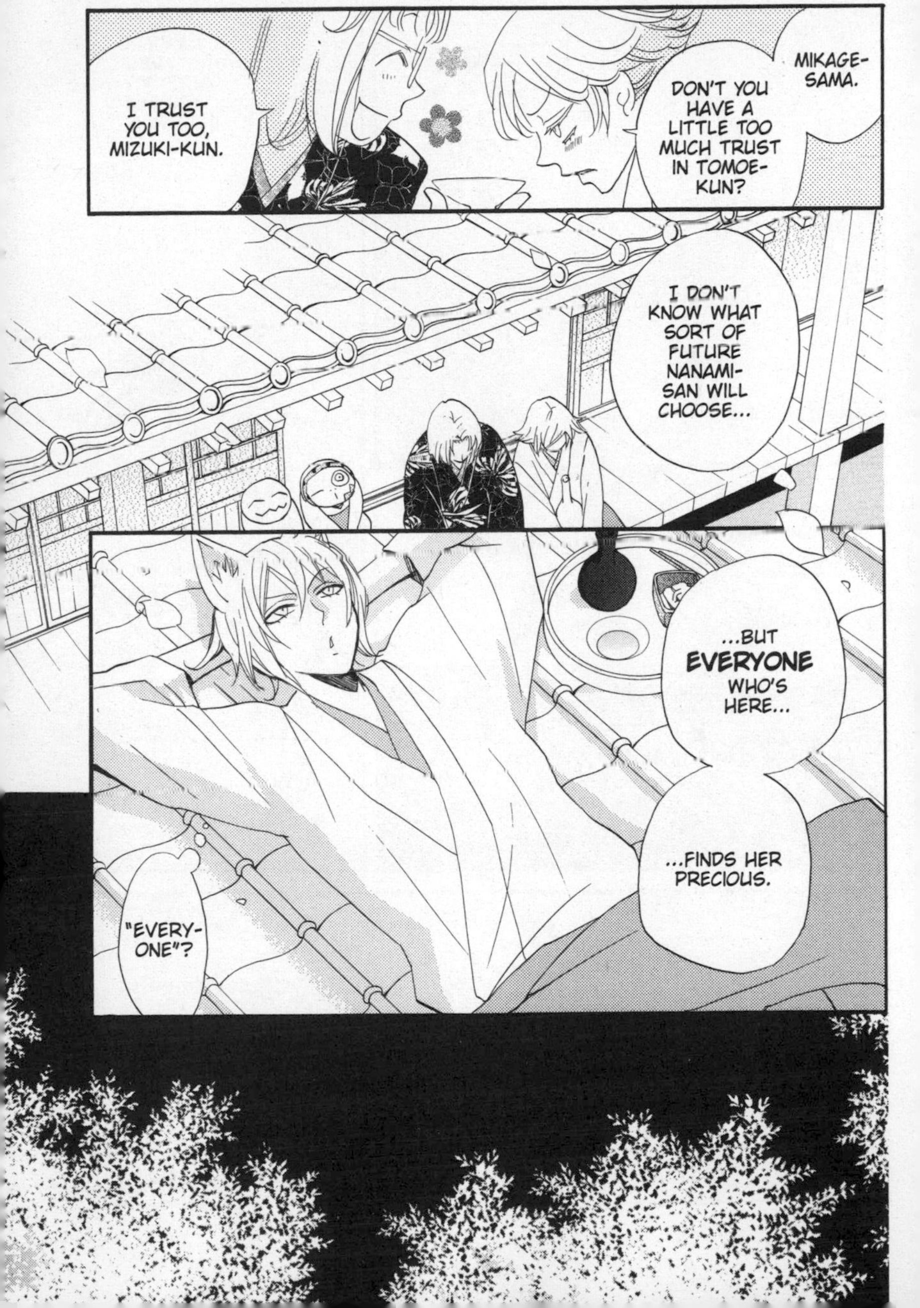
MIKAGE-SAMA.
DON'T YOU HAVE A LITTLE TOO MUCH TRUST IN TOMOE-KUN?
I TRUST YOU TOO, MIZUKI-KUN.
I DON'T KNOW WHAT SORT OF FUTURE NANAMI-SAN WILL CHOOSE...
...BUT EVERYONE WHO'S HERE...
...FINDS HER PRECIOUS.
"EVERY-ONE"?

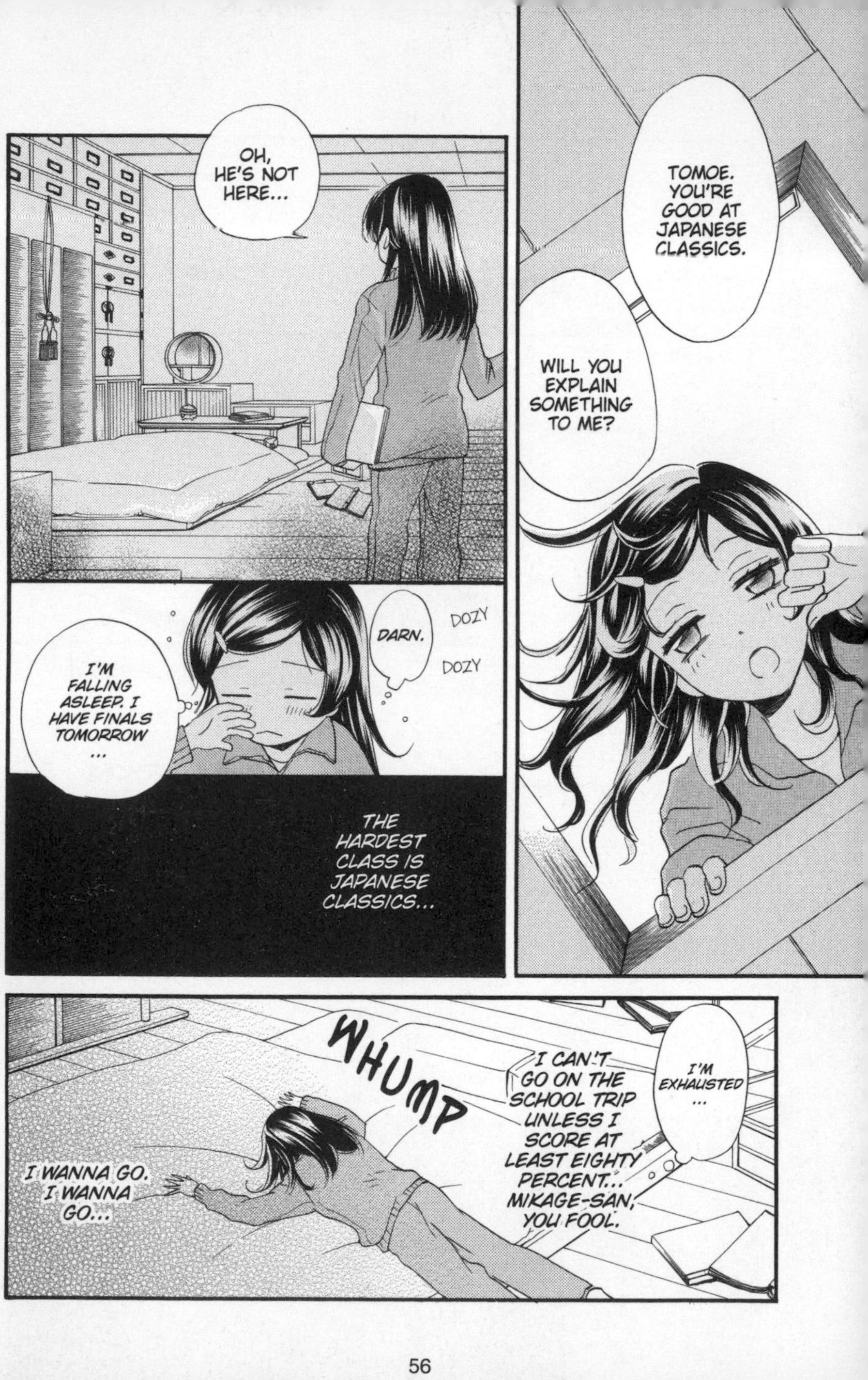
TOMOE. YOU'RE GOOD AT JAPANESE CLASSICS.
WILL YOU EXPLAIN SOMETHING TO ME?
OH, HE'S NOT HERE...
DOZY
DOZY
DARN.
I'M FALLING ASLEEP. I HAVE FINALS TOMORROW ...
THE HARDEST CLASS IS JAPANESE CLASSICS...
I'M EXHAUSTED ...
I CAN'T GO ON THE SCHOOL TRIP UNLESS I SCORE AT LEAST EIGHTY PERCENT... MIKAGE-SAN, YOU FOOL.
WHUMP
I WANNA GO. I WANNA GO...

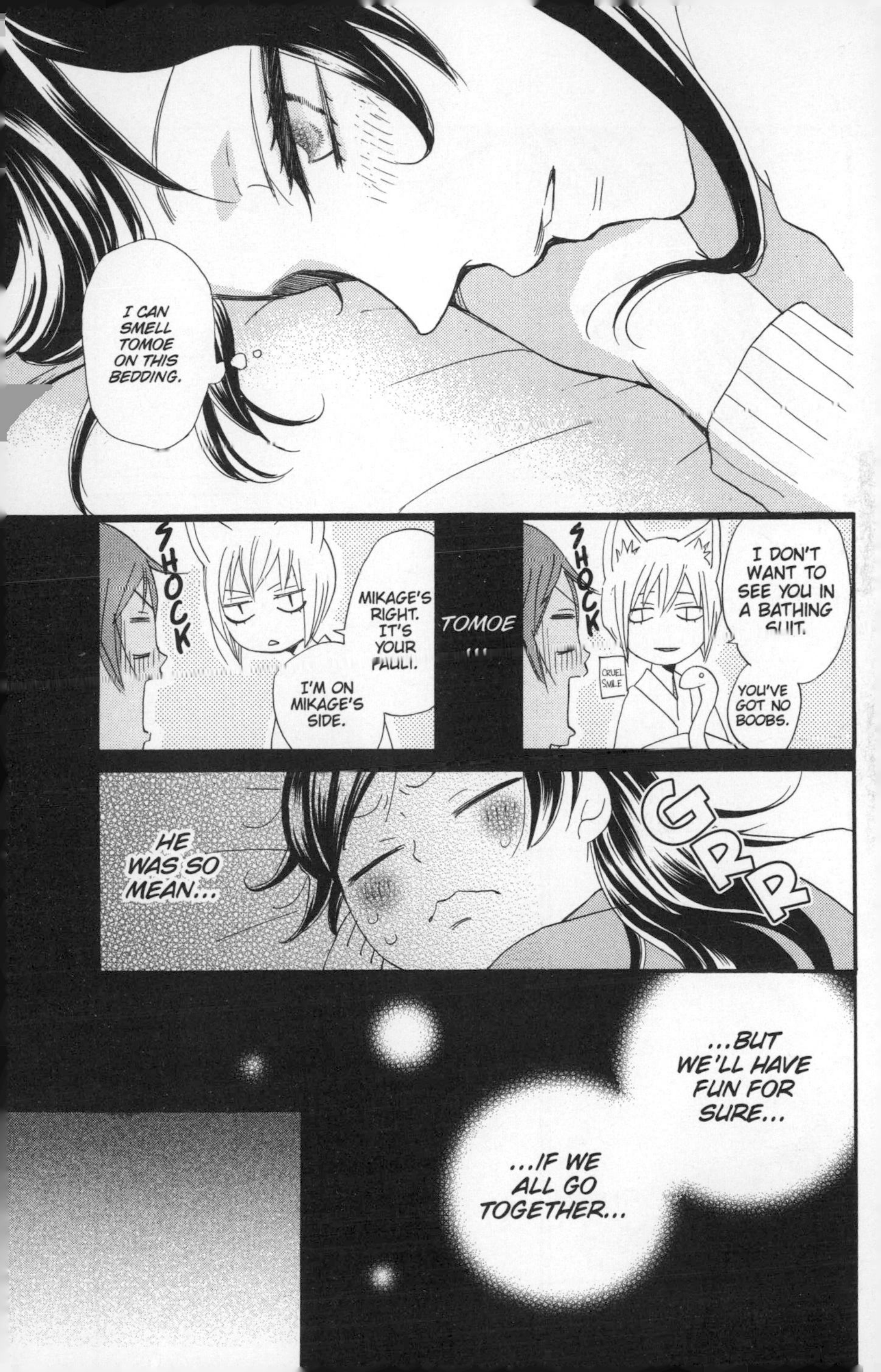
I CAN SMELL TOMOE ON THIS BEDDING.
SHOCK
I DON'T WANT TO SEE YOU IN A BATHING SUIT.
CRUEL SMILE
YOU'VE GOT NO BOOBS.
TOMOE ...
SHOCK
MIKAGE'S RIGHT. IT'S YOUR FAULT.
I'M ON MIKAGE'S SIDE.
GRR
HE WAS SO MEAN...
...BUT WE'LL HAVE FUN FOR SURE...
...IF WE ALL GO TOGETHER...

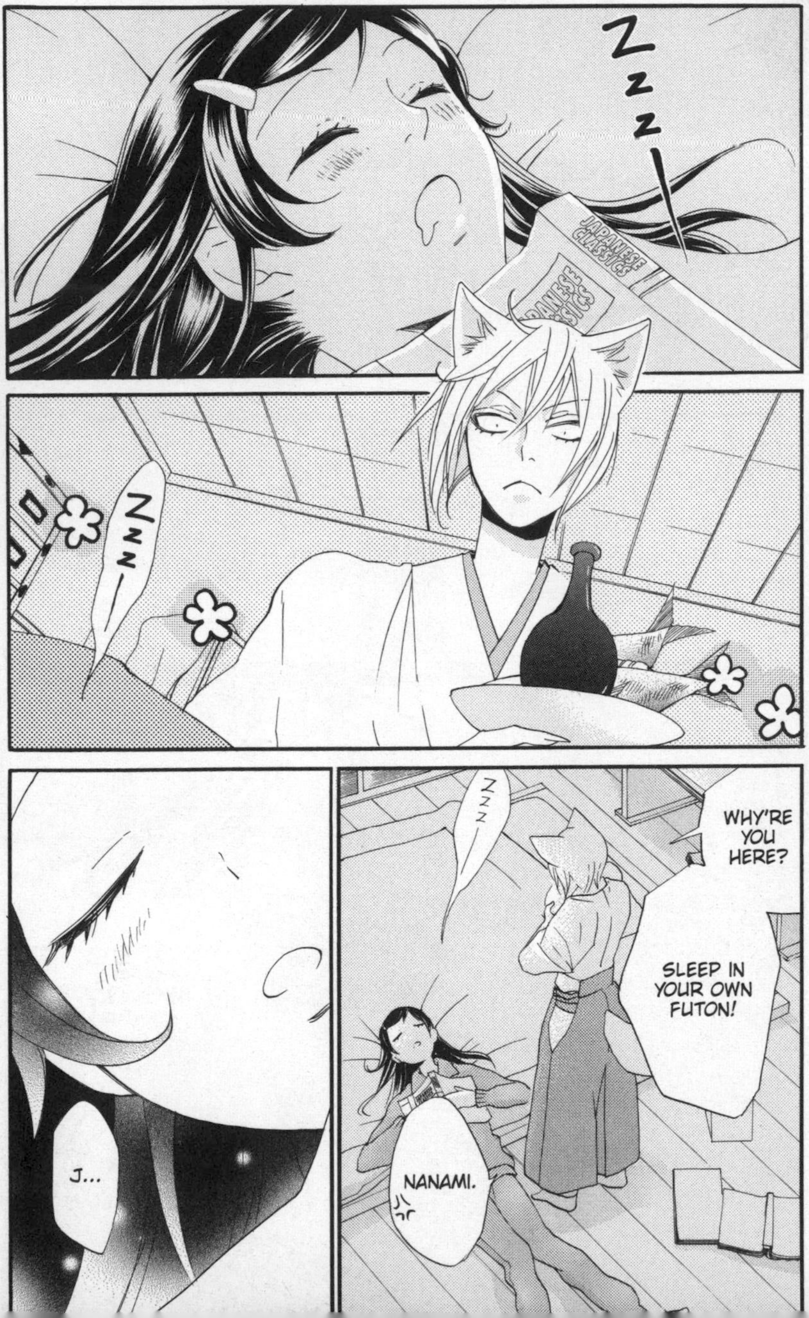
ZZZ
JAPANESE CLASSICS
ZZZ
WHY'RE YOU HERE?
ZZZ
SLEEP IN YOUR OWN FUTON!
NANAMI.
J...

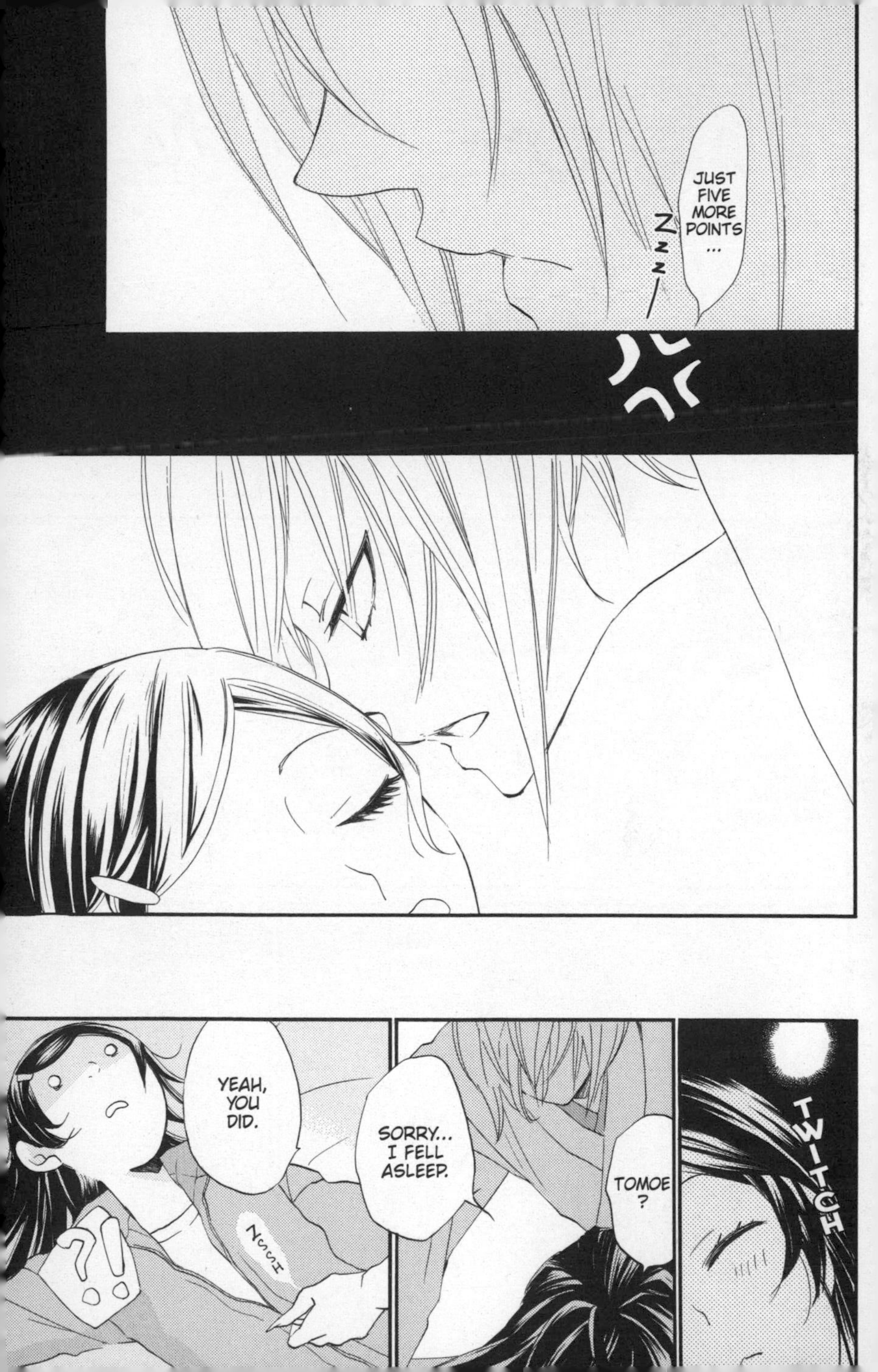
JUST FIVE MORE POINTS ...
Z z z
TWITCH
TOMOE?
SORRY... I FELL ASLEEP.
YEAH, YOU DID.
ZSSH

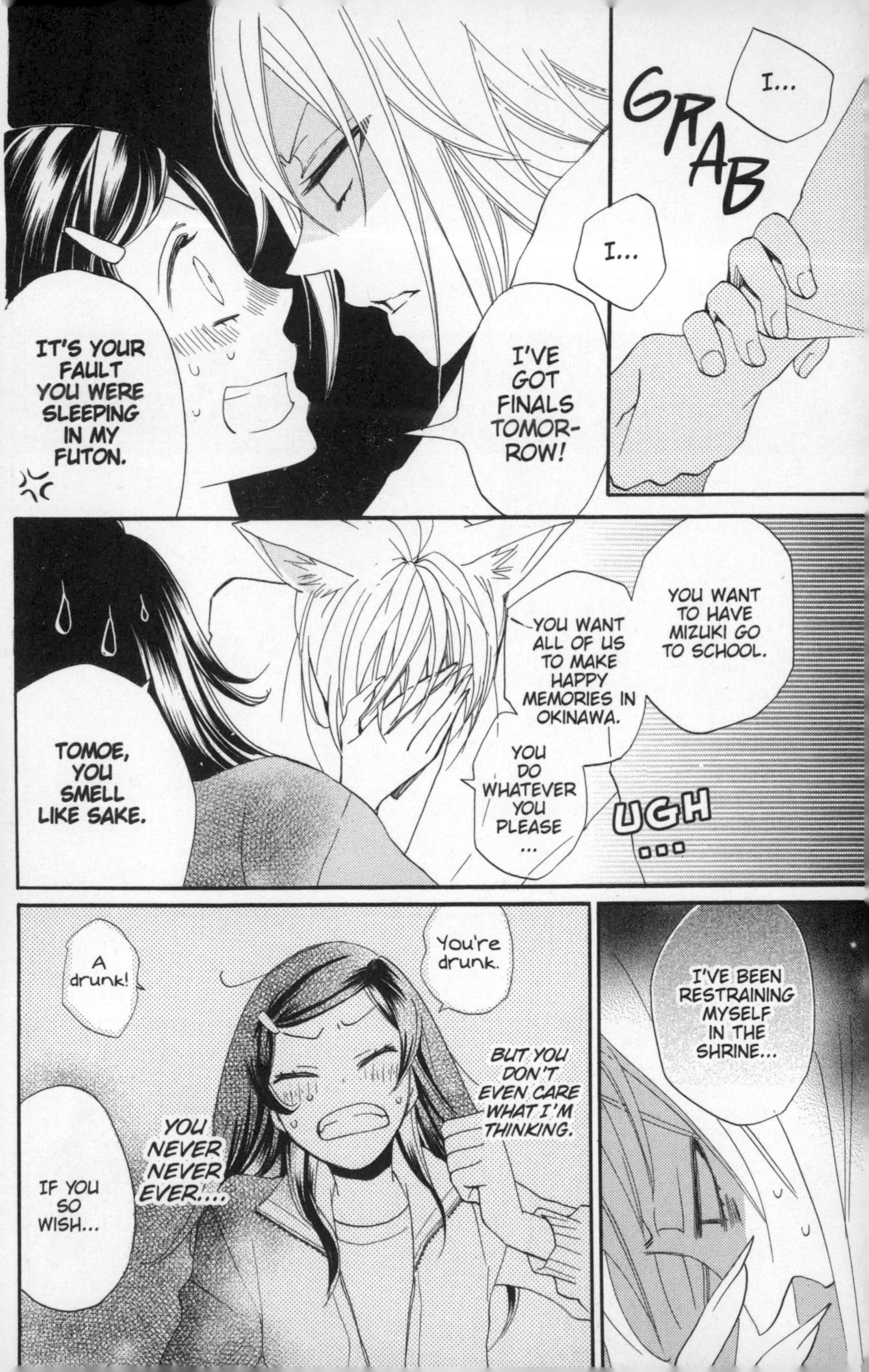
I...
GRAB
I...
I'VE GOT FINALS TOMORROW!
IT'S YOUR FAULT YOU WERE SLEEPING IN MY FUTON.
YOU WANT TO HAVE MIZUKI GO TO SCHOOL.
YOU WANT ALL OF US TO MAKE HAPPY MEMORIES IN OKINAWA.
UGH...
YOU DO WHATEVER YOU PLEASE...
TOMOE, YOU SMELL LIKE SAKE.
I'VE BEEN RESTRAINING MYSELF IN THE SHRINE...
You're drunk.
A drunk!
BUT YOU DON'T EVEN CARE WHAT I'M THINKING.
YOU NEVER NEVER EVER....
IF YOU SO WISH...

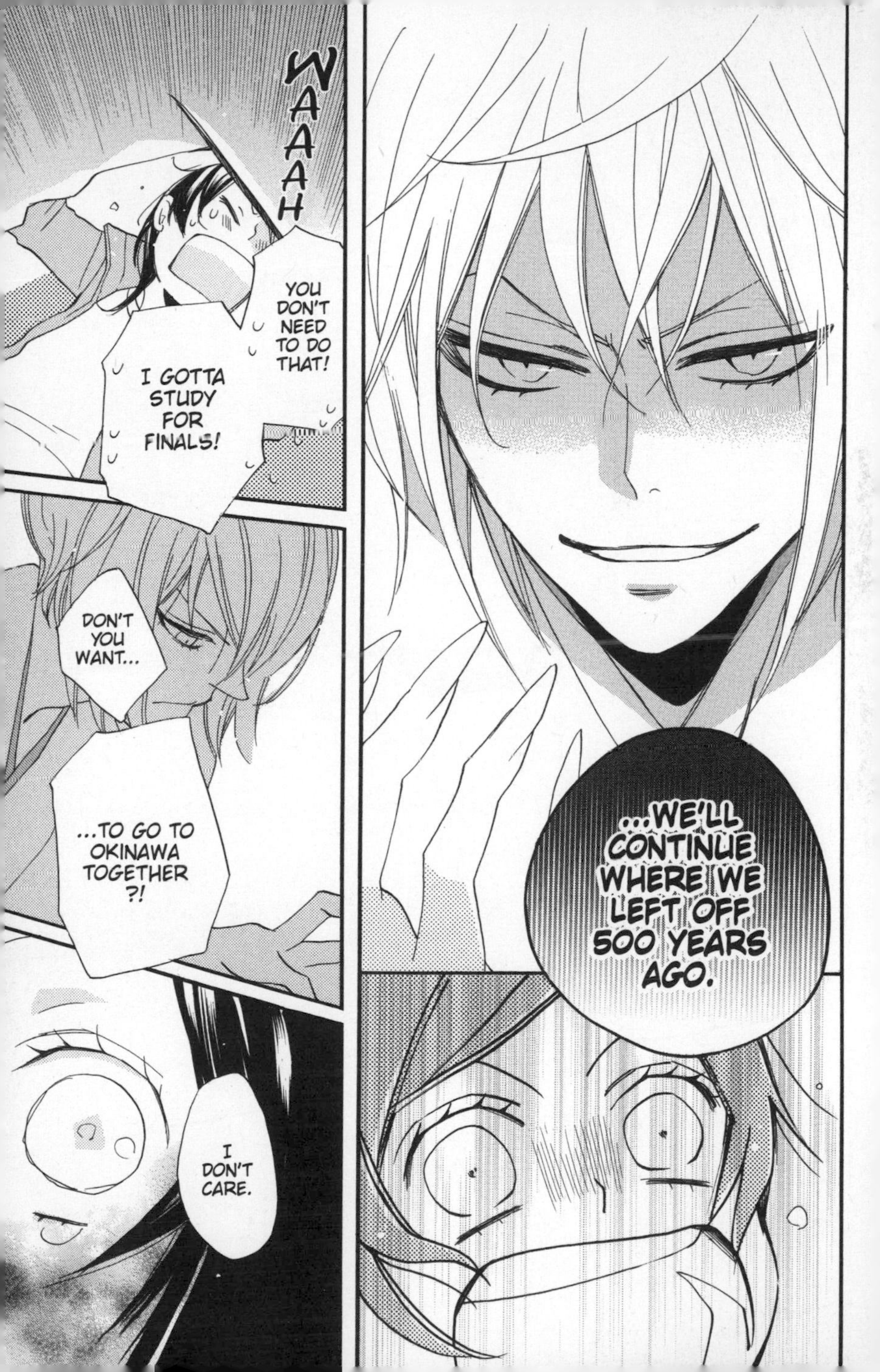
...WE'LL CONTINUE WHERE WE LEFT OFF 500 YEARS AGO.
WAAAAH
YOU DON'T NEED TO DO THAT!
I GOTTA STUDY FOR FINALS!
DON'T YOU WANT...
...TO GO TO OKINAWA TOGETHER ?!
I DON'T CARE.

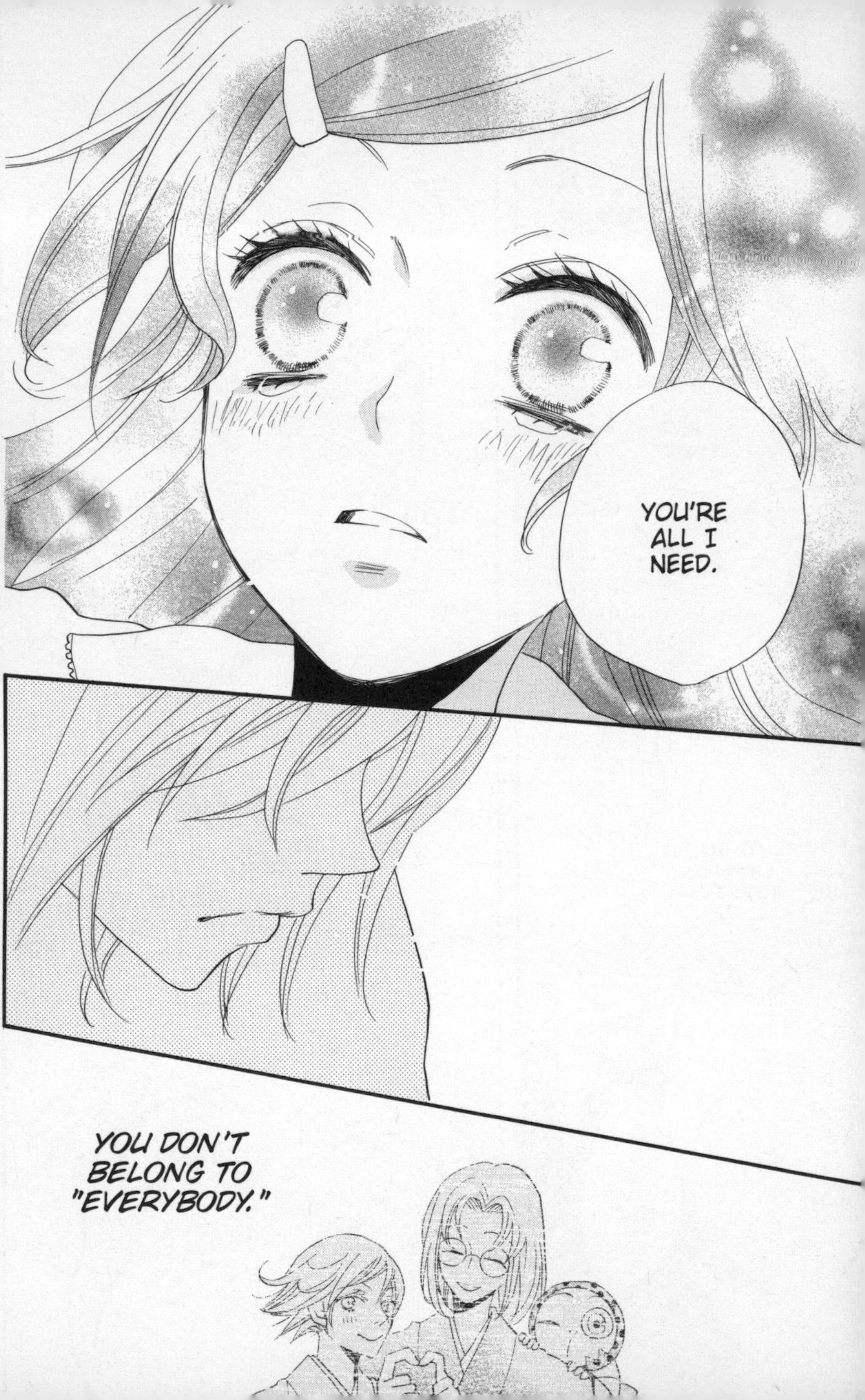
YOU'RE ALL I NEED.
YOU DON'T BELONG TO "EVERYBODY."

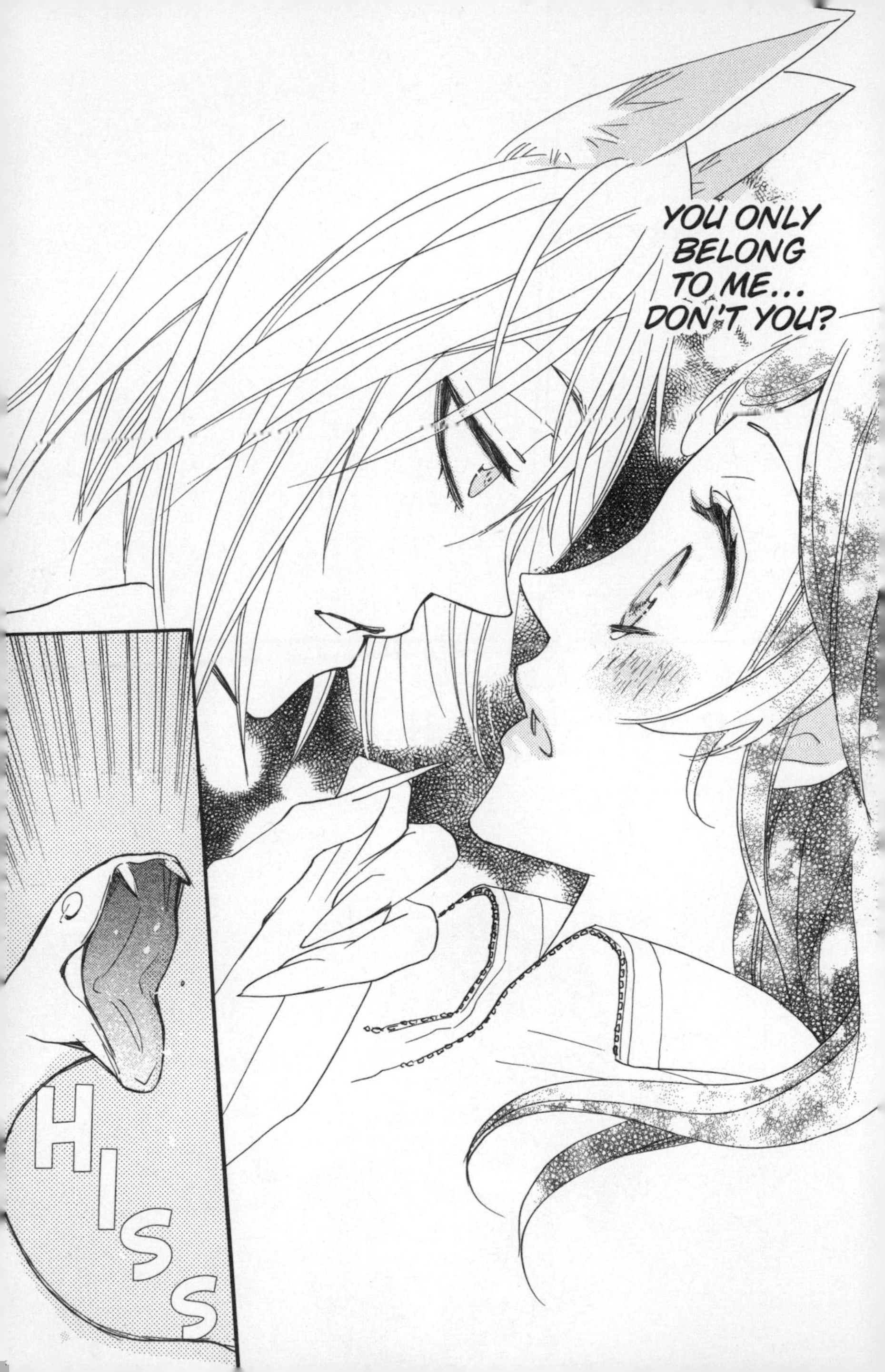
YOU ONLY BELONG TO ME... DON'T YOU?
HISS

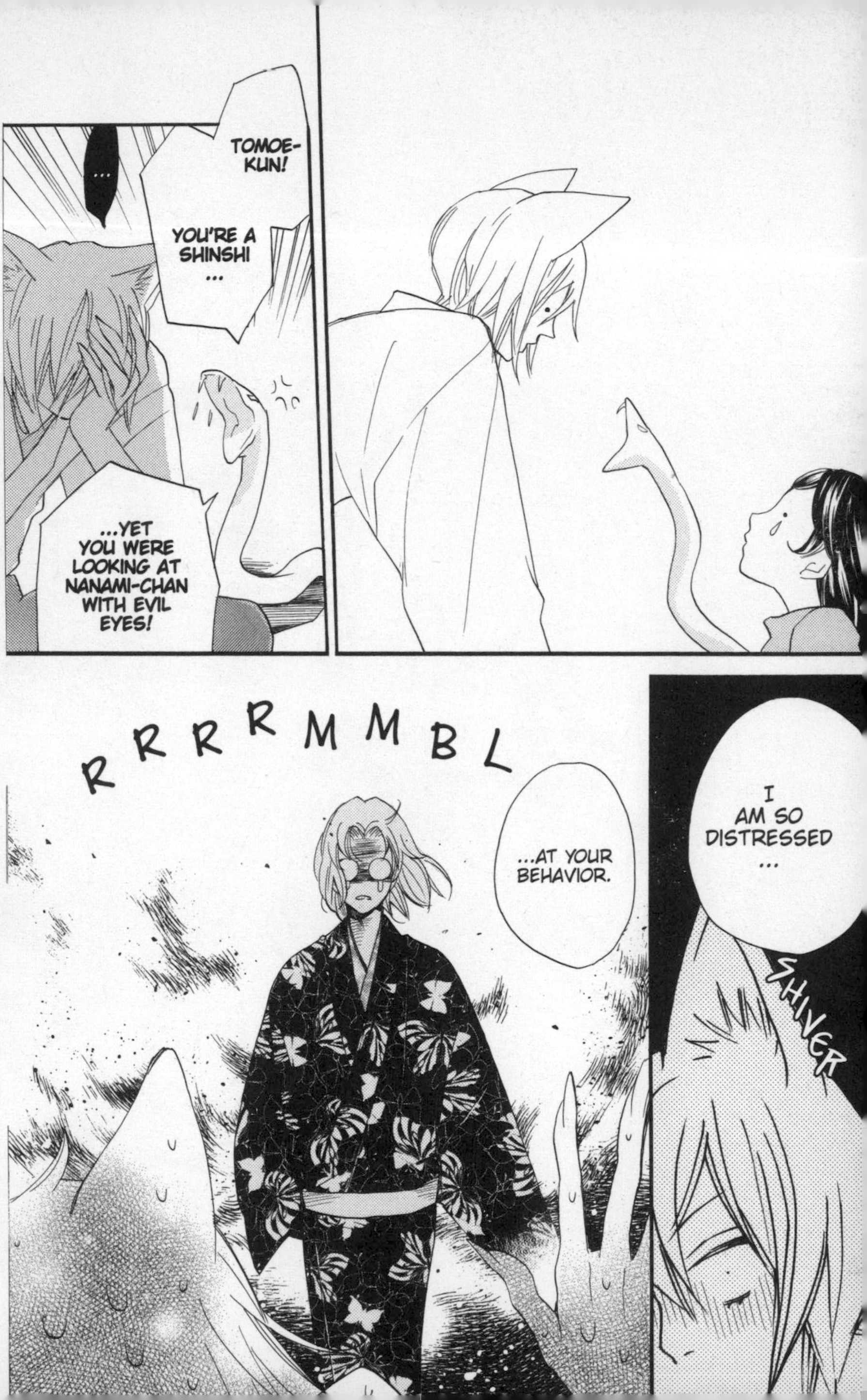
TOMOE-KUN!
YOU'RE A SHINSHI ...
...
...YET YOU WERE LOOKING AT NANAMI-CHAN WITH EVIL EYES!
I AM SO DISTRESSED ...
SHIVER
...AT YOUR BEHAVIOR.
RRRRMMBL

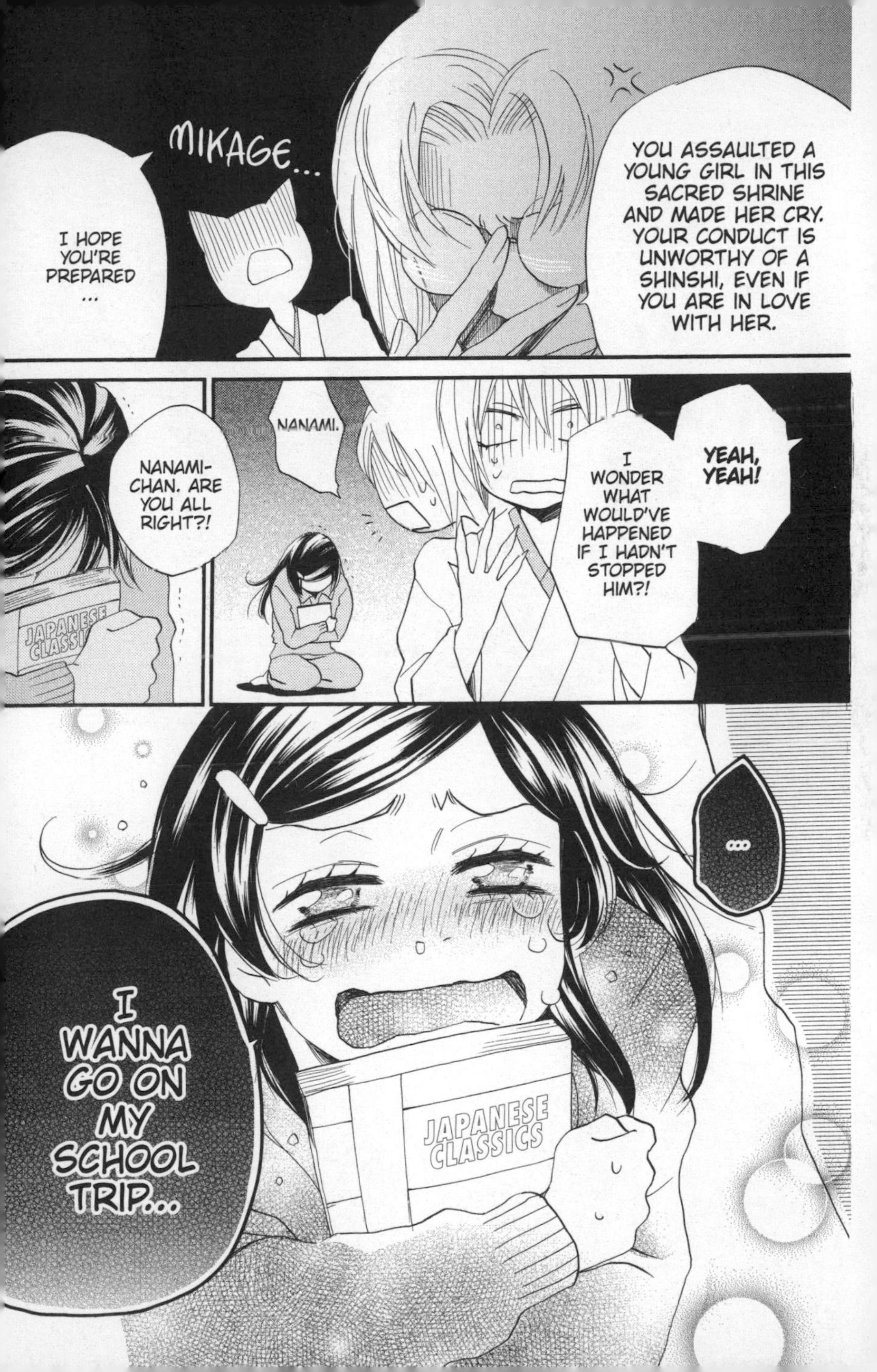
YOU ASSAULTED A YOUNG GIRL IN THIS SACRED SHRINE AND MADE HER CRY. YOUR CONDUCT IS UNWORTHY OF A SHINSHI, EVEN IF YOU ARE IN LOVE WITH HER.
MIKAGE...
I HOPE YOU'RE PREPARED ...
YEAH, YEAH!
I WONDER WHAT WOULD'VE HAPPENED IF I HADN'T STOPPED HIM?!
NANAMI.
NANAMI-CHAN. ARE YOU ALL RIGHT?!
JAPANESE CLASSICS
...
I WANNA GO ON MY SCHOOL TRIP...
JAPANESE CLASSICS

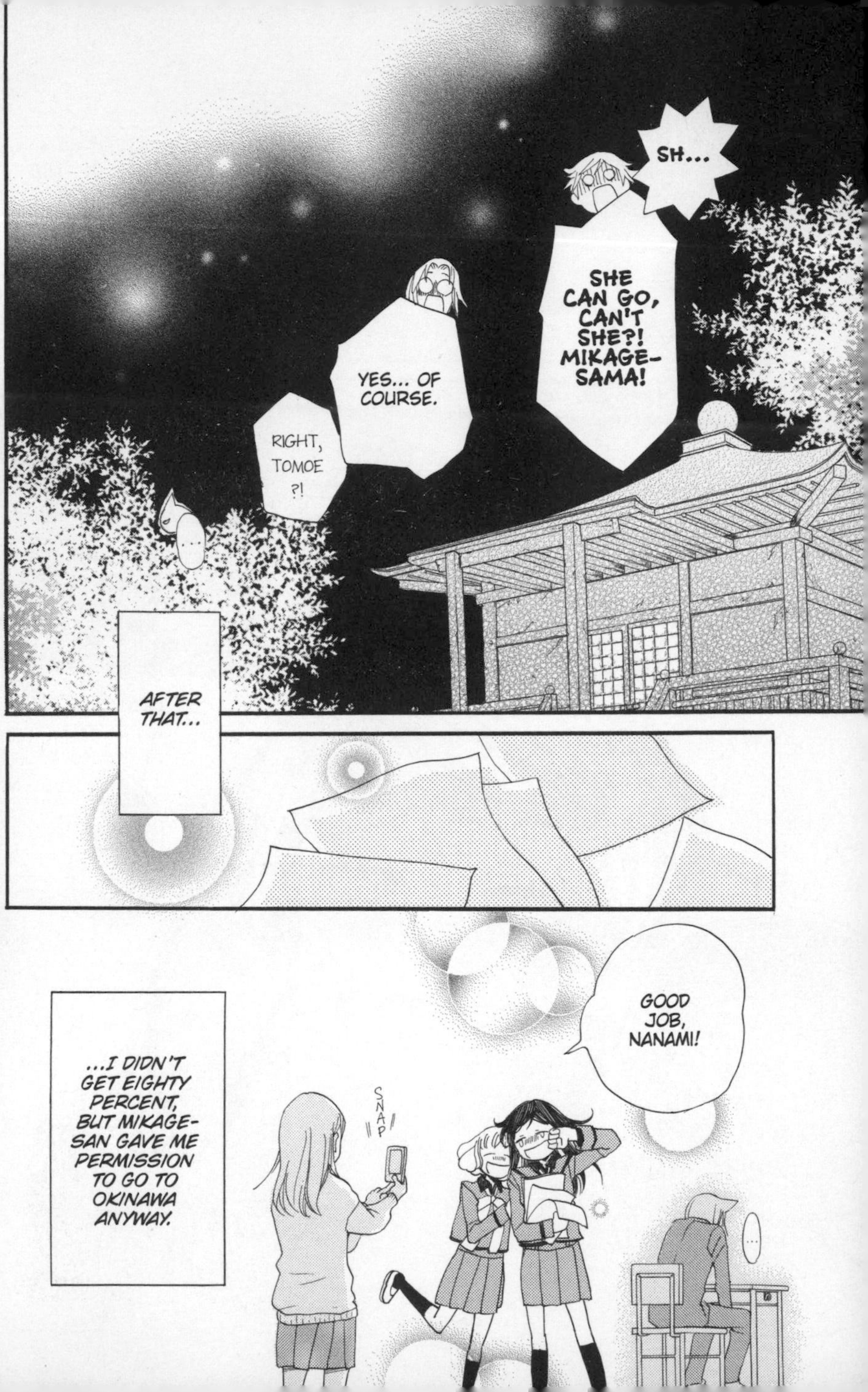

SH...
SHE CAN GO, CAN'T SHE?! MIKAGE-SAMA!
YES... OF COURSE.
RIGHT, TOMOE ?!
...
AFTER THAT...
GOOD JOB, NANAMI!
...
SNAP
...I DIDN'T GET EIGHTY PERCENT, BUT MIKAGE-SAN GAVE ME PERMISSION TO GO TO OKINAWA ANYWAY.

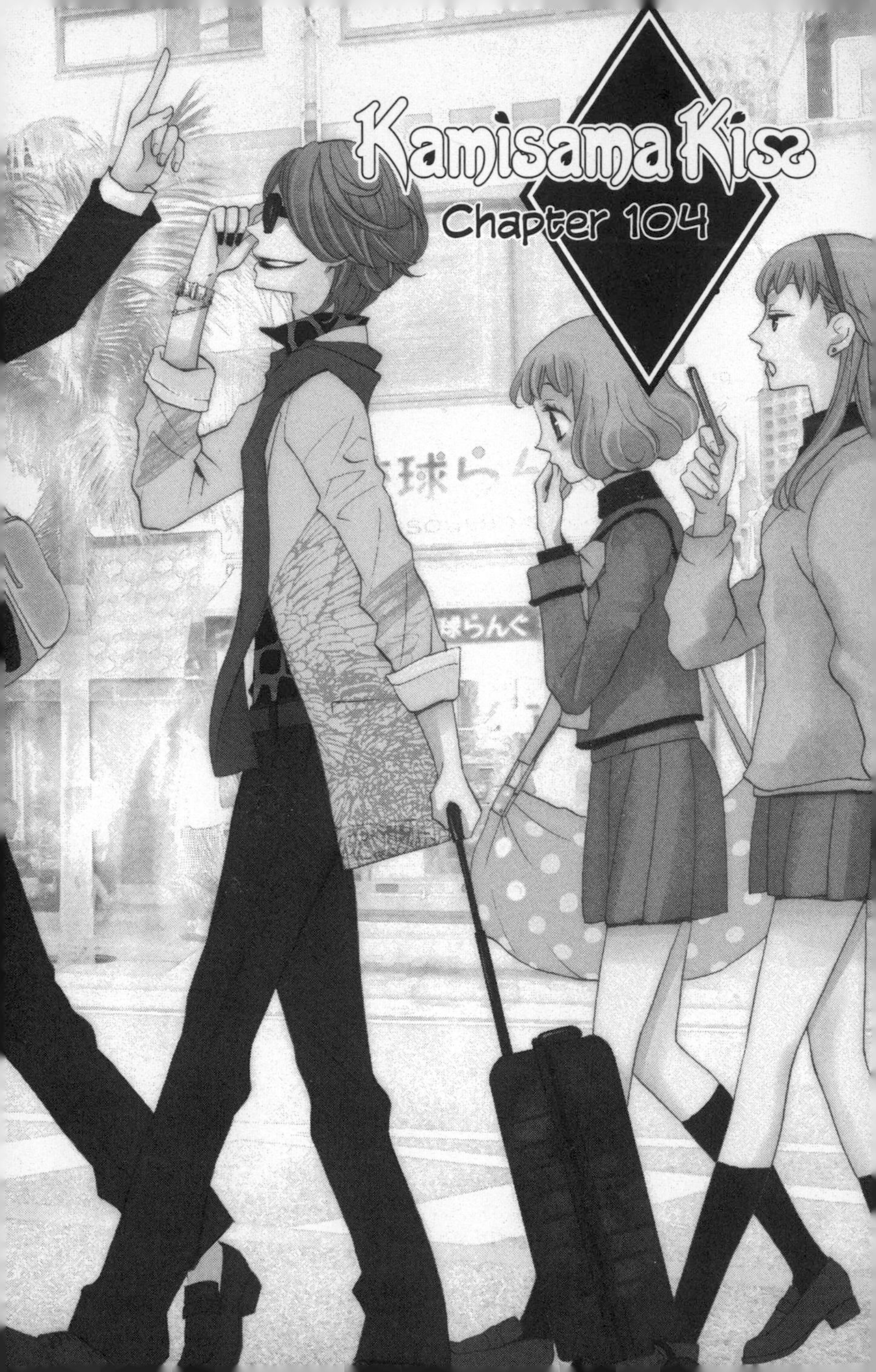
Kamisama Kiss
Chapter 104

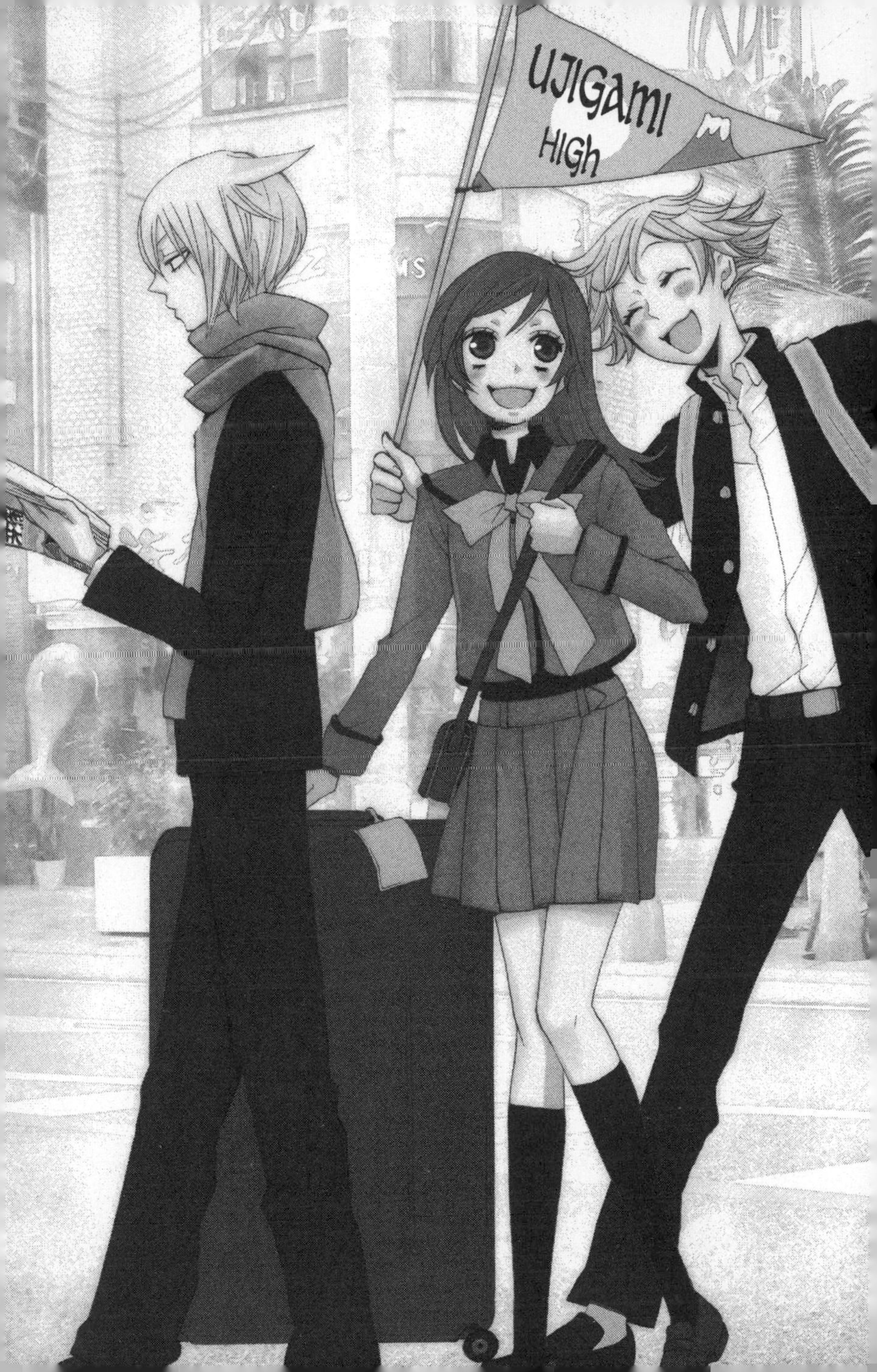
UJIGAMI
HIGh

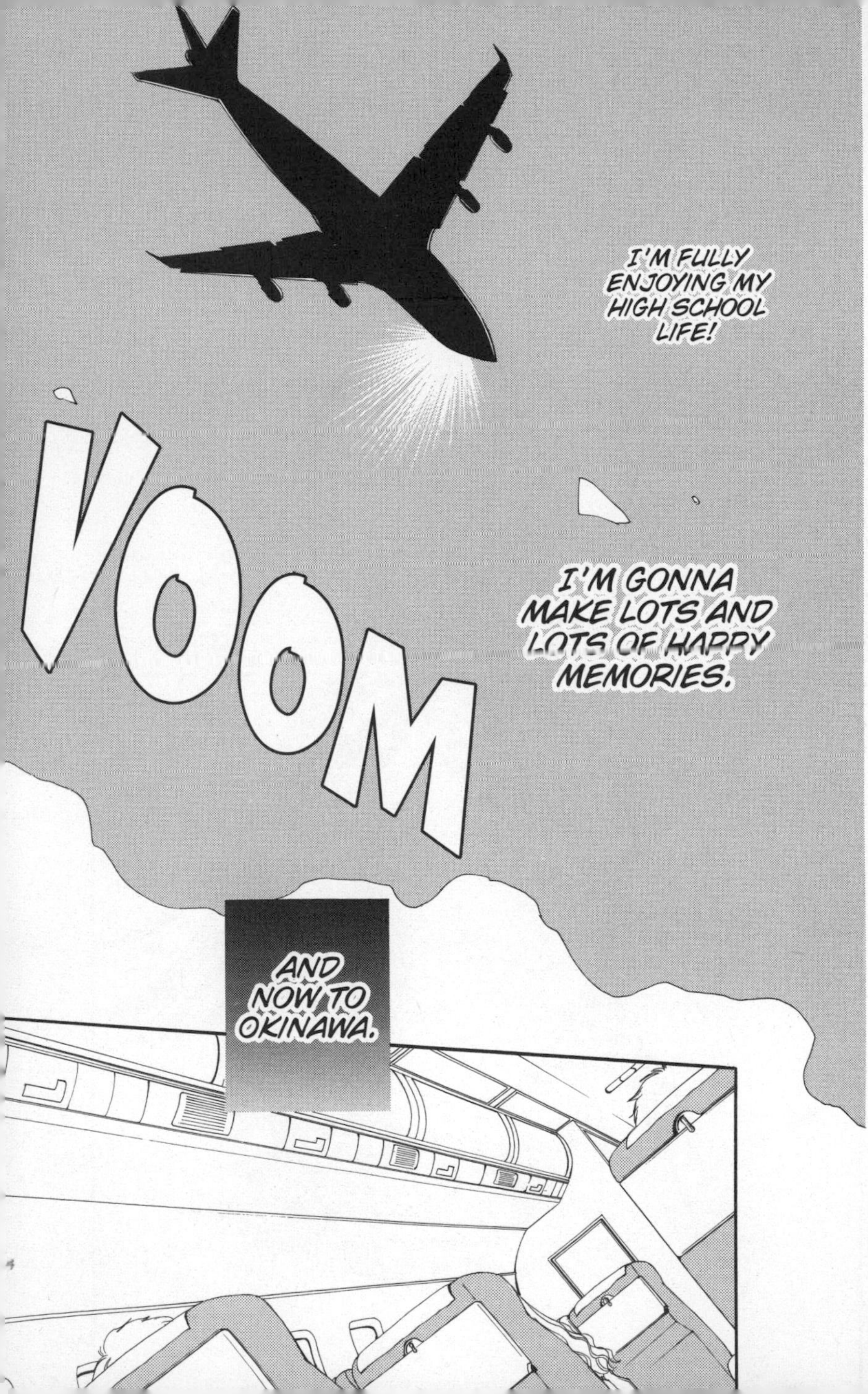
I'M FULLY ENJOYING MY HIGH SCHOOL LIFE!
I'M GONNA MAKE LOTS AND LOTS OF HAPPY MEMORIES.
VOOM
AND NOW TO OKINAWA.

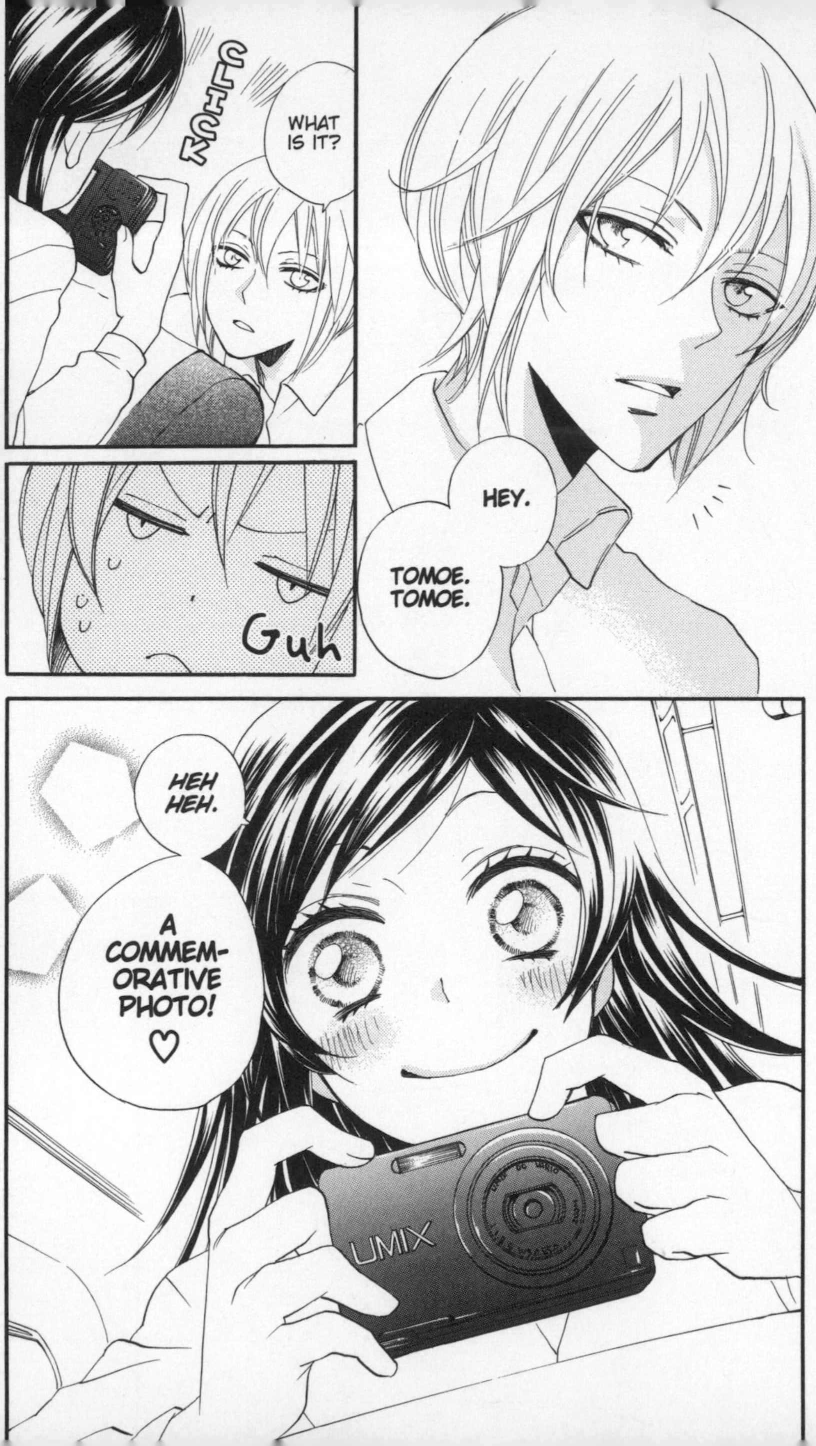
HEY.
TOMOE. TOMOE.
WHAT IS IT?
CLICK
Guh
HEH HEH.
A COMMEM-ORATIVE PHOTO! ♡
UMIX

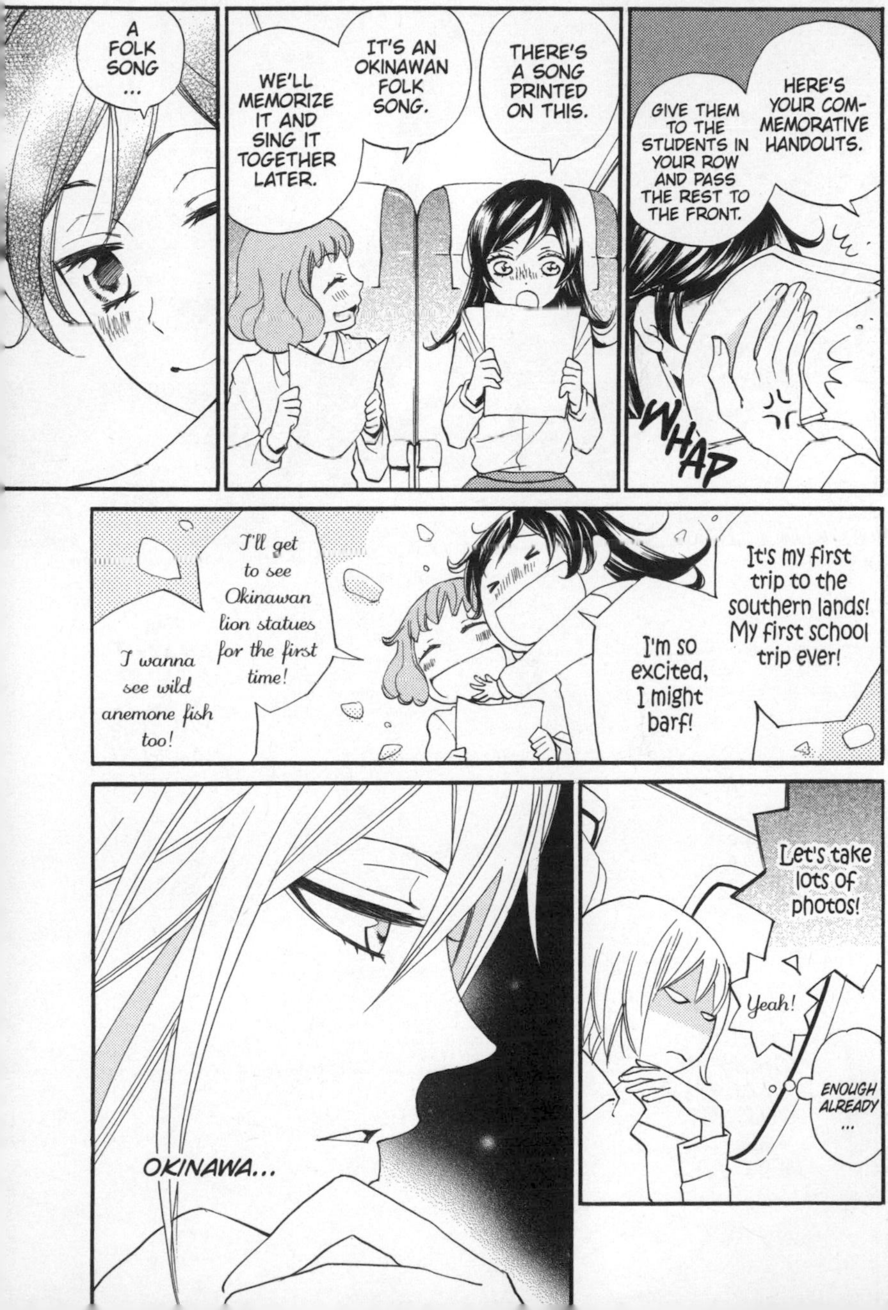
HERE'S YOUR COM-MEMORATIVE HANDOUTS.
GIVE THEM TO THE STUDENTS IN YOUR ROW AND PASS THE REST TO THE FRONT.
WHAP
THERE'S A SONG PRINTED ON THIS.
IT'S AN OKINAWAN FOLK SONG.
WE'LL MEMORIZE IT AND SING IT TOGETHER LATER.
A FOLK SONG ...
It's my first trip to the southern lands! My first school trip ever!
I'm so excited, I might barf!
I'll get to see Okinawan lion statues for the first time!
I wanna see wild anemone fish too!
Let's take lots of photos!
Yeah!
ENOUGH ALREADY ...
OKINAWA...

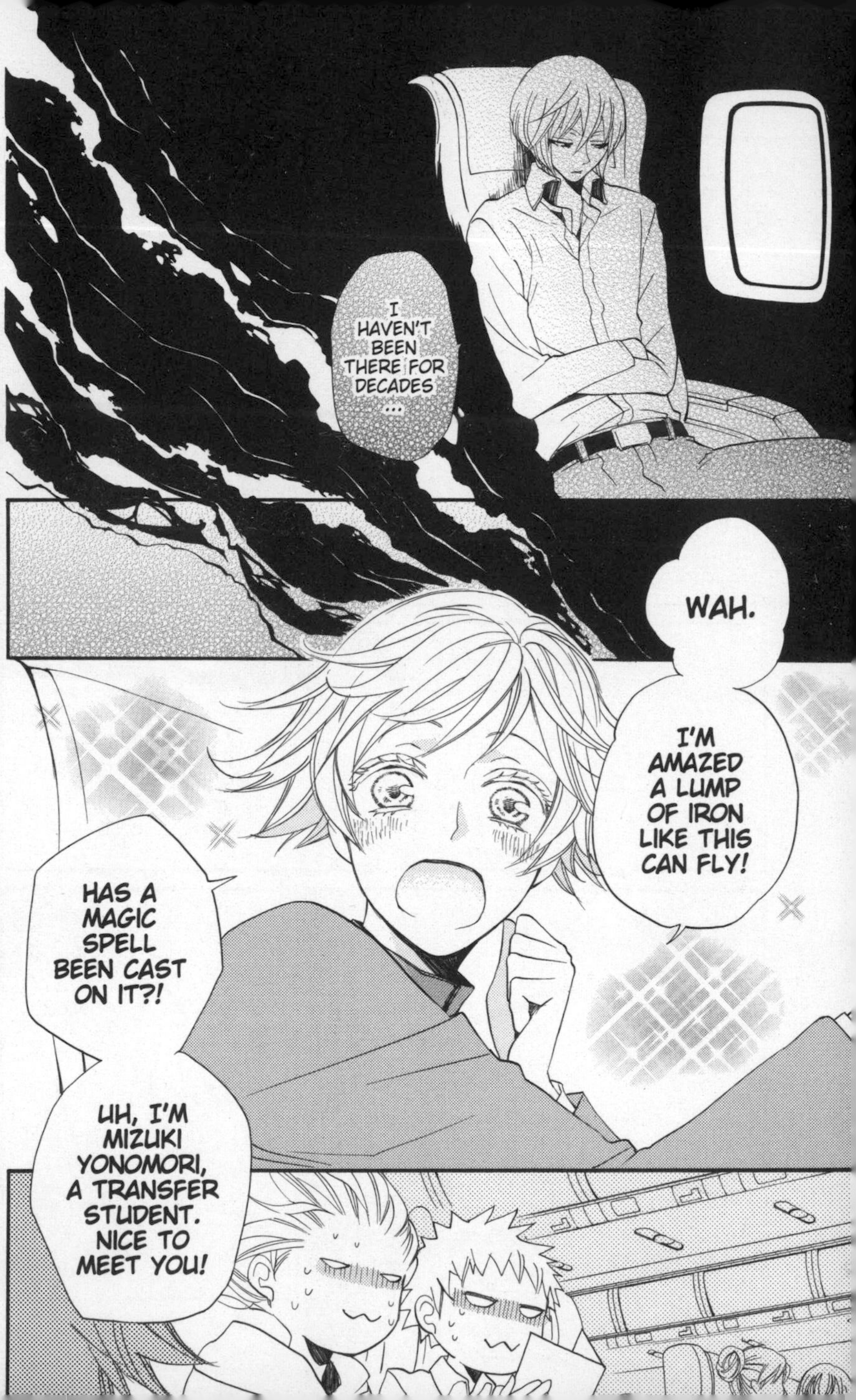
I HAVEN'T BEEN THERE FOR DECADES ...
WAH.
I'M AMAZED A LUMP OF IRON LIKE THIS CAN FLY!
HAS A MAGIC SPELL BEEN CAST ON IT?!
UH, I'M MIZUKI YONOMORI, A TRANSFER STUDENT. NICE TO MEET YOU!

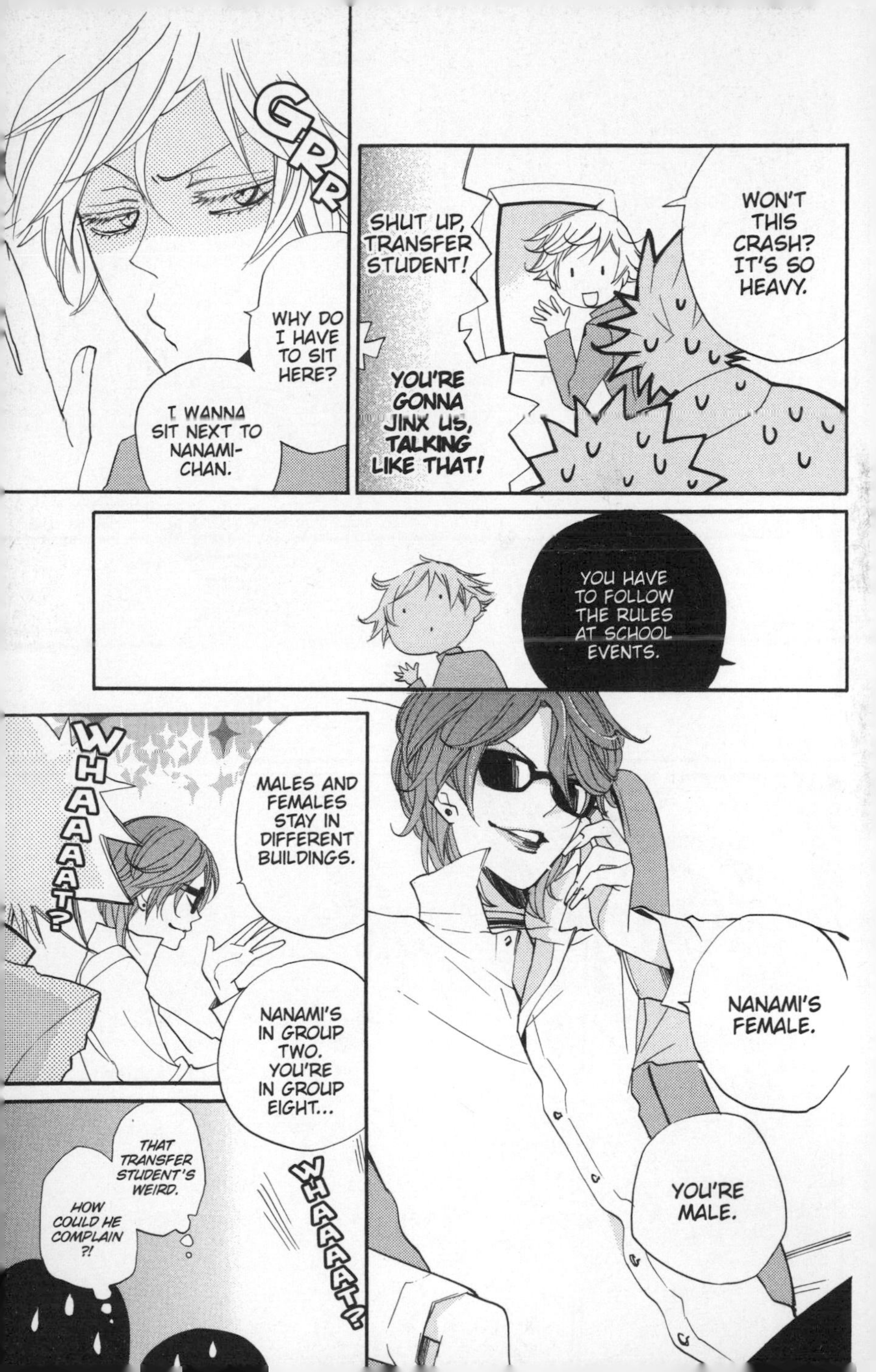
WON'T THIS CRASH? IT'S SO HEAVY.
SHUT UP, TRANSFER STUDENT!
YOU'RE GONNA JINX US, TALKING LIKE THAT!
GRR
WHY DO I HAVE TO SIT HERE?
I WANNA SIT NEXT TO NANAMI-CHAN.
YOU HAVE TO FOLLOW THE RULES AT SCHOOL EVENTS.
NANAMI'S FEMALE.
YOU'RE MALE.
MALES AND FEMALES STAY IN DIFFERENT BUILDINGS.
WHAAAAAT?
NANAMI'S IN GROUP TWO. YOU'RE IN GROUP EIGHT...
WHAAAAAAT?
THAT TRANSFER STUDENT'S WEIRD.
HOW COULD HE COMPLAIN ?!

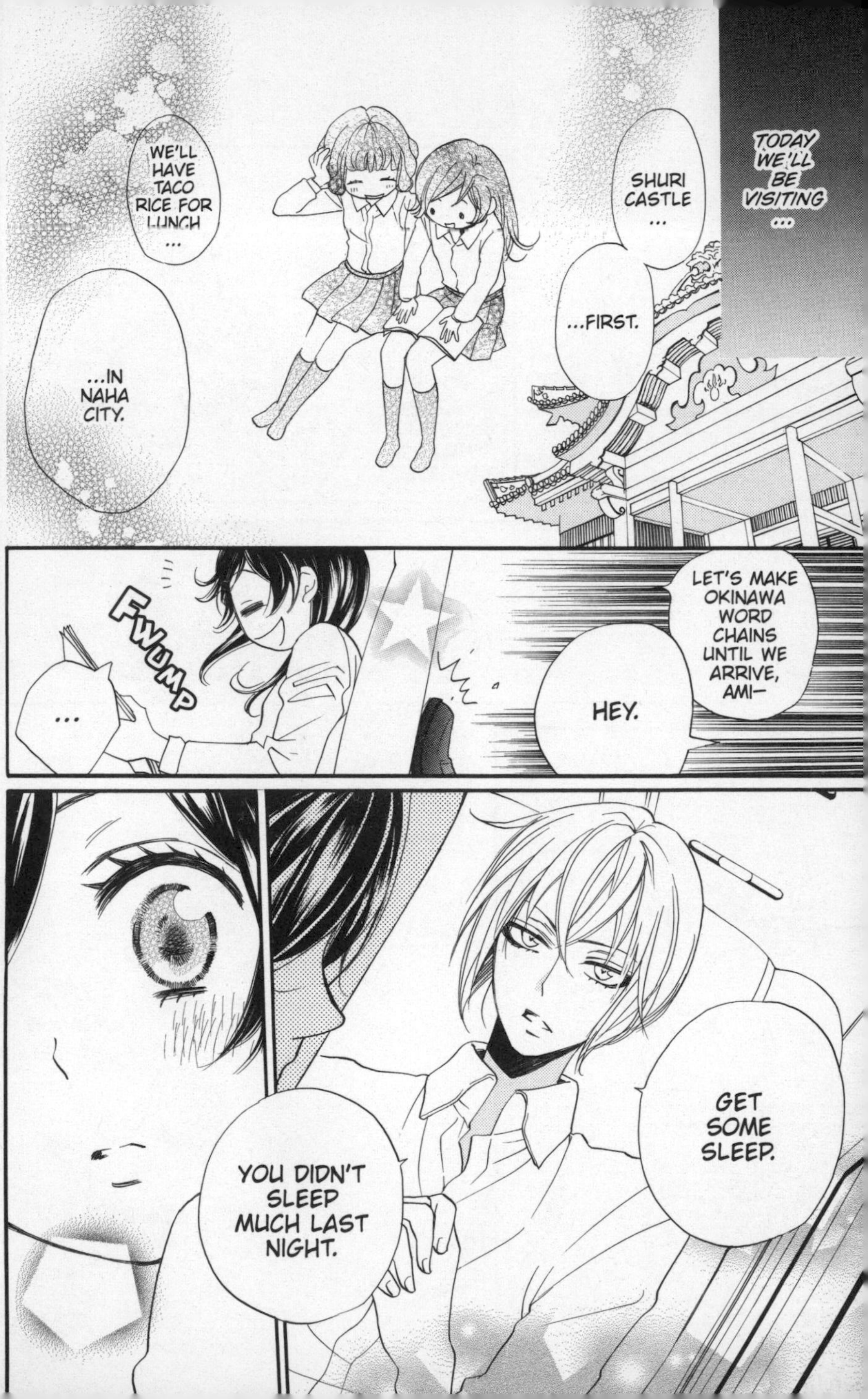
TODAY WE'LL BE VISITING...
SHURI CASTLE...
...FIRST.
WE'LL HAVE TACO RICE FOR LUNCH...
...IN NAHA CITY.
LET'S MAKE OKINAWA WORD CHAINS UNTIL WE ARRIVE, AMI—
HEY.
FWUMP
...
GET SOME SLEEP.
YOU DIDN'T SLEEP MUCH LAST NIGHT.

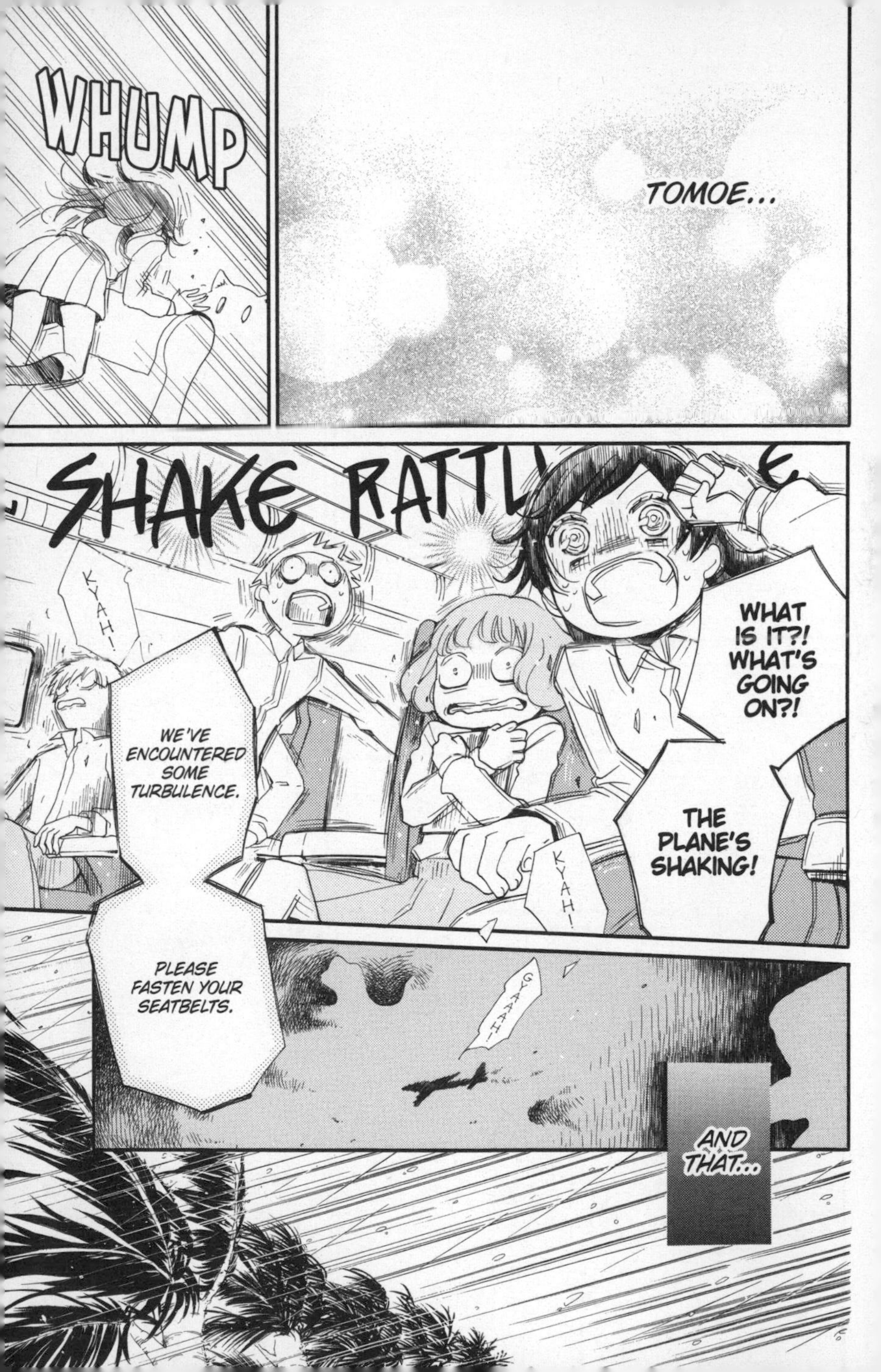
TOMOE...
WHUMP
SHAKE RATTL
WHAT IS IT?! WHAT'S GOING ON?!
THE PLANE'S SHAKING!
KYAH!
KYAH!
WE'VE ENCOUNTERED SOME TURBULENCE.
GYAAAH!
PLEASE FASTEN YOUR SEATBELTS.
AND THAT...

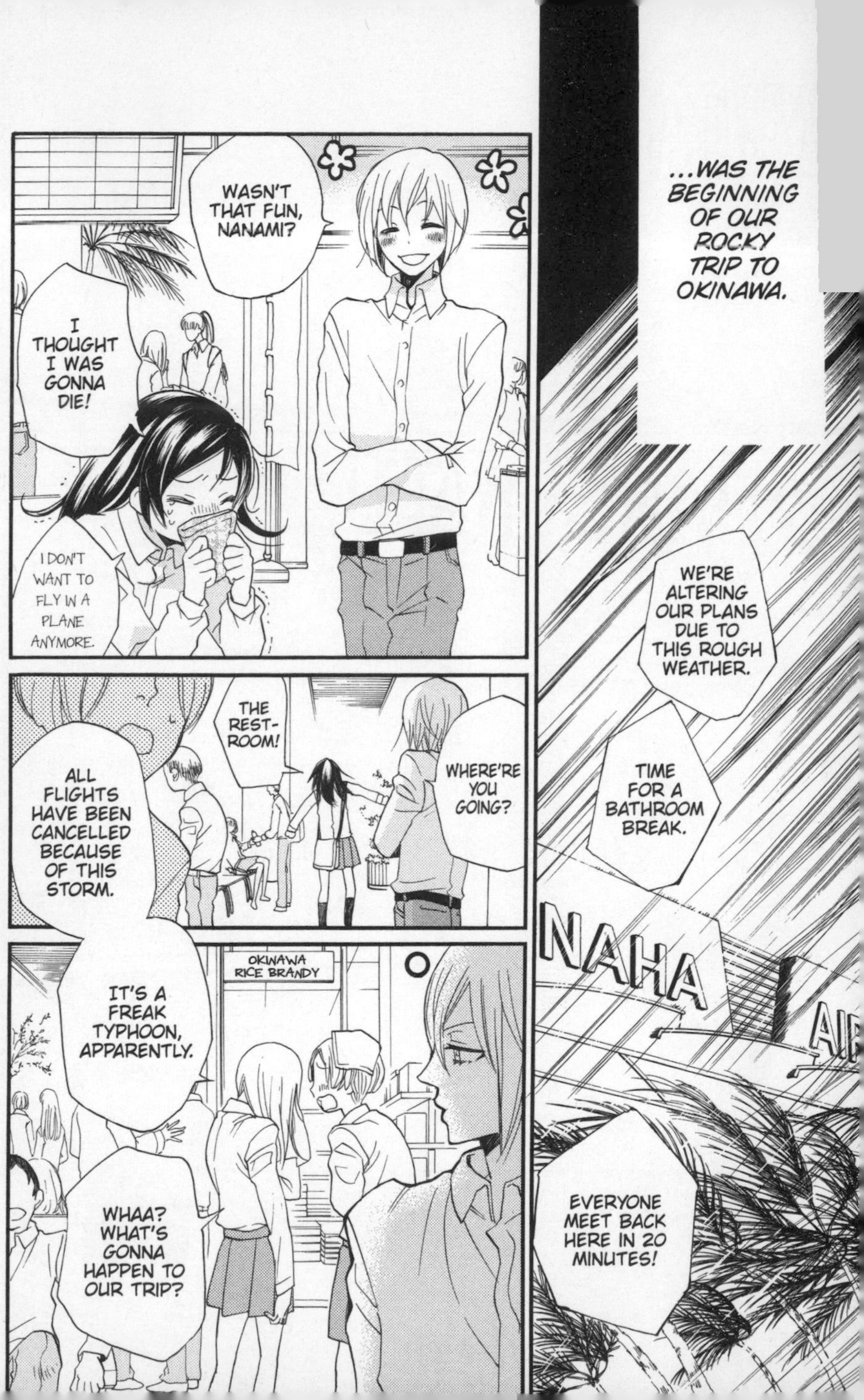
...WAS THE BEGINNING OF OUR ROCKY TRIP TO OKINAWA.
WE'RE ALTERING OUR PLANS DUE TO THIS ROUGH WEATHER.
TIME FOR A BATHROOM BREAK.
NAHA
EVERYONE MEET BACK HERE IN 20 MINUTES!
WASN'T THAT FUN, NANAMI?
I THOUGHT I WAS GONNA DIE!
I DON'T WANT TO FLY IN A PLANE ANYMORE.
WHERE'RE YOU GOING?
THE REST-ROOM!
ALL FLIGHTS HAVE BEEN CANCELLED BECAUSE OF THIS STORM.
OKINAWA RICE BRANDY
IT'S A FREAK TYPHOON, APPARENTLY.
WHAA? WHAT'S GONNA HAPPEN TO OUR TRIP?

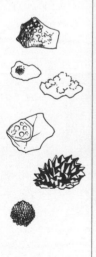

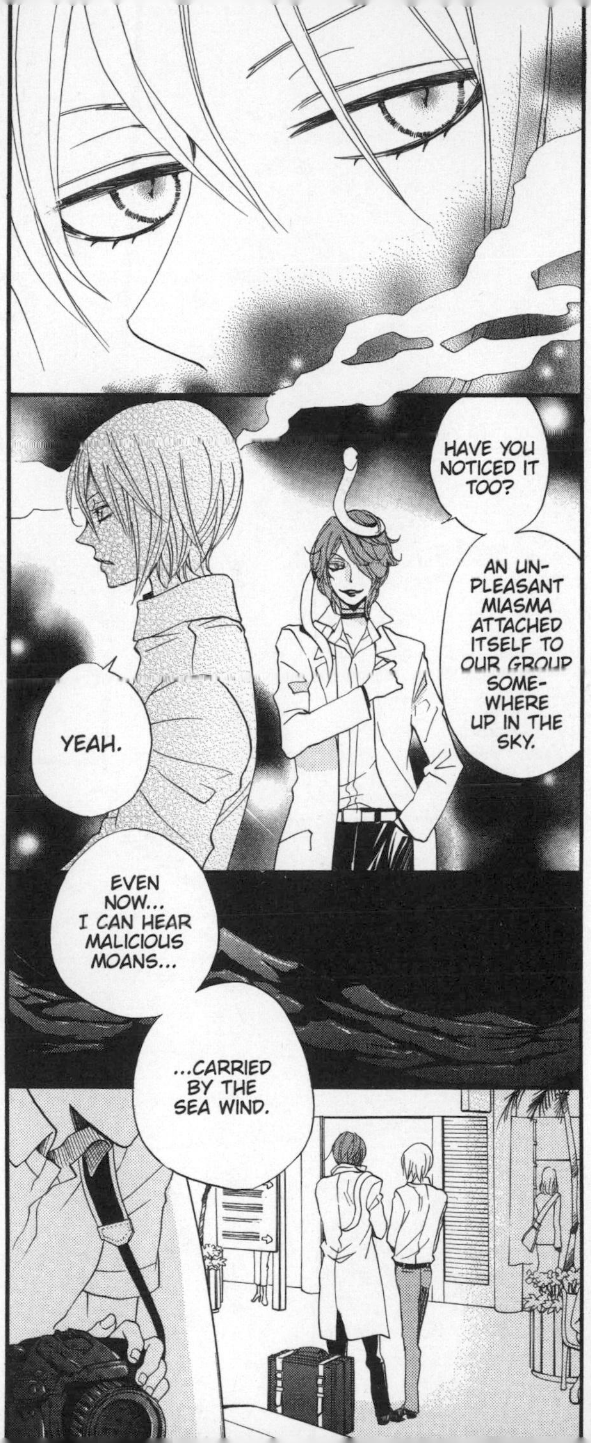
HAVE YOU NOTICED IT TOO?
AN UN-PLEASANT MIASMA ATTACHED ITSELF TO OUR GROUP SOME-WHERE UP IN THE SKY.
YEAH.
EVEN NOW... I CAN HEAR MALICIOUS MOANS...
...CARRIED BY THE SEA WIND.

I have a Glass display Box on my work desk with stones in it.

When I'm tired, I look at the stones to recharge myself.

The stones are colorful and very Beautiful.

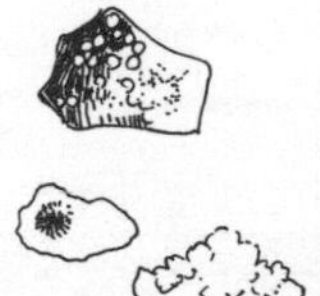

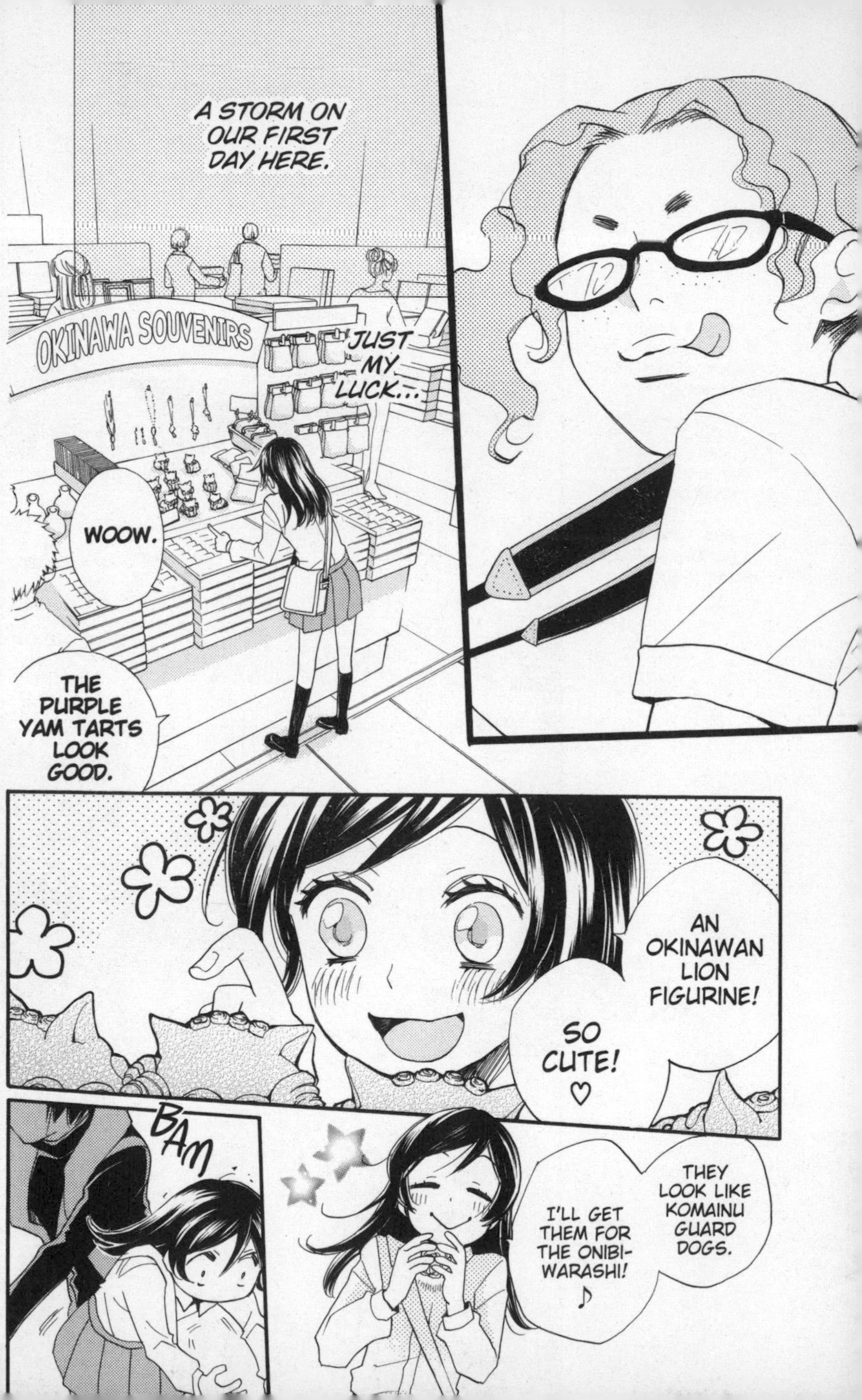
A STORM ON OUR FIRST DAY HERE.
OKINAWA SOUVENIRS
JUST MY LUCK...
WOOW.
THE PURPLE YAM TARTS LOOK GOOD.
AN OKINAWAN LION FIGURINE!
SO CUTE! ♡
BAM
THEY LOOK LIKE KOMAINU GUARD DOGS.
I'LL GET THEM FOR THE ONIBI-WARASHI! ♪

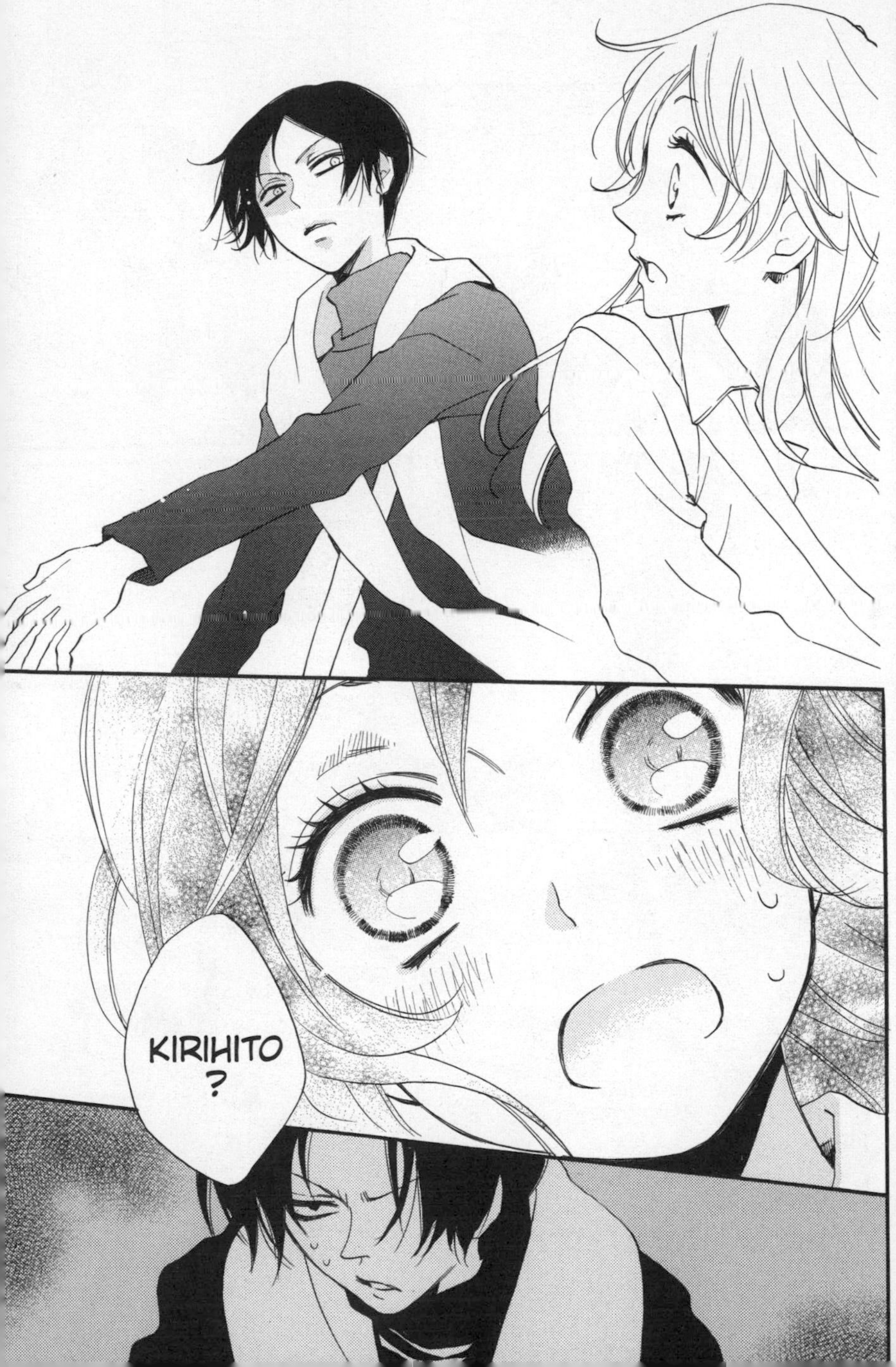
KIRIHITO
?

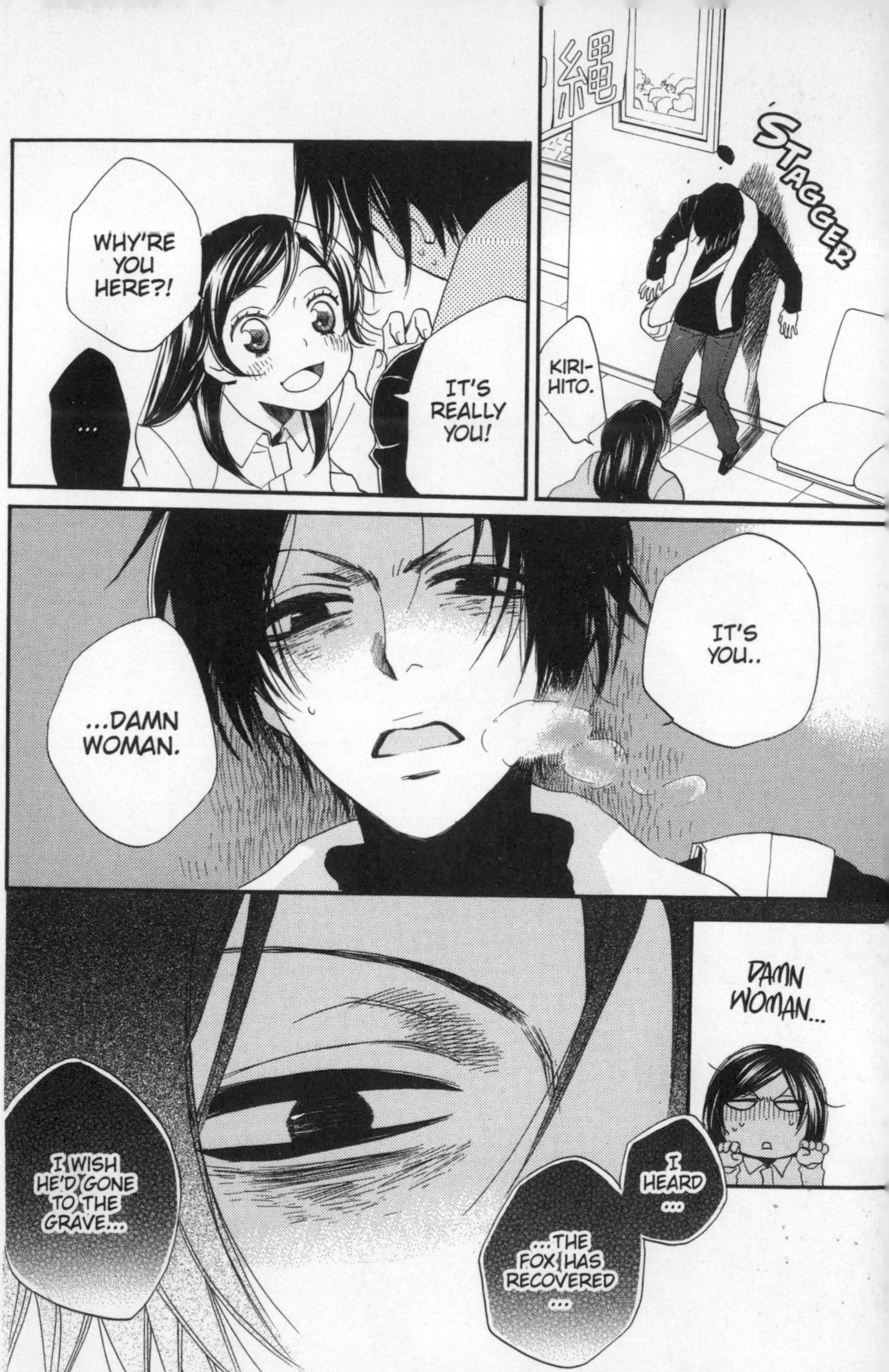
STAGGER
KIRI-HITO.
WHY'RE YOU HERE?!
IT'S REALLY YOU!
...
IT'S YOU..
...DAMN WOMAN.
DAMN WOMAN...
I HEARD ...
...THE FOX HAS RECOVERED ...
I WISH HE'D GONE TO THE GRAVE...

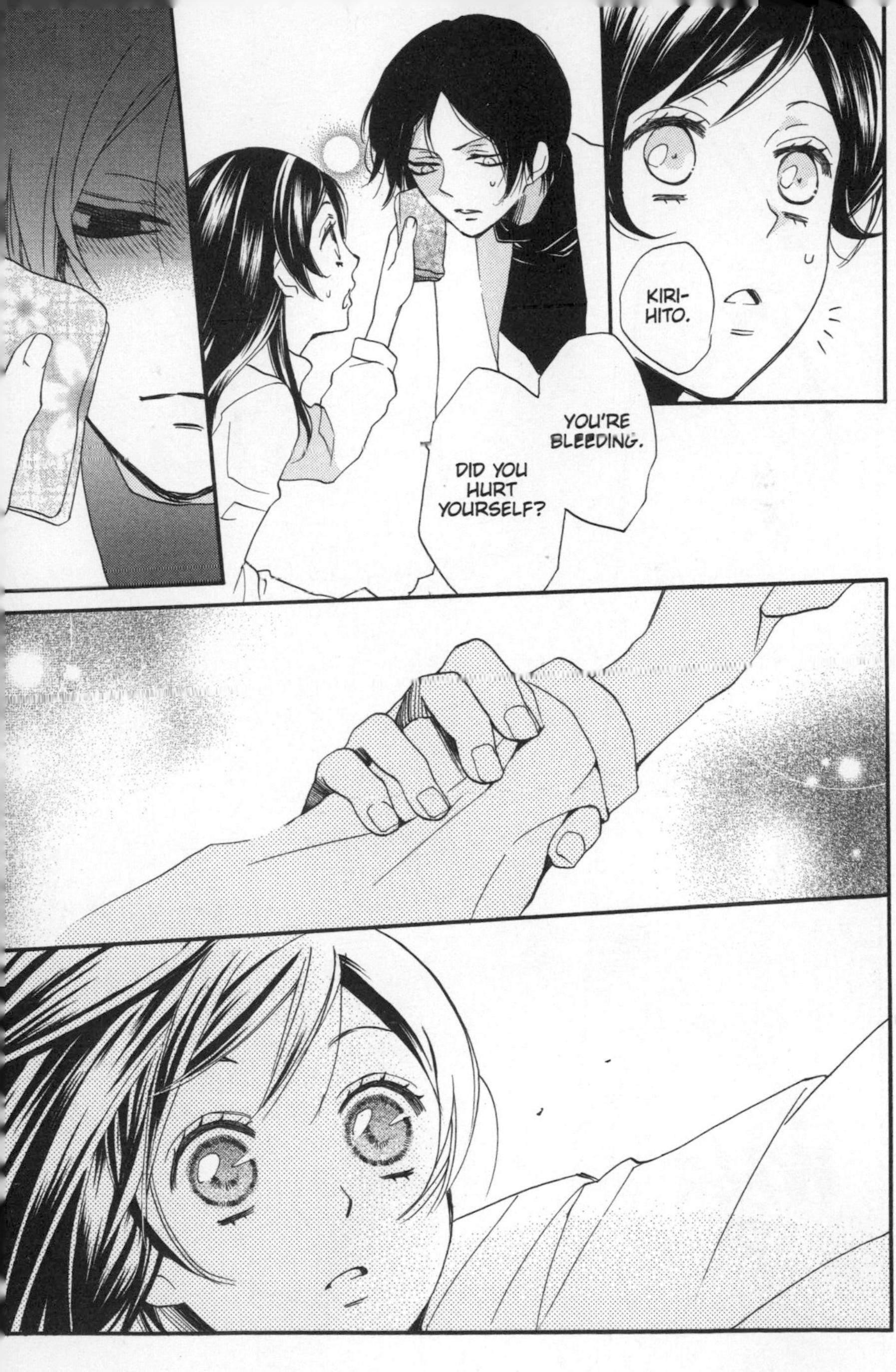
KIRI-HITO.
YOU'RE BLEEDING.
DID YOU HURT YOURSELF?

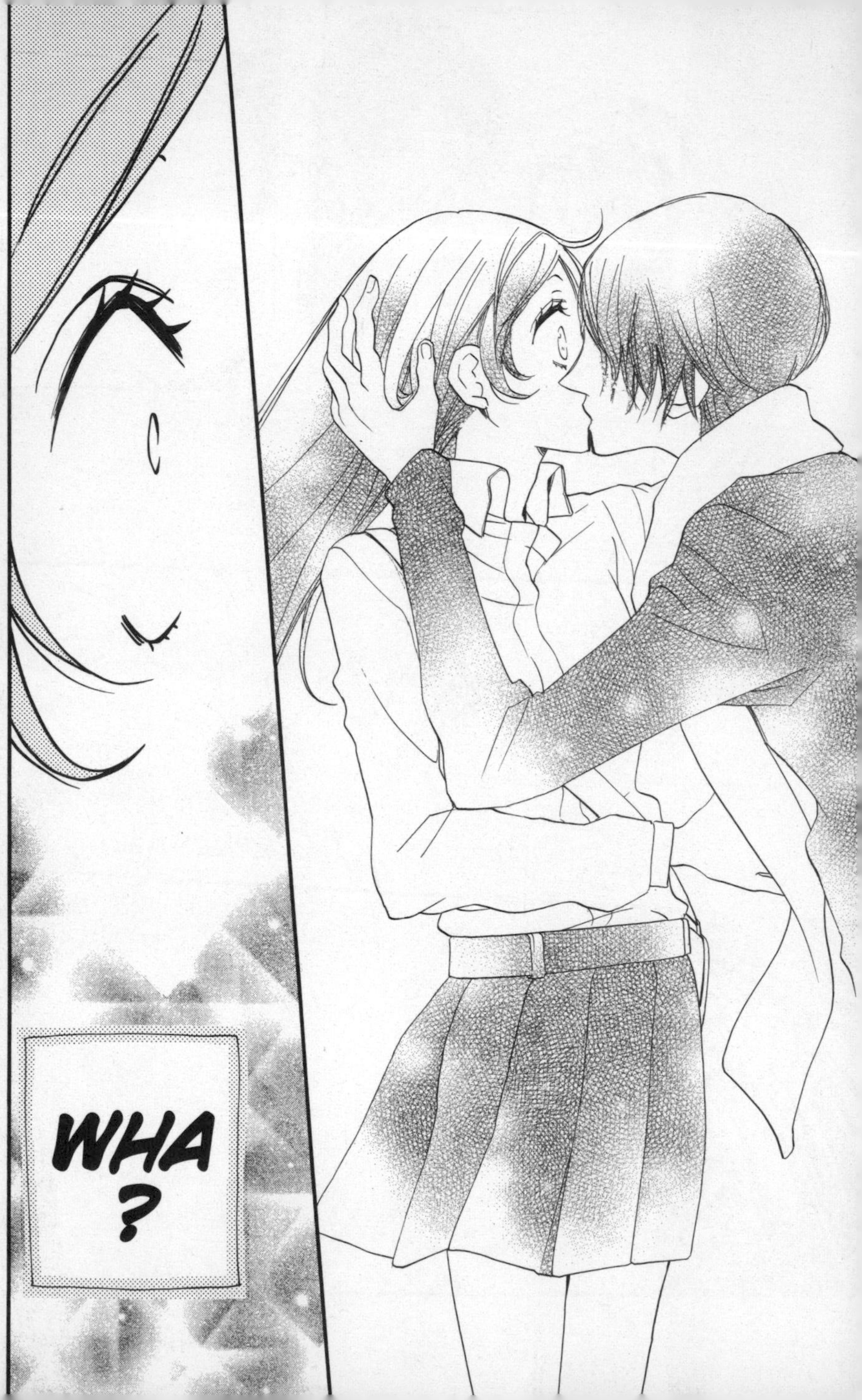
WHA?

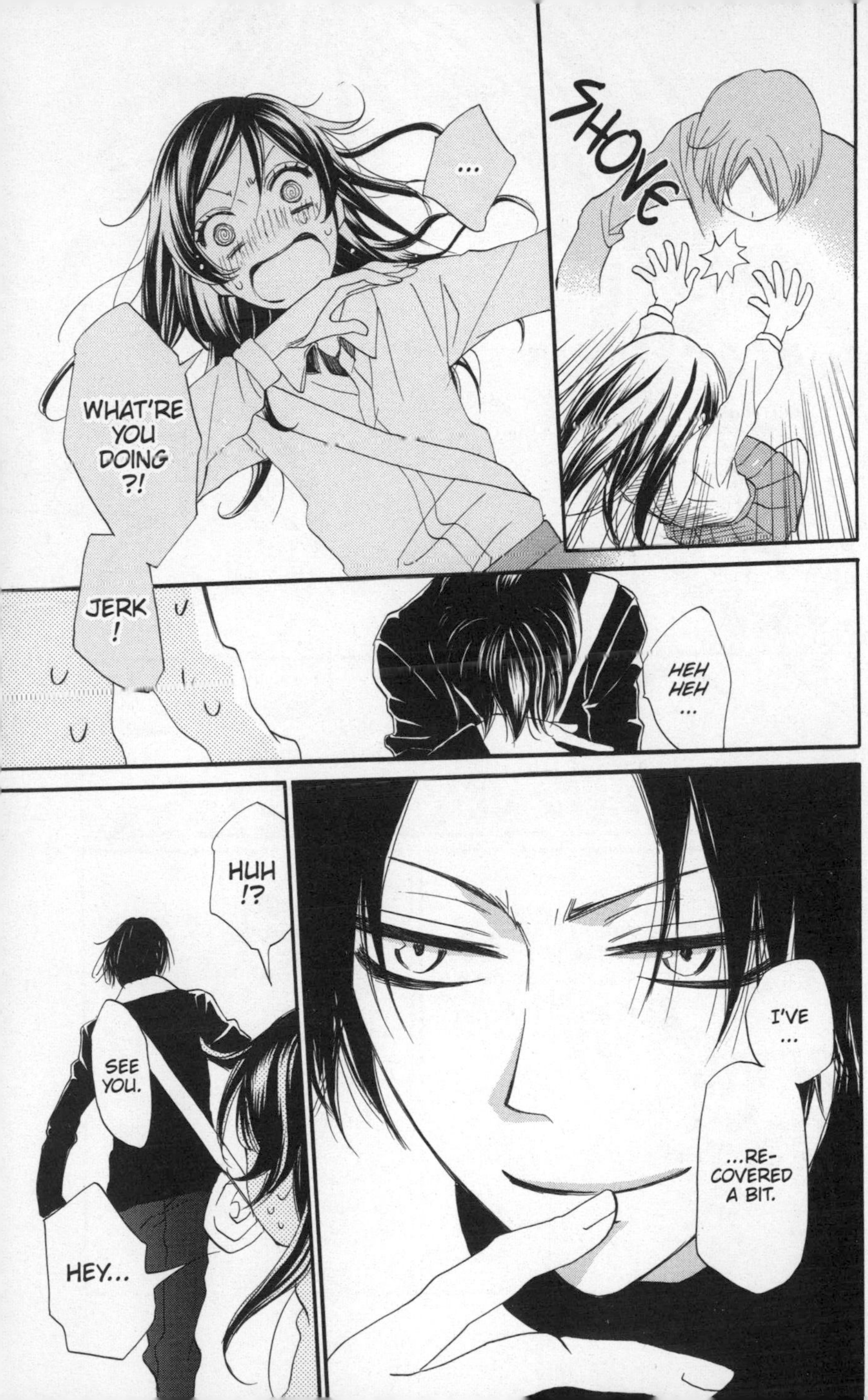
SHOVE
...
WHAT'RE YOU DOING ?!
JERK !
HEH HEH ...
I'VE ...
...RE-COVERED A BIT.
HUH !?
SEE YOU.
HEY...

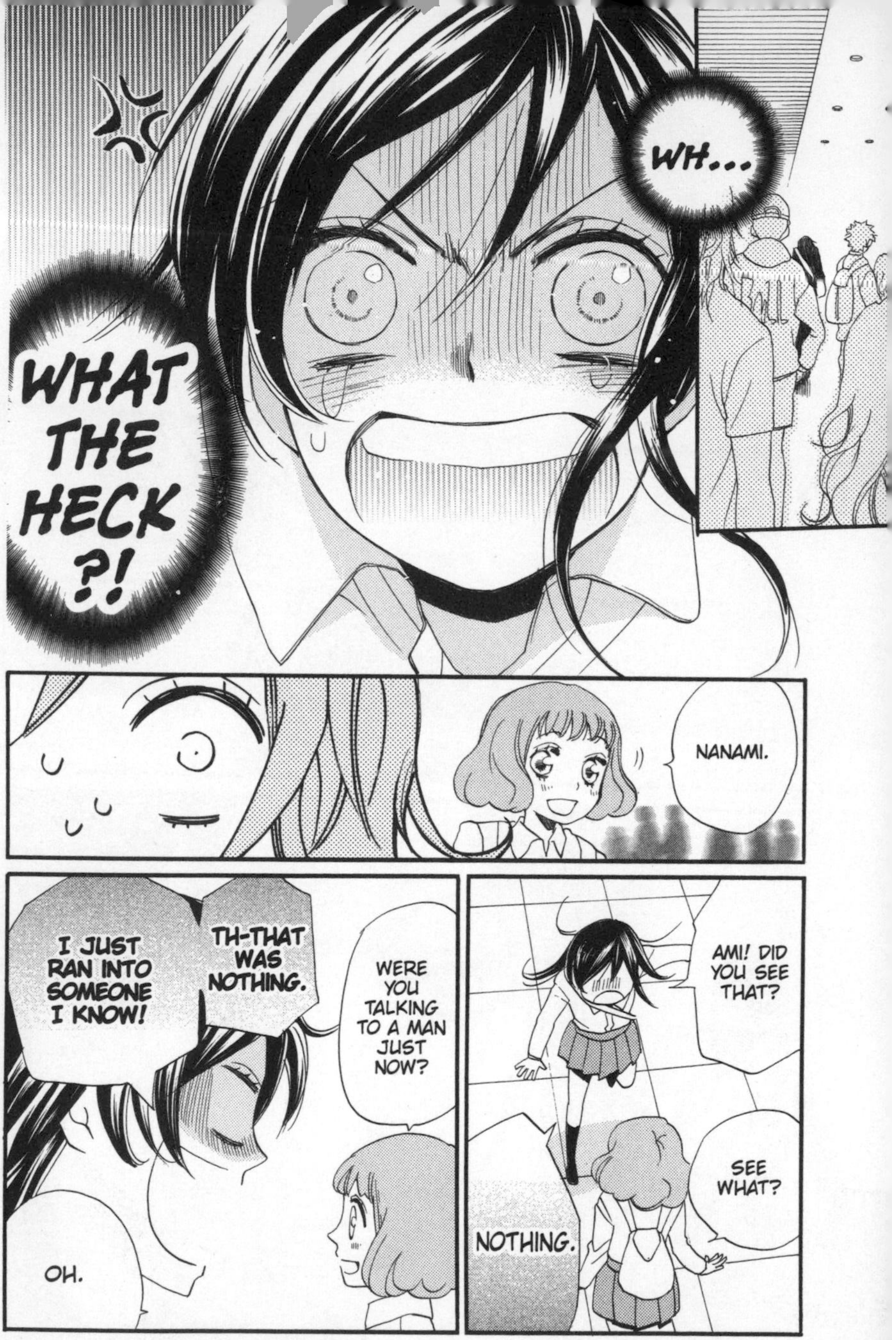
WH...
WHAT THE HECK ?!
NANAMI.
AMI! DID YOU SEE THAT?
SEE WHAT?
NOTHING.
WERE YOU TALKING TO A MAN JUST NOW?
TH-THAT WAS NOTHING.
I JUST RAN INTO SOMEONE I KNOW!
OH.

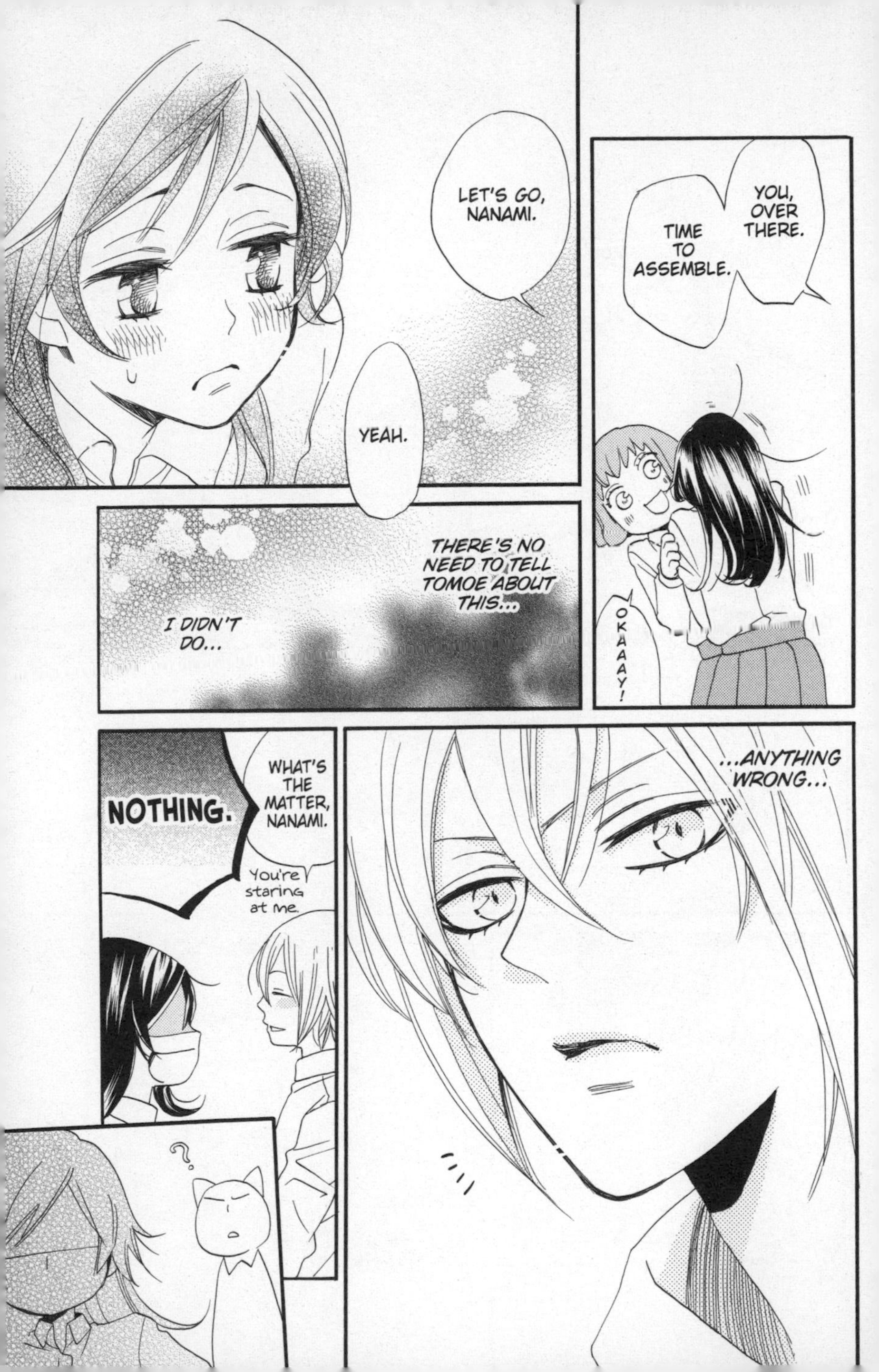
YOU, OVER THERE.
TIME TO ASSEMBLE.
OKAAAY!
LET'S GO, NANAMI.
YEAH.
THERE'S NO NEED TO TELL TOMOE ABOUT THIS...
I DIDN'T DO...
...ANYTHING WRONG...
WHAT'S THE MATTER, NANAMI.
NOTHING.
You're staring at me.
?

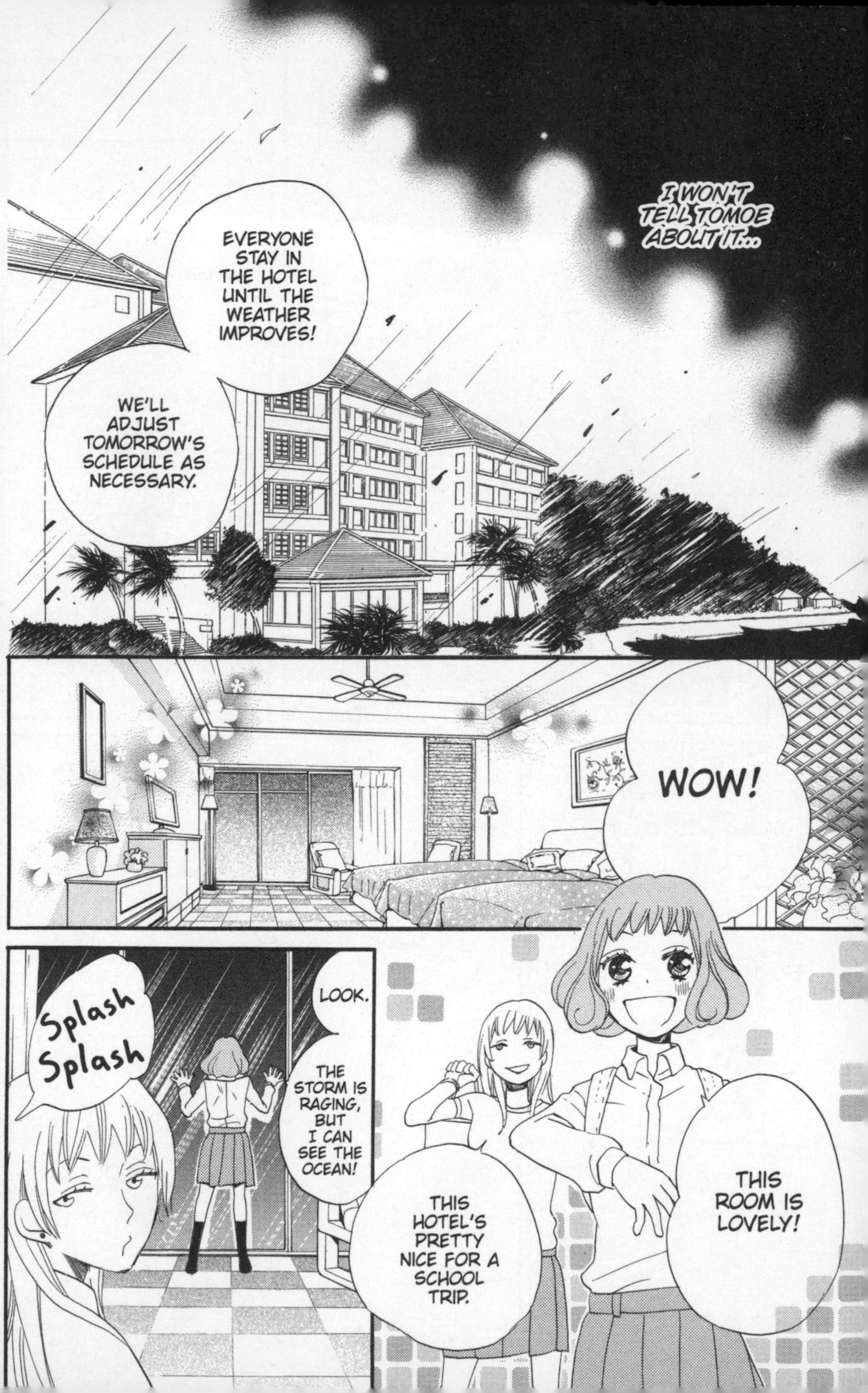
I WON'T TELL TOMOE ABOUT IT...
EVERYONE STAY IN THE HOTEL UNTIL THE WEATHER IMPROVES!
WE'LL ADJUST TOMORROW'S SCHEDULE AS NECESSARY.
WOW!
THIS ROOM IS LOVELY!
THIS HOTEL'S PRETTY NICE FOR A SCHOOL TRIP.
LOOK.
THE STORM IS RAGING, BUT I CAN SEE THE OCEAN!
Splash Splash

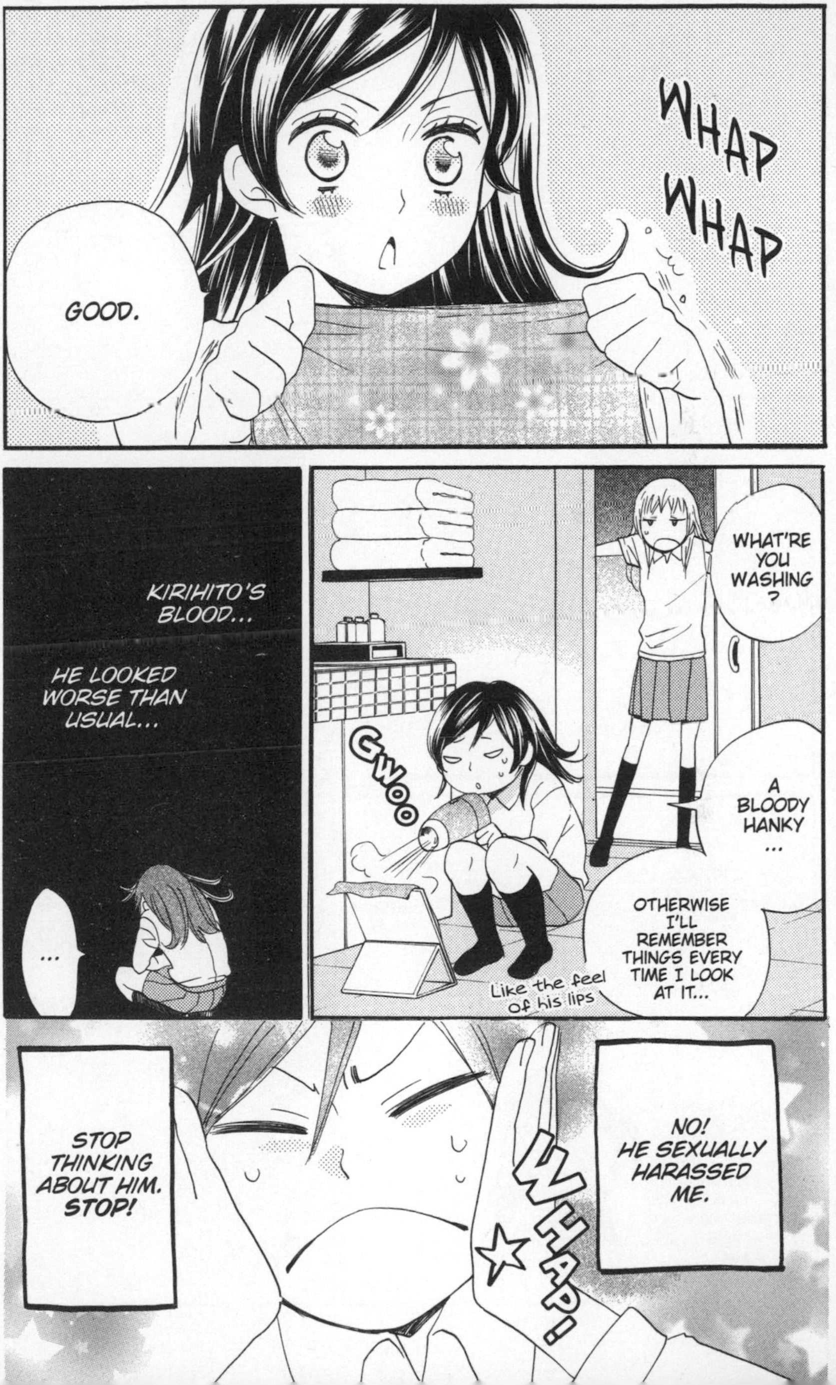
WHAP WHAP
GOOD.
WHAT'RE YOU WASHING?
A BLOODY HANKY...
OTHERWISE I'LL REMEMBER THINGS EVERY TIME I LOOK AT IT...
Like the feel of his lips
GWOO
KIRIHITO'S BLOOD...
HE LOOKED WORSE THAN USUAL...
...
NO! HE SEXUALLY HARASSED ME.
WHAP!
STOP THINKING ABOUT HIM. STOP!

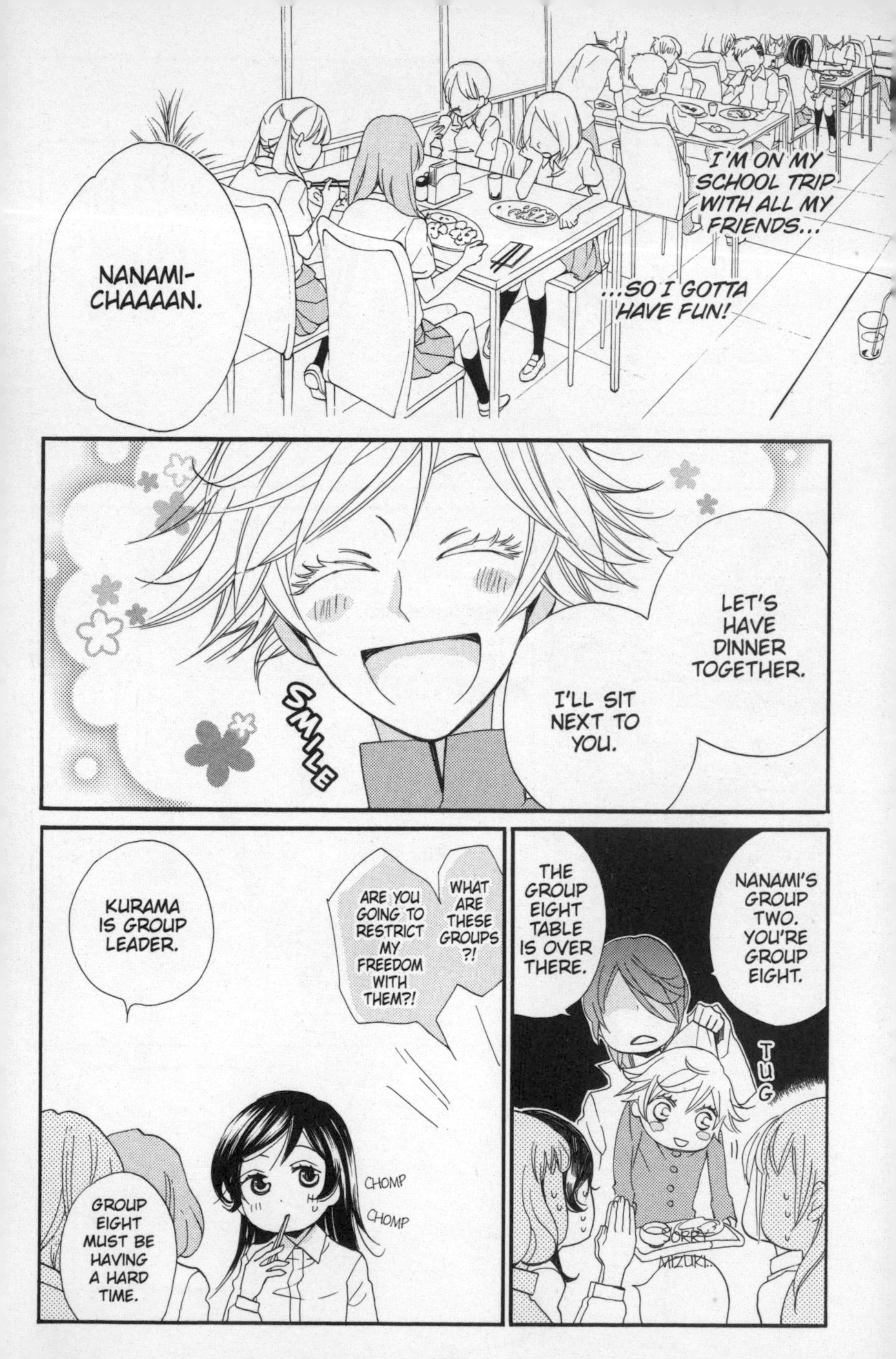
I'M ON MY SCHOOL TRIP WITH ALL MY FRIENDS...
...SO I GOTTA HAVE FUN!
NANAMI-CHAAAAN.
LET'S HAVE DINNER TOGETHER.
I'LL SIT NEXT TO YOU.
SMILE
NANAMI'S GROUP TWO. YOU'RE GROUP EIGHT.
THE GROUP EIGHT TABLE IS OVER THERE.
TUG
SORRY MIZUKI...
WHAT ARE THESE GROUPS?!
ARE YOU GOING TO RESTRICT MY FREEDOM WITH THEM?!
KURAMA IS GROUP LEADER.
CHOMP
CHOMP
GROUP EIGHT MUST BE HAVING A HARD TIME.

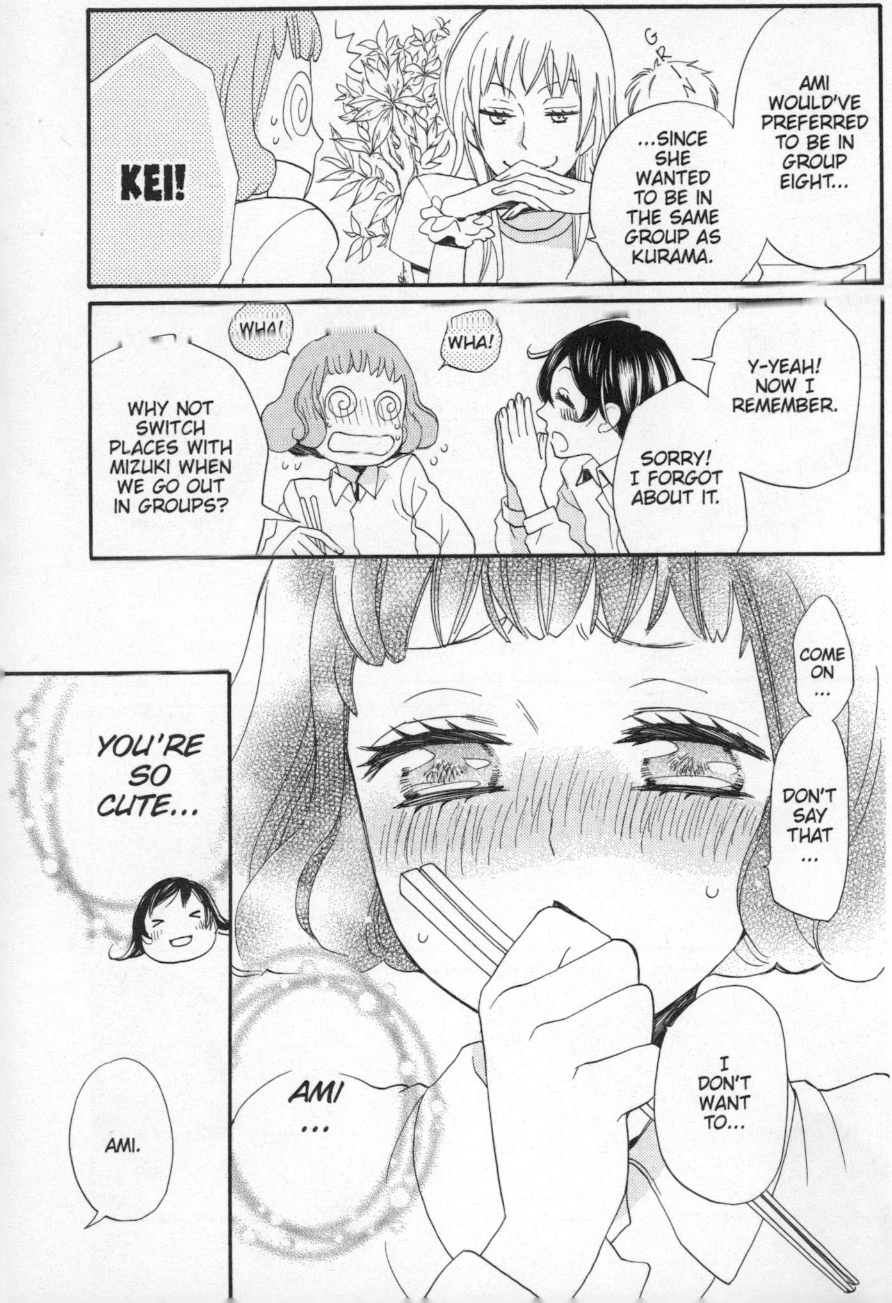
AMI WOULD'VE PREFERRED TO BE IN GROUP EIGHT...
GRIN
...SINCE SHE WANTED TO BE IN THE SAME GROUP AS KURAMA.
KEI!
Y-YEAH! NOW I REMEMBER.
SORRY! I FORGOT ABOUT IT.
WHA!
WHA!
WHY NOT SWITCH PLACES WITH MIZUKI WHEN WE GO OUT IN GROUPS?
COME ON ...
DON'T SAY THAT ...
I DON'T WANT TO...
AMI ...
YOU'RE SO CUTE...
AMI.

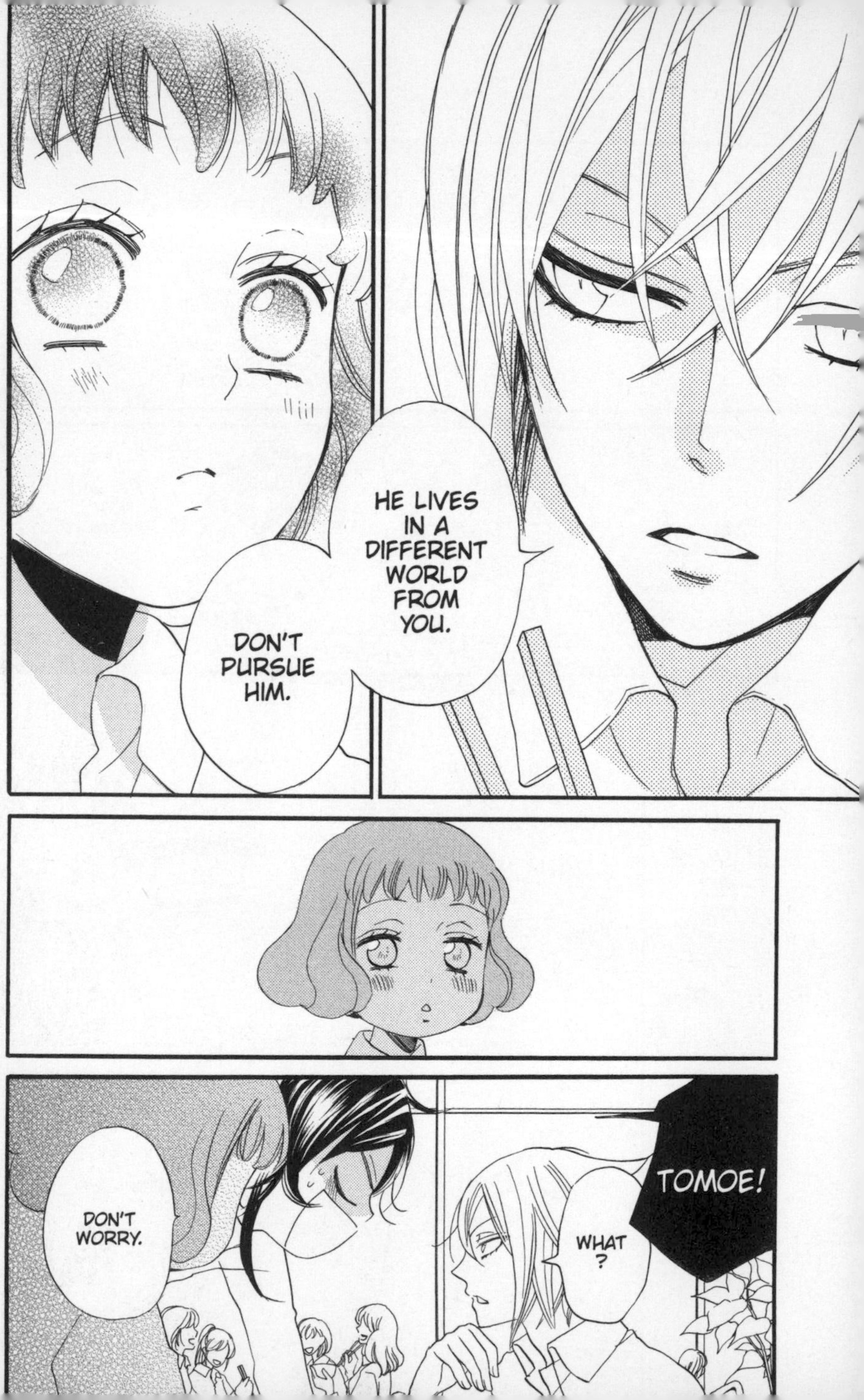
HE LIVES IN A DIFFERENT WORLD FROM YOU.
DON'T PURSUE HIM.
TOMOE!
WHAT?
DON'T WORRY.

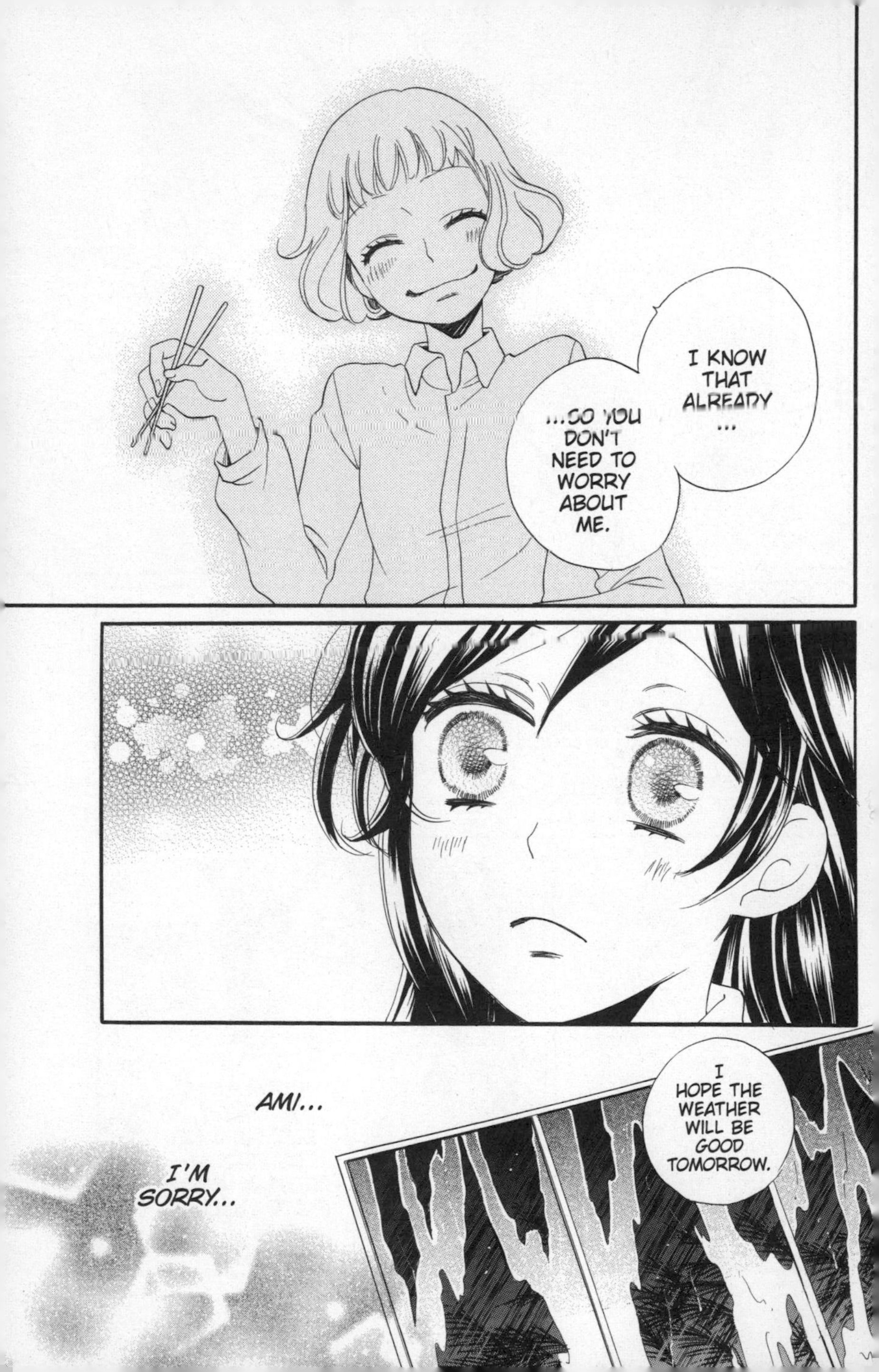
I KNOW THAT ALREADY ...
...SO YOU DON'T NEED TO WORRY ABOUT ME.
I HOPE THE WEATHER WILL BE GOOD TOMORROW.
AMI...
I'M SORRY...

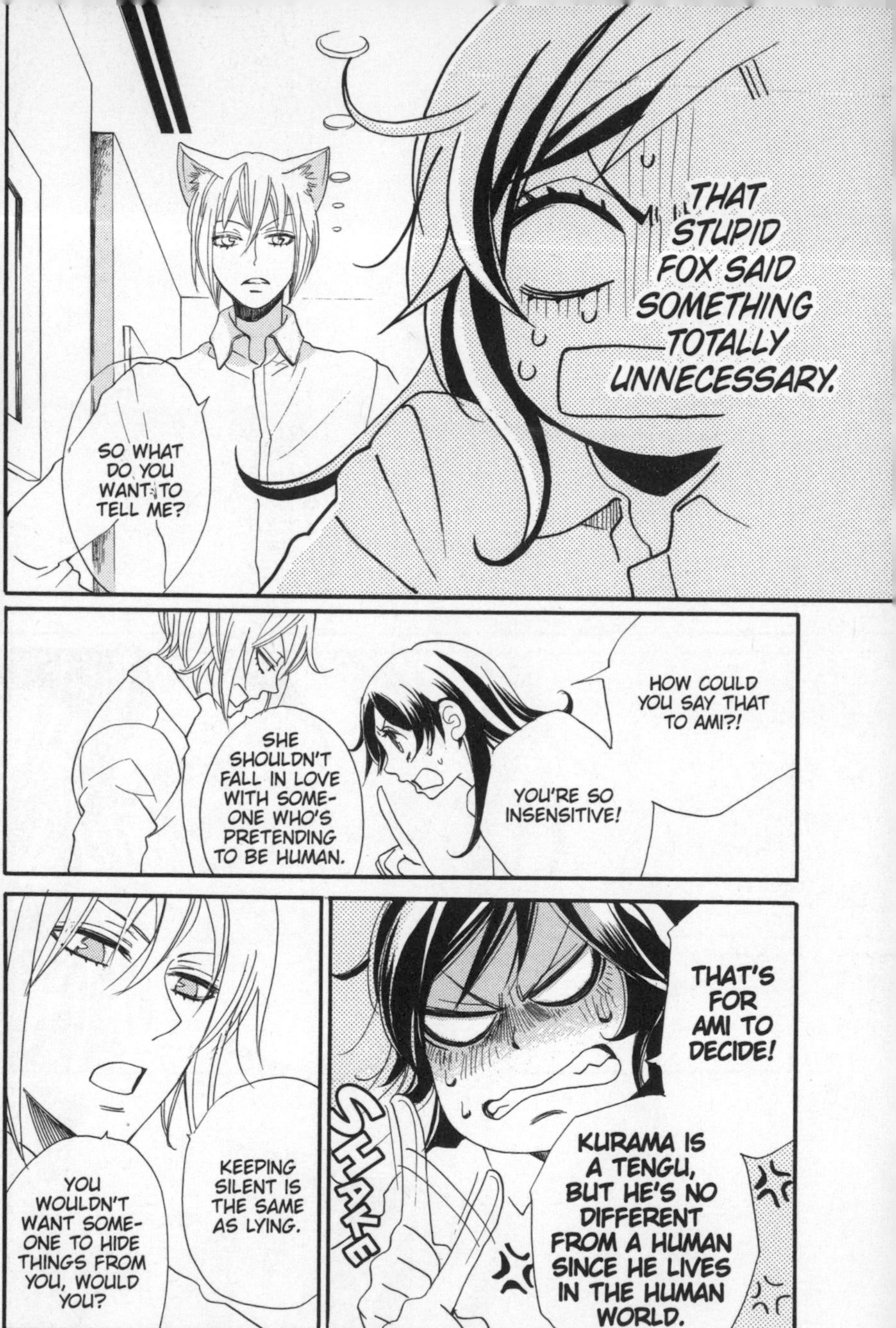
THAT STUPID FOX SAID SOMETHING TOTALLY UNNECESSARY.
SO WHAT DO YOU WANT TO TELL ME?
HOW COULD YOU SAY THAT TO AMI?!
YOU'RE SO INSENSITIVE!
SHE SHOULDN'T FALL IN LOVE WITH SOME-ONE WHO'S PRETENDING TO BE HUMAN.
THAT'S FOR AMI TO DECIDE!
SHAKE
KURAMA IS A TENGU, BUT HE'S NO DIFFERENT FROM A HUMAN SINCE HE LIVES IN THE HUMAN WORLD.
KEEPING SILENT IS THE SAME AS LYING.
YOU WOULDN'T WANT SOME-ONE TO HIDE THINGS FROM YOU, WOULD YOU?

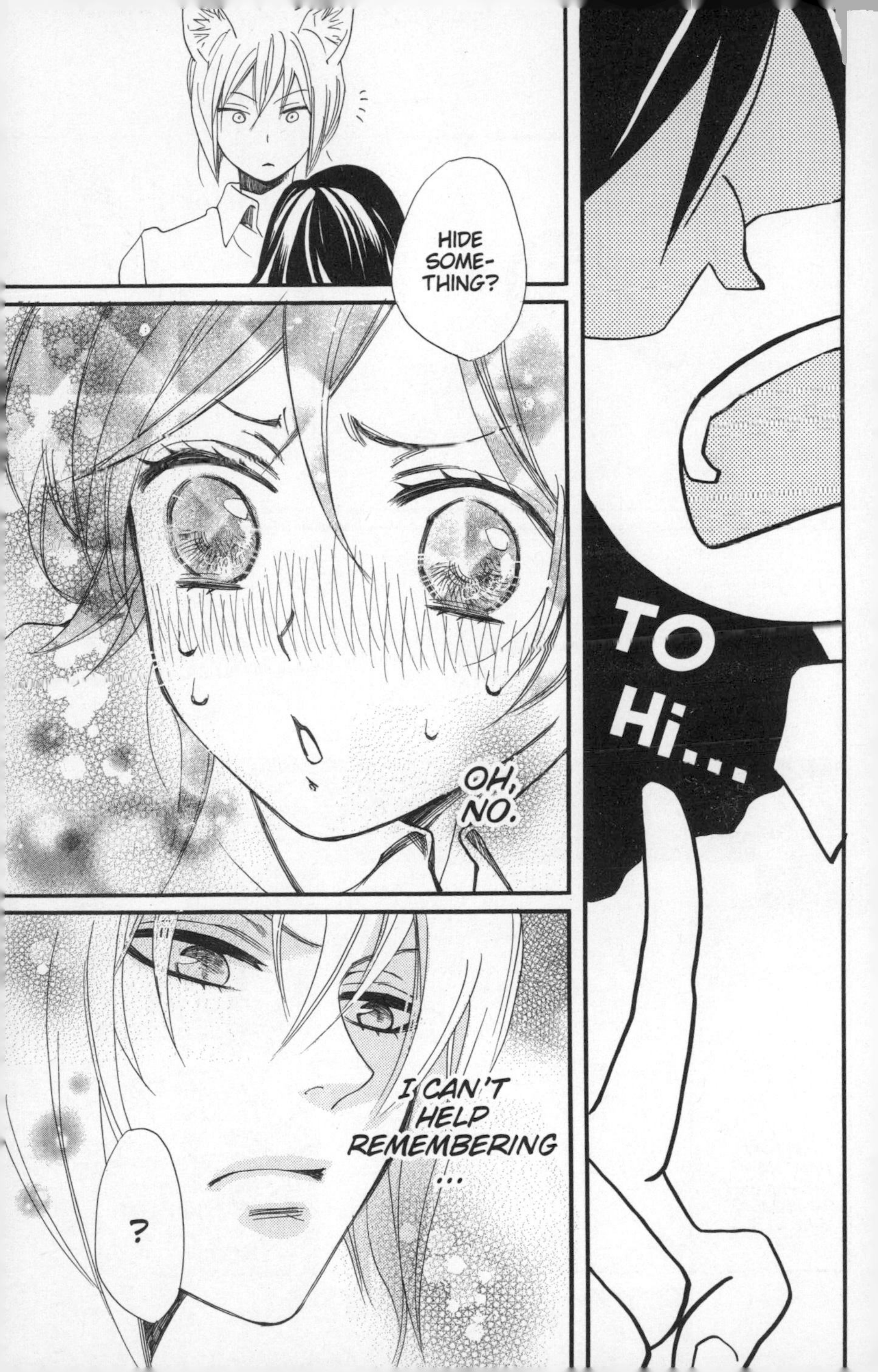
TO Hi...
HIDE SOME-THING?
OH, NO.
I CAN'T HELP REMEMBERING...
?

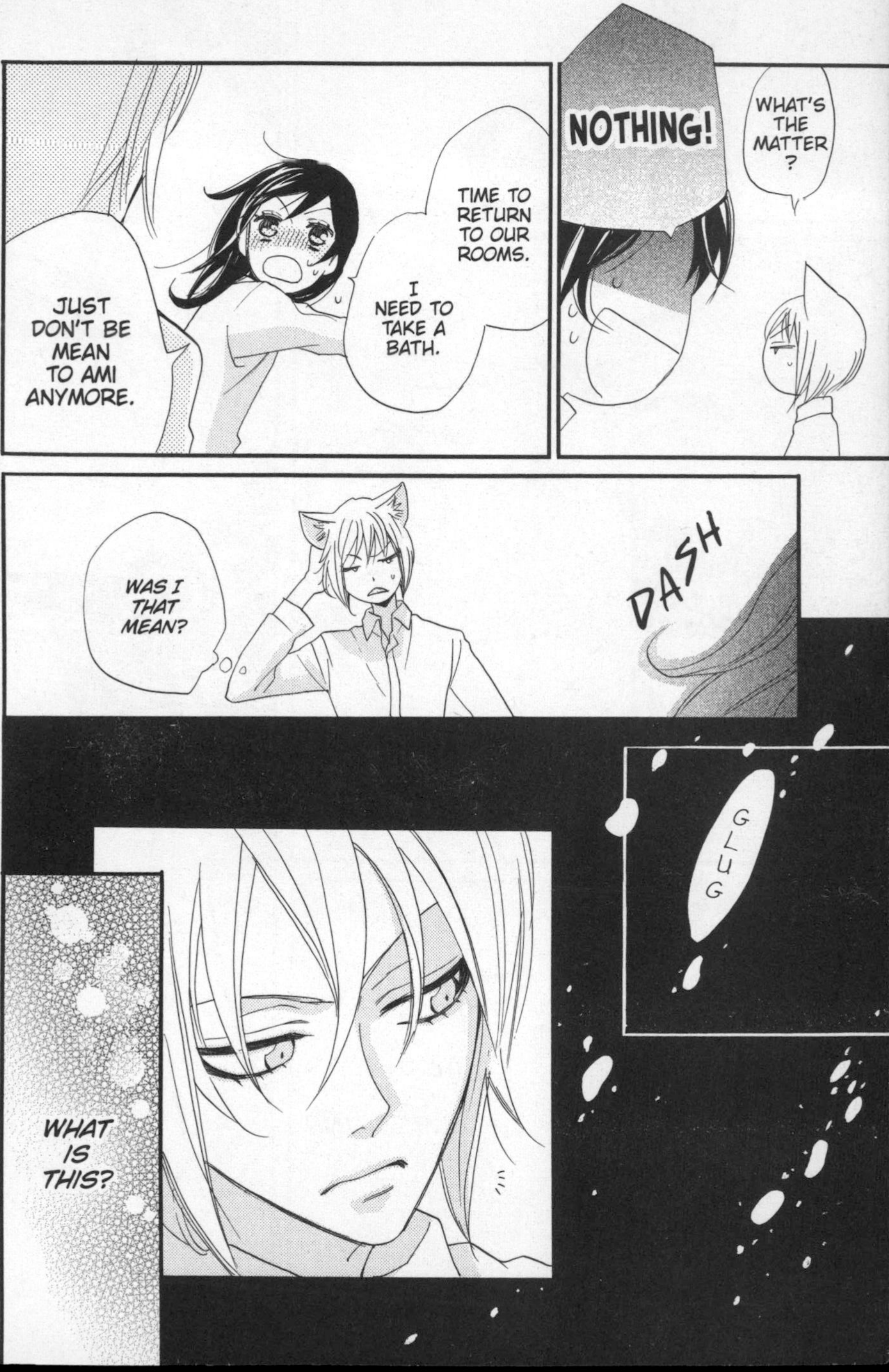
WHAT'S THE MATTER?
NOTHING!
TIME TO RETURN TO OUR ROOMS.
I NEED TO TAKE A BATH.
JUST DON'T BE MEAN TO AMI ANYMORE.
DASH
WAS I THAT MEAN?
GLUG
WHAT IS THIS?

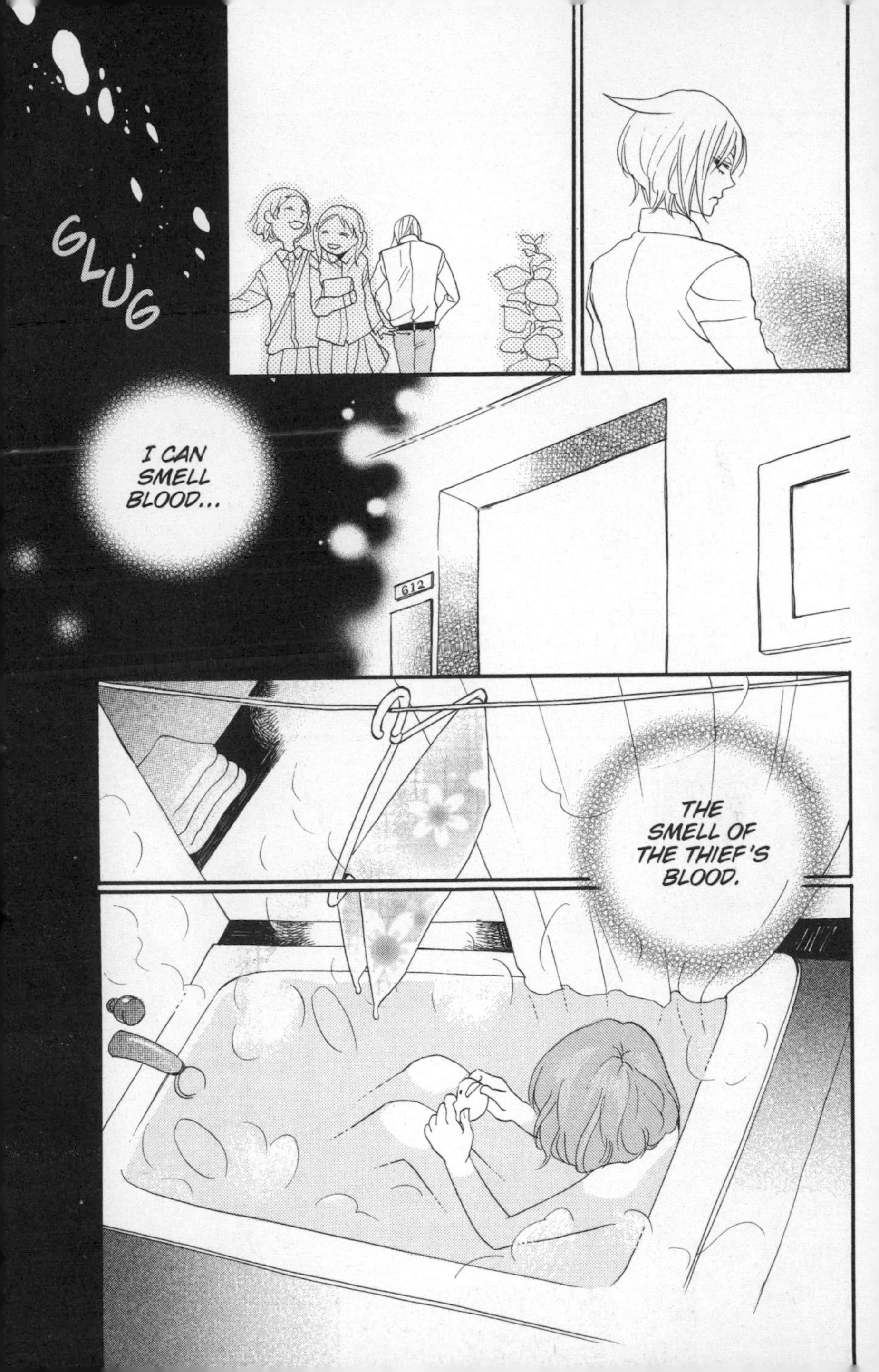
GLUG
I CAN SMELL BLOOD...
612
THE SMELL OF THE THIEF'S BLOOD.

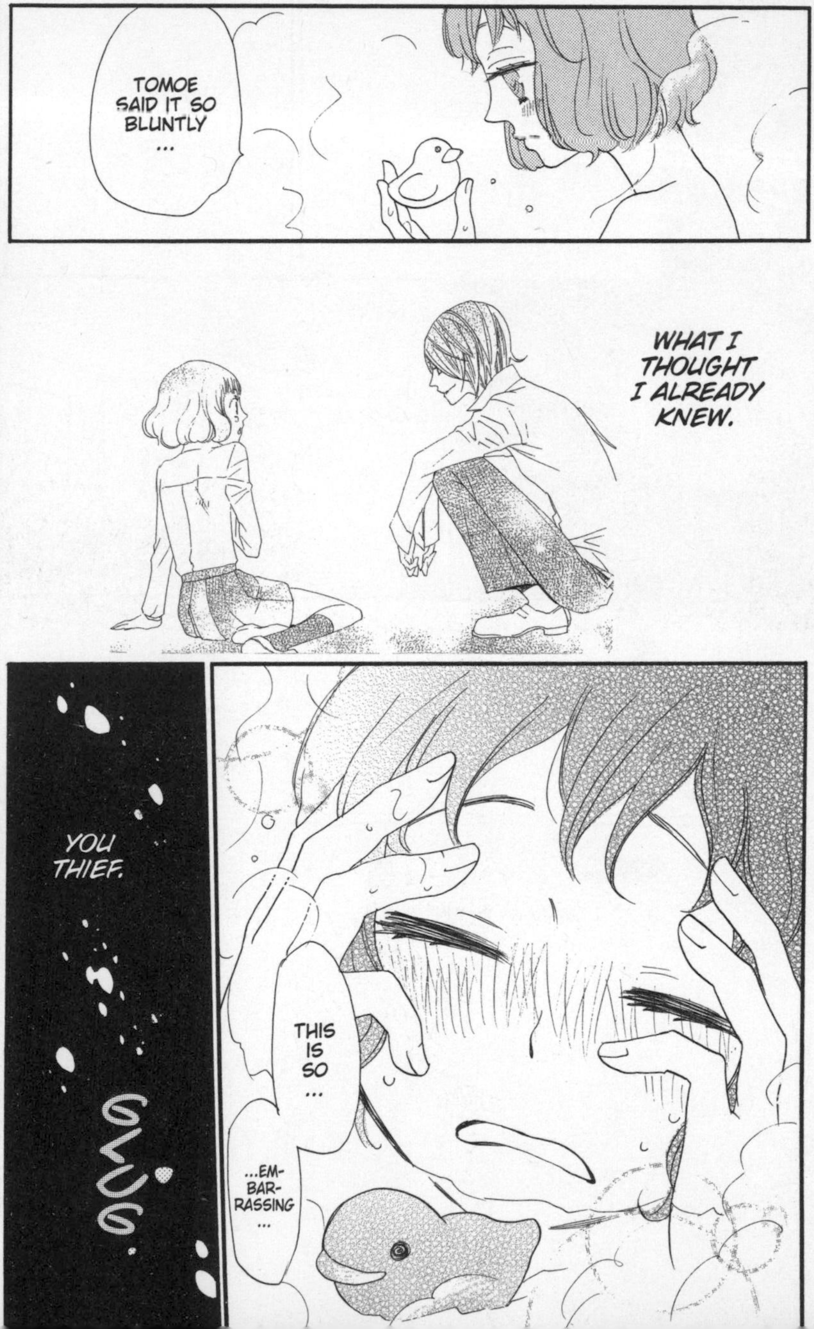
TOMOE SAID IT SO BLUNTLY ...
WHAT I THOUGHT I ALREADY KNEW.
THIS IS SO ...
...EM-BAR-RASSING ...
YOU THIEF.

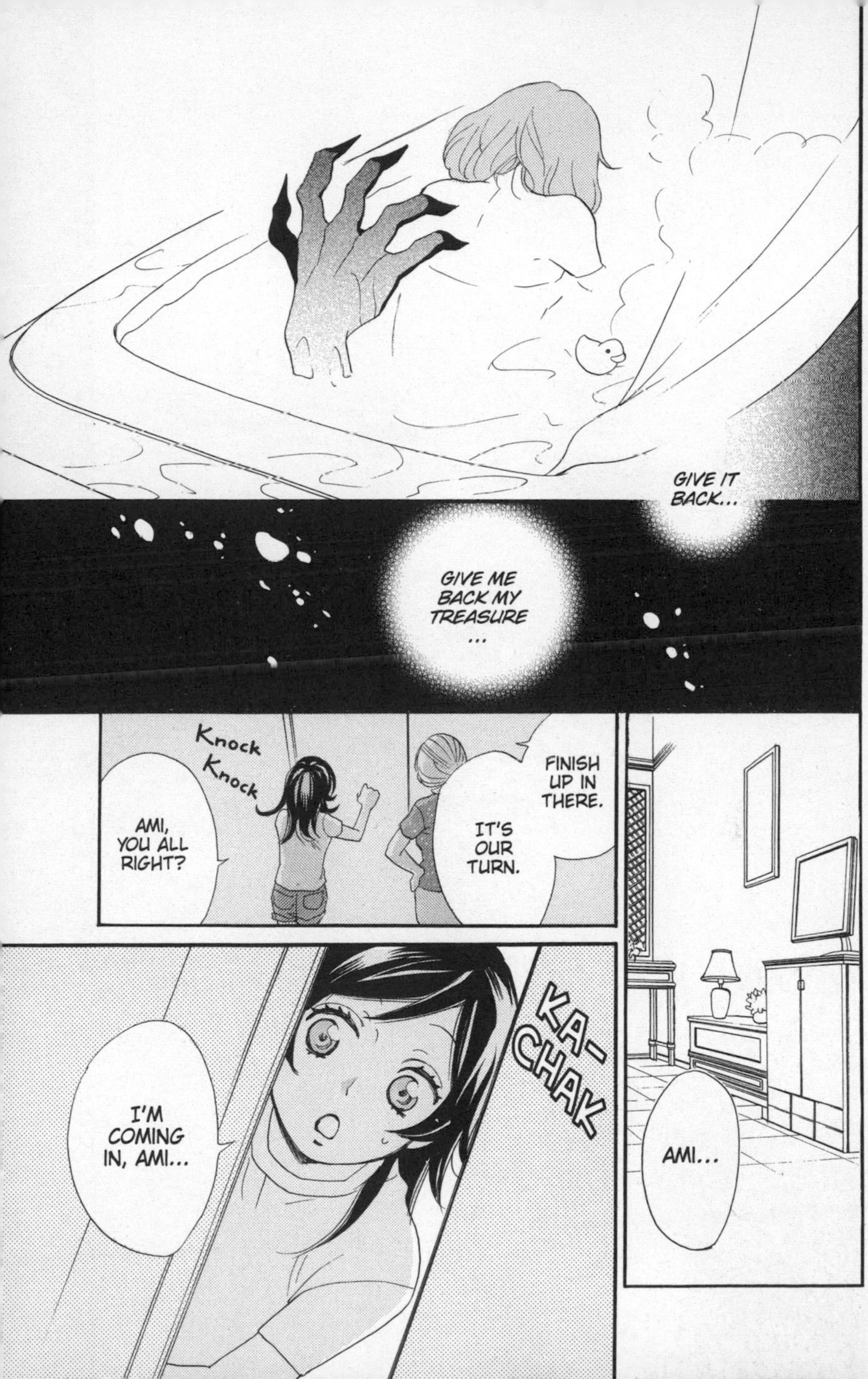
GIVE IT BACK...
GIVE ME BACK MY TREASURE ...
AMI...
FINISH UP IN THERE.
IT'S OUR TURN.
Knock Knock
AMI, YOU ALL RIGHT?
KA-CHAK
I'M COMING IN, AMI...

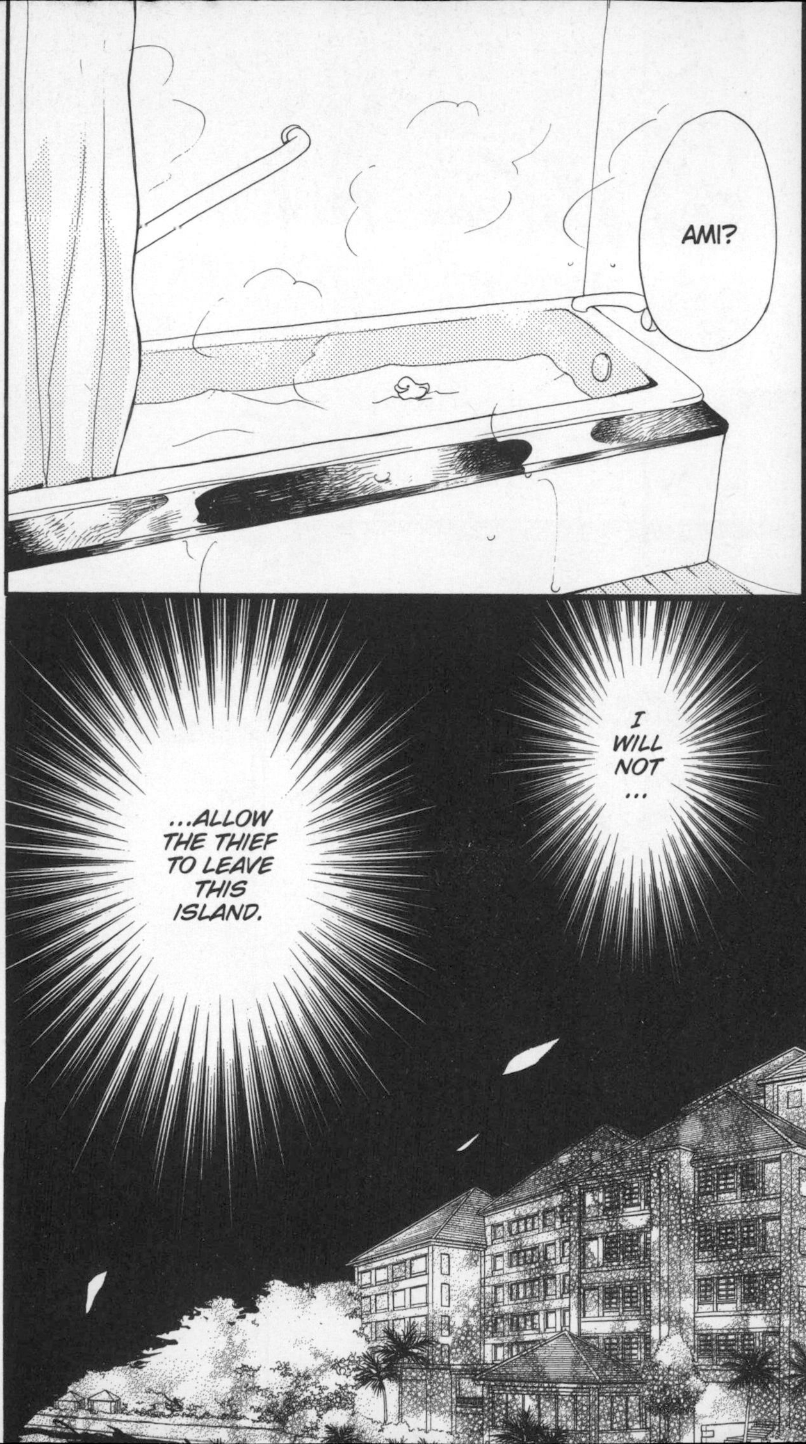
AMI?
I WILL NOT ...
...ALLOW THE THIEF TO LEAVE THIS ISLAND.

Chapter 105

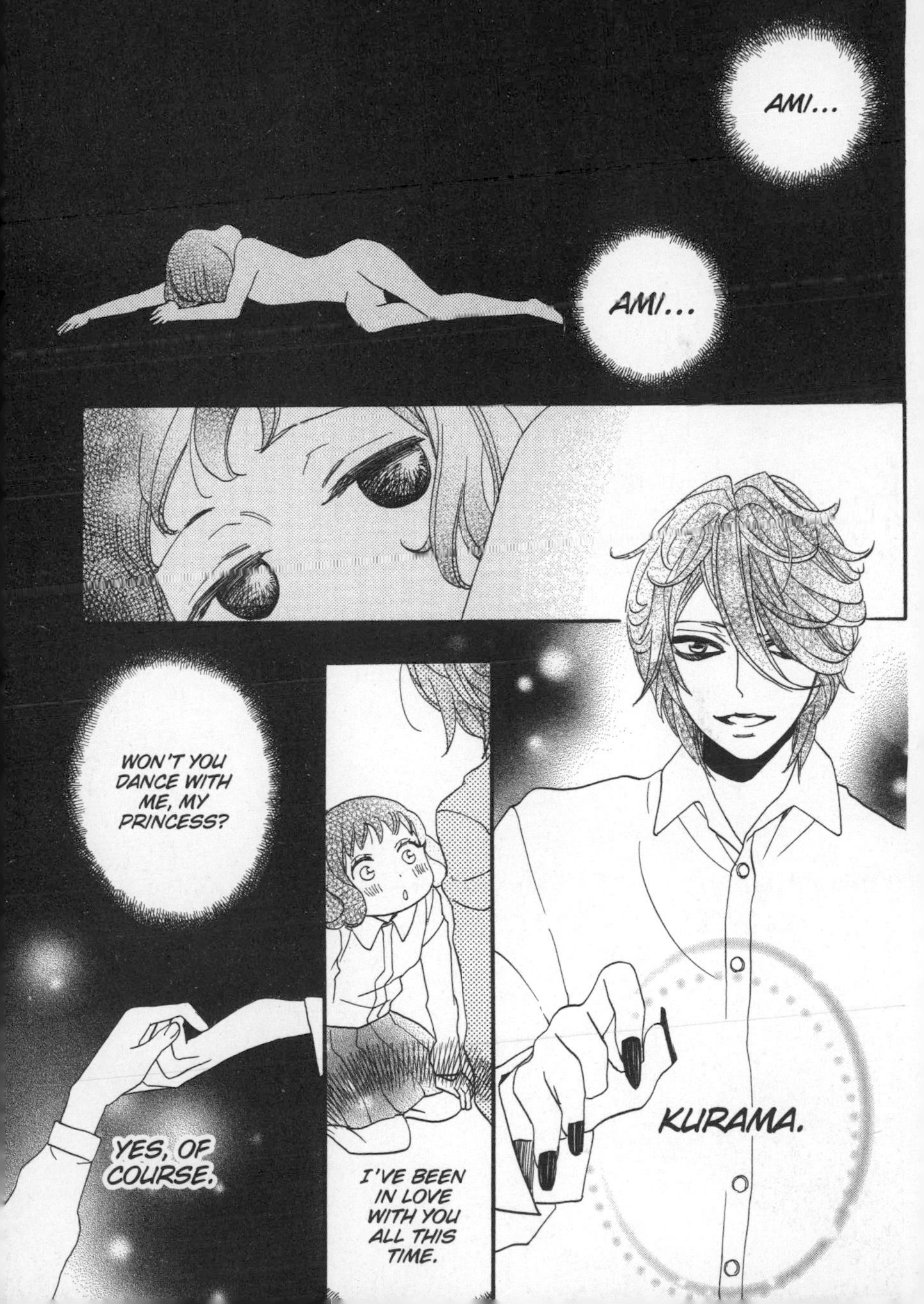
AMI...
AMI...
KURAMA.
I'VE BEEN IN LOVE WITH YOU ALL THIS TIME.
WON'T YOU DANCE WITH ME, MY PRINCESS?
YES, OF COURSE.

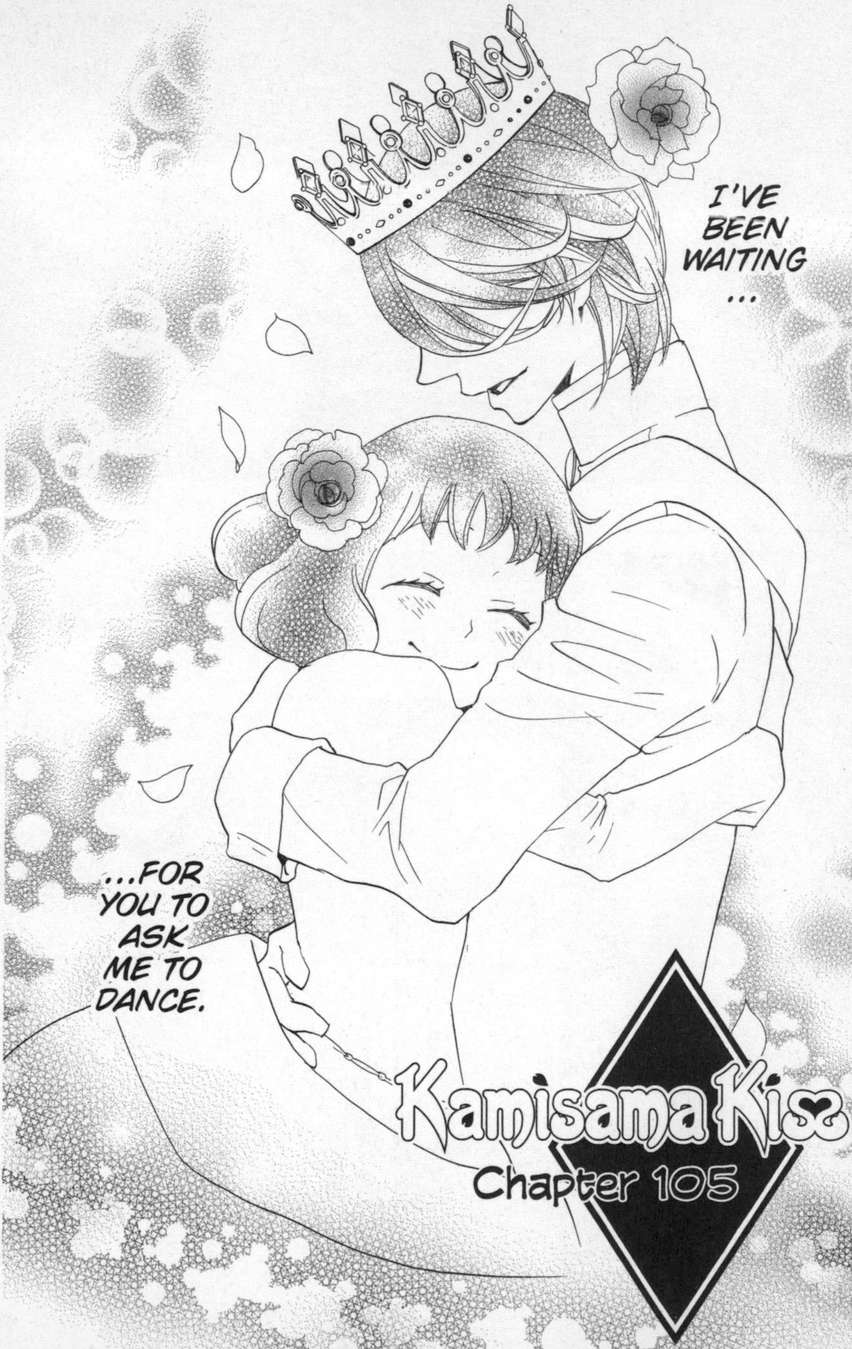
I'VE BEEN WAITING ...
...FOR YOU TO ASK ME TO DANCE.
Kamisama Kiss
Chapter 105

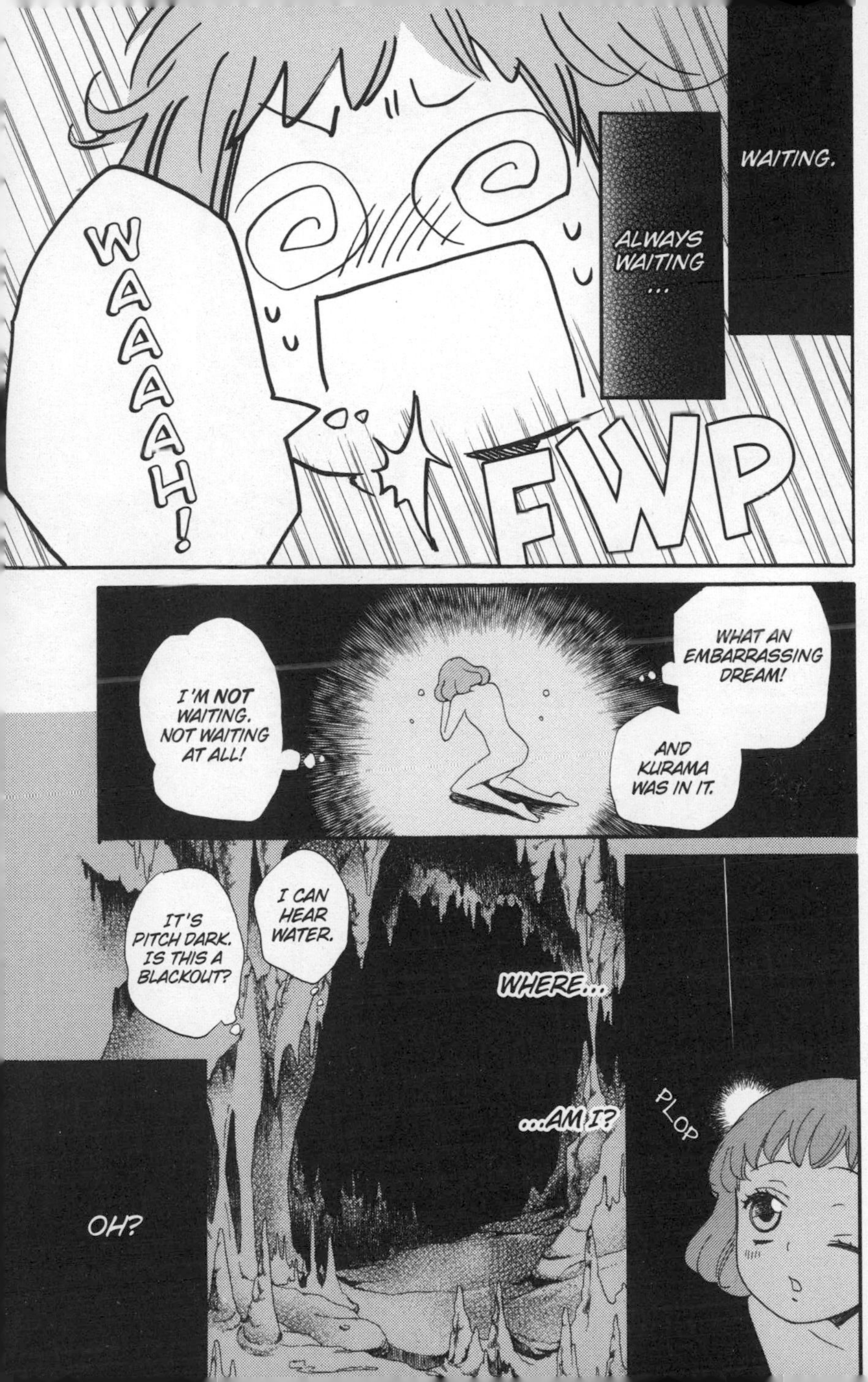
WAITING.
ALWAYS WAITING ...
WAAAAAH!
FWP
WHAT AN EMBARRASSING DREAM!
AND KURAMA WAS IN IT.
I'M NOT WAITING. NOT WAITING AT ALL!
I CAN HEAR WATER.
IT'S PITCH DARK. IS THIS A BLACKOUT?
WHERE...
...AM I?
PLOP
OH?

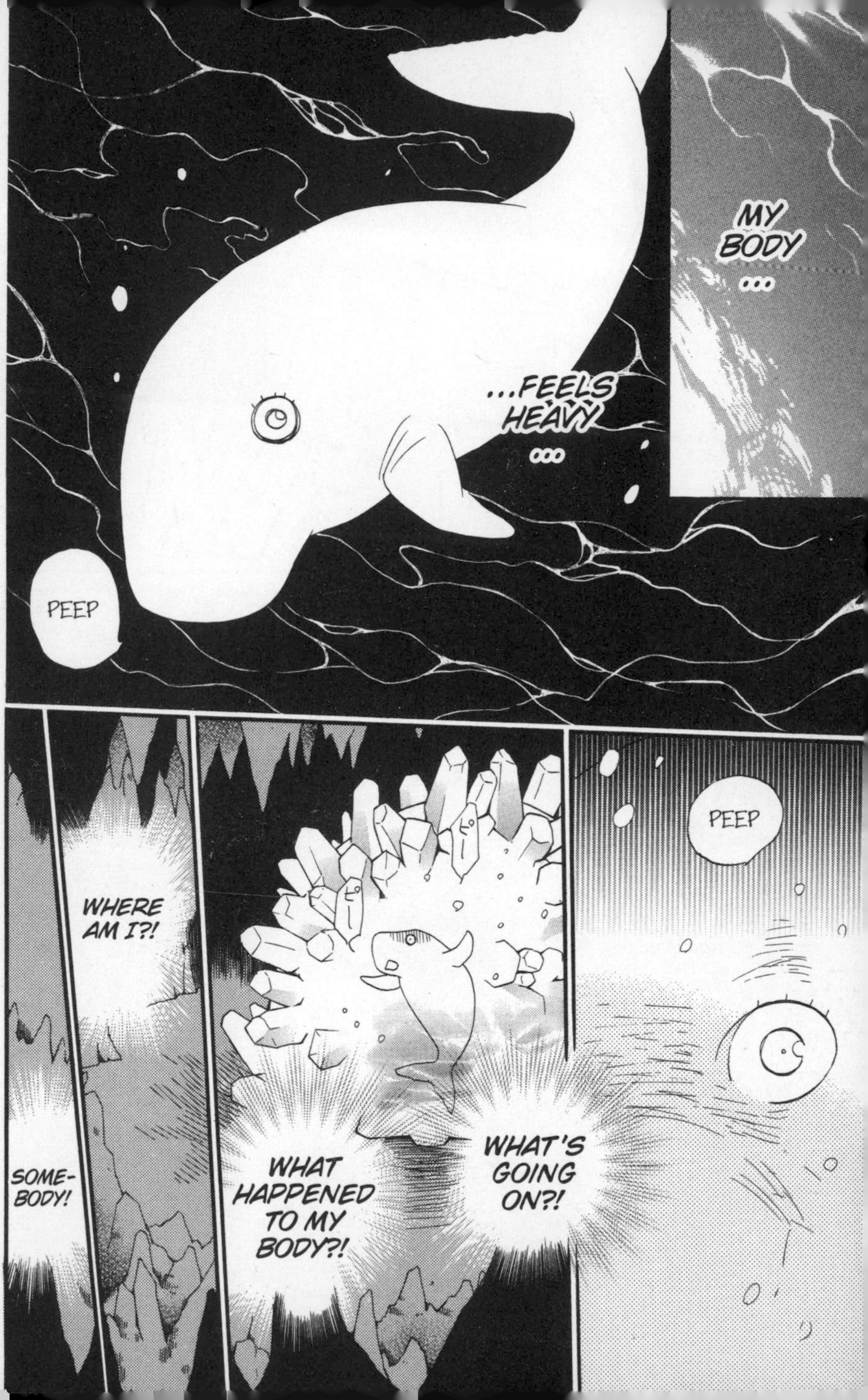
MY BODY ...
...FEELS HEAVY ...
PEEP
PEEP
WHAT'S GOING ON?!
WHAT HAPPENED TO MY BODY?!
WHERE AM I?!
SOME-BODY!

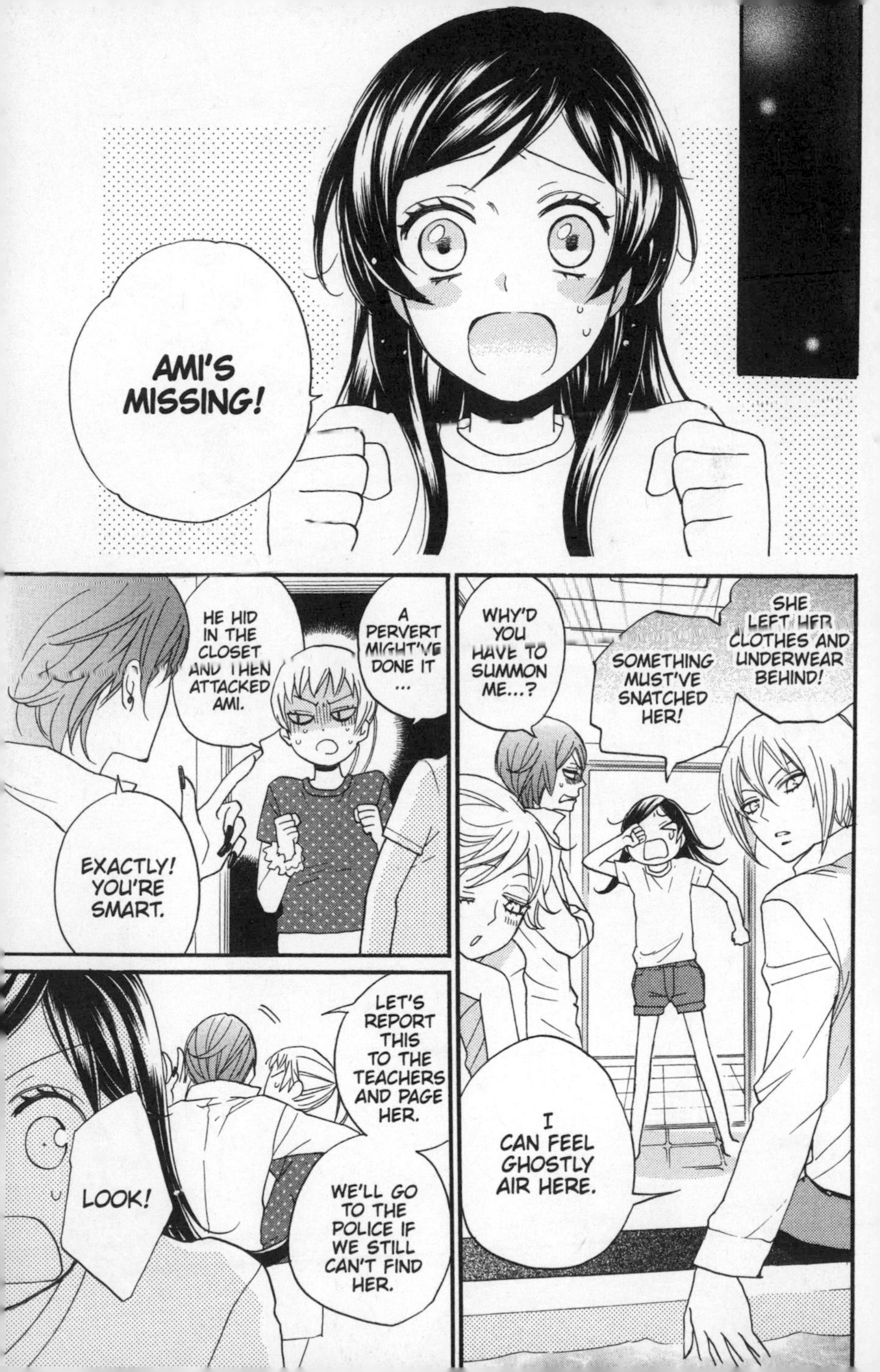
AMI'S MISSING!
SHE LEFT HER CLOTHES AND UNDERWEAR BEHIND!
SOMETHING MUST'VE SNATCHED HER!
WHY'D YOU HAVE TO SUMMON ME...?
I CAN FEEL GHOSTLY AIR HERE.
A PERVERT MIGHT'VE DONE IT...
HE HID IN THE CLOSET AND THEN ATTACKED AMI.
EXACTLY! YOU'RE SMART.
LET'S REPORT THIS TO THE TEACHERS AND PAGE HER.
WE'LL GO TO THE POLICE IF WE STILL CAN'T FIND HER.
LOOK!

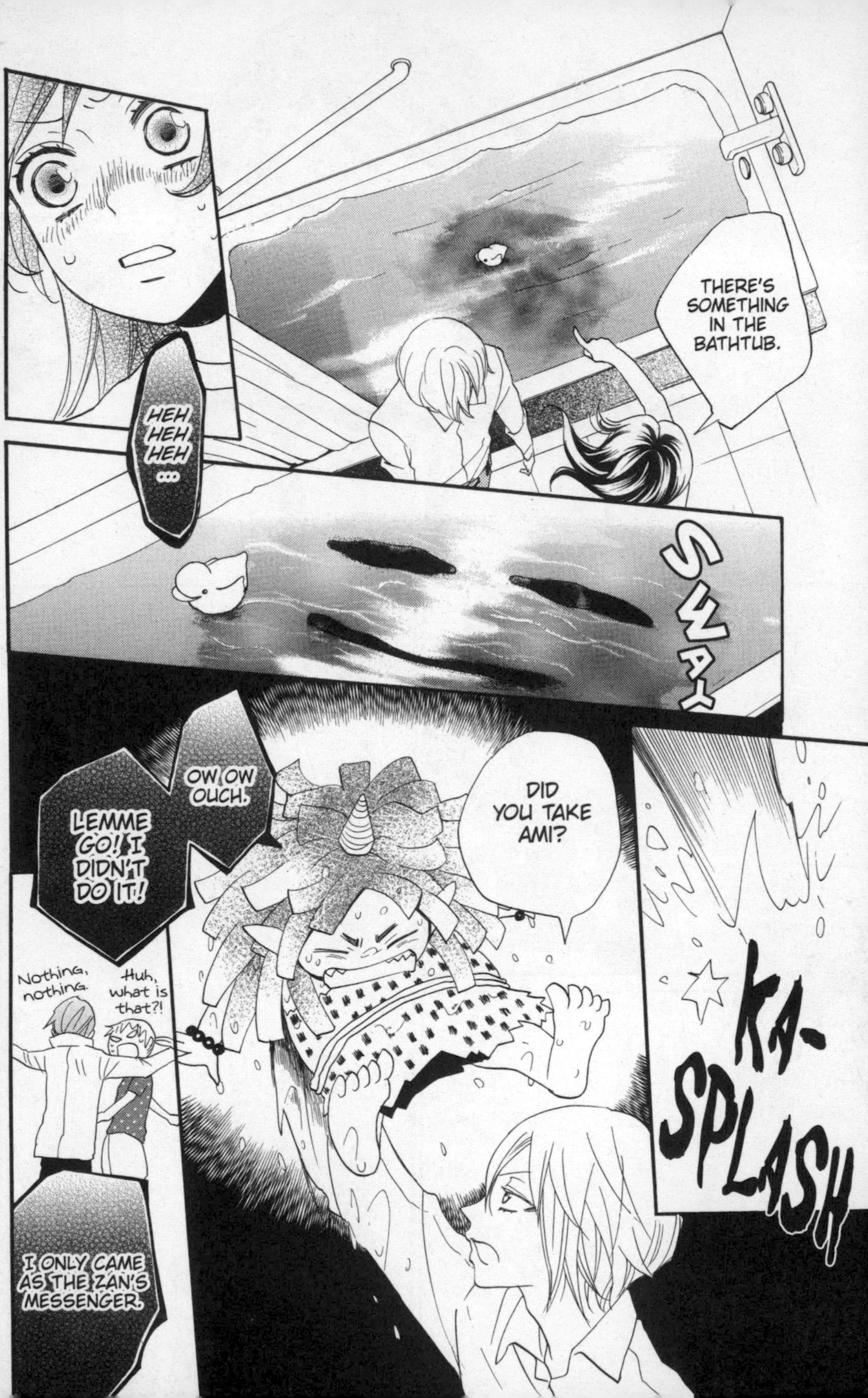
THERE'S SOMETHING IN THE BATHTUB.
HEH HEH HEH...
SWAY
KA-SPLASH
DID YOU TAKE AMI?
OW OW OUCH.
LEMME GO! I DIDN'T DO IT!
Huh, what is that?!
Nothing, nothing.
I ONLY CAME AS THE ZAN'S MESSENGER.

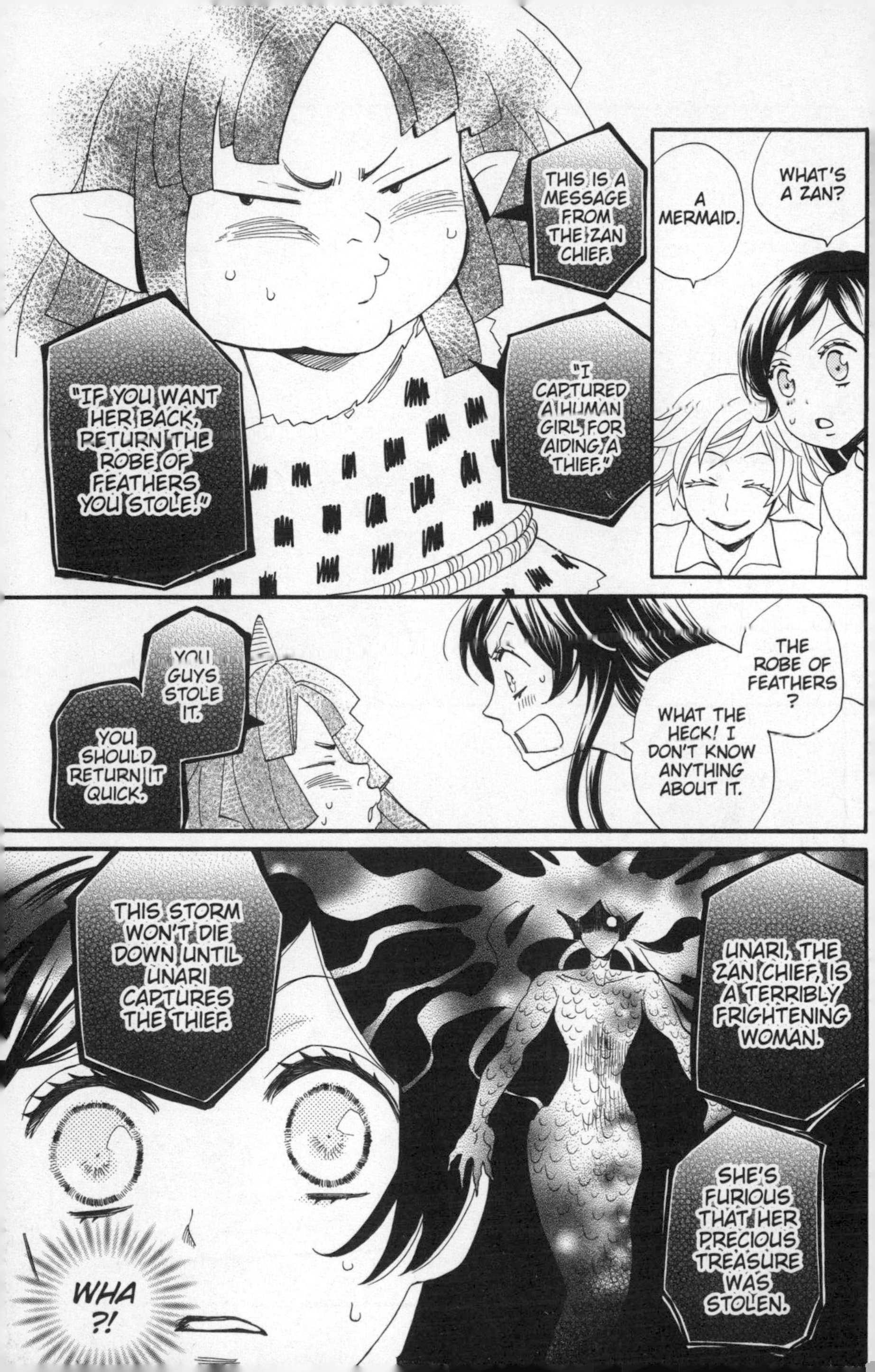
WHAT'S A ZAN?
A MERMAID.
THIS IS A MESSAGE FROM THE ZAN CHIEF.
"I CAPTURED A HUMAN GIRL FOR AIDING A THIEF."
"IF YOU WANT HER BACK, RETURN THE ROBE OF FEATHERS YOU STOLE."
THE ROBE OF FEATHERS ?
WHAT THE HECK! I DON'T KNOW ANYTHING ABOUT IT.
YOU GUYS STOLE IT.
YOU SHOULD RETURN IT QUICK.
UNARI, THE ZAN CHIEF, IS A TERRIBLY FRIGHTENING WOMAN.
SHE'S FURIOUS THAT HER PRECIOUS TREASURE WAS STOLEN.
THIS STORM WON'T DIE DOWN UNTIL UNARI CAPTURES THE THIEF.
WHA ?!

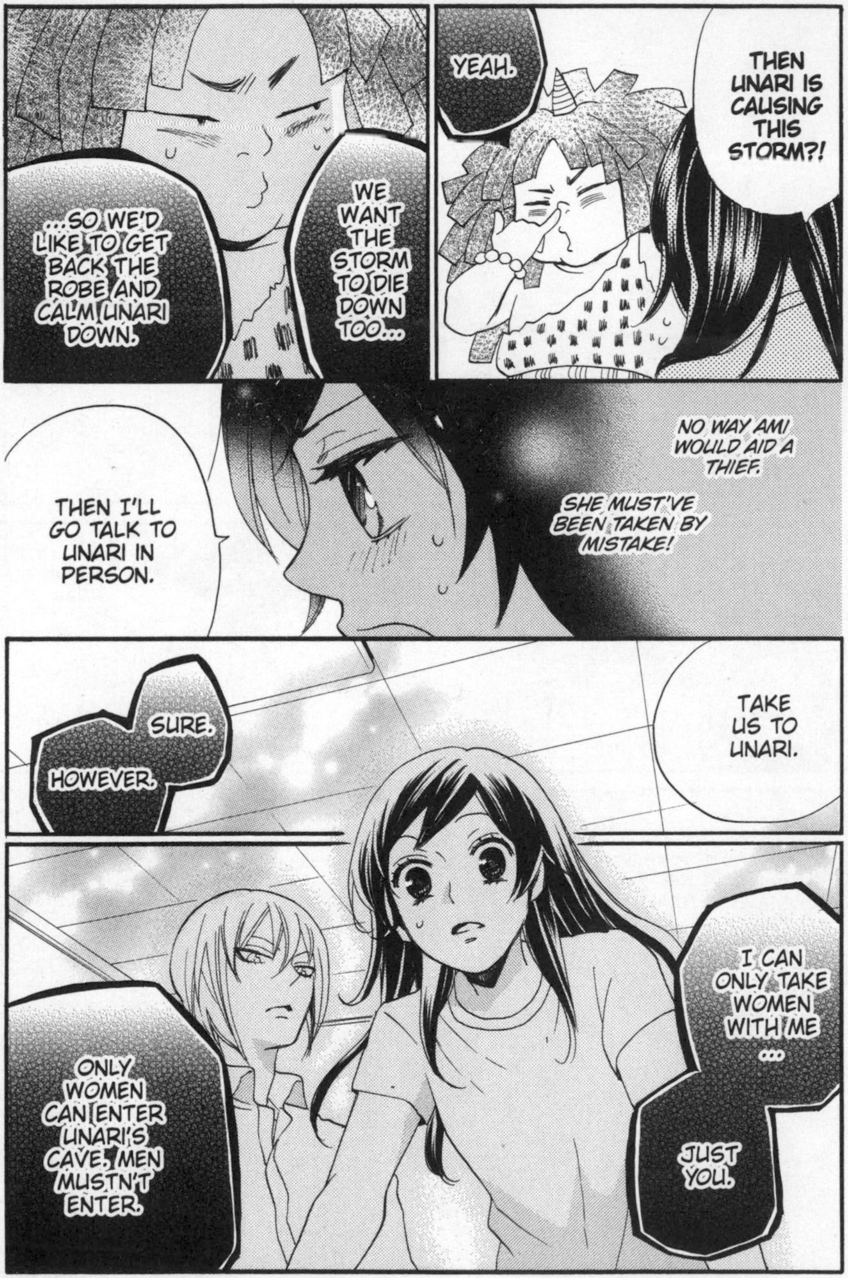
THEN UNARI IS CAUSING THIS STORM?!
YEAH.
WE WANT THE STORM TO DIE DOWN TOO...
...SO WE'D LIKE TO GET BACK THE ROBE AND CALM UNARI DOWN.
NO WAY AMI WOULD AID A THIEF.
SHE MUST'VE BEEN TAKEN BY MISTAKE!
THEN I'LL GO TALK TO UNARI IN PERSON.
TAKE US TO UNARI.
SURE.
HOWEVER.
I CAN ONLY TAKE WOMEN WITH ME ...
JUST YOU.
ONLY WOMEN CAN ENTER UNARI'S CAVE, MEN MUSTN'T ENTER.

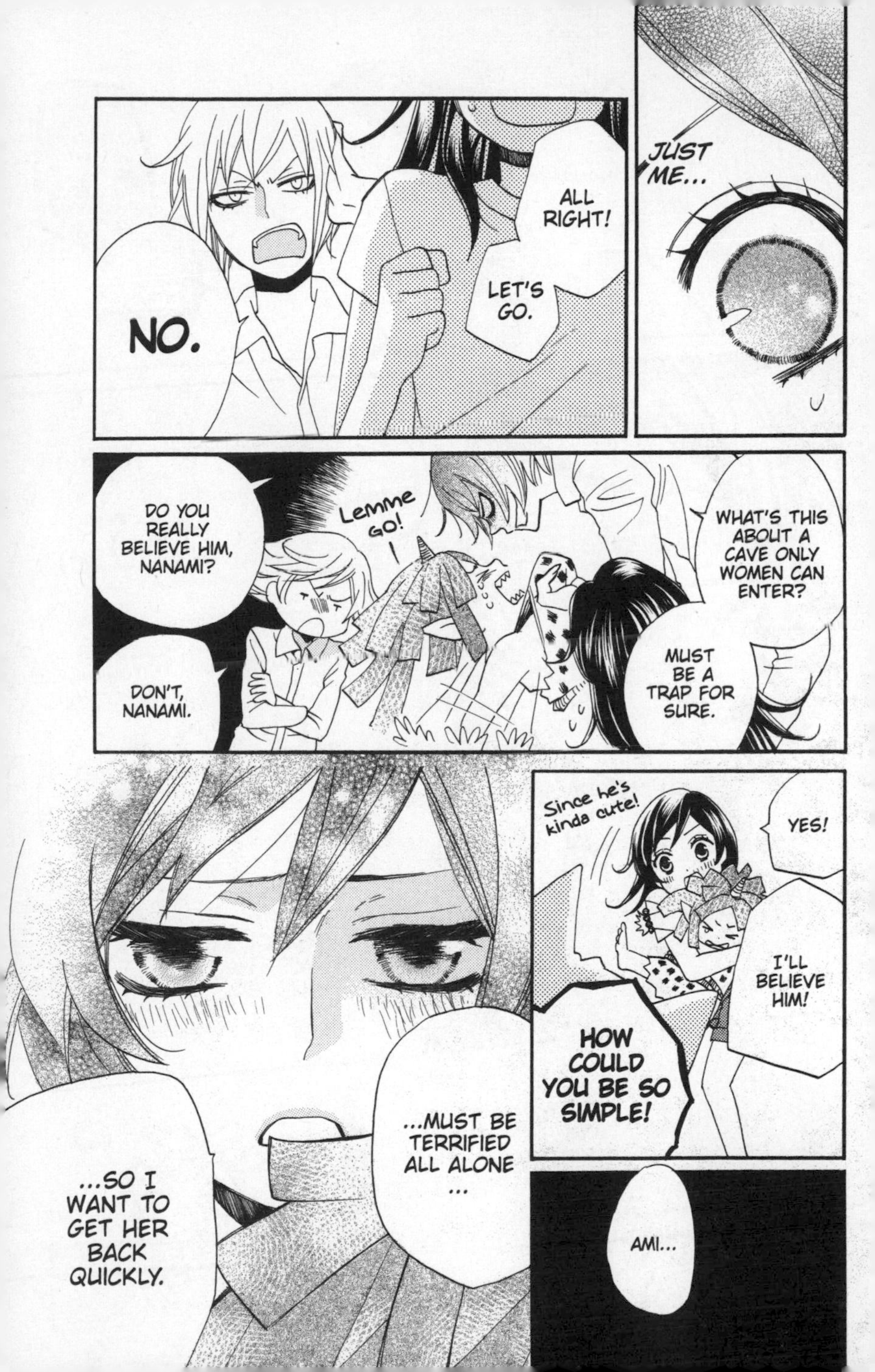
JUST ME...
ALL RIGHT!
LET'S GO.
NO.
WHAT'S THIS ABOUT A CAVE ONLY WOMEN CAN ENTER?
MUST BE A TRAP FOR SURE.
Lemme go!
DO YOU REALLY BELIEVE HIM, NANAMI?
DON'T, NANAMI.
YES!
Since he's kinda cute!
I'LL BELIEVE HIM!
HOW COULD YOU BE SO SIMPLE!
AMI...
...MUST BE TERRIFIED ALL ALONE ...
...SO I WANT TO GET HER BACK QUICKLY.

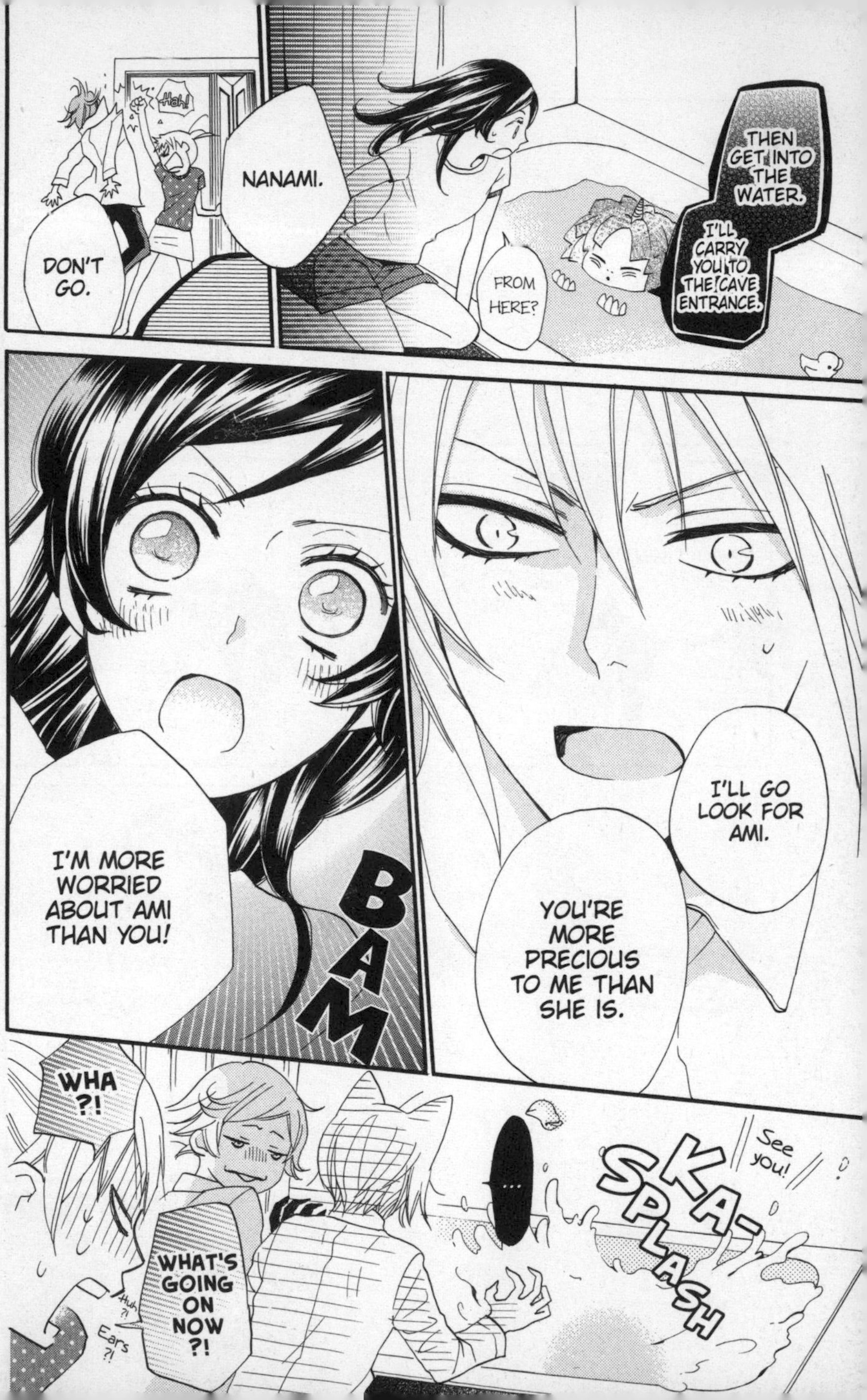
THEN GET INTO THE WATER.
I'LL CARRY YOU TO THE CAVE ENTRANCE.
FROM HERE?
NANAMI.
Hah!
DON'T GO.
I'LL GO LOOK FOR AMI.
YOU'RE MORE PRECIOUS TO ME THAN SHE IS.
I'M MORE WORRIED ABOUT AMI THAN YOU!
BAM
See you!
KA-SPLASH
...
WHA?!
WHAT'S GOING ON NOW?!
Huh?!
Ears?!

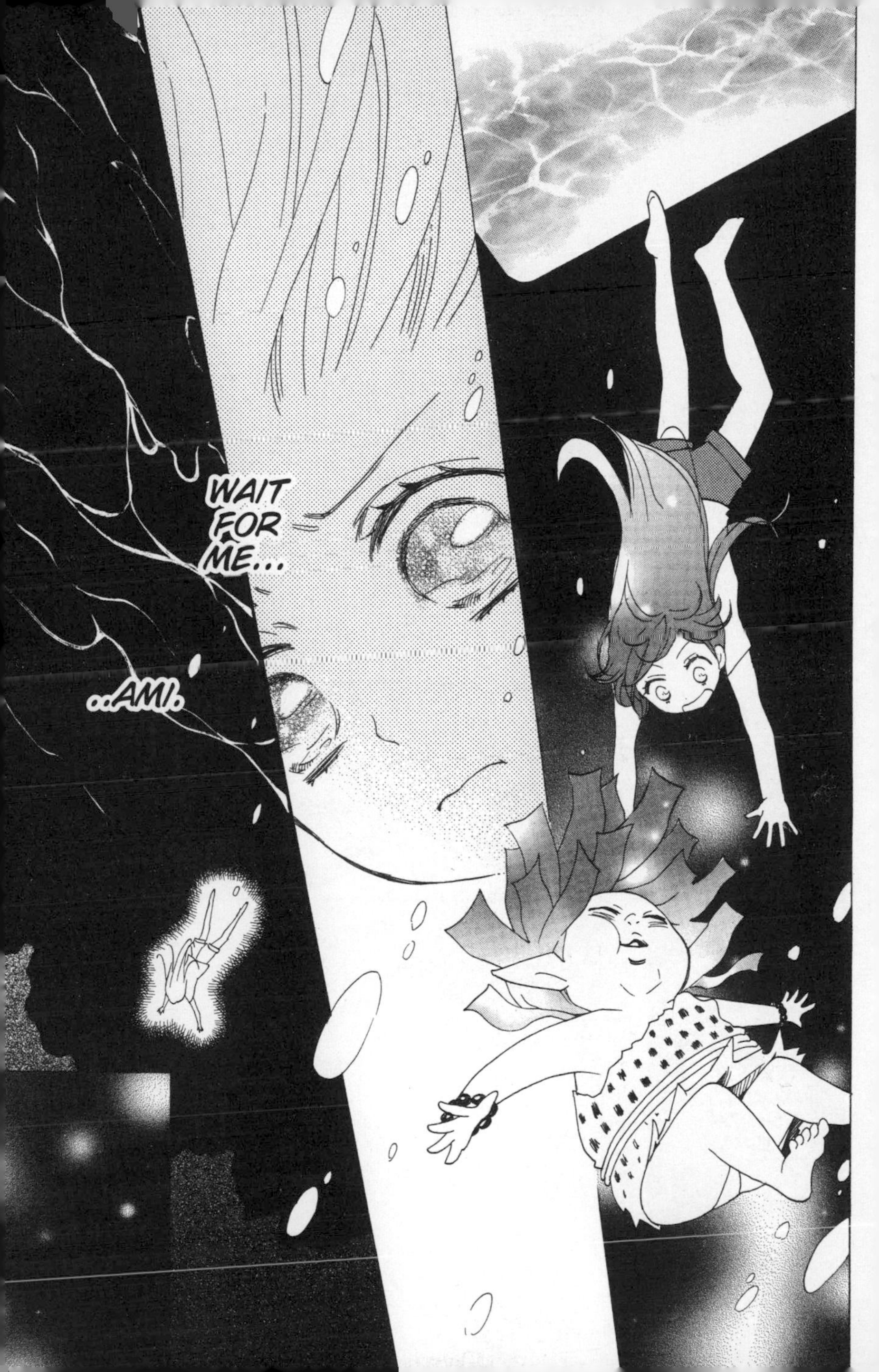
WAIT FOR ME...
..AMI.

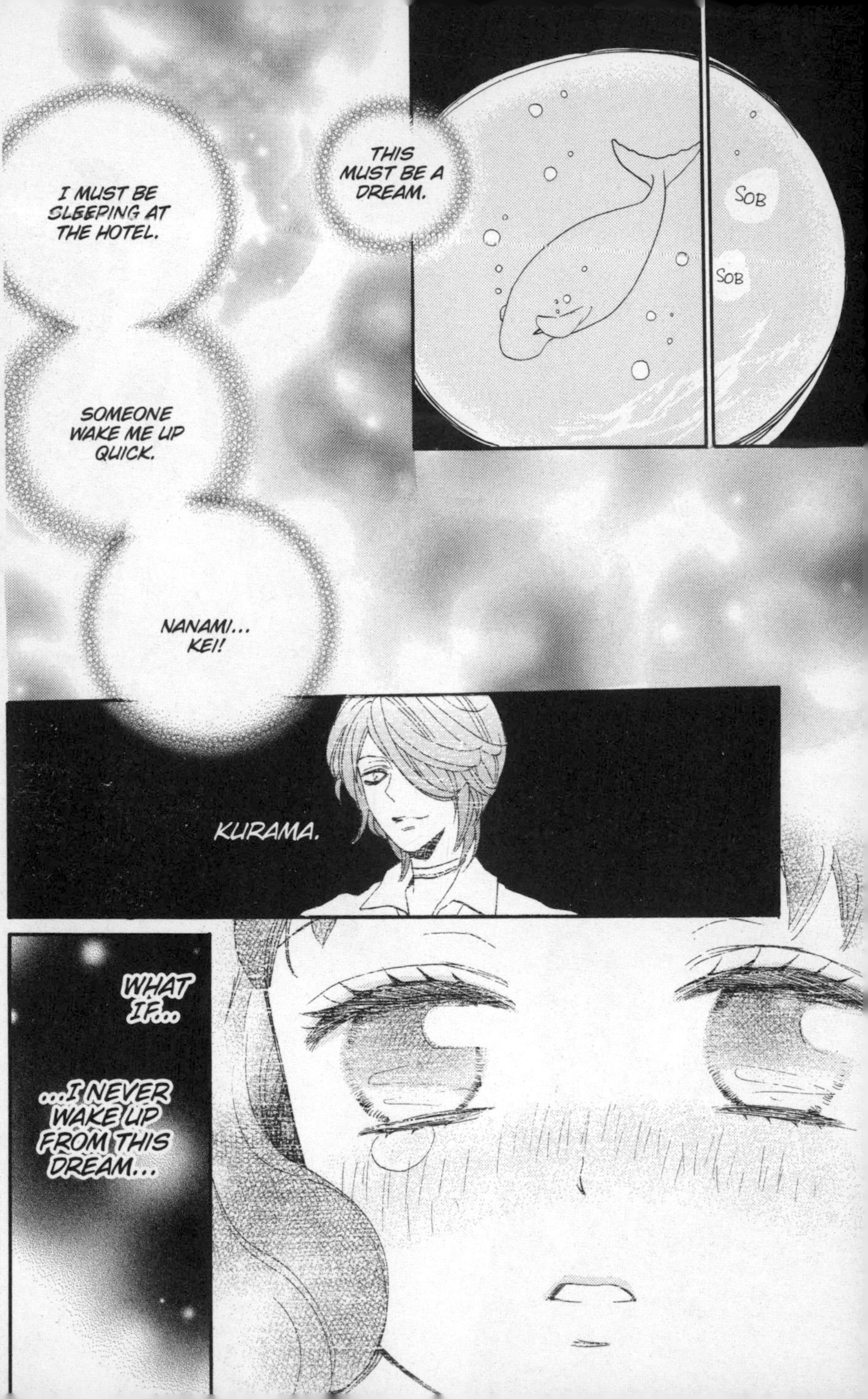
SOB
SOB
THIS MUST BE A DREAM.
I MUST BE SLEEPING AT THE HOTEL.
SOMEONE WAKE ME UP QUICK.
NANAMI... KEI!
KURAMA.
WHAT IF...
...I NEVER WAKE UP FROM THIS DREAM...

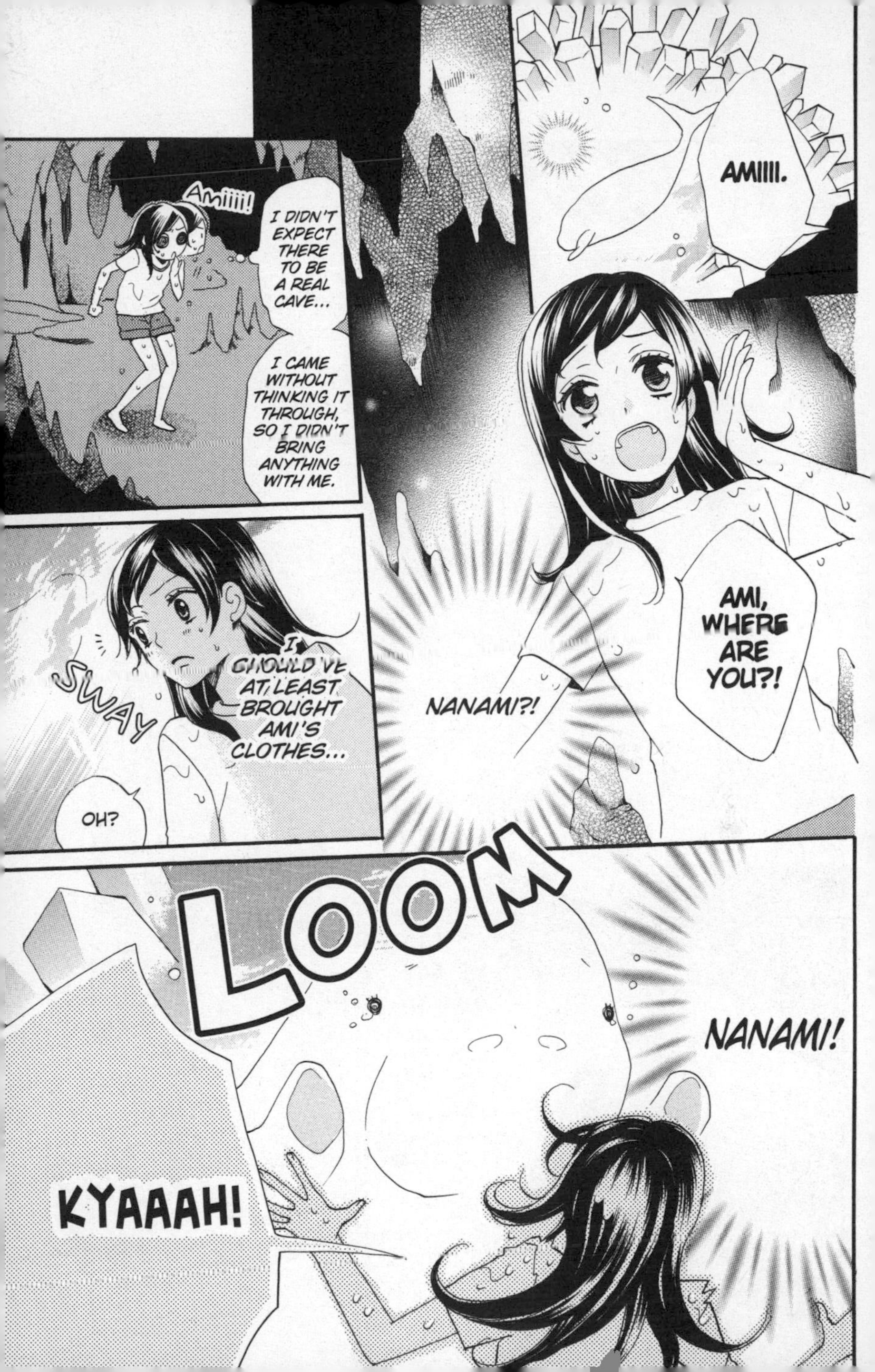
AMIIII.
Amiiii!
I DIDN'T EXPECT THERE TO BE A REAL CAVE...
I CAME WITHOUT THINKING IT THROUGH, SO I DIDN'T BRING ANYTHING WITH ME.
AMI, WHERE ARE YOU?!
NANAMI?!
I SHOULD'VE AT LEAST BROUGHT AMI'S CLOTHES...
SWAY
OH?
LOOM
NANAMI!
KYAAAH!

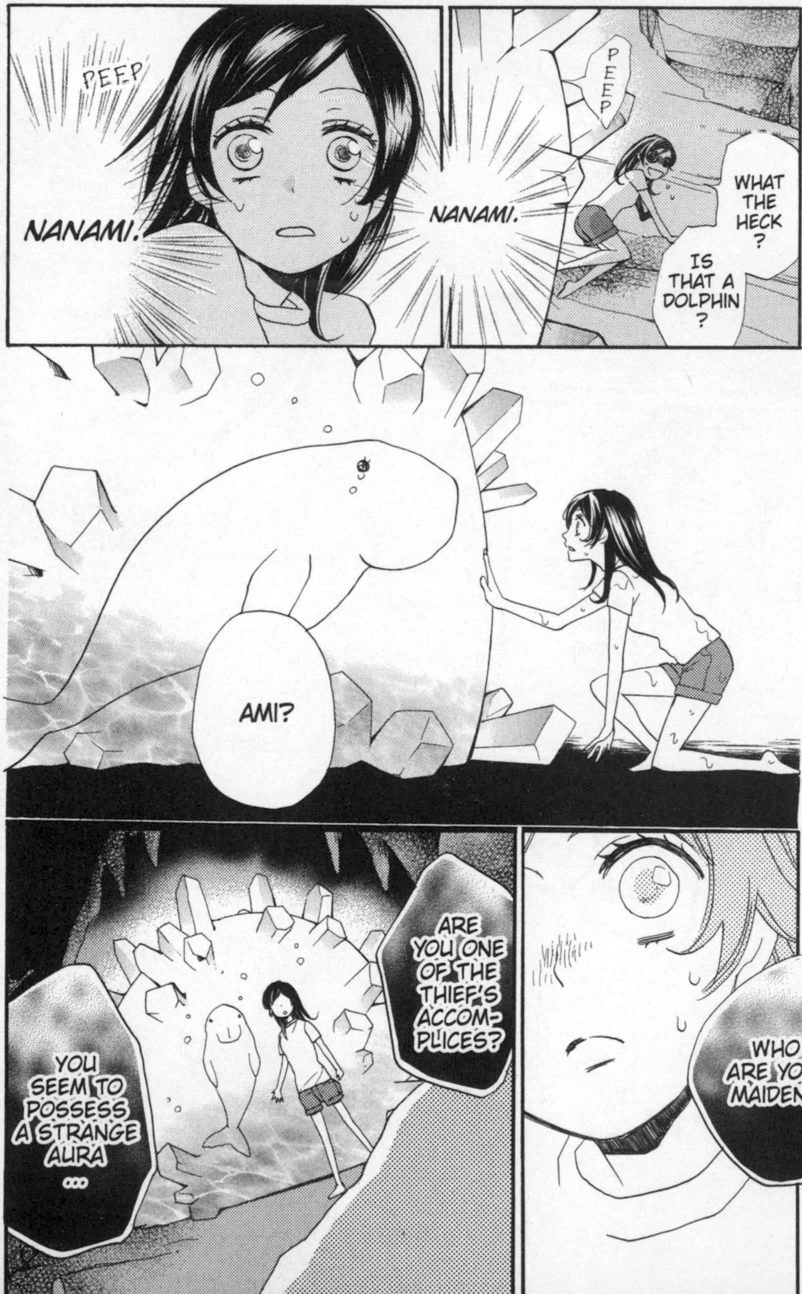
PEEP PEEP
WHAT THE HECK?
IS THAT A DOLPHIN?
PEEP
NANAMI.
NANAMI.
AMI?
WHO ARE YOU, MAIDEN?
ARE YOU ONE OF THE THIEF'S ACCOMPLICES?
YOU SEEM TO POSSESS A STRANGE AURA...

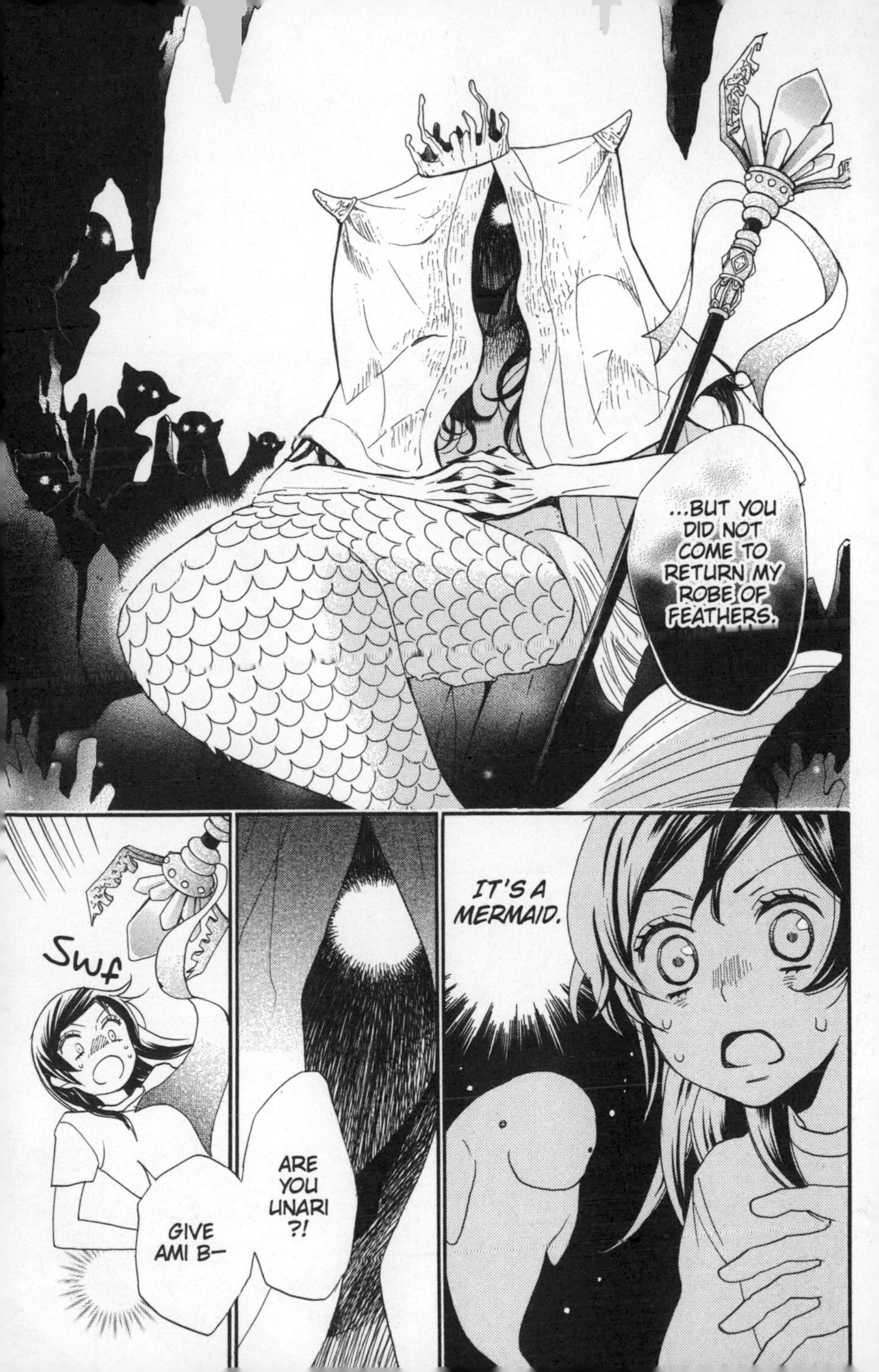
...BUT YOU DID NOT COME TO RETURN MY ROBE OF FEATHERS.
IT'S A MERMAID.
ARE YOU UNARI?!
Swf
GIVE AMI B—

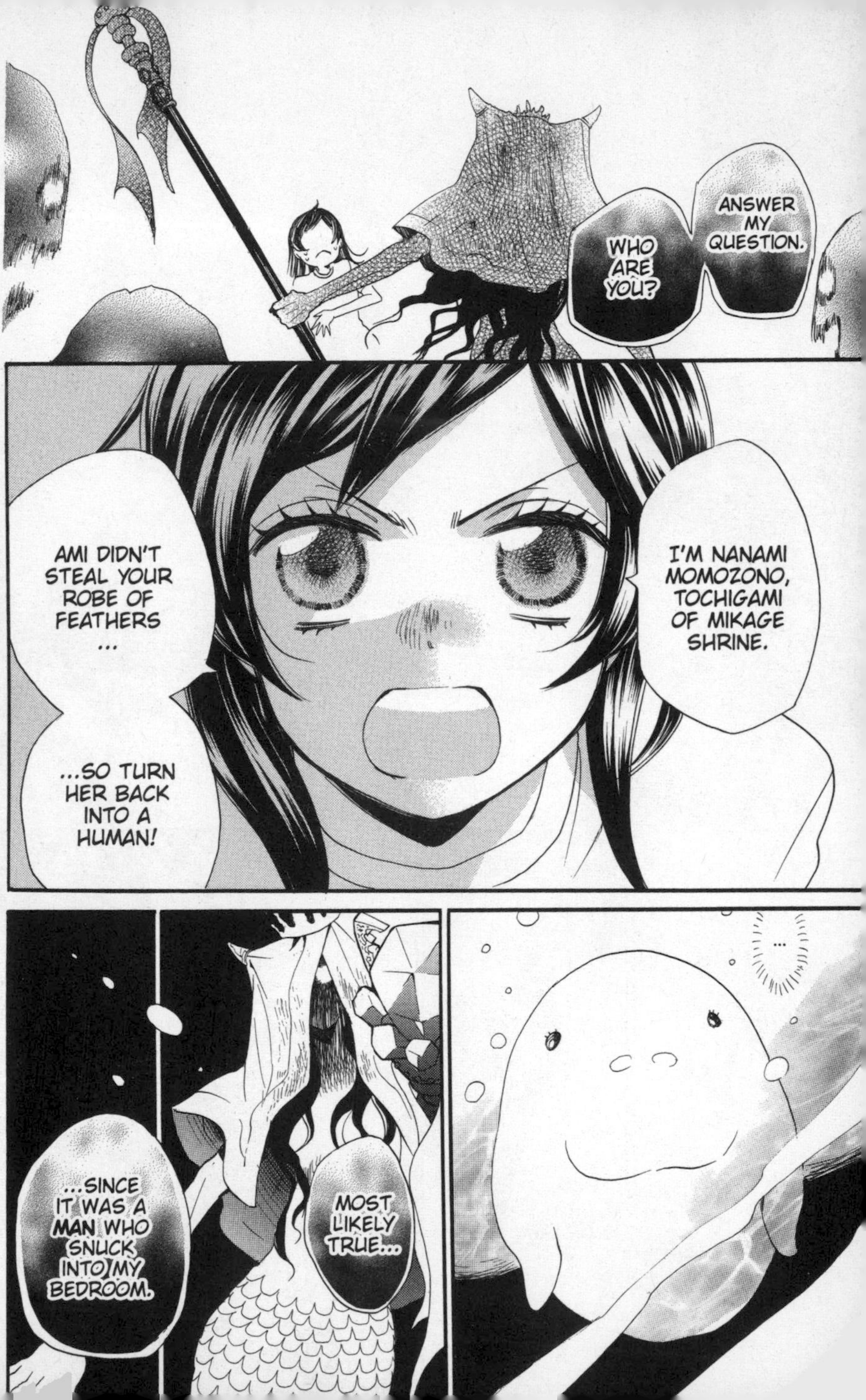
ANSWER MY QUESTION.
WHO ARE YOU?
I'M NANAMI MOMOZONO, TOCHIGAMI OF MIKAGE SHRINE.
AMI DIDN'T STEAL YOUR ROBE OF FEATHERS ...
...SO TURN HER BACK INTO A HUMAN!
...
MOST LIKELY TRUE...
...SINCE IT WAS A MAN WHO SNUCK INTO MY BEDROOM.

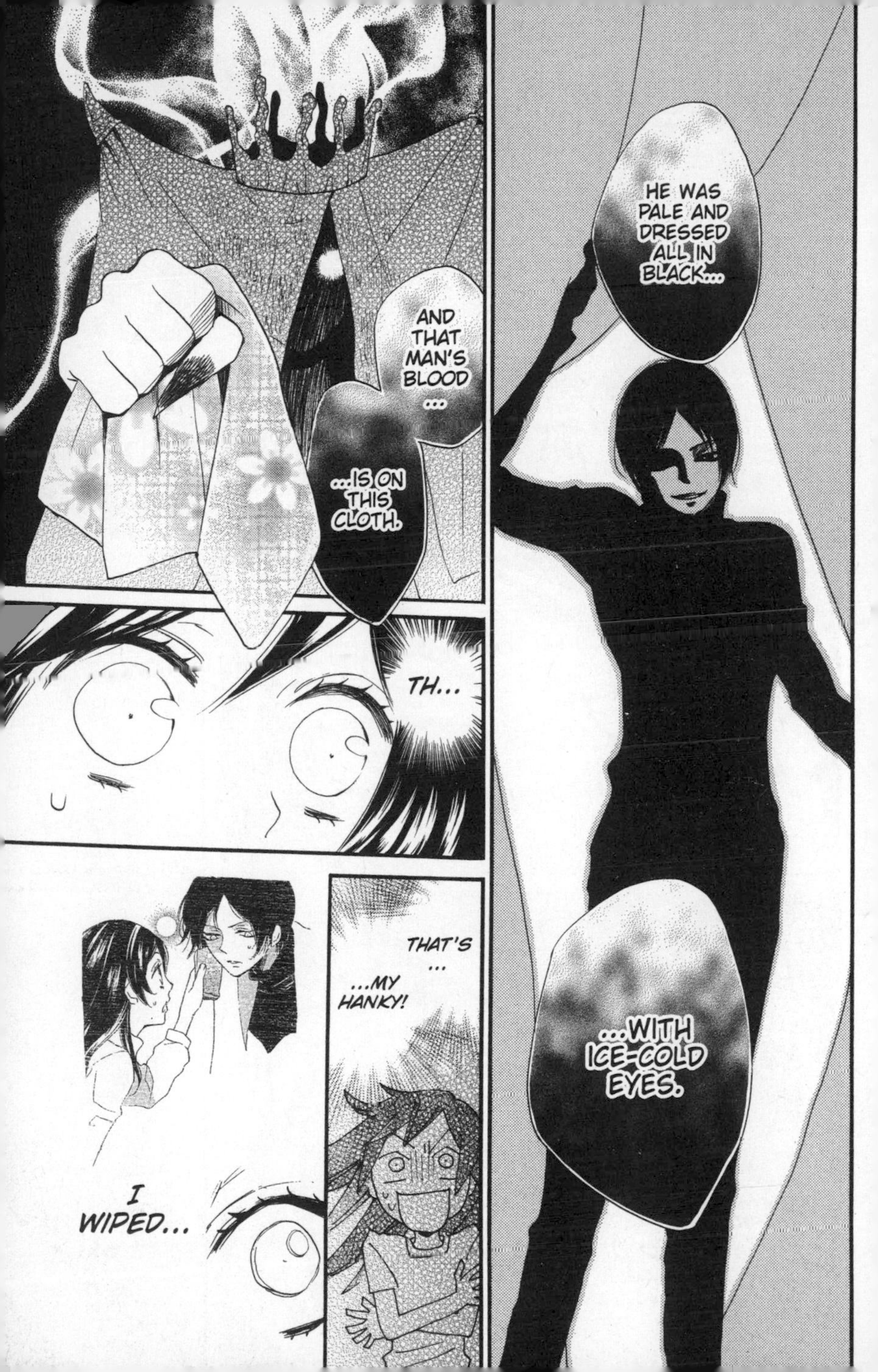
HE WAS PALE AND DRESSED ALL IN BLACK...
...WITH ICE-COLD EYES.
AND THAT MAN'S BLOOD...
...IS ON THIS CLOTH.
TH...
THAT'S...
...MY HANKY!
I WIPED...

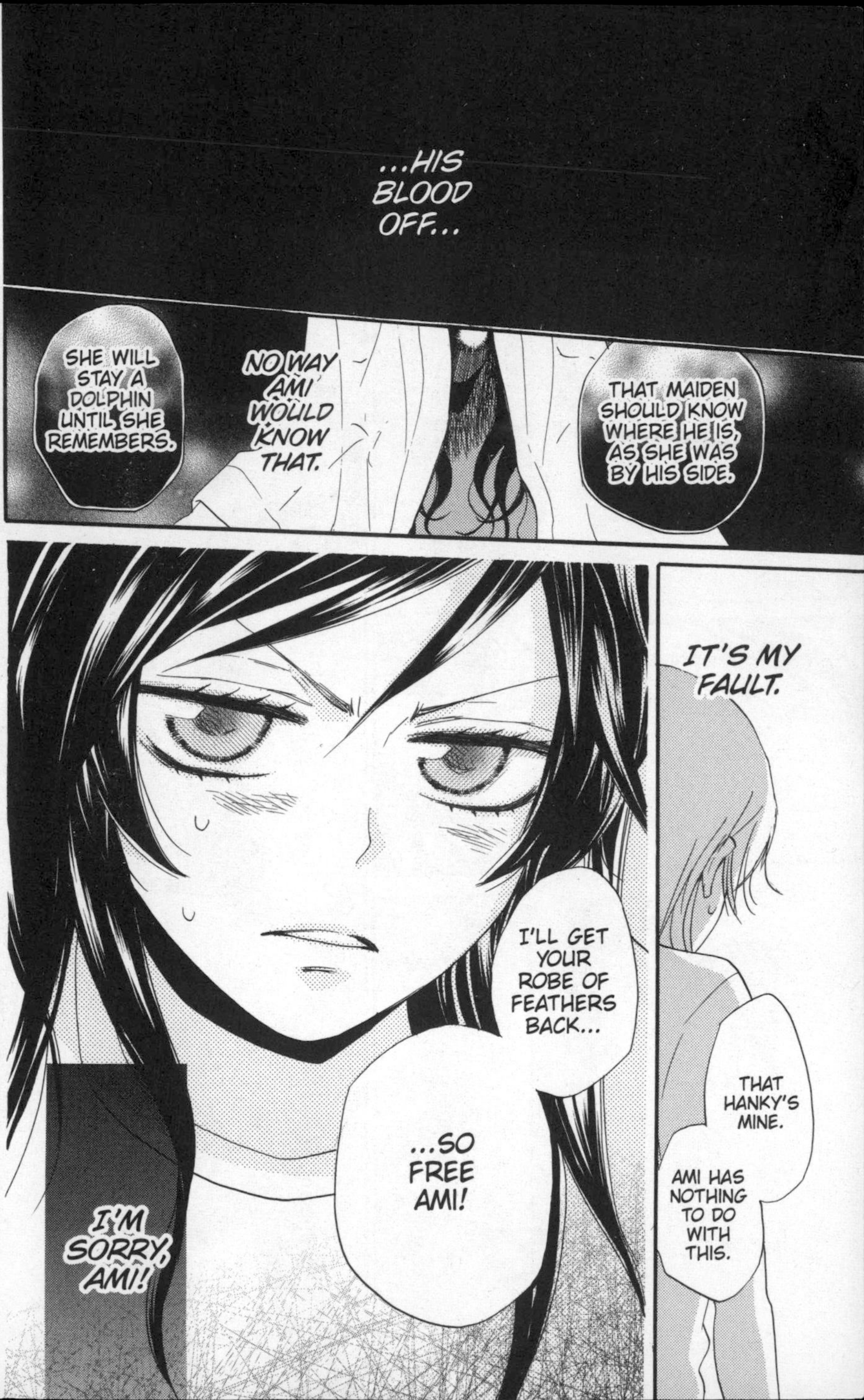
...HIS BLOOD OFF...
THAT MAIDEN SHOULD KNOW WHERE HE IS, AS SHE WAS BY HIS SIDE.
NO WAY AMI WOULD KNOW THAT.
SHE WILL STAY A DOLPHIN UNTIL SHE REMEMBERS.
IT'S MY FAULT.
THAT HANKY'S MINE.
AMI HAS NOTHING TO DO WITH THIS.
I'LL GET YOUR ROBE OF FEATHERS BACK...
...SO FREE AMI!
I'M SORRY, AMI!

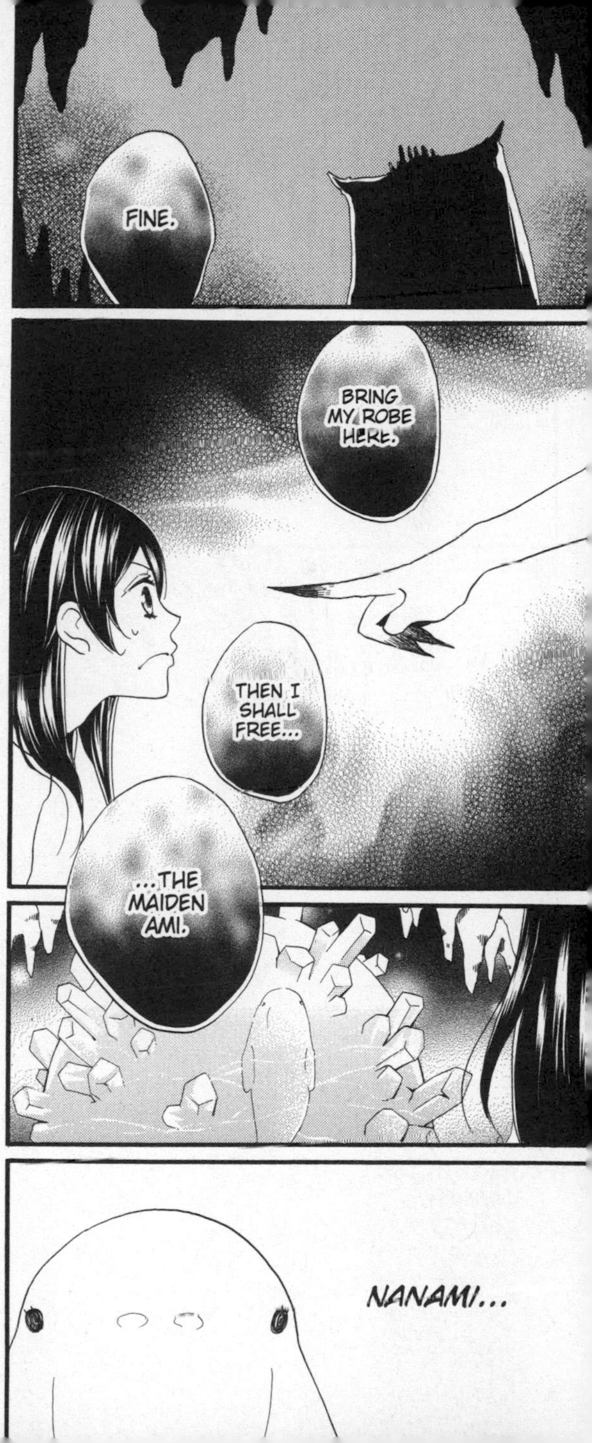
FINE.
BRING MY ROBE HERE.
THEN I SHALL FREE...
...THE MAIDEN AMI.
NANAMI...

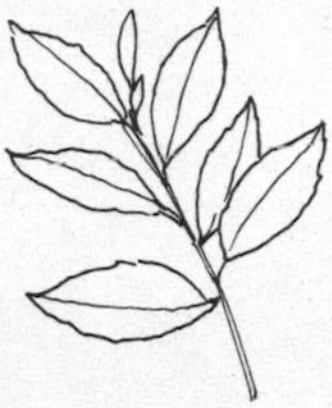

This year I've set up a little Shinto shrine at my home.

So I water the cleyera japonica every day. I need to replace them twice a month, but I don't want to replace a good branch, because some branches wither fast while others stay fresh for a long time.

Watering them every day enables me to spend the whole day feeling refreshed and good.

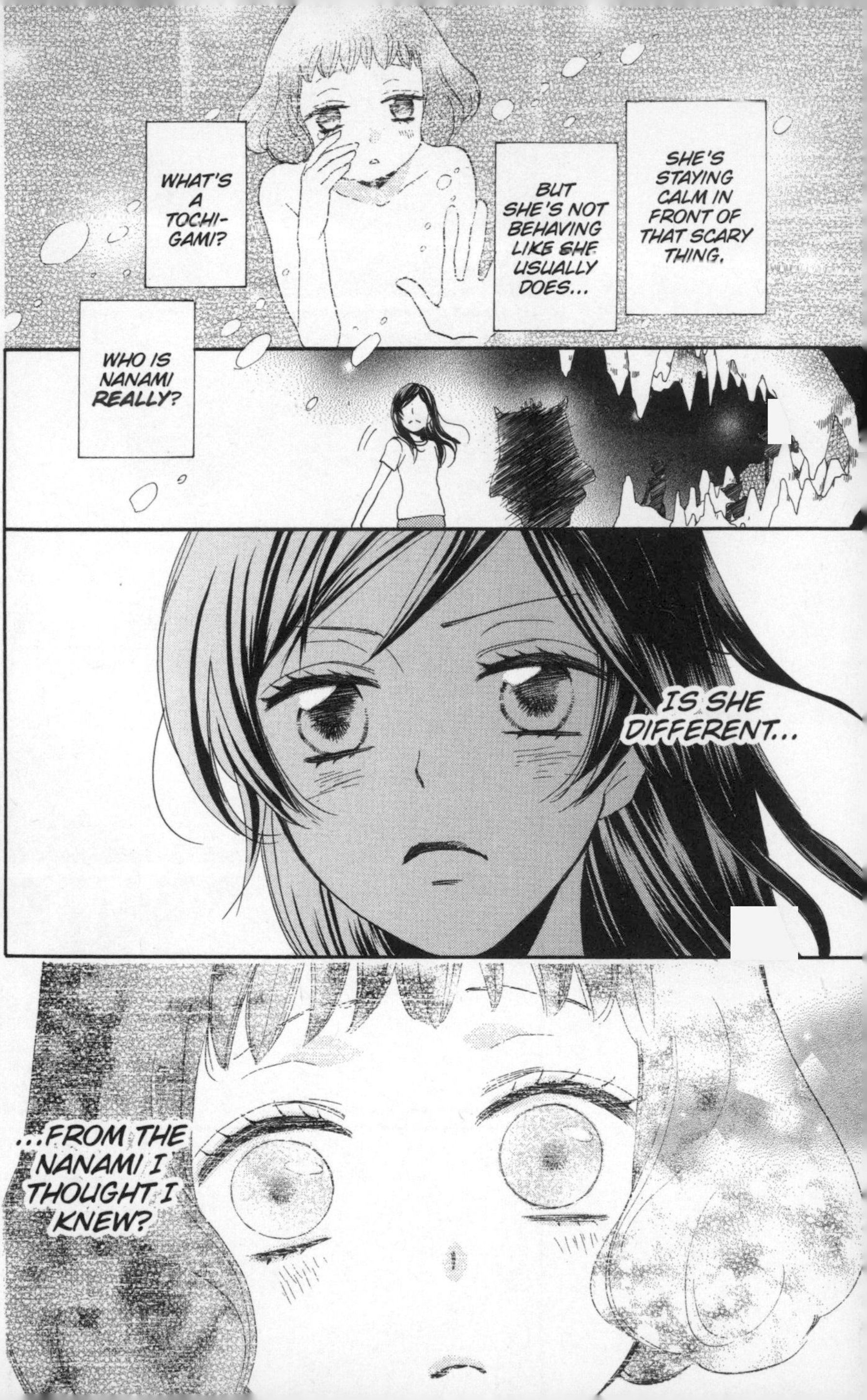
SHE'S STAYING CALM IN FRONT OF THAT SCARY THING.
BUT SHE'S NOT BEHAVING LIKE SHE USUALLY DOES...
WHAT'S A TOCHI-GAMI?
WHO IS NANAMI REALLY?
IS SHE DIFFERENT...
...FROM THE NANAMI I THOUGHT I KNEW?

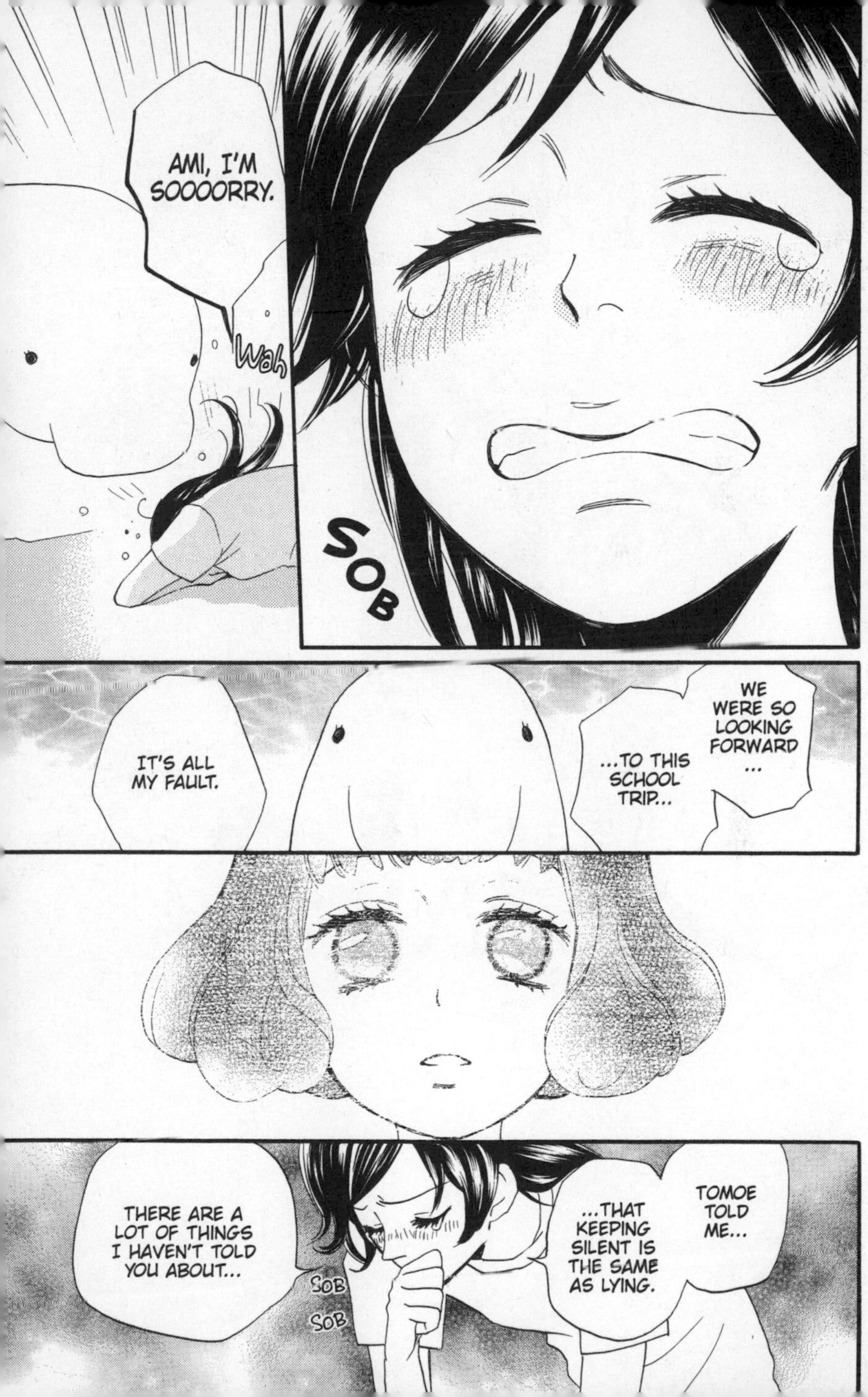
SOB
AMI, I'M SOOOORRY.
Wah
WE WERE SO LOOKING FORWARD...
...TO THIS SCHOOL TRIP...
IT'S ALL MY FAULT.
TOMOE TOLD ME...
...THAT KEEPING SILENT IS THE SAME AS LYING.
SOB
SOB
THERE ARE A LOT OF THINGS I HAVEN'T TOLD YOU ABOUT...

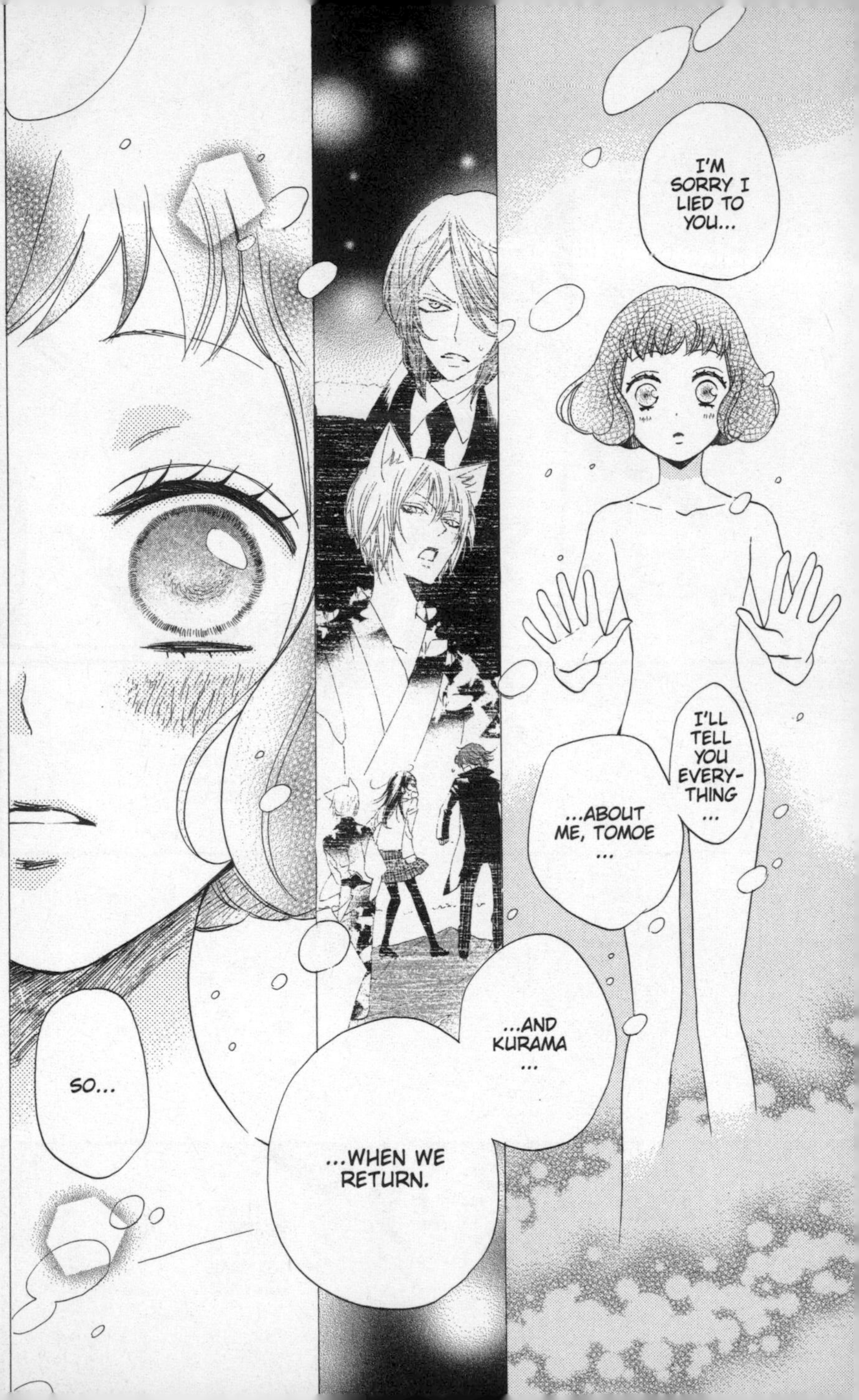
I'M SORRY I LIED TO YOU...
I'LL TELL YOU EVERYTHING...
...ABOUT ME, TOMOE...
...AND KURAMA...
...WHEN WE RETURN.
SO...

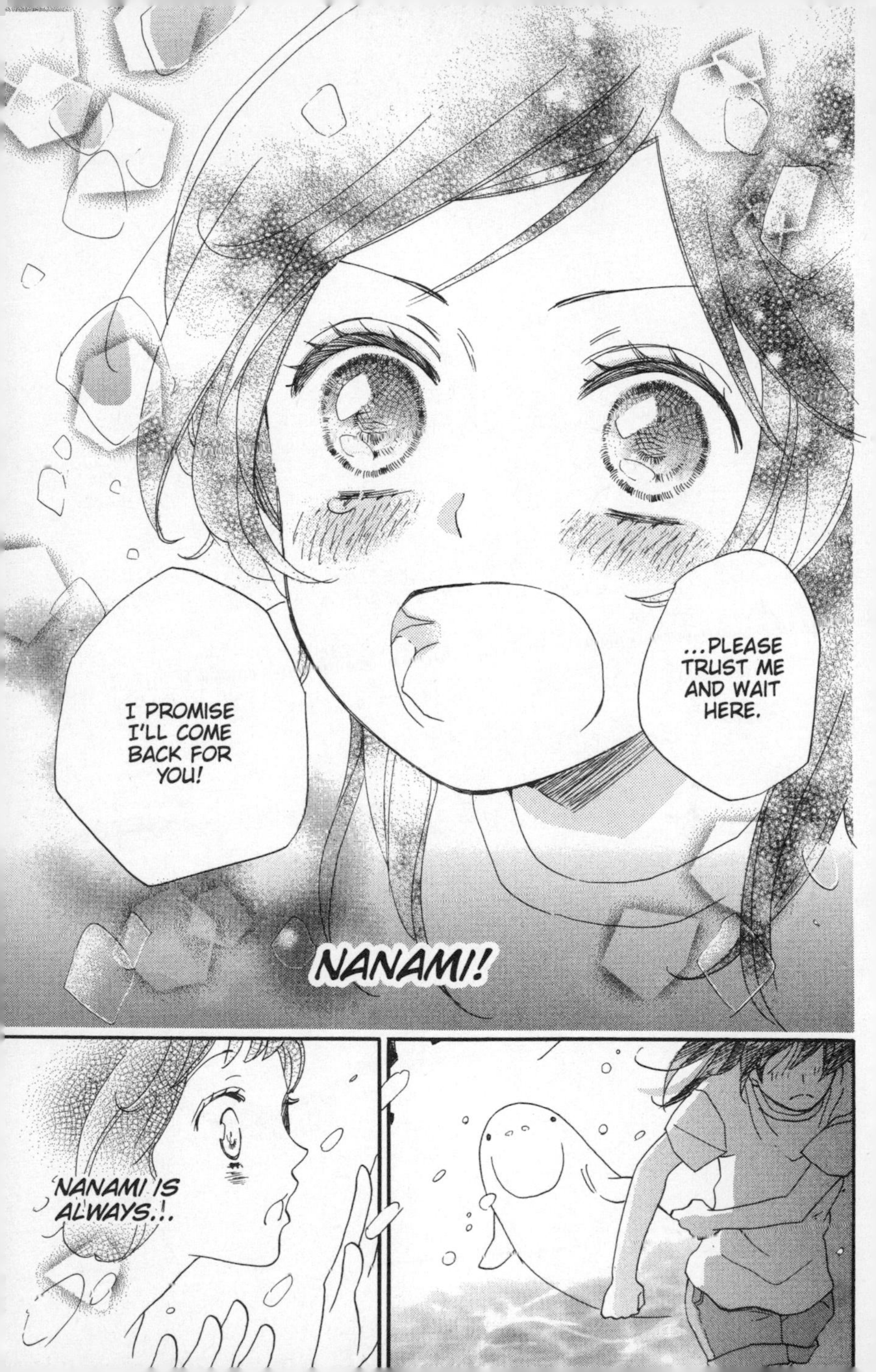
...PLEASE TRUST ME AND WAIT HERE.
I PROMISE I'LL COME BACK FOR YOU!
NANAMI!
NANAMI IS ALWAYS.!..

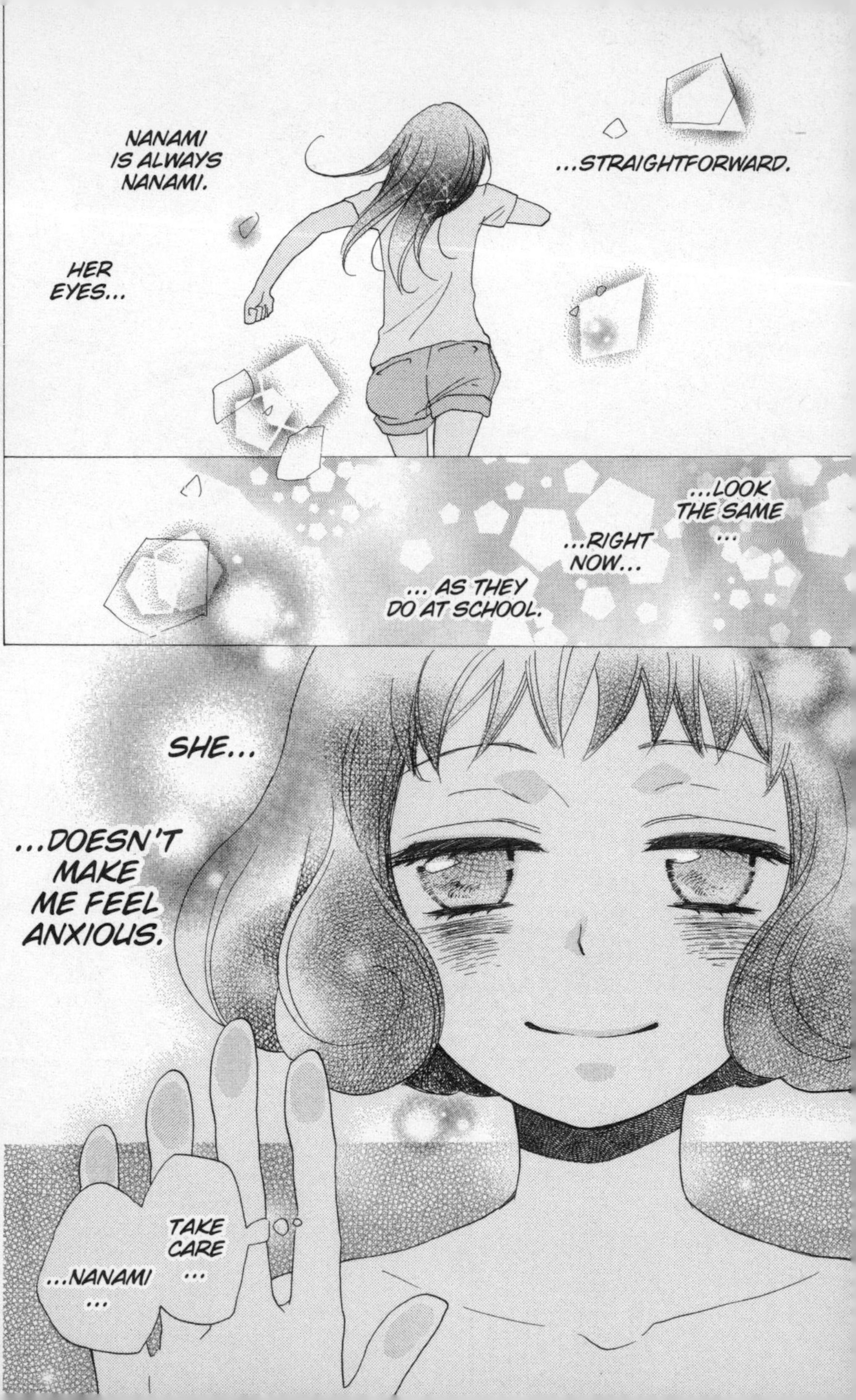
...STRAIGHTFORWARD.
NANAMI IS ALWAYS NANAMI.
HER EYES...
...LOOK THE SAME ...
...RIGHT NOW...
... AS THEY DO AT SCHOOL.
SHE...
...DOESN'T MAKE ME FEEL ANXIOUS.
TAKE CARE ...
...NANAMI ...

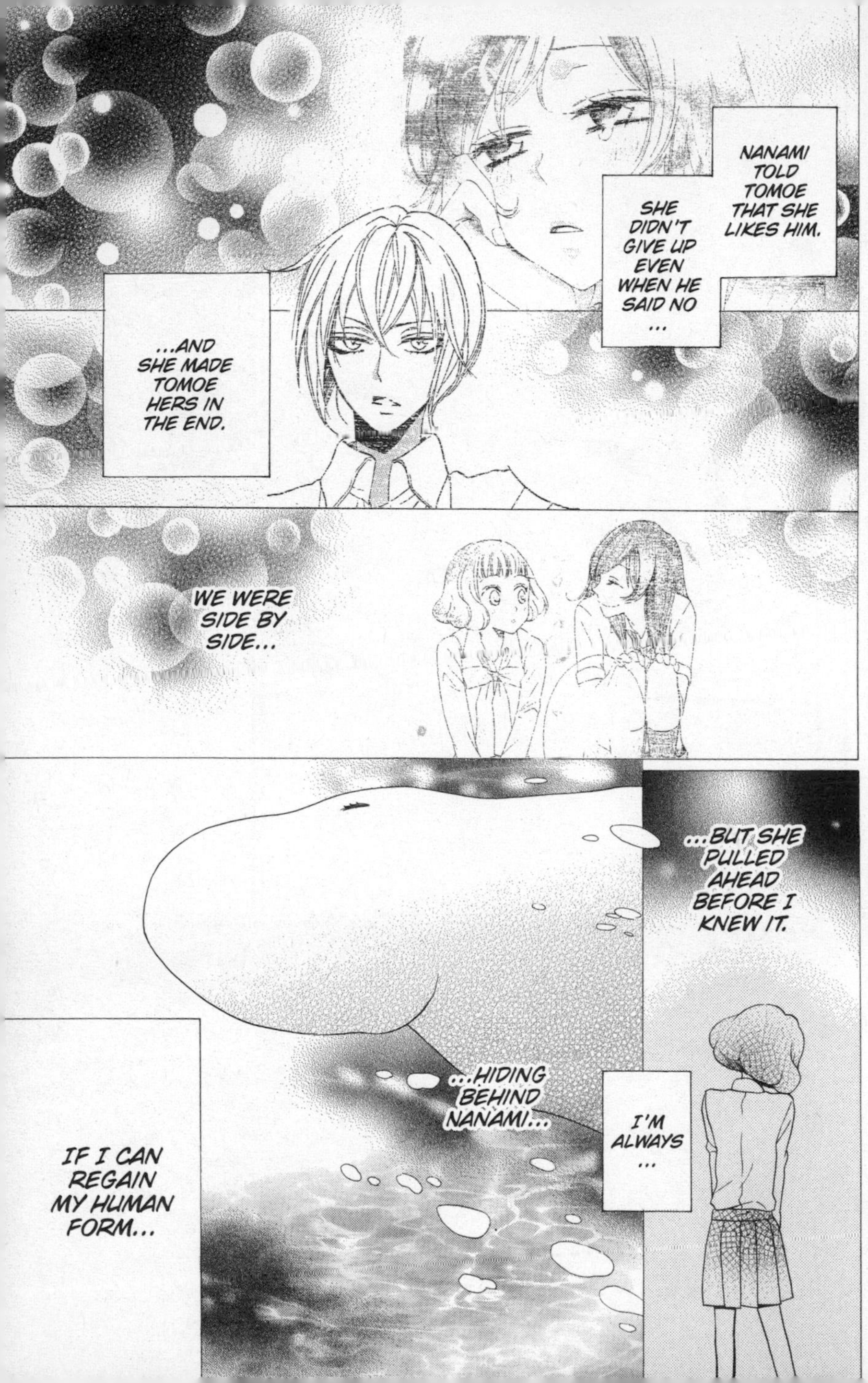
NANAMI TOLD TOMOE THAT SHE LIKES HIM.
SHE DIDN'T GIVE UP EVEN WHEN HE SAID NO ...
...AND SHE MADE TOMOE HERS IN THE END.
WE WERE SIDE BY SIDE...
...BUT SHE PULLED AHEAD BEFORE I KNEW IT.
I'M ALWAYS ...
...HIDING BEHIND NANAMI...
IF I CAN REGAIN MY HUMAN FORM...

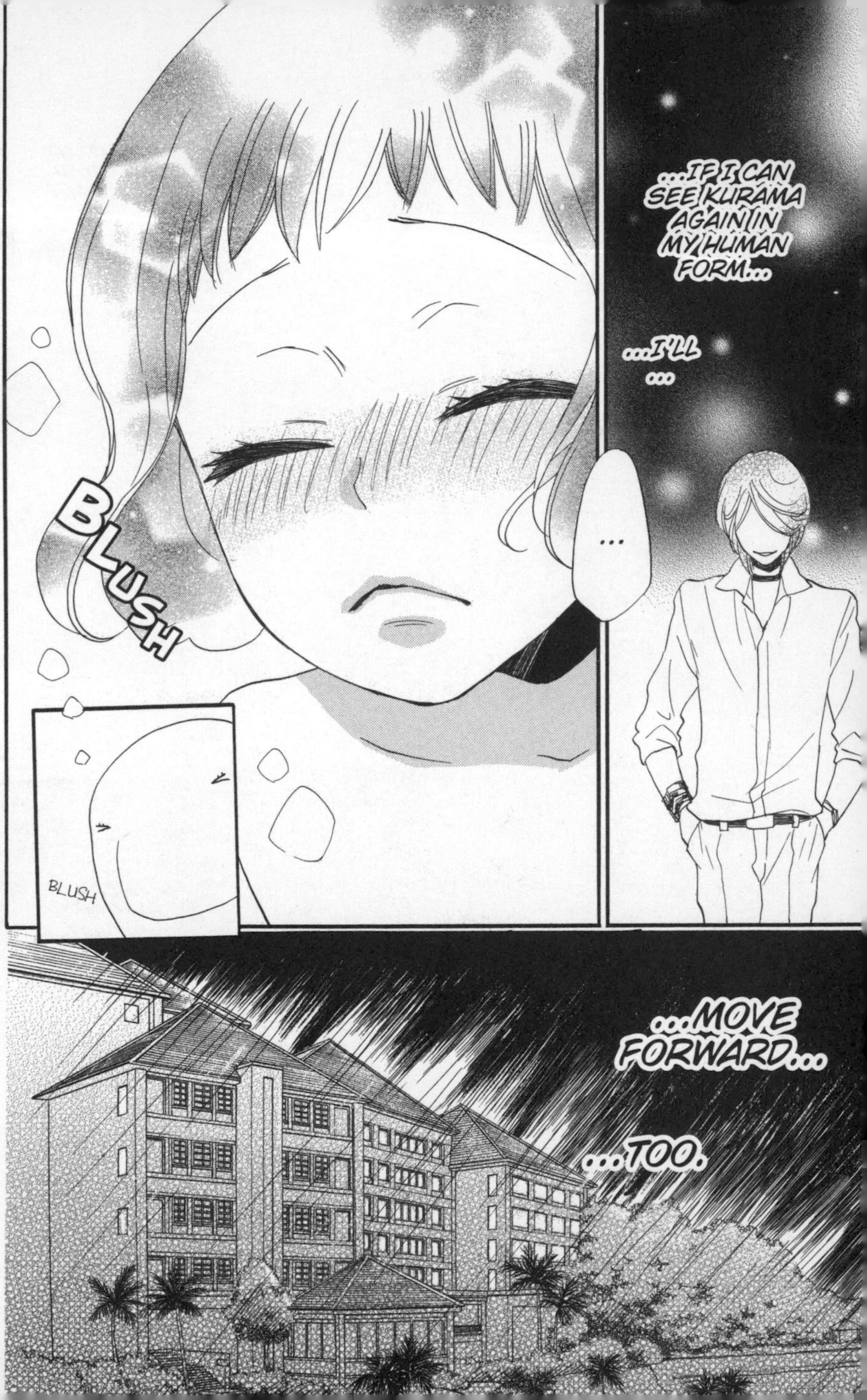
...IF I CAN SEE KURAMA AGAIN IN MY HUMAN FORM...
...I'LL ...
...
BLUSH
BLUSH
...MOVE FORWARD...
...TOO.

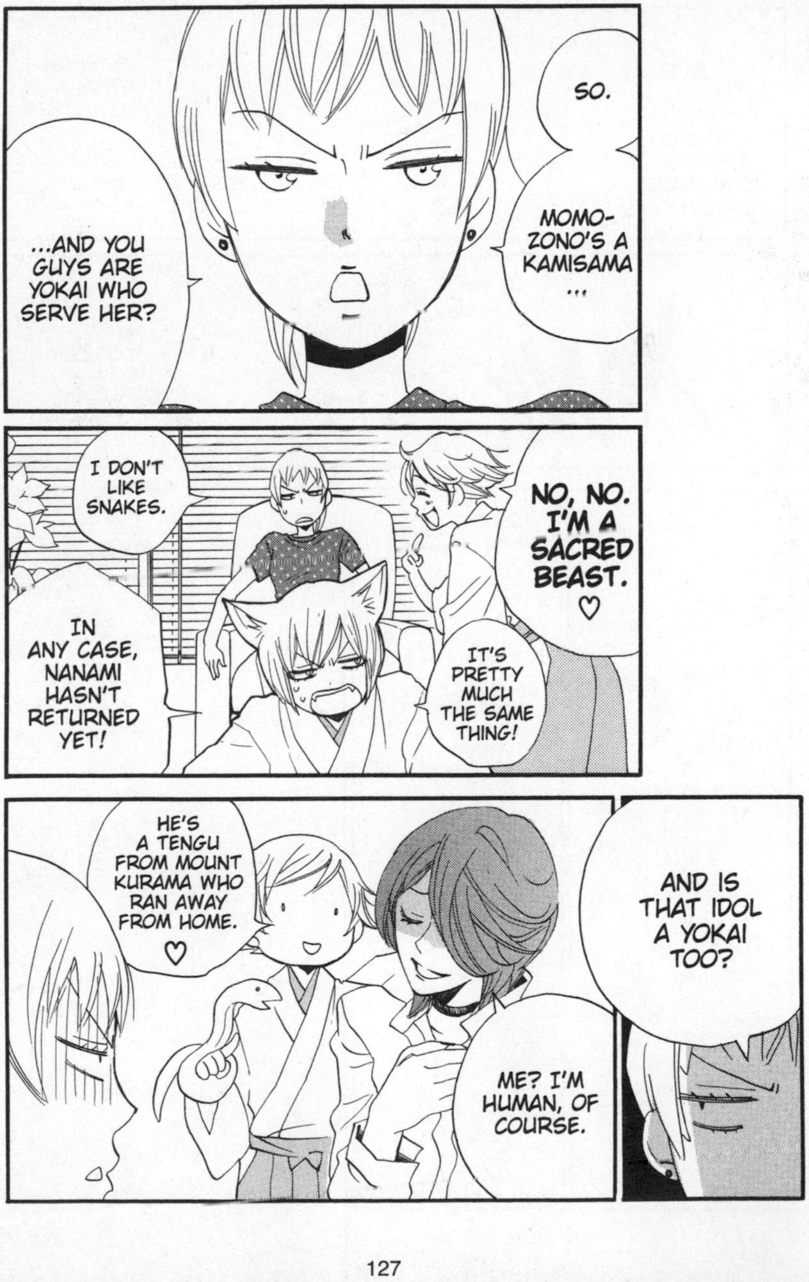
SO.
MOMO-ZONO'S A KAMISAMA...
...AND YOU GUYS ARE YOKAI WHO SERVE HER?
NO, NO. I'M A SACRED BEAST. ♡
I DON'T LIKE SNAKES.
IT'S PRETTY MUCH THE SAME THING!
IN ANY CASE, NANAMI HASN'T RETURNED YET!
AND IS THAT IDOL A YOKAI TOO?
ME? I'M HUMAN, OF COURSE.
HE'S A TENGU FROM MOUNT KURAMA WHO RAN AWAY FROM HOME. ♡

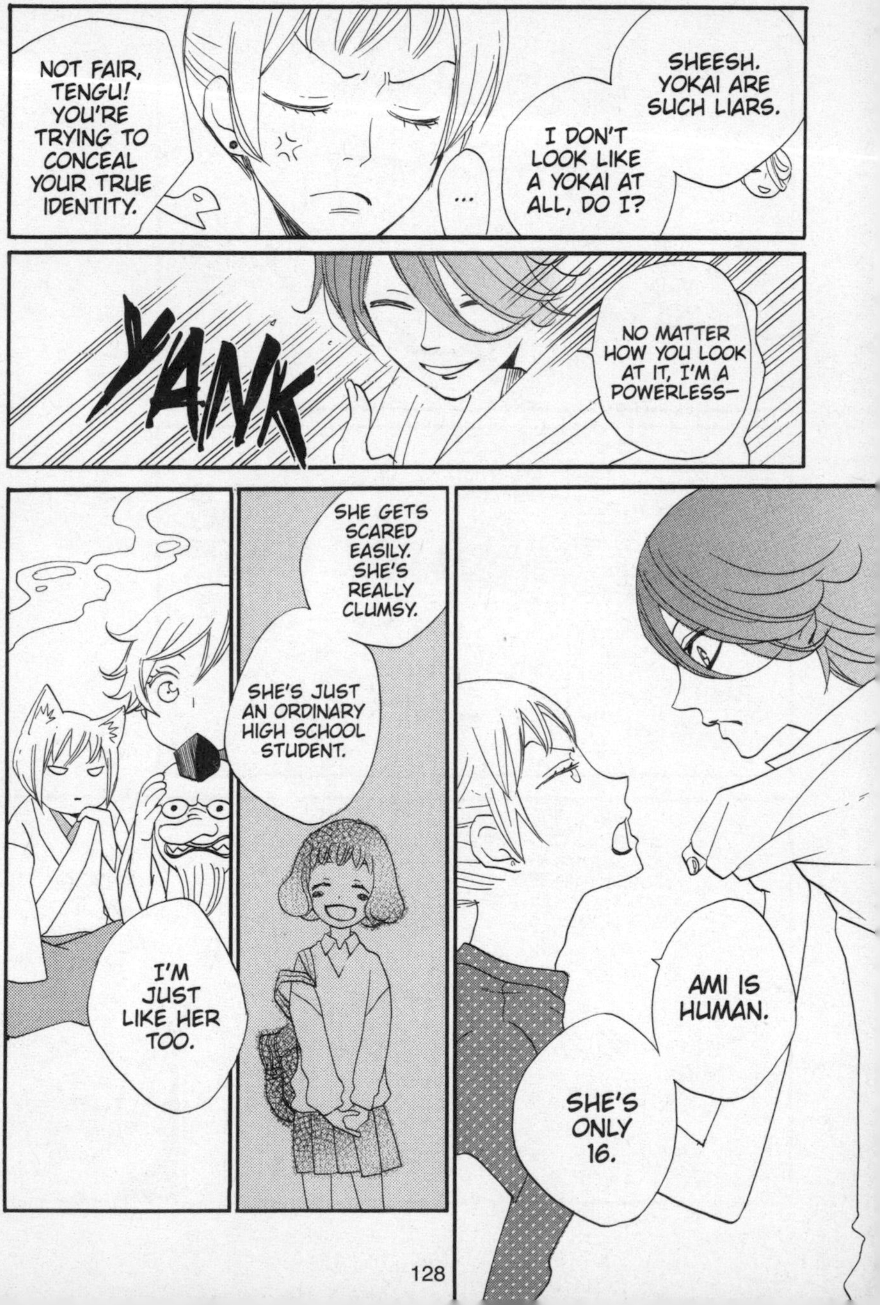
SHEESH. YOKAI ARE SUCH LIARS.
I DON'T LOOK LIKE A YOKAI AT ALL, DO I?
...
NOT FAIR, TENGU! YOU'RE TRYING TO CONCEAL YOUR TRUE IDENTITY.
NO MATTER HOW YOU LOOK AT IT, I'M A POWERLESS—
YANK
AMI IS HUMAN.
SHE'S ONLY 16.
SHE GETS SCARED EASILY. SHE'S REALLY CLUMSY.
SHE'S JUST AN ORDINARY HIGH SCHOOL STUDENT.
I'M JUST LIKE HER TOO.

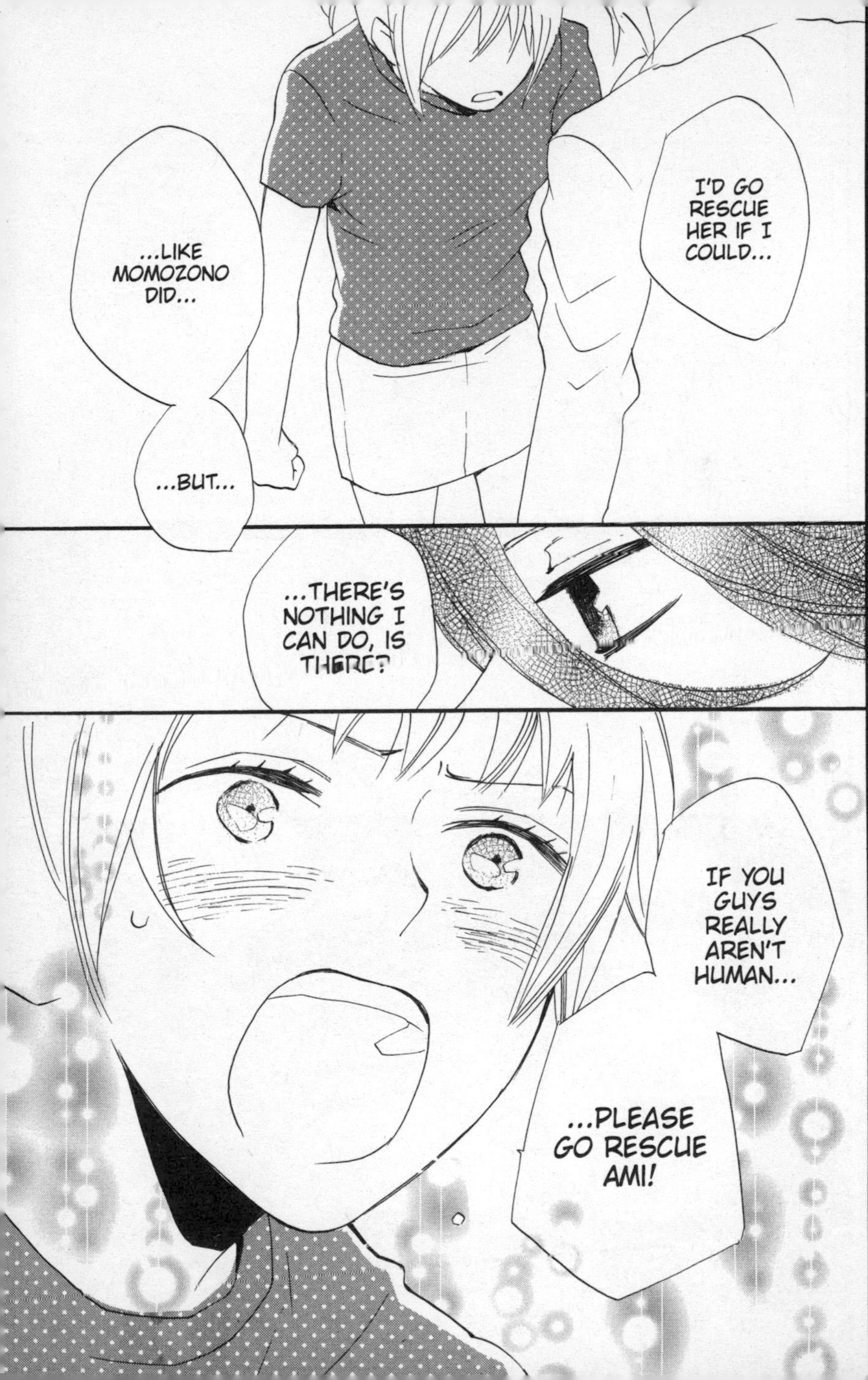
I'D GO RESCUE HER IF I COULD...
...LIKE MOMOZONO DID...
...BUT...
...THERE'S NOTHING I CAN DO, IS THERE?
IF YOU GUYS REALLY AREN'T HUMAN...
...PLEASE GO RESCUE AMI!

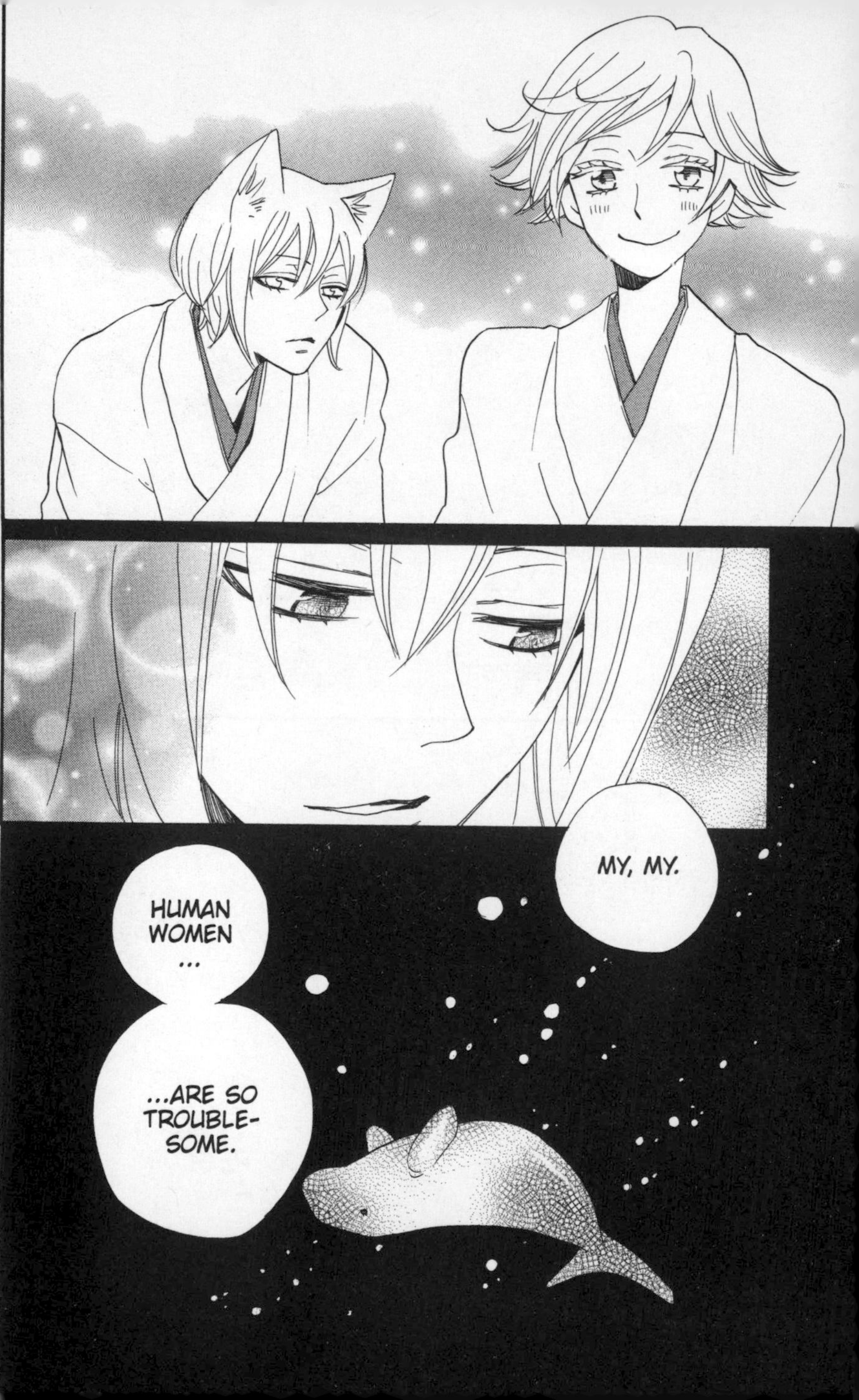
MY, MY.
HUMAN WOMEN ...
...ARE SO TROUBLE-SOME.

Chapter 106

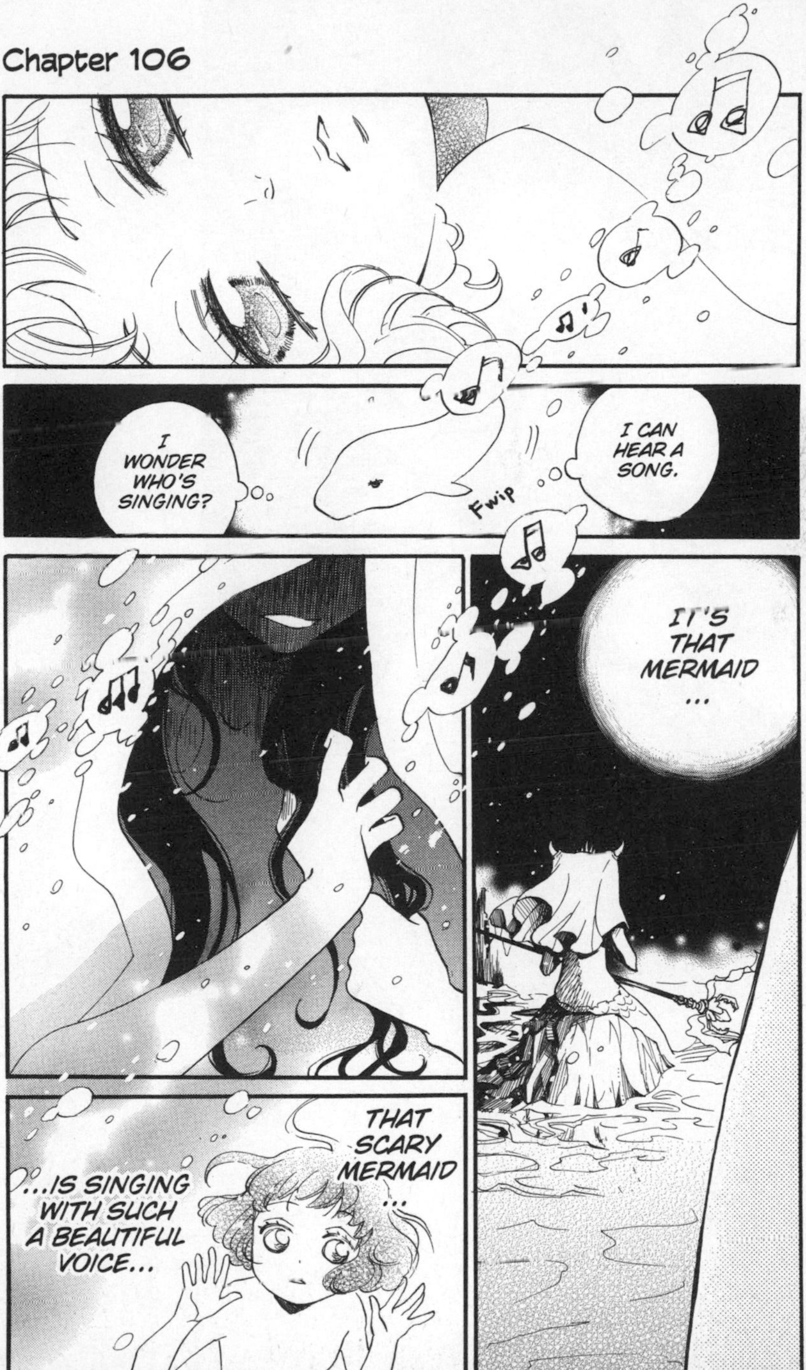
I CAN HEAR A SONG.
Fwip
I WONDER WHO'S SINGING?
IT'S THAT MERMAID...
THAT SCARY MERMAID...
...IS SINGING WITH SUCH A BEAUTIFUL VOICE...

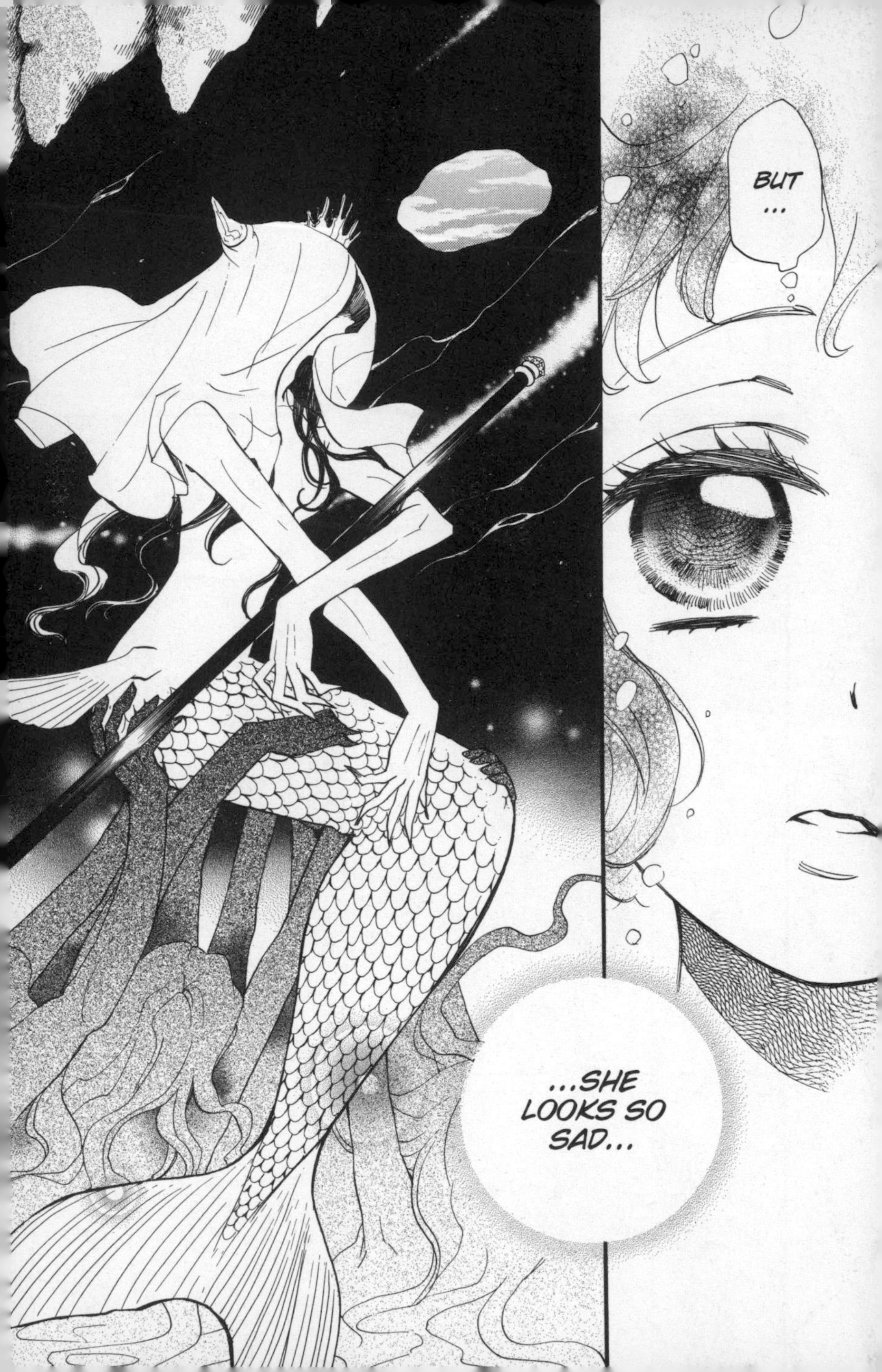
BUT ...
...SHE LOOKS SO SAD...

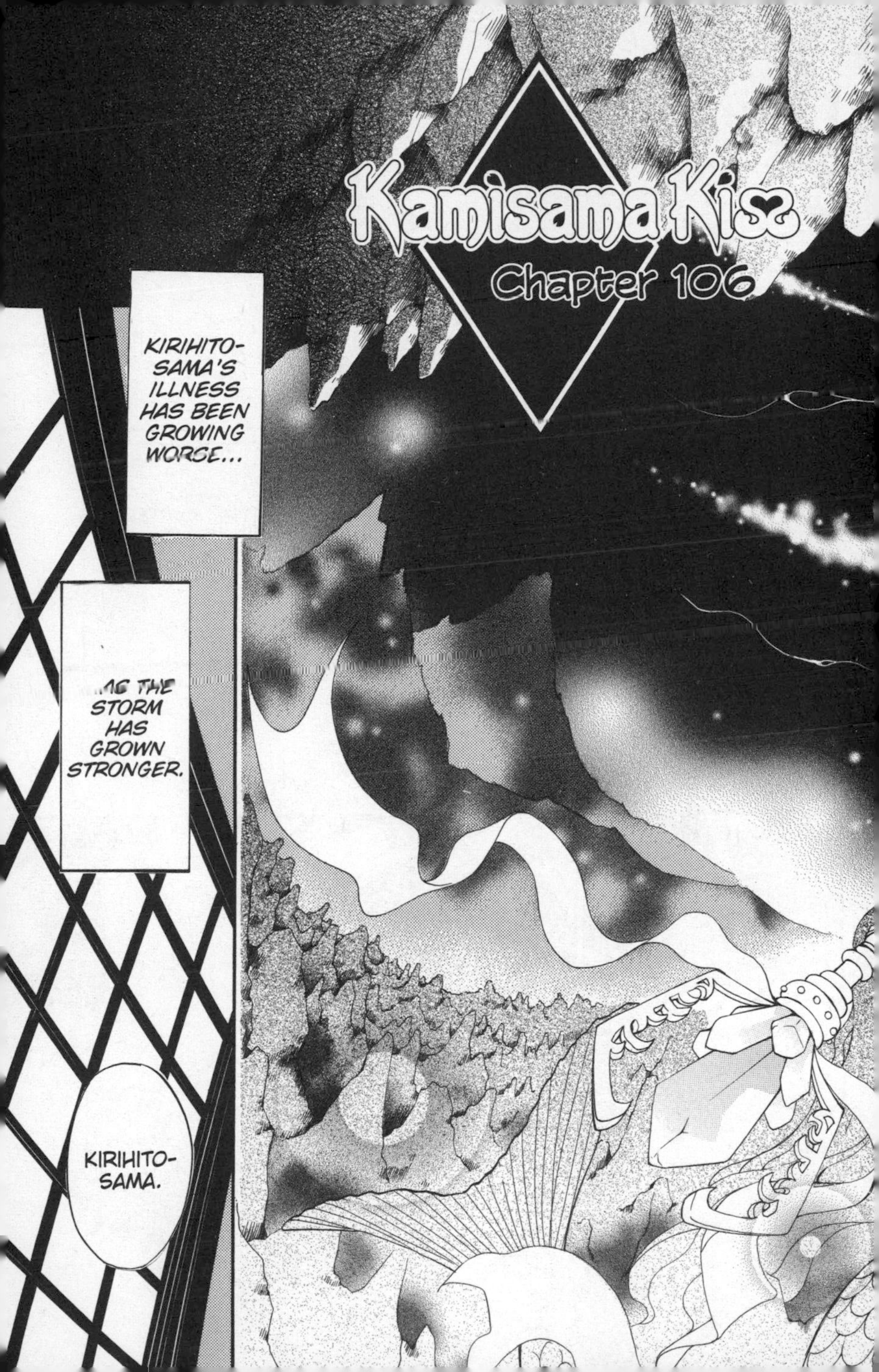
Kamisama Kiss
Chapter 106
KIRIHITO-SAMA'S ILLNESS HAS BEEN GROWING WORSE...
THE STORM HAS GROWN STRONGER.
KIRIHITO-SAMA.

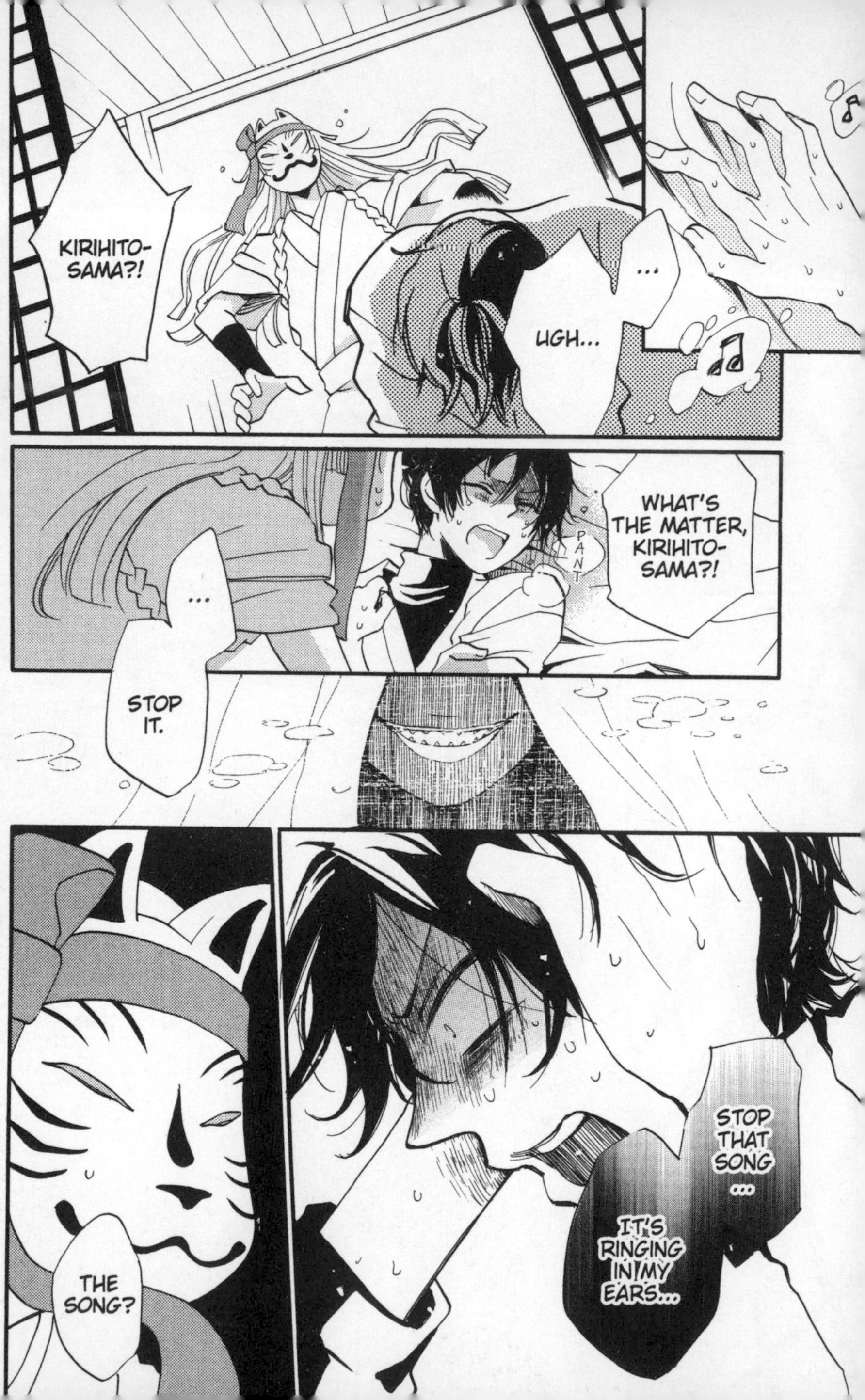
...
UGH...
KIRIHITO-SAMA?!
WHAT'S THE MATTER, KIRIHITO-SAMA?!
PANT
...
STOP IT.
STOP THAT SONG...
IT'S RINGING IN MY EARS...
THE SONG?

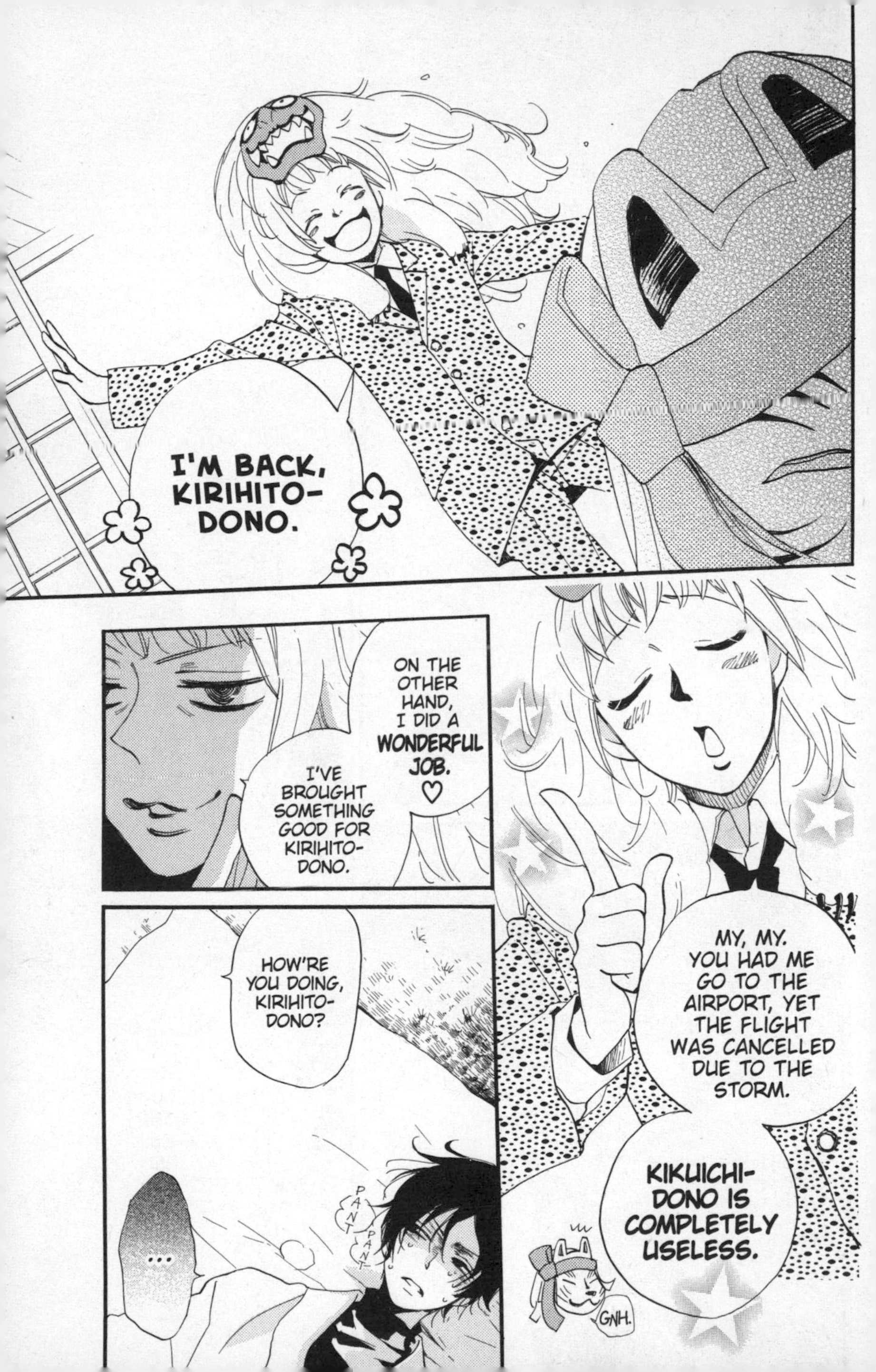
I'M BACK, KIRIHITO-DONO.
MY, MY. YOU HAD ME GO TO THE AIRPORT, YET THE FLIGHT WAS CANCELLED DUE TO THE STORM.
KIKUICHI-DONO IS COMPLETELY USELESS.
GNH.
ON THE OTHER HAND, I DID A WONDERFUL JOB. ♡
I'VE BROUGHT SOMETHING GOOD FOR KIRIHITO-DONO.
HOW'RE YOU DOING, KIRIHITO-DONO?
PANT PANT
...

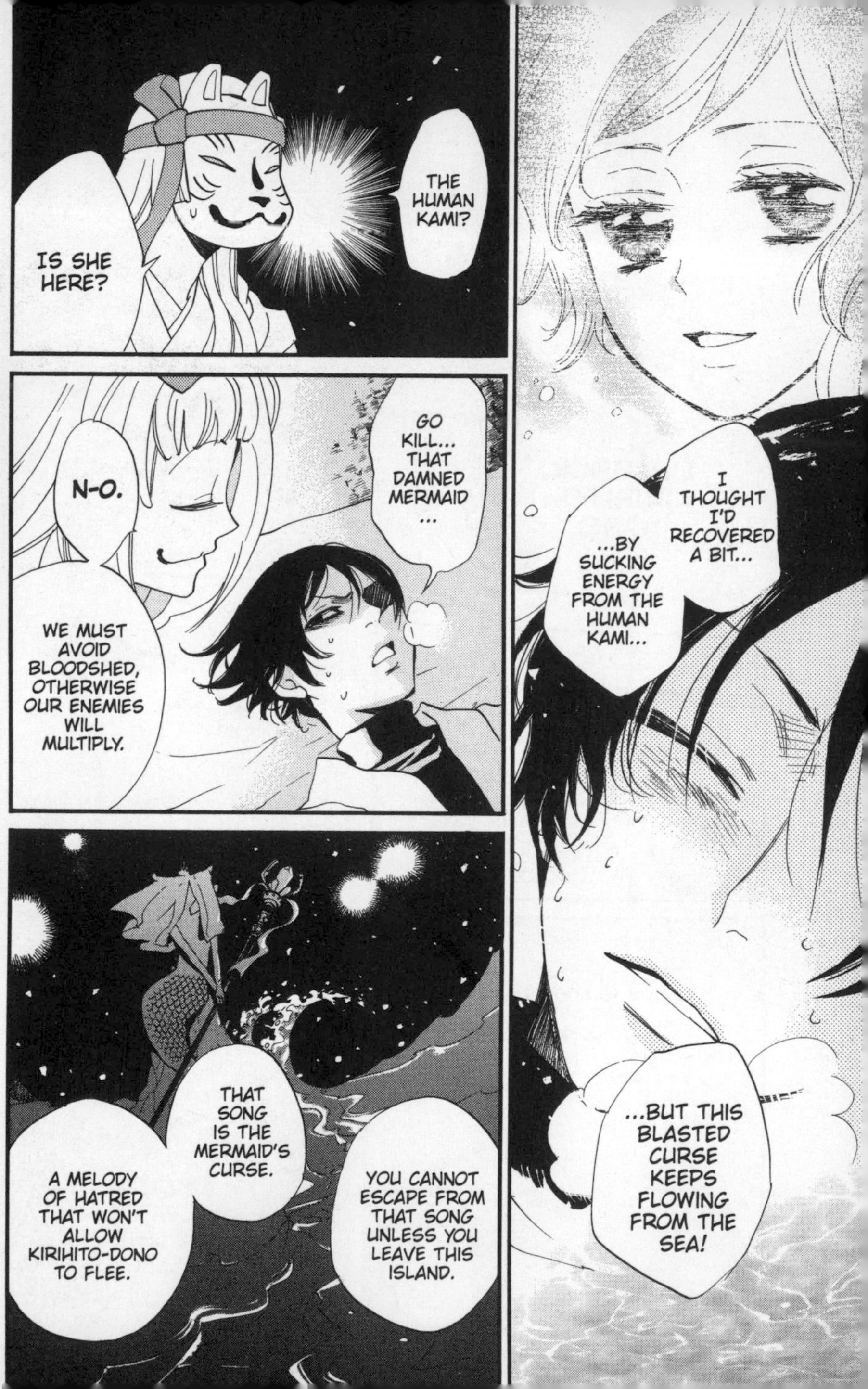
I THOUGHT I'D RECOVERED A BIT...
...BY SUCKING ENERGY FROM THE HUMAN KAMI...
...BUT THIS BLASTED CURSE KEEPS FLOWING FROM THE SEA!
THE HUMAN KAMI?
IS SHE HERE?
GO KILL... THAT DAMNED MERMAID ...
N-O.
WE MUST AVOID BLOODSHED, OTHERWISE OUR ENEMIES WILL MULTIPLY.
THAT SONG IS THE MERMAID'S CURSE.
YOU CANNOT ESCAPE FROM THAT SONG UNLESS YOU LEAVE THIS ISLAND.
A MELODY OF HATRED THAT WON'T ALLOW KIRIHITO-DONO TO FLEE.

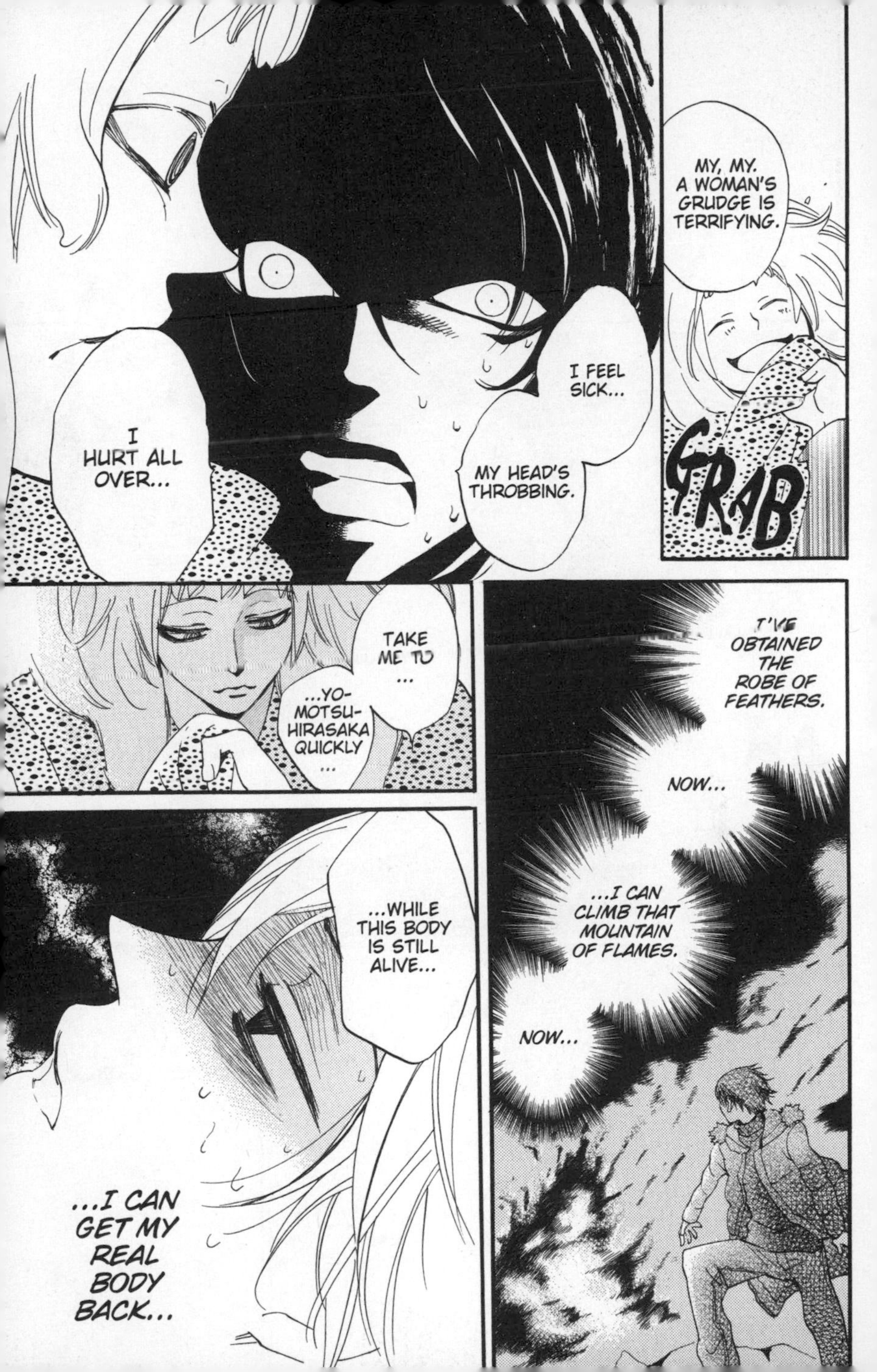
MY, MY. A WOMAN'S GRUDGE IS TERRIFYING.
GRAB
I FEEL SICK...
MY HEAD'S THROBBING.
I HURT ALL OVER...
I'VE OBTAINED THE ROBE OF FEATHERS.
NOW...
...I CAN CLIMB THAT MOUNTAIN OF FLAMES.
NOW...
TAKE ME TO ...
...YO-MOTSU-HIRASAKA QUICKLY ...
...WHILE THIS BODY IS STILL ALIVE...
...I CAN GET MY REAL BODY BACK...

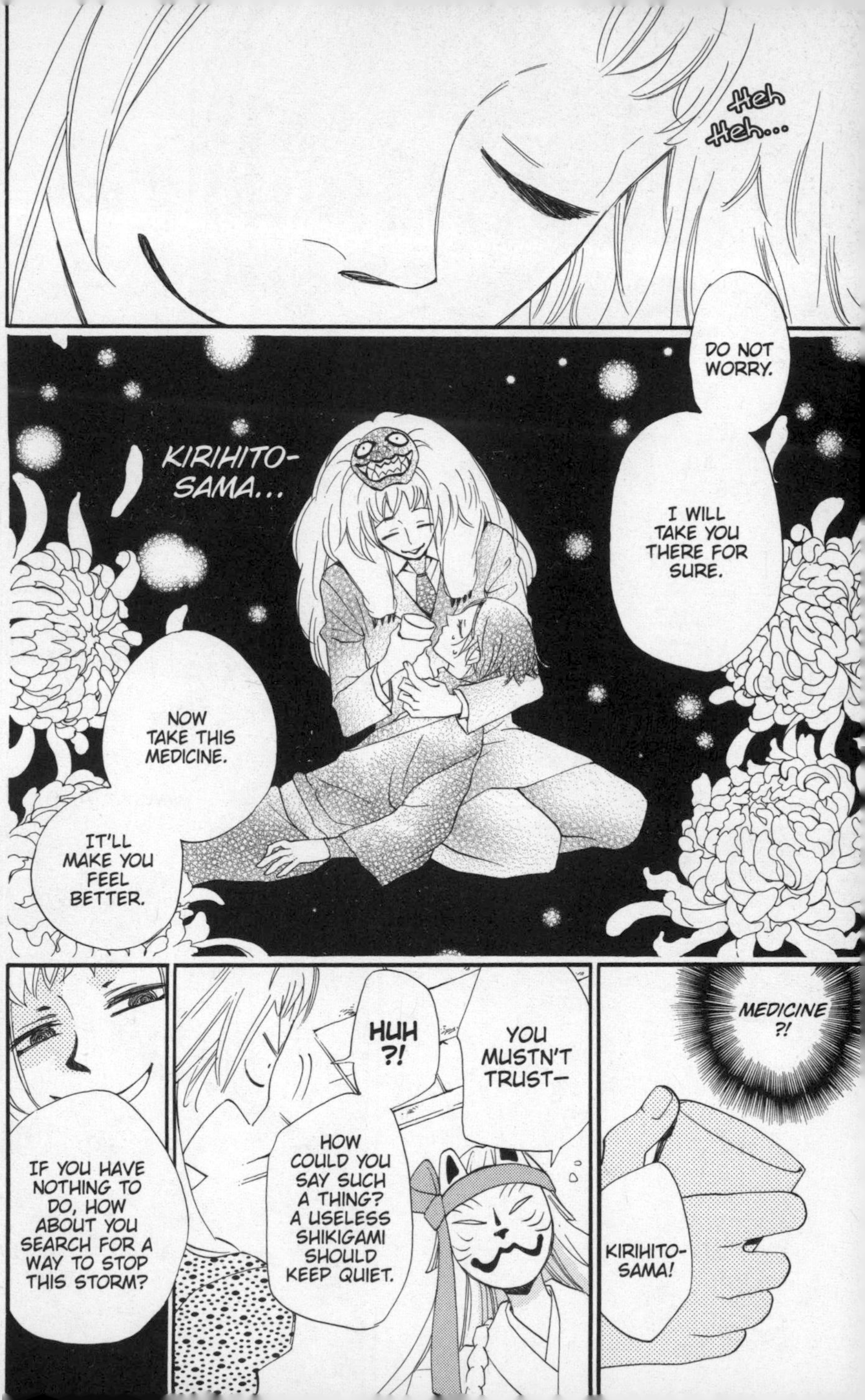
Heh Heh...
DO NOT WORRY.
I WILL TAKE YOU THERE FOR SURE.
KIRIHITO-SAMA...
NOW TAKE THIS MEDICINE.
IT'LL MAKE YOU FEEL BETTER.
MEDICINE?!
KIRIHITO-SAMA!
YOU MUSTN'T TRUST—
HUH?!
HOW COULD YOU SAY SUCH A THING? A USELESS SHIKIGAMI SHOULD KEEP QUIET.
IF YOU HAVE NOTHING TO DO, HOW ABOUT YOU SEARCH FOR A WAY TO STOP THIS STORM?

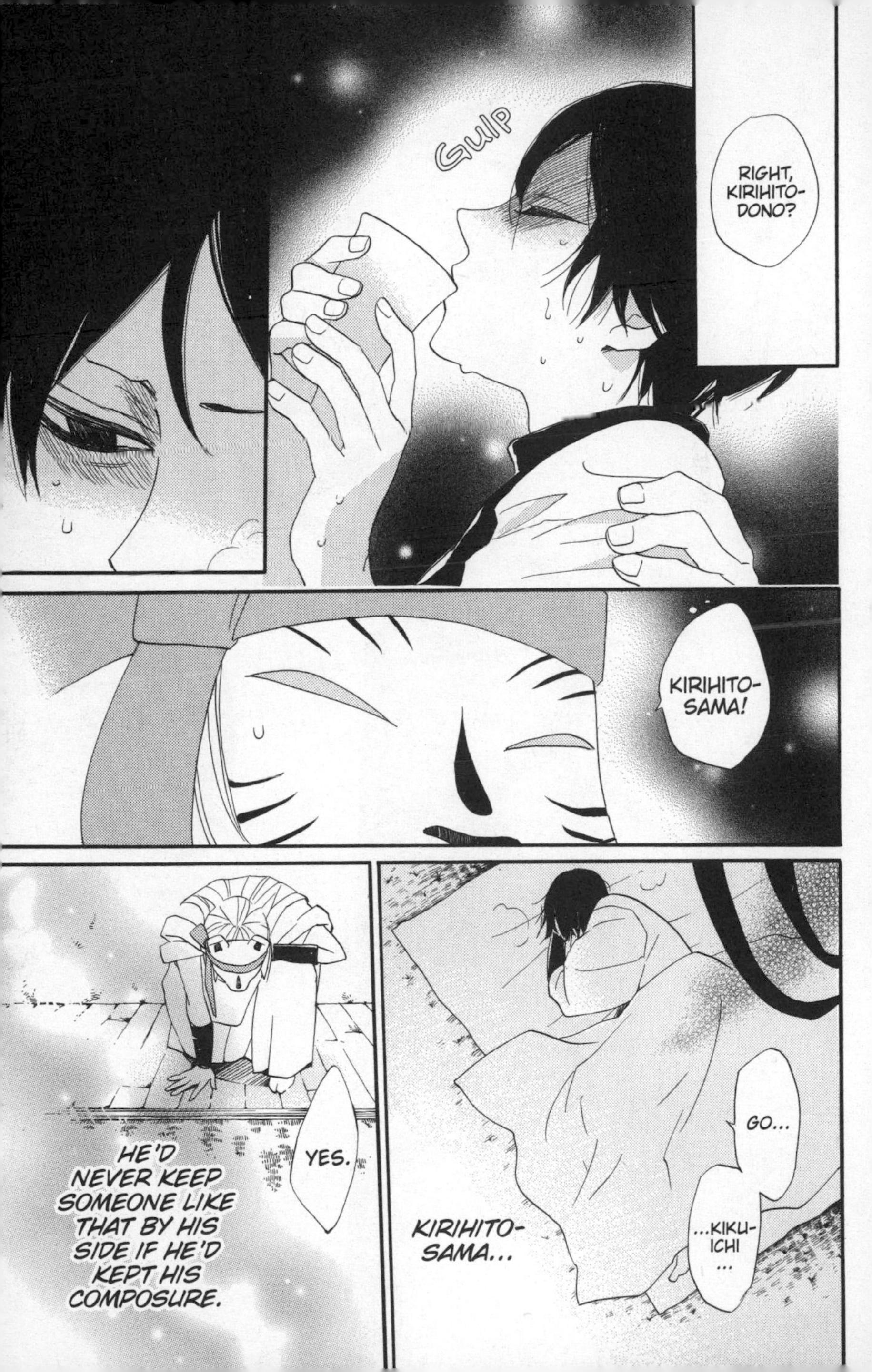
RIGHT, KIRIHITO-DONO?
Gulp
KIRIHITO-SAMA!
GO...
...KIKU-CHI ...
KIRIHITO-SAMA...
YES.
HE'D NEVER KEEP SOMEONE LIKE THAT BY HIS SIDE IF HE'D KEPT HIS COMPOSURE.

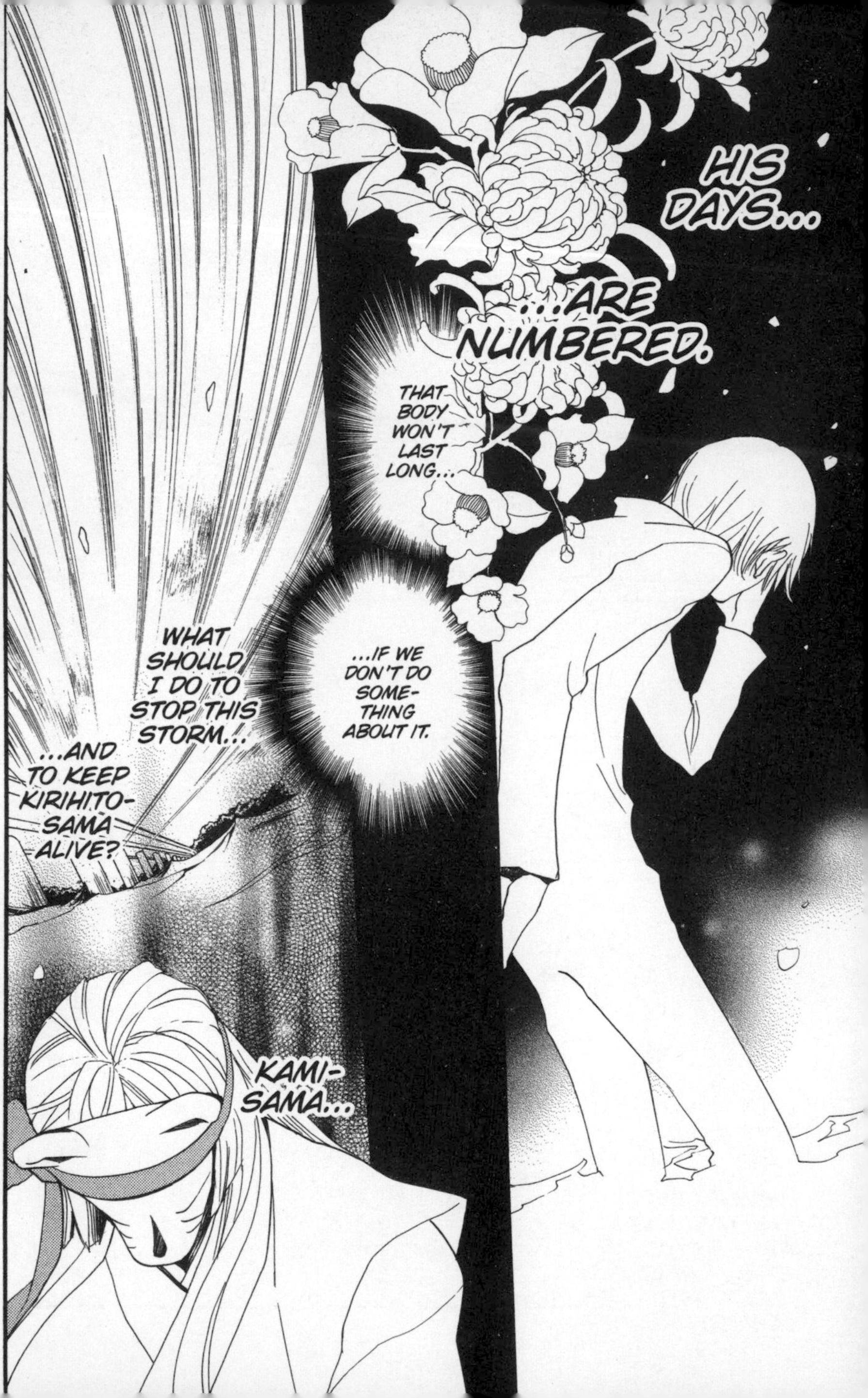
HIS DAYS...
...ARE NUMBERED.
THAT BODY WON'T LAST LONG...
...IF WE DON'T DO SOME-THING ABOUT IT.
WHAT SHOULD I DO TO STOP THIS STORM...
...AND TO KEEP KIRIHITO-SAMA ALIVE?
KAMI-SAMA...

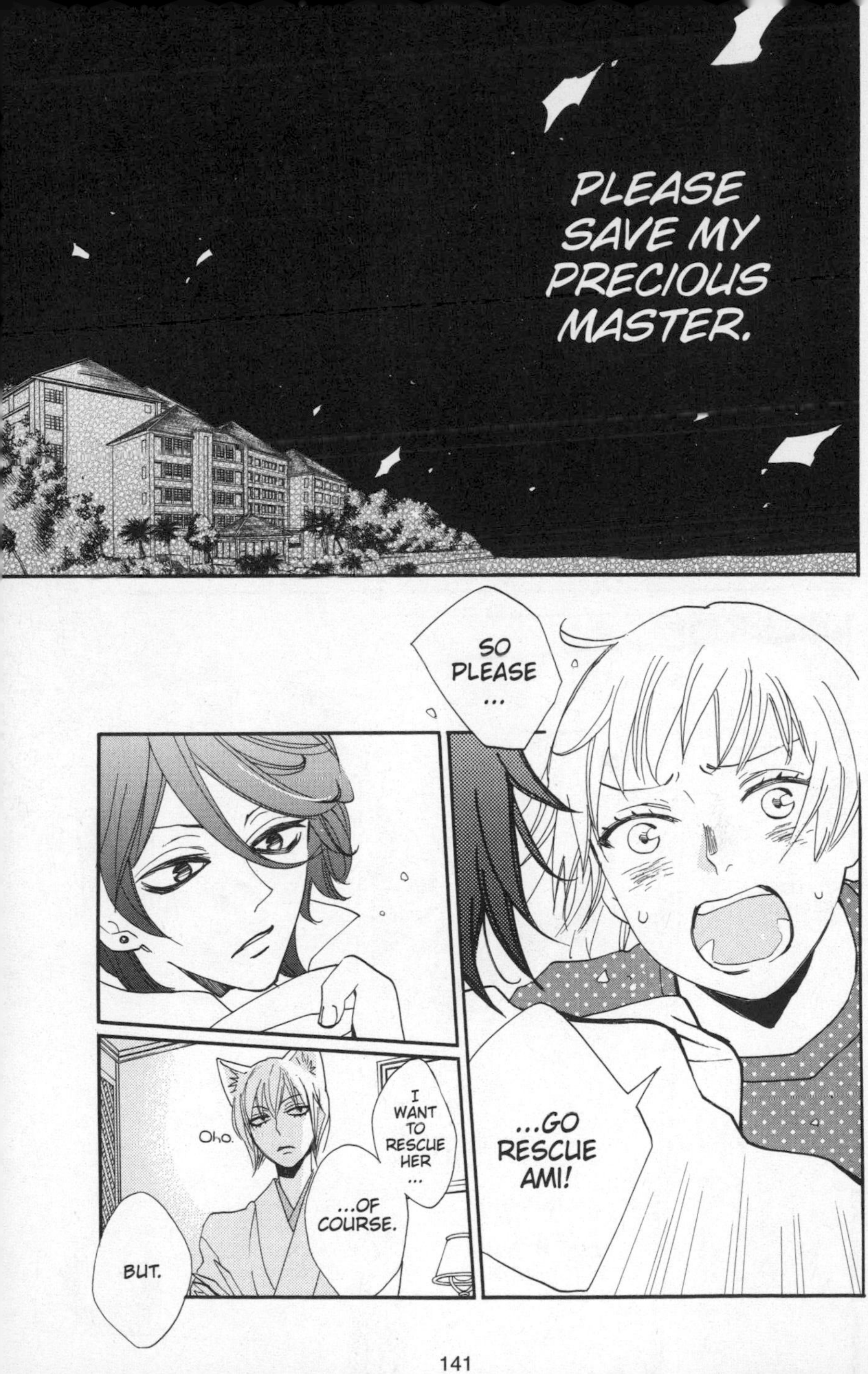
PLEASE SAVE MY PRECIOUS MASTER.
SO PLEASE ...
...GO RESCUE AMI!
I WANT TO RESCUE HER ...
...OF COURSE.
Oho.
BUT.

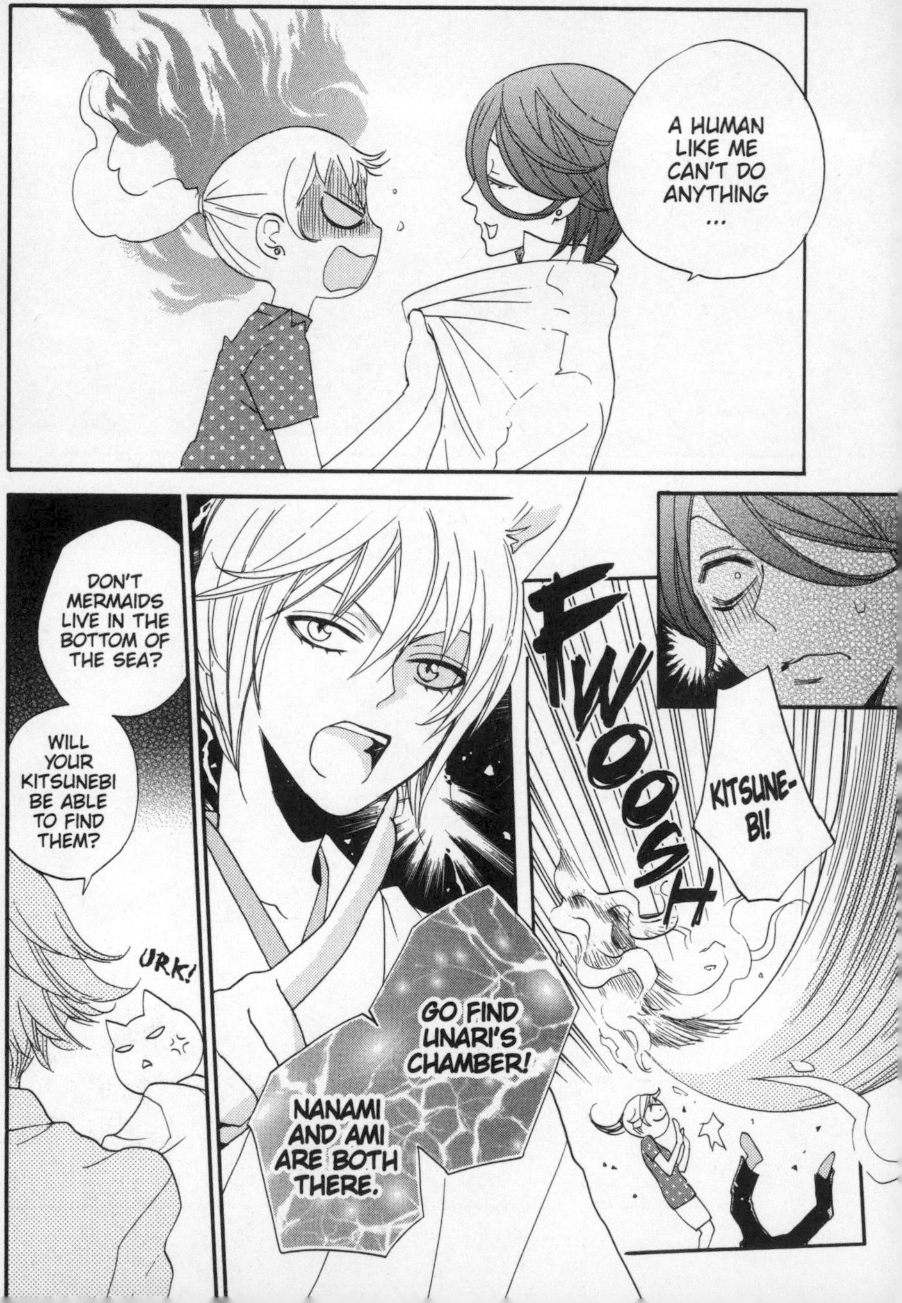
A HUMAN LIKE ME CAN'T DO ANYTHING ...
KITSUNE-BI!
FWOOSH
GO FIND UNARI'S CHAMBER!
NANAMI AND AMI ARE BOTH THERE.
DON'T MERMAIDS LIVE IN THE BOTTOM OF THE SEA?
WILL YOUR KITSUNEBI BE ABLE TO FIND THEM?
URK!

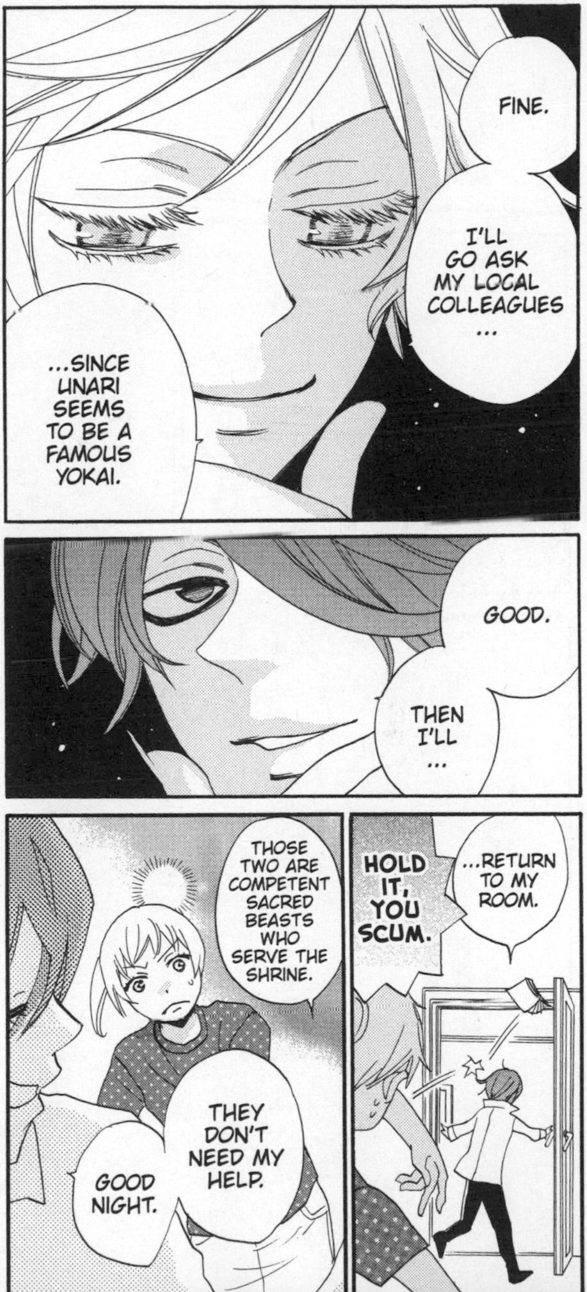
FINE.
I'LL GO ASK MY LOCAL COLLEAGUES ...
...SINCE UNARI SEEMS TO BE A FAMOUS YOKAI.
GOOD.
THEN I'LL ...
...RETURN TO MY ROOM.
HOLD IT, YOU SCUM.
THOSE TWO ARE COMPETENT SACRED BEASTS WHO SERVE THE SHRINE.
THEY DON'T NEED MY HELP.
GOOD NIGHT.

I do squats every day to train my legs and lower back since I spend a long time working at my desk.

I started at 30 squats four months ago, but now I'm able to do 60 squats. I can now climb stairs easily. I hope I'll be able to continue doing them.

I wasn't able to see cherry blossoms much this year. I'm looking forward to next year!

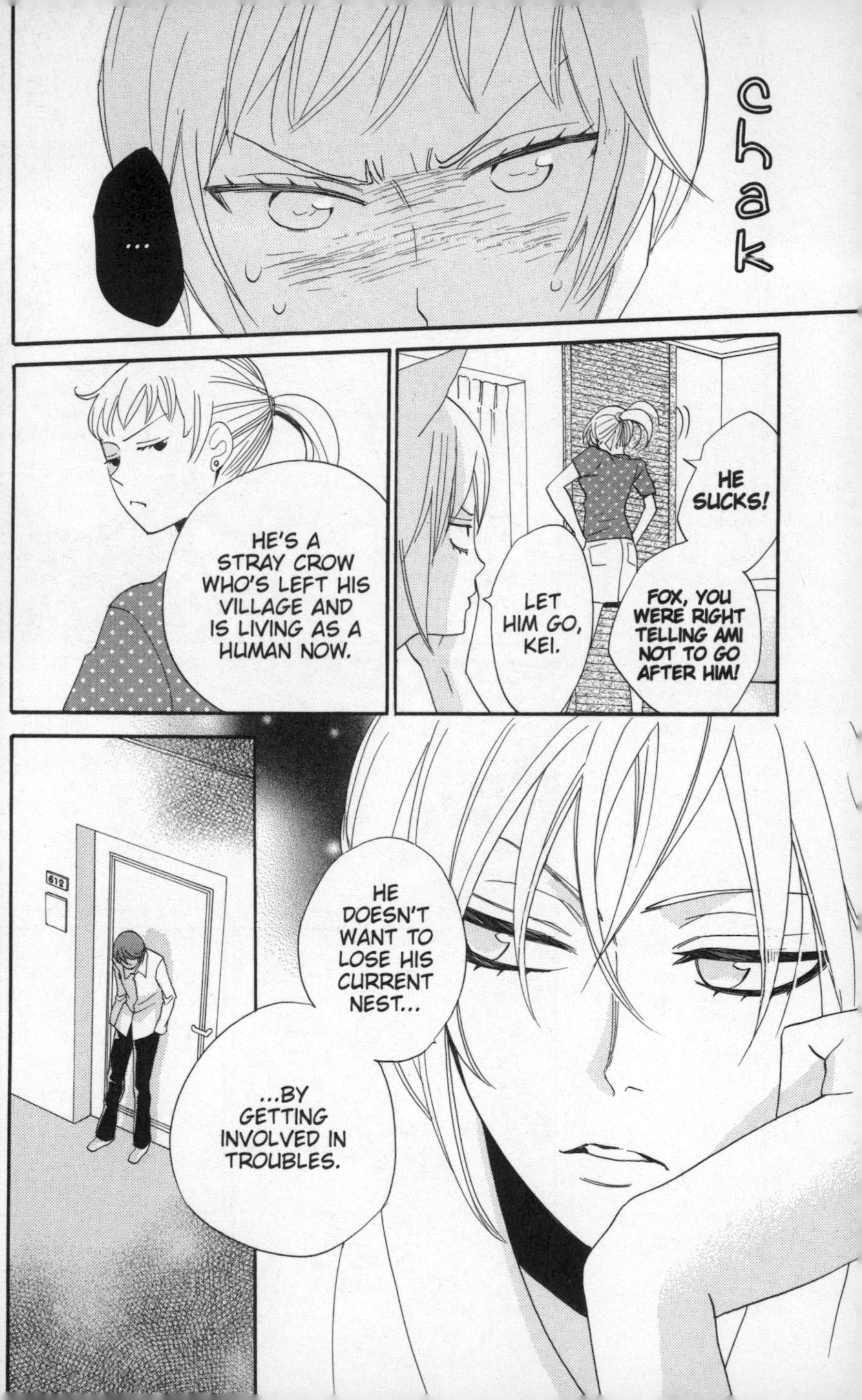
chak
...
HE SUCKS!
FOX, YOU WERE RIGHT TELLING AMI NOT TO GO AFTER HIM!
LET HIM GO, KEI.
HE'S A STRAY CROW WHO'S LEFT HIS VILLAGE AND IS LIVING AS A HUMAN NOW.
HE DOESN'T WANT TO LOSE HIS CURRENT NEST...
...BY GETTING INVOLVED IN TROUBLES.
612

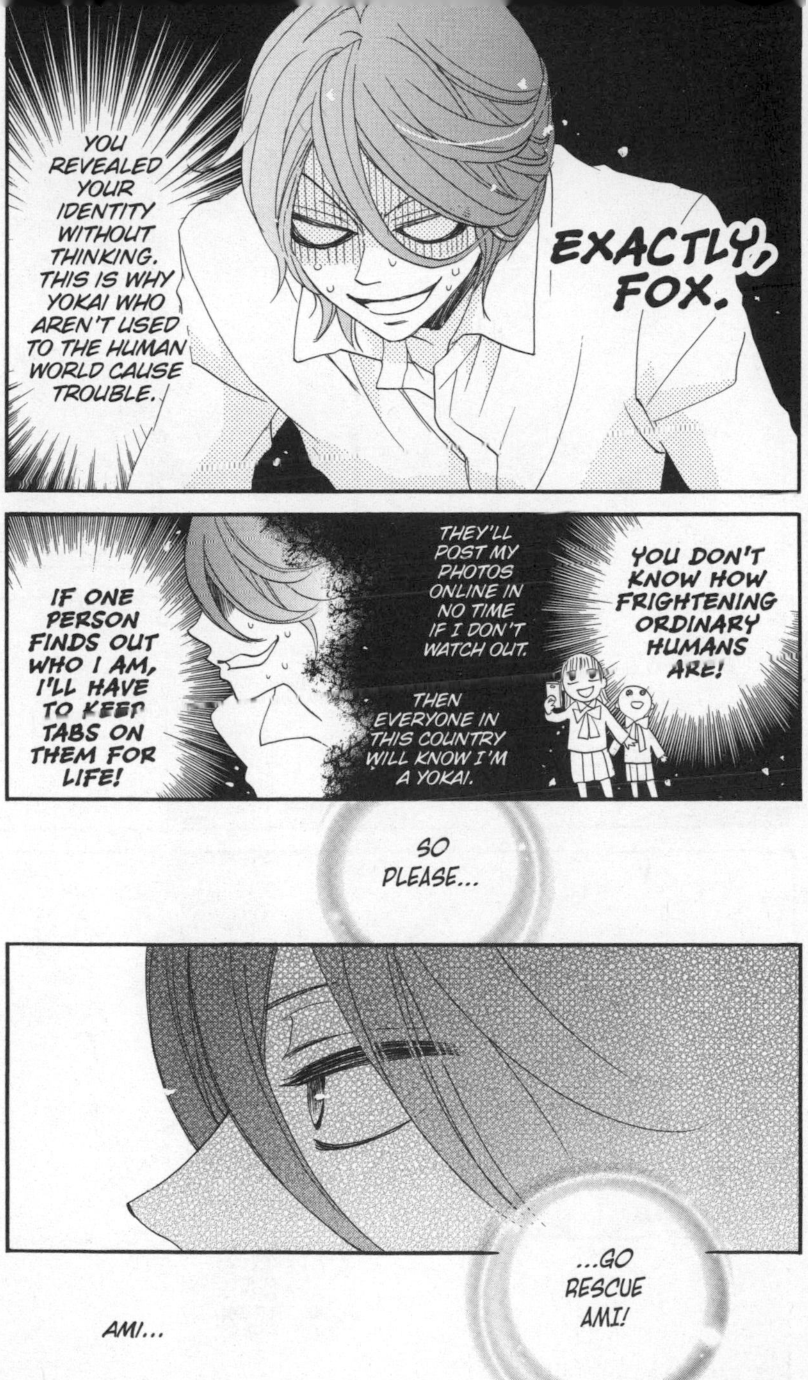
EXACTLY, FOX.
YOU REVEALED YOUR IDENTITY WITHOUT THINKING. THIS IS WHY YOKAI WHO AREN'T USED TO THE HUMAN WORLD CAUSE TROUBLE.
YOU DON'T KNOW HOW FRIGHTENING ORDINARY HUMANS ARE!
THEY'LL POST MY PHOTOS ONLINE IN NO TIME IF I DON'T WATCH OUT.
THEN EVERYONE IN THIS COUNTRY WILL KNOW I'M A YOKAI.
IF ONE PERSON FINDS OUT WHO I AM, I'LL HAVE TO KEEP TABS ON THEM FOR LIFE!
SO PLEASE...
...GO RESCUE AMI!
AMI...

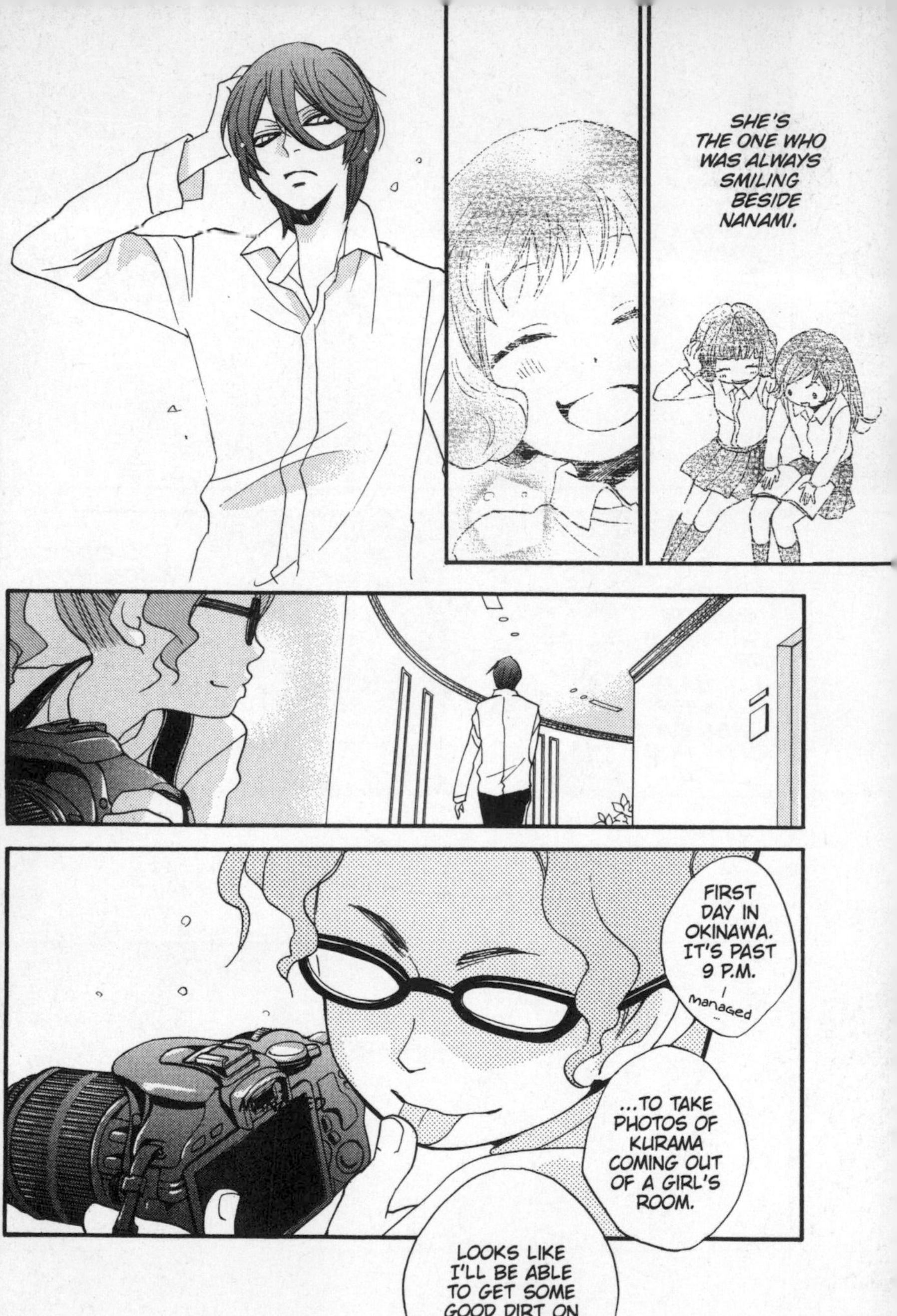
SHE'S THE ONE WHO WAS ALWAYS SMILING BESIDE NANAMI.
FIRST DAY IN OKINAWA. IT'S PAST 9 P.M.
I managed...
...TO TAKE PHOTOS OF KURAMA COMING OUT OF A GIRL'S ROOM.
LOOKS LIKE I'LL BE ABLE TO GET SOME GOOD DIRT ON THIS TRIP.

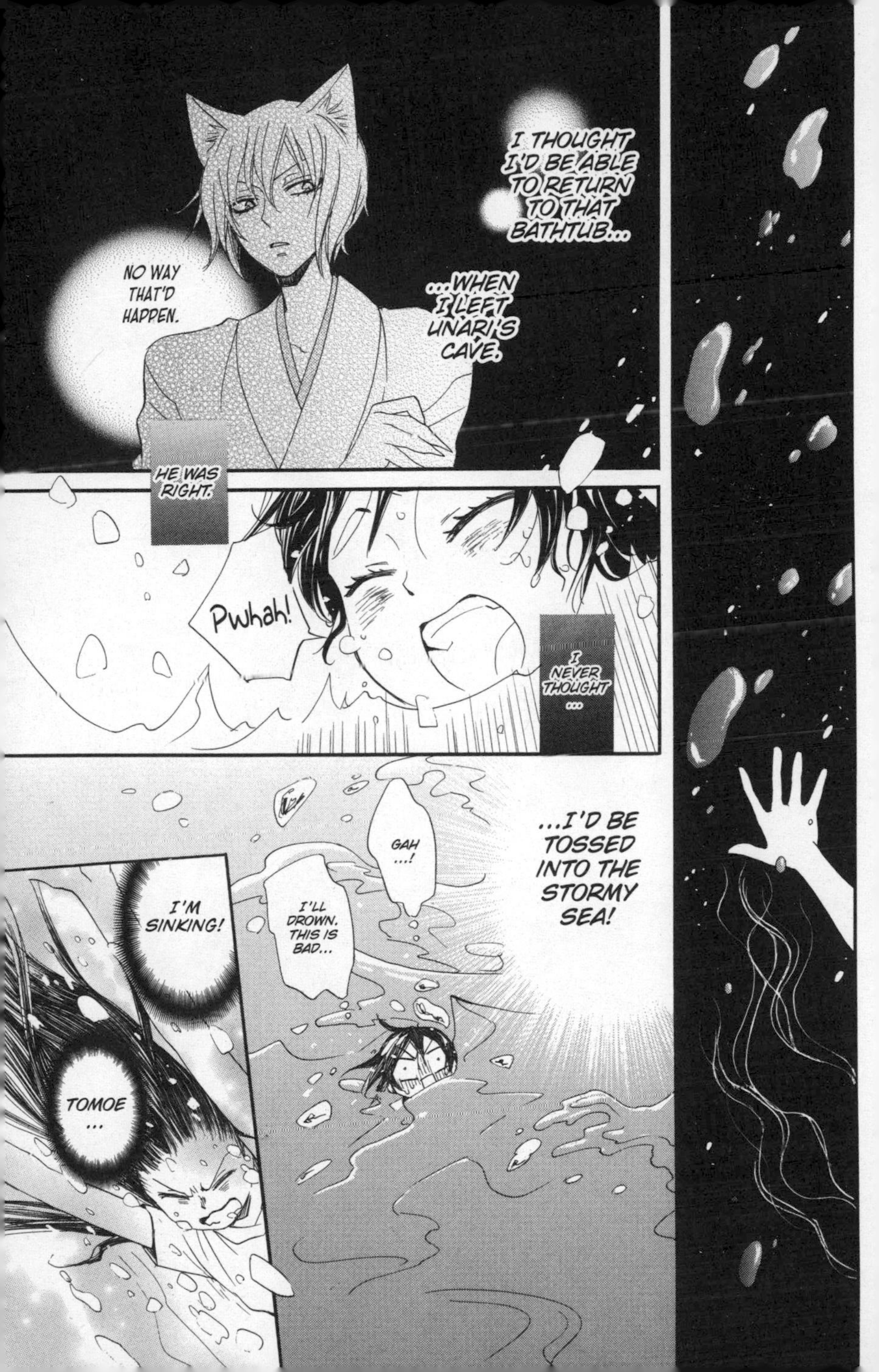
I THOUGHT I'D BE ABLE TO RETURN TO THAT BATHTUB...
...WHEN I LEFT UNARI'S CAVE.
NO WAY THAT'D HAPPEN.
HE WAS RIGHT.
I NEVER THOUGHT...
Pwhah!
...I'D BE TOSSED INTO THE STORMY SEA!
GAH...!
I'LL DROWN. THIS IS BAD...
I'M SINKING!
TOMOE...

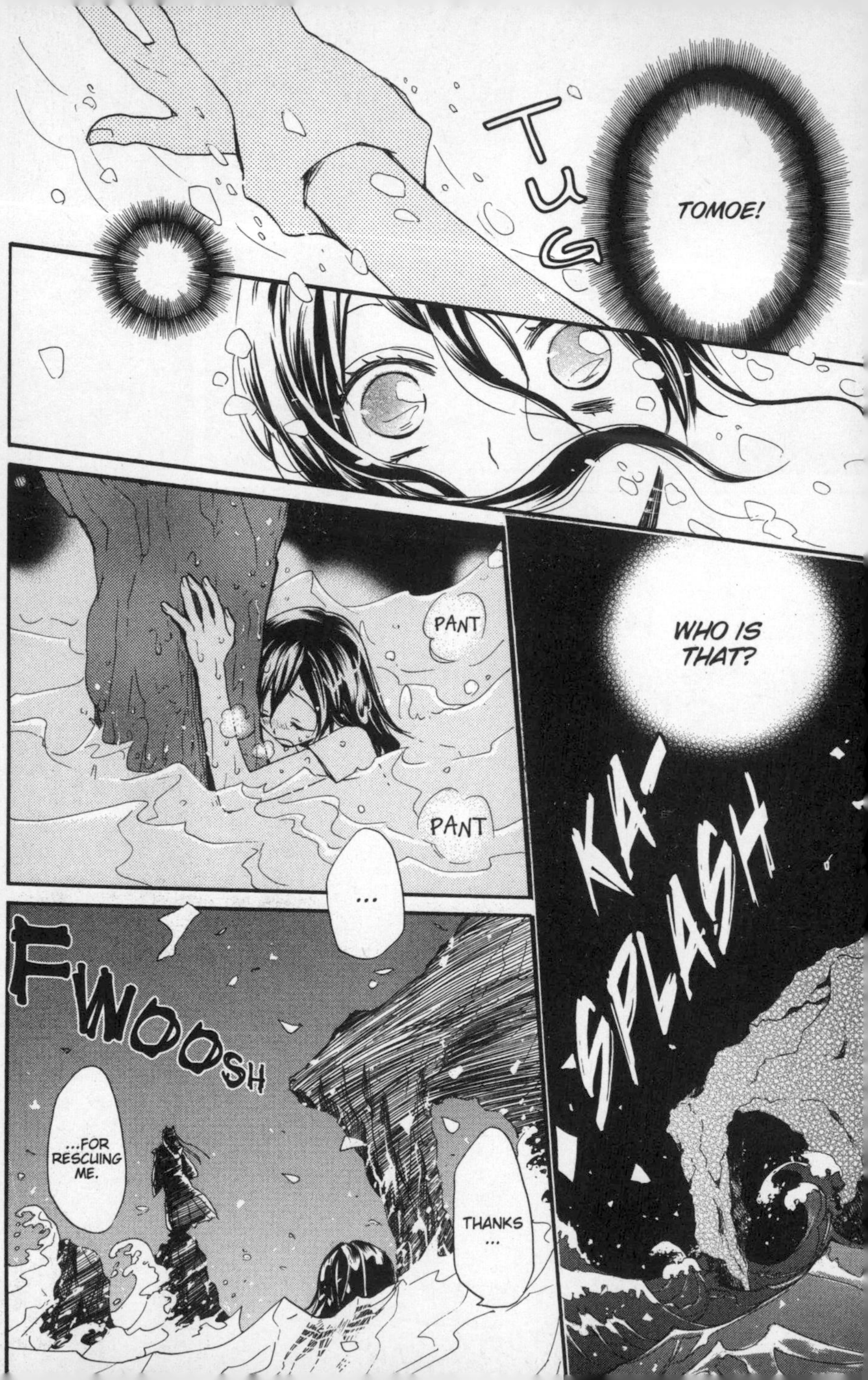
TUG
TOMOE!
WHO IS THAT?
KA-SPLASH
PANT
PANT
...
FWOOSH
THANKS...
...FOR RESCUING ME.

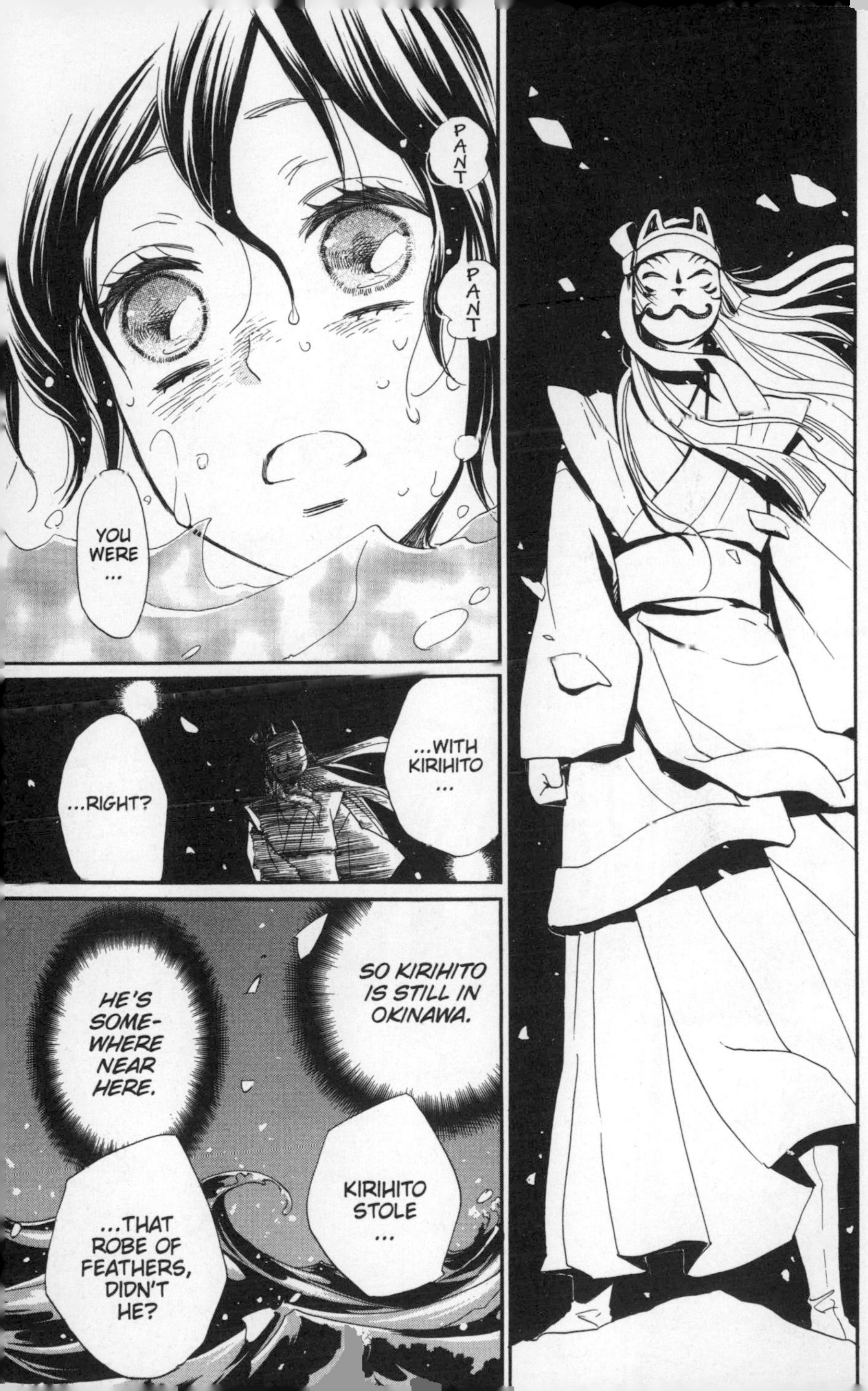
PANT
PANT
YOU WERE ...
...WITH KIRIHITO ...
...RIGHT?
SO KIRIHITO IS STILL IN OKINAWA.
HE'S SOME-WHERE NEAR HERE.
KIRIHITO STOLE ...
...THAT ROBE OF FEATHERS, DIDN'T HE?

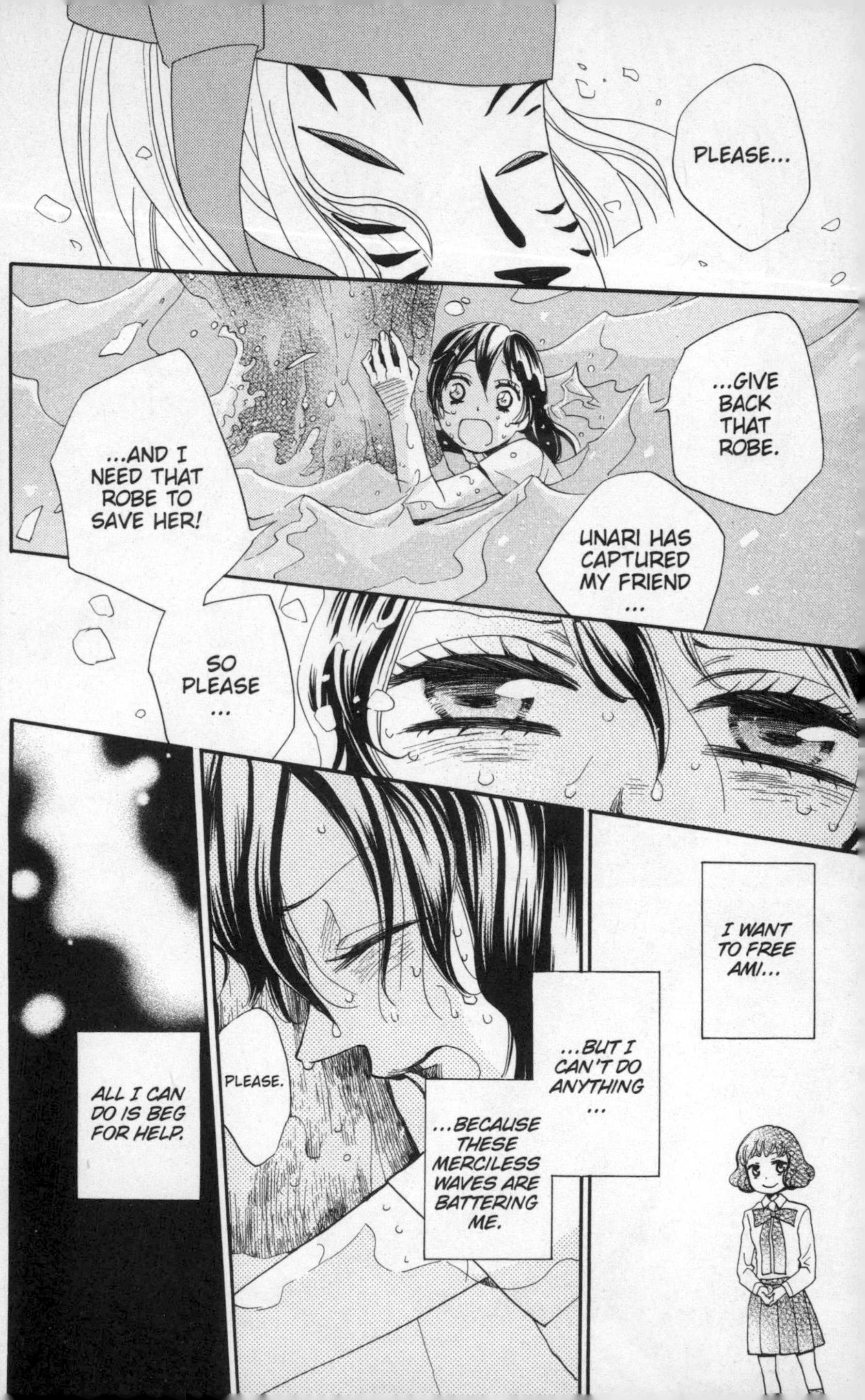
PLEASE...
...GIVE BACK THAT ROBE.
UNARI HAS CAPTURED MY FRIEND ...
...AND I NEED THAT ROBE TO SAVE HER!
SO PLEASE ...
I WANT TO FREE AMI...
...BUT I CAN'T DO ANYTHING ...
...BECAUSE THESE MERCILESS WAVES ARE BATTERING ME.
PLEASE.
ALL I CAN DO IS BEG FOR HELP.

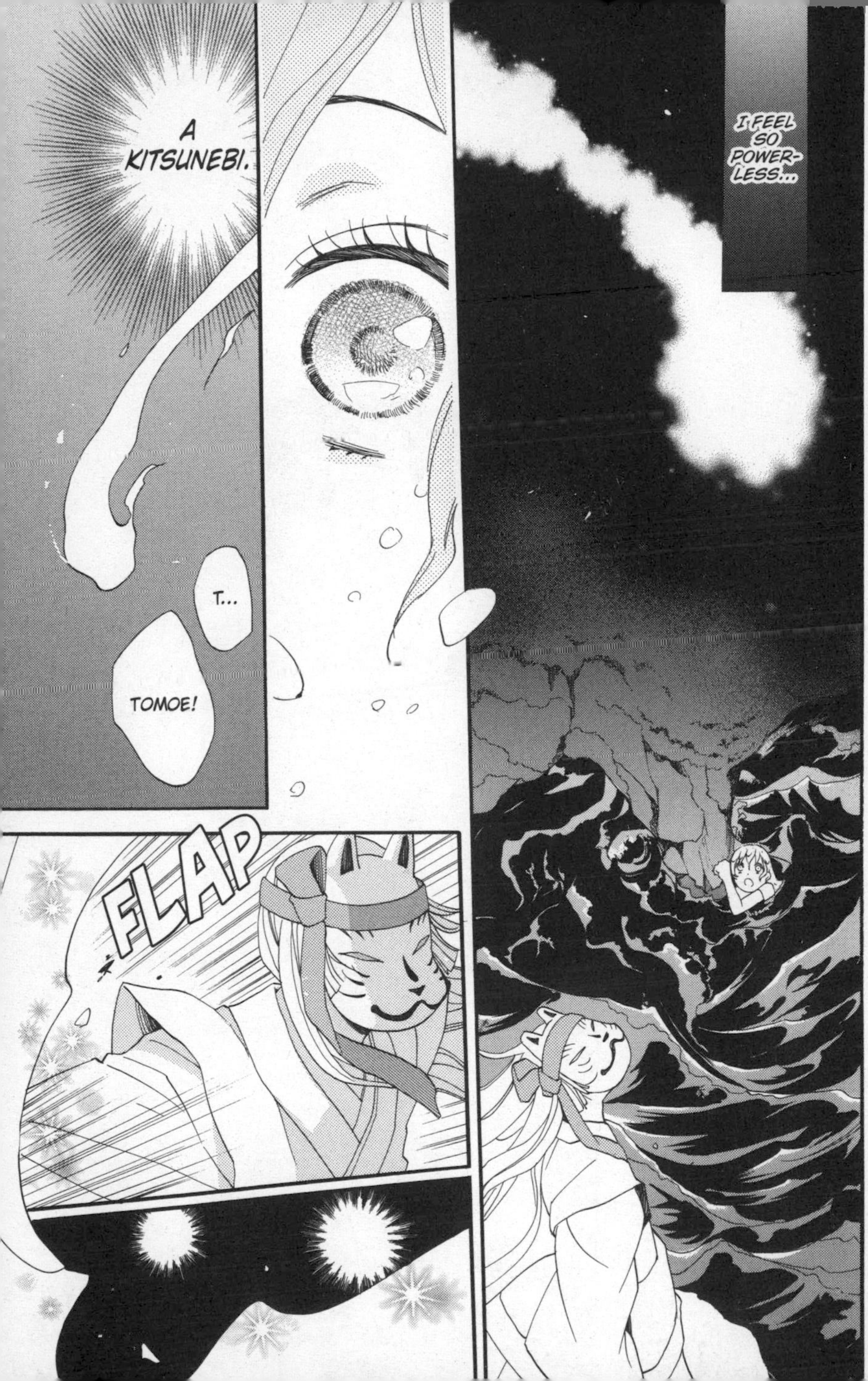
I FEEL SO POWER-LESS...
A KITSUNEBI.
T...
TOMOE!
FLAP

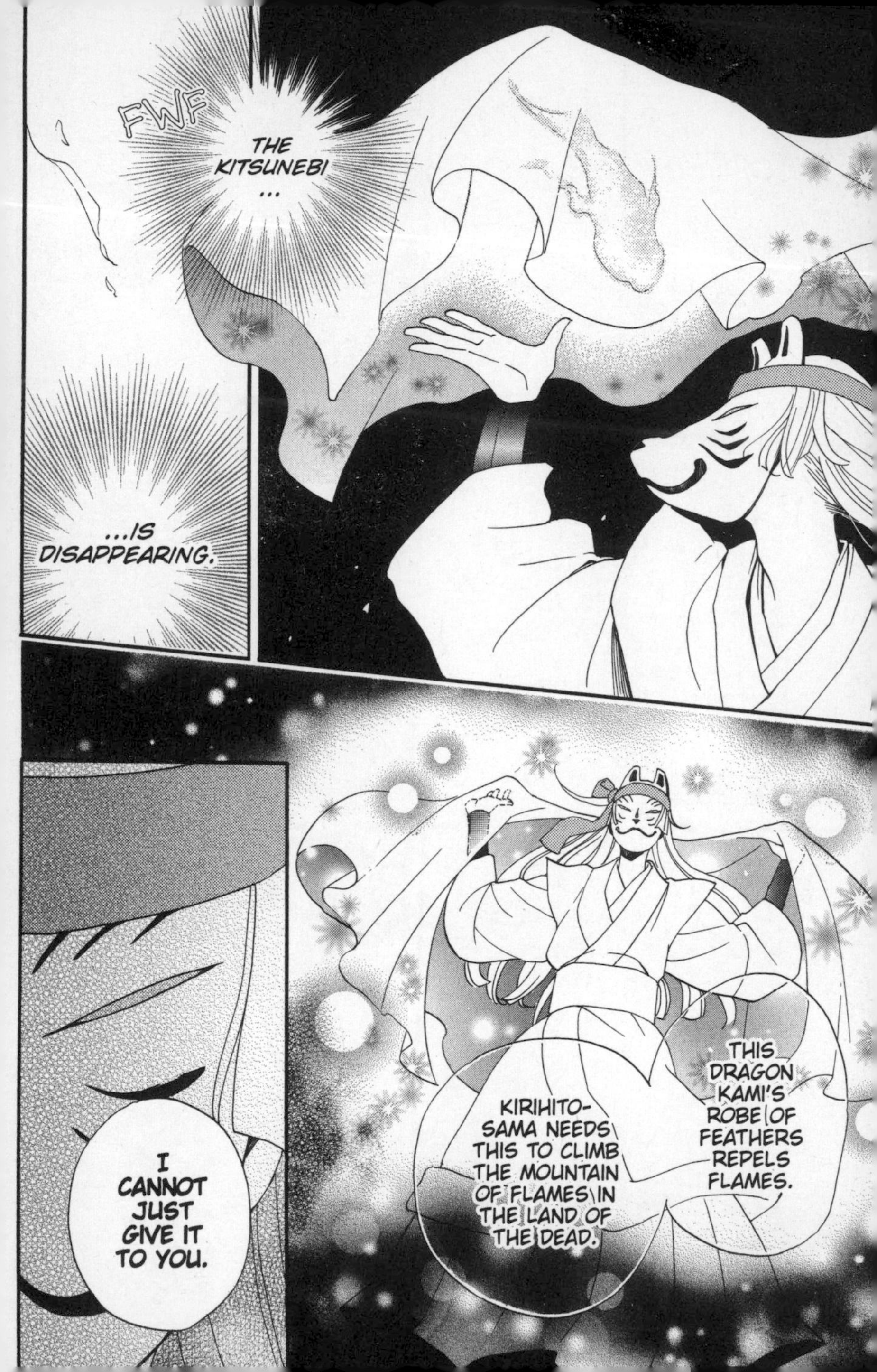
FWF
THE KITSUNEBI ...
...IS DISAPPEARING.
THIS DRAGON KAMI'S ROBE OF FEATHERS REPELS FLAMES.
KIRIHITO-SAMA NEEDS THIS TO CLIMB THE MOUNTAIN OF FLAMES IN THE LAND OF THE DEAD.
I CANNOT JUST GIVE IT TO YOU.

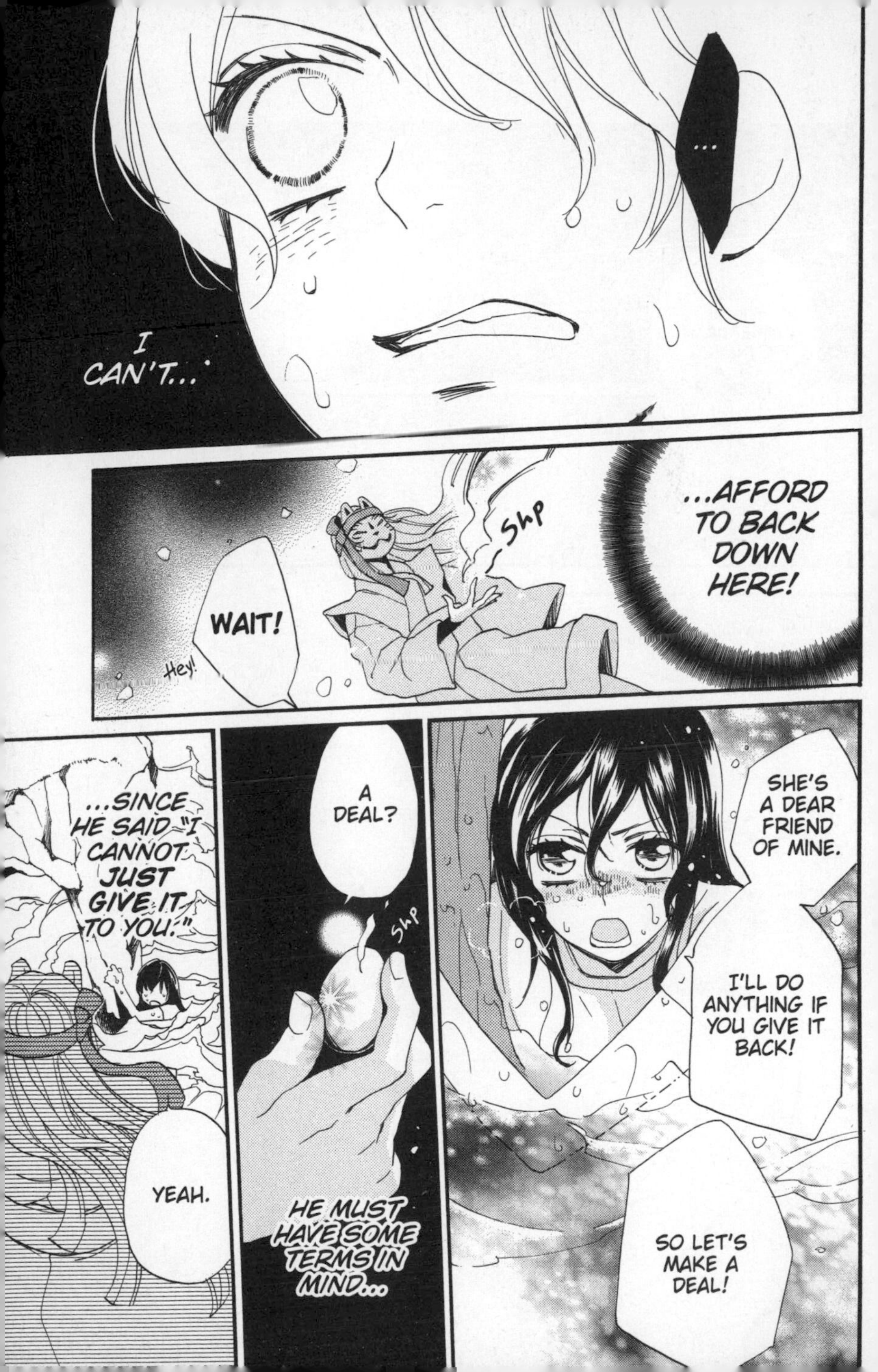
...
I CAN'T...
...AFFORD TO BACK DOWN HERE!
Shp
WAIT!
Hey!
SHE'S A DEAR FRIEND OF MINE.
I'LL DO ANYTHING IF YOU GIVE IT BACK!
SO LET'S MAKE A DEAL!
A DEAL?
Shp
HE MUST HAVE SOME TERMS IN MIND...
...SINCE HE SAID "I CANNOT JUST GIVE IT TO YOU."
YEAH.

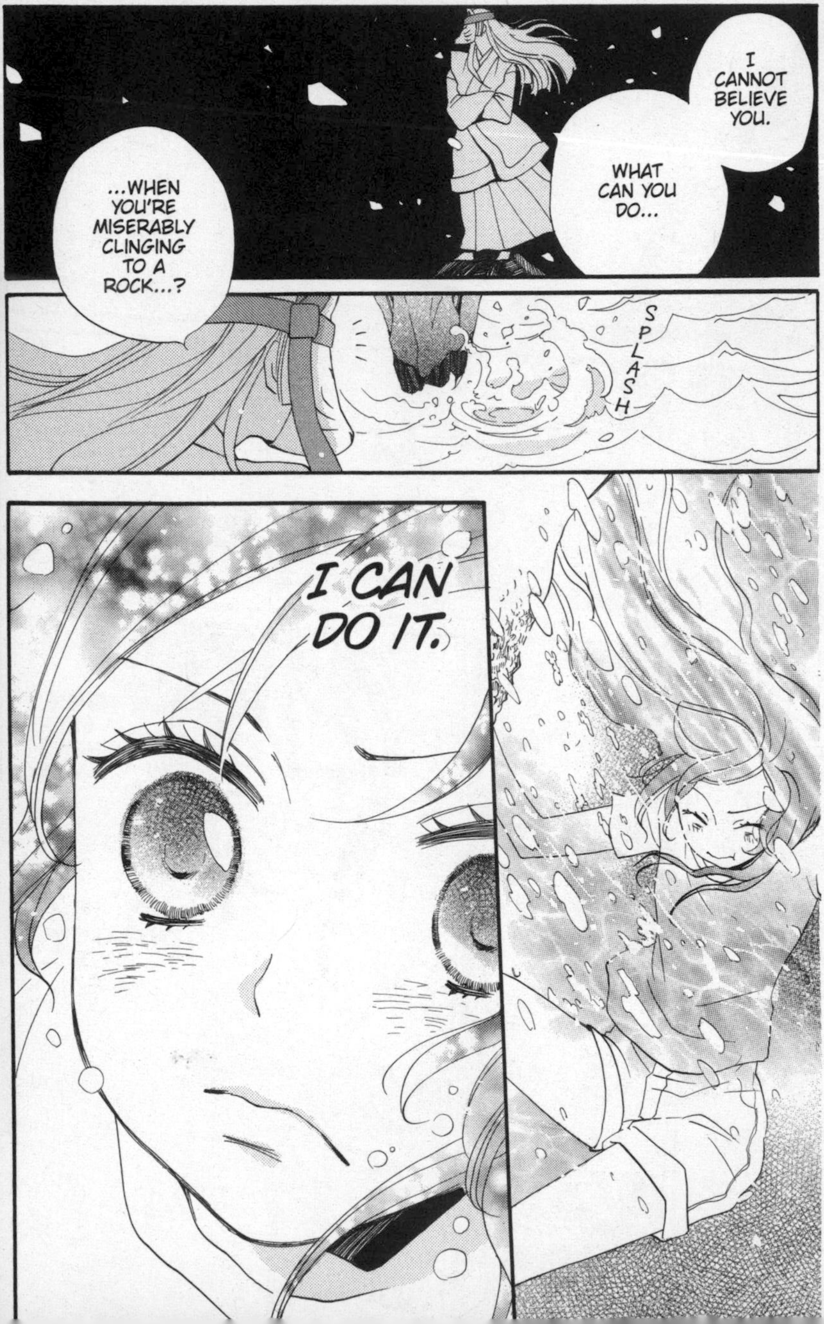
I CANNOT BELIEVE YOU.
WHAT CAN YOU DO...
...WHEN YOU'RE MISERABLY CLINGING TO A ROCK...?
SPLASH
I CAN DO IT.

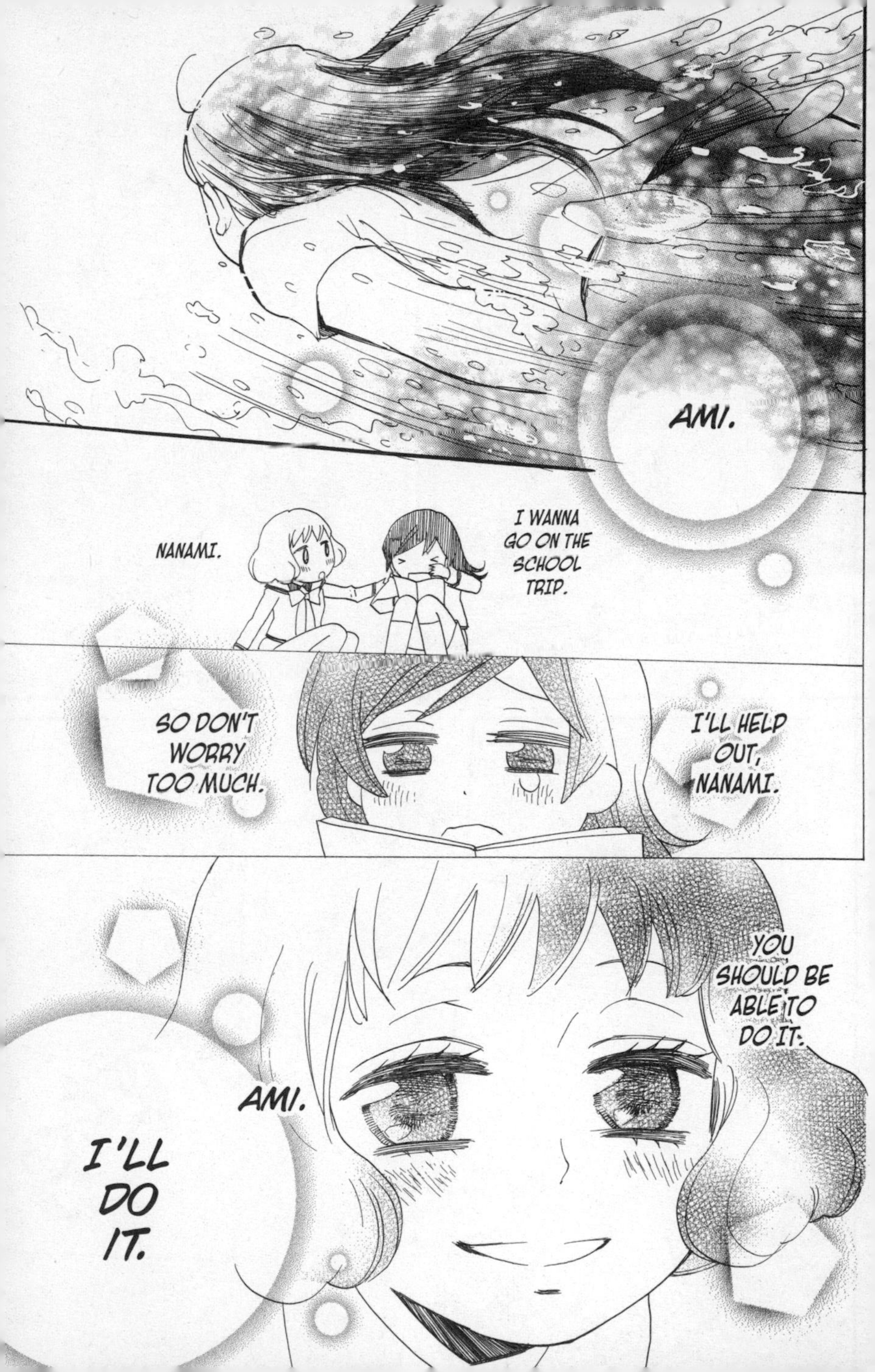
AMI.
I WANNA GO ON THE SCHOOL TRIP.
NANAMI.
I'LL HELP OUT, NANAMI.
SO DON'T WORRY TOO MUCH.
YOU SHOULD BE ABLE TO DO IT.
AMI.
I'LL DO IT.

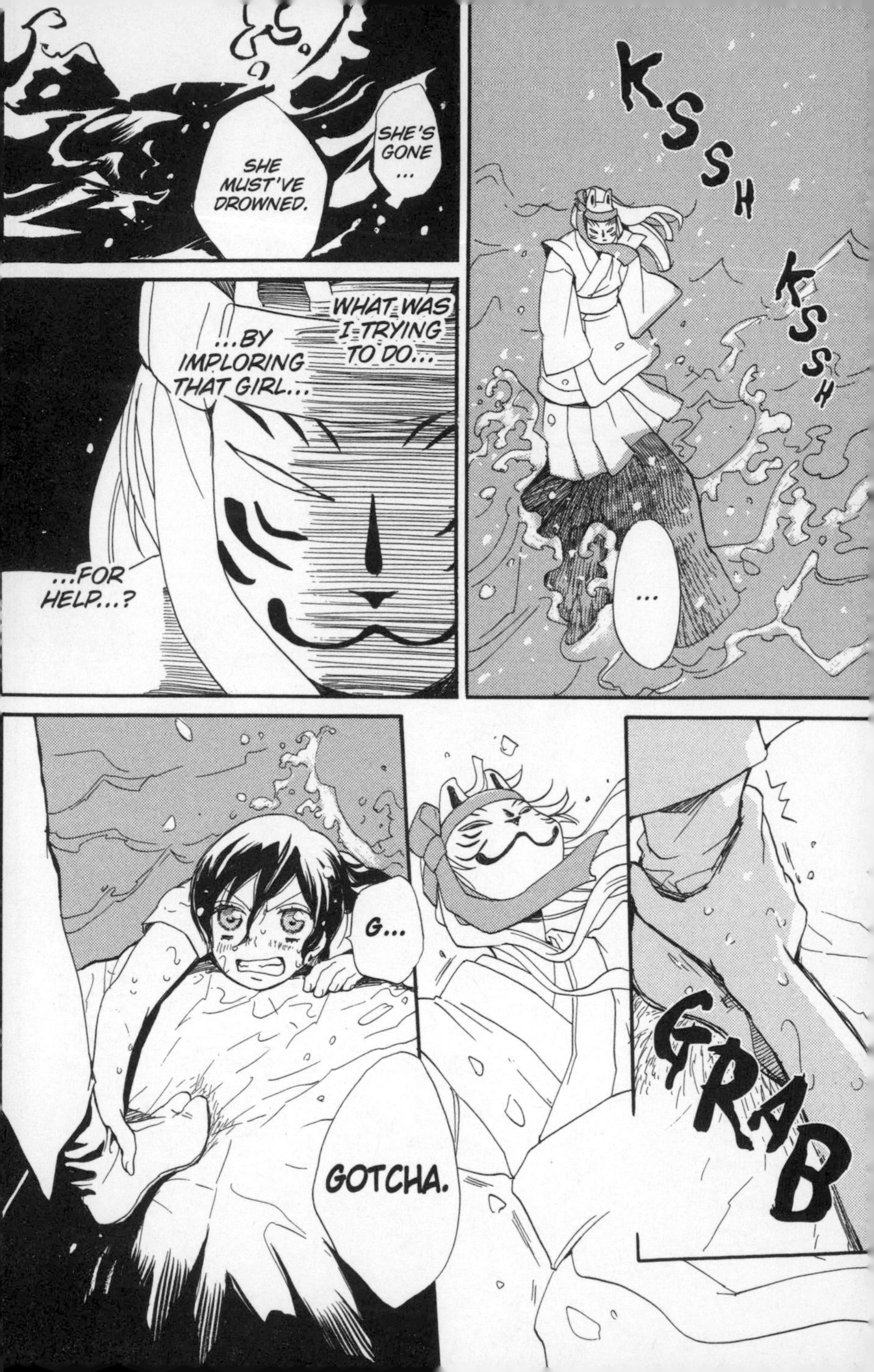
KSSSH
KSSSH
...
SHE'S GONE...
SHE MUST'VE DROWNED.
WHAT WAS I TRYING TO DO...
...BY IMPLORING THAT GIRL...
...FOR HELP...?
GRAB
G...
GOTCHA.

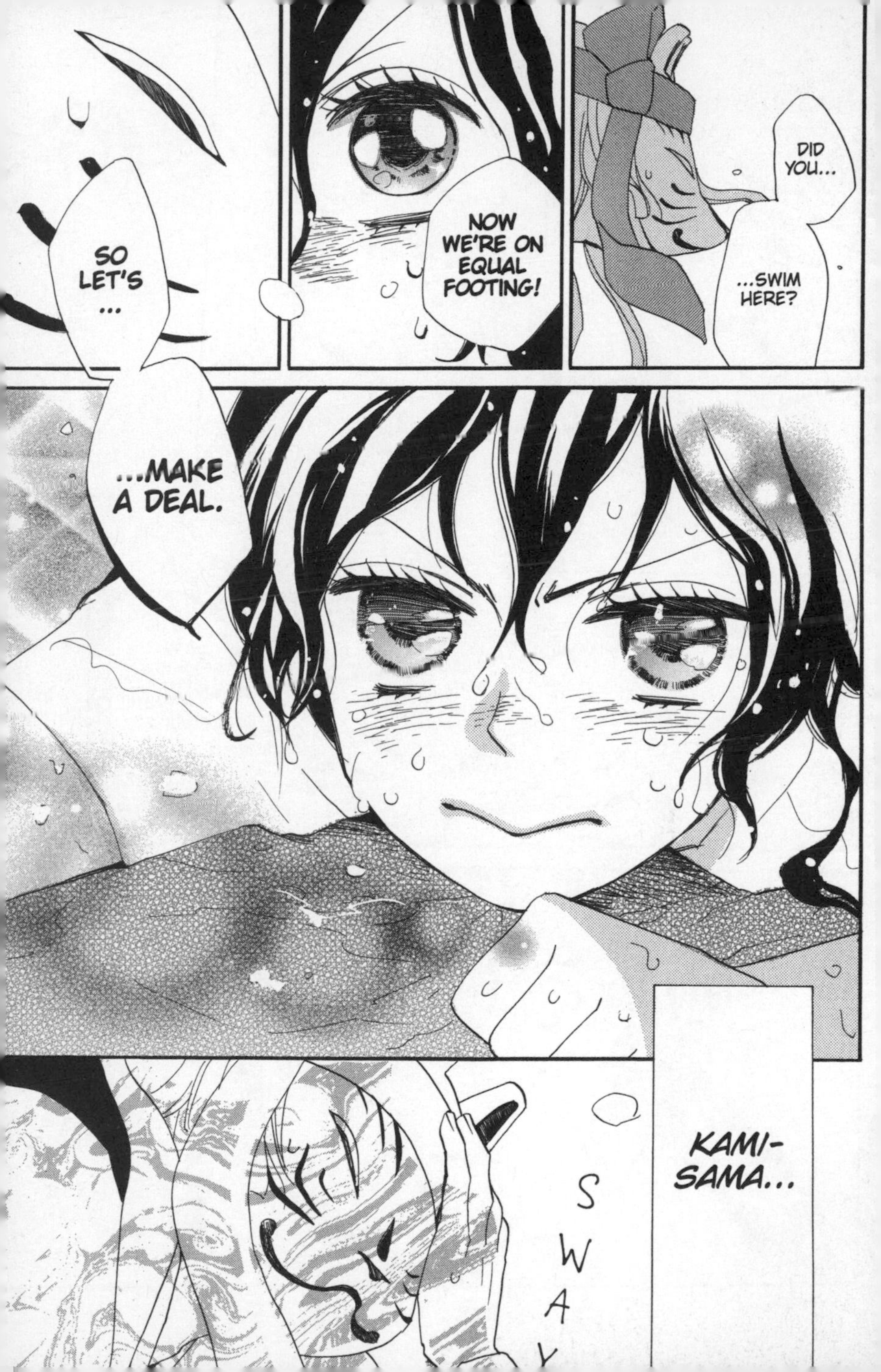
DID YOU...
...SWIM HERE?
NOW WE'RE ON EQUAL FOOTING!
SO LET'S ...
...MAKE A DEAL.
KAMI-SAMA...
SWAY

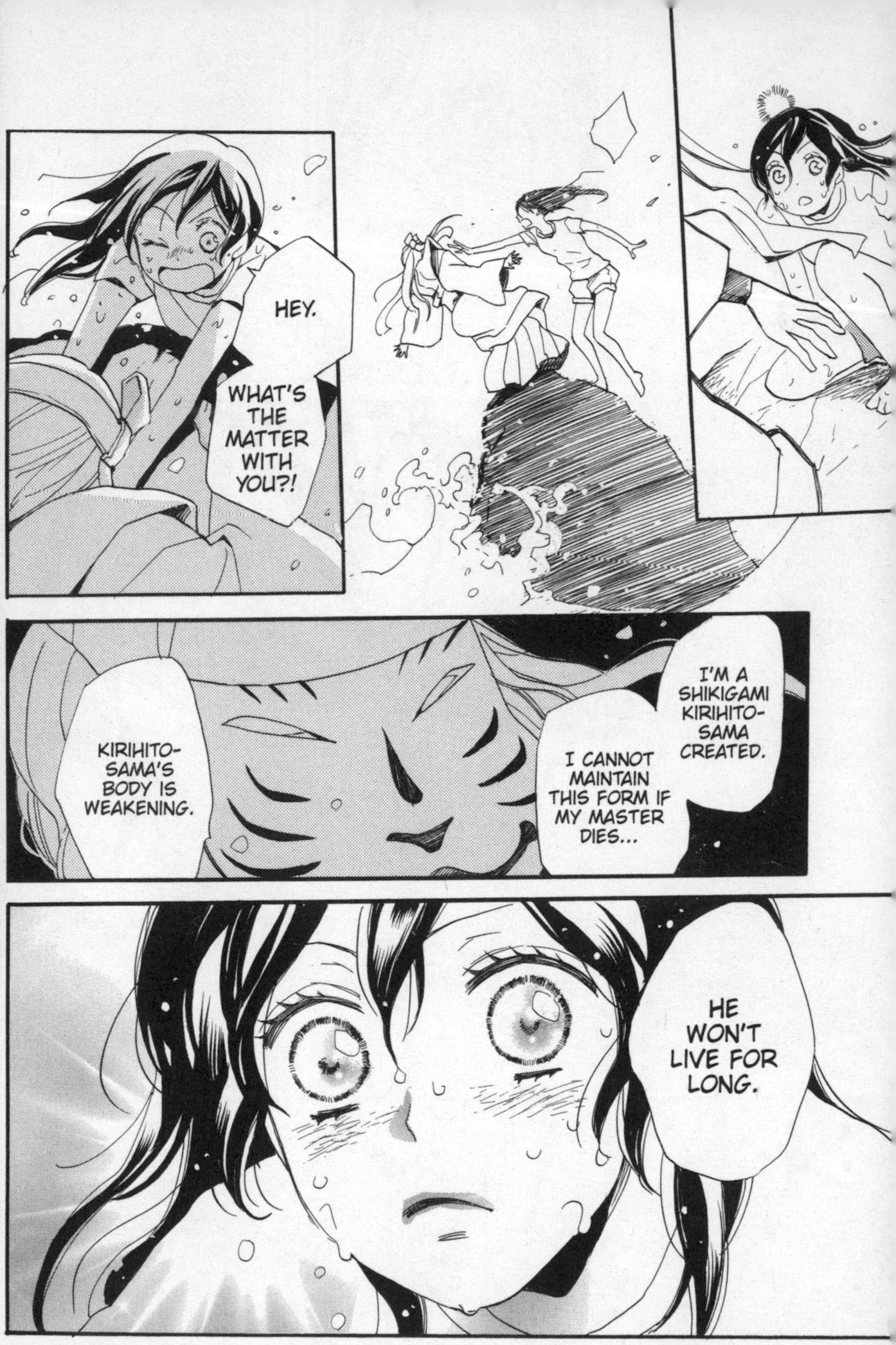
HEY.
WHAT'S THE MATTER WITH YOU?!
I'M A SHIKIGAMI KIRIHITO-SAMA CREATED.
I CANNOT MAINTAIN THIS FORM IF MY MASTER DIES...
KIRIHITO-SAMA'S BODY IS WEAKENING.
HE WON'T LIVE FOR LONG.

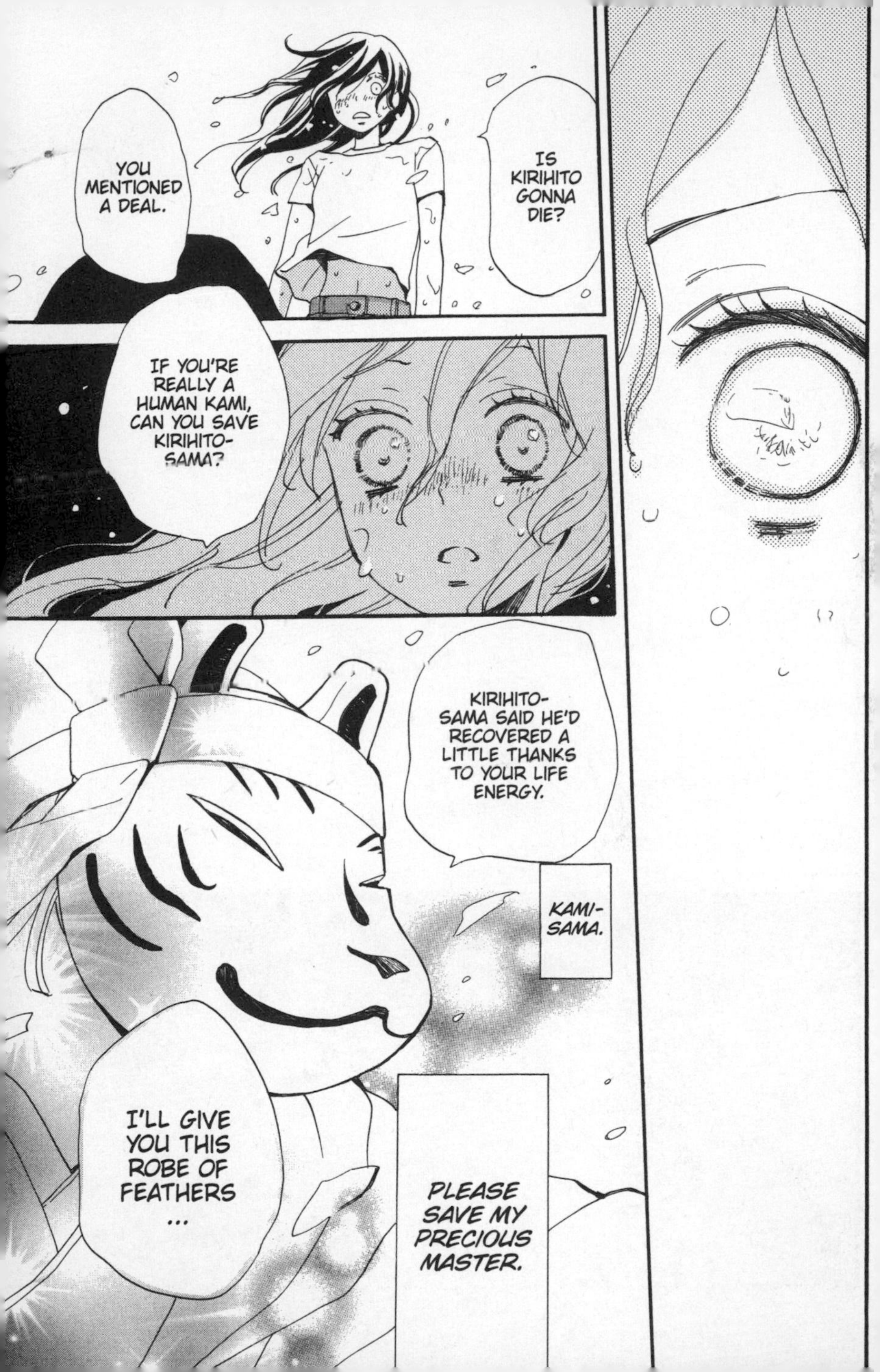
IS KIRIHITO GONNA DIE?
YOU MENTIONED A DEAL.
IF YOU'RE REALLY A HUMAN KAMI, CAN YOU SAVE KIRIHITO-SAMA?
KIRIHITO-SAMA SAID HE'D RECOVERED A LITTLE THANKS TO YOUR LIFE ENERGY.
KAMI-SAMA.
I'LL GIVE YOU THIS ROBE OF FEATHERS ...
PLEASE SAVE MY PRECIOUS MASTER.

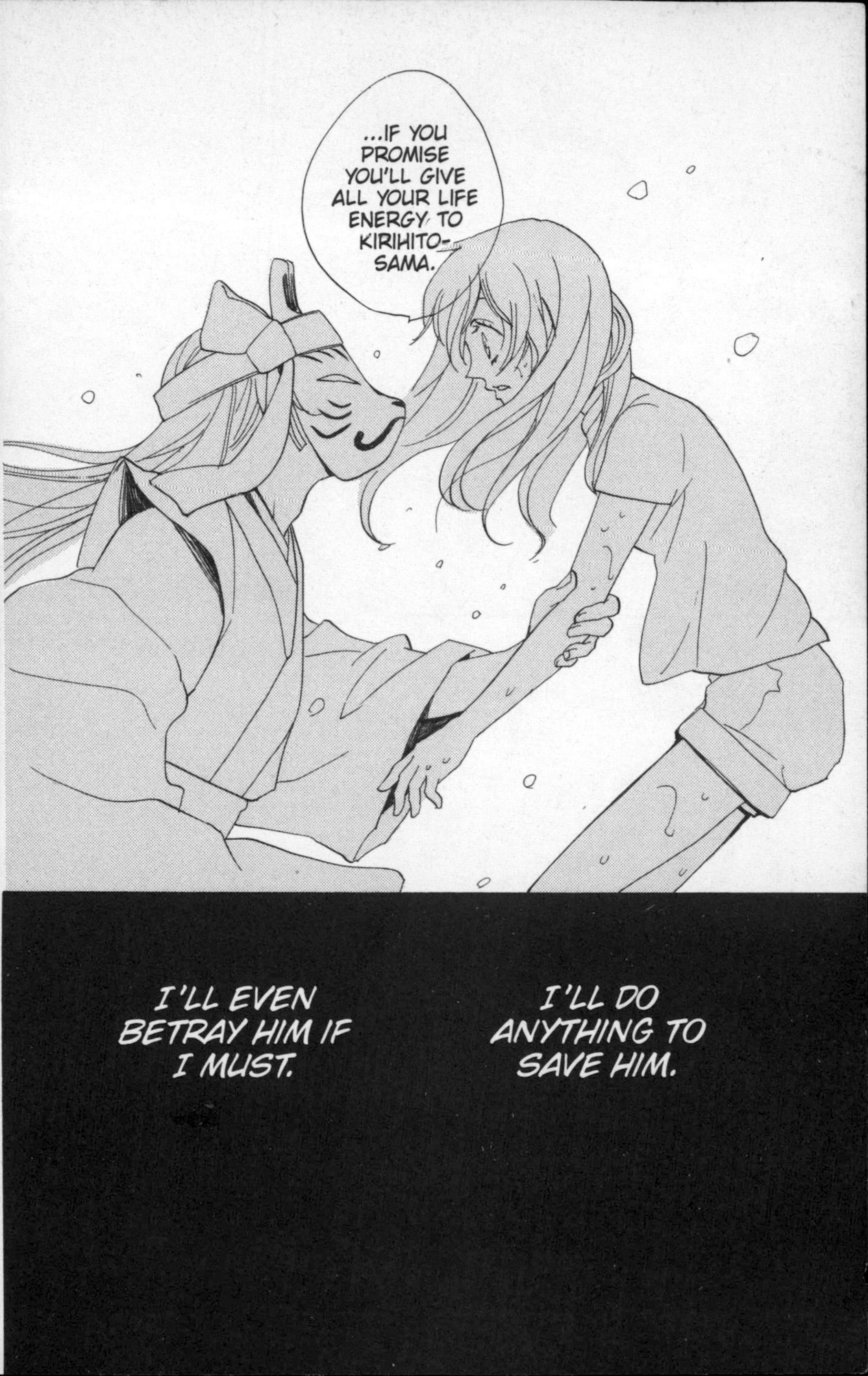
...IF YOU PROMISE YOU'LL GIVE ALL YOUR LIFE ENERGY TO KIRIHITO-SAMA.
I'LL DO ANYTHING TO SAVE HIM.
I'LL EVEN BETRAY HIM IF I MUST.

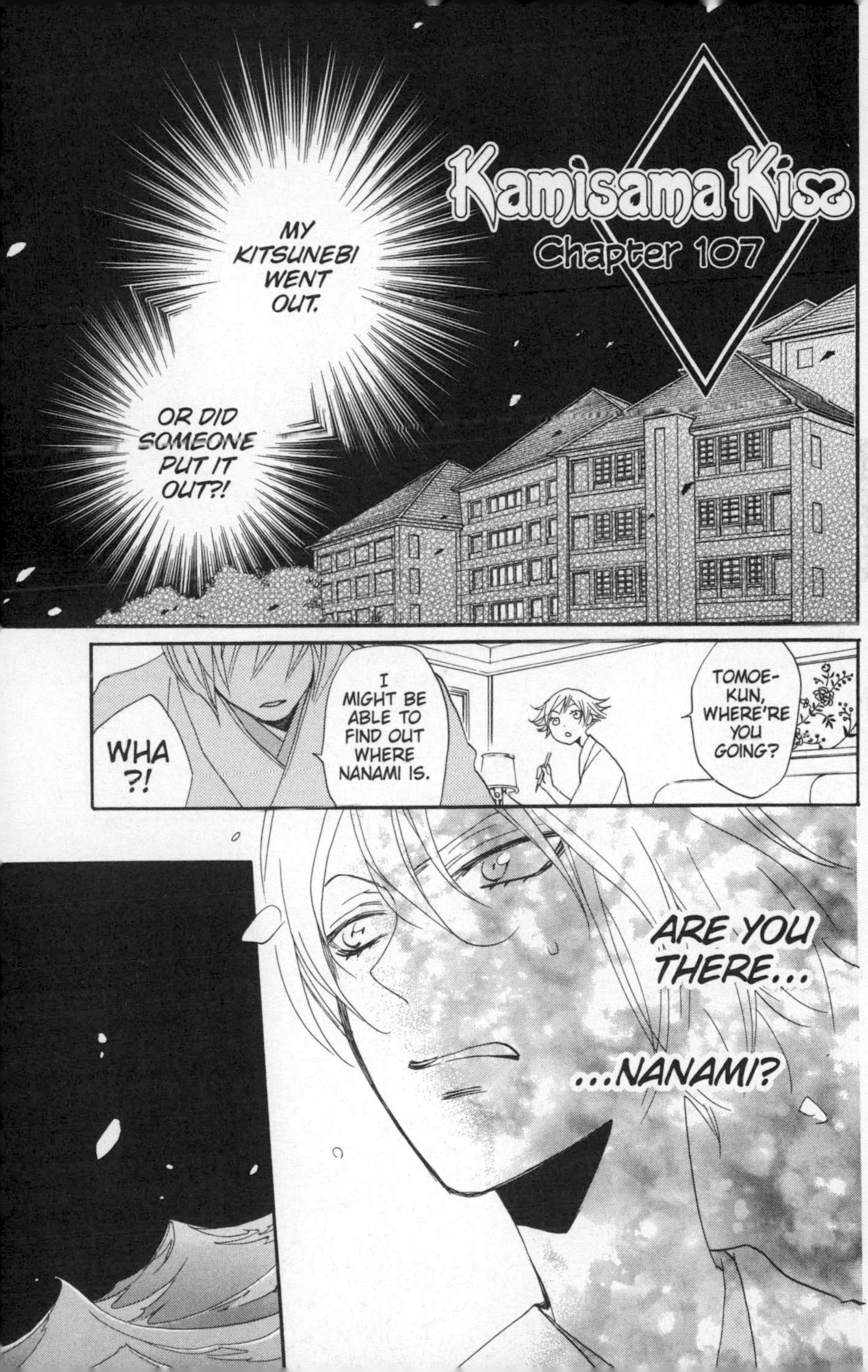
Kamisama Kiss
Chapter 107
MY KITSUNEBI WENT OUT.
OR DID SOMEONE PUT IT OUT?!
TOMOE-KUN, WHERE'RE YOU GOING?
I MIGHT BE ABLE TO FIND OUT WHERE NANAMI IS.
WHA ?!
ARE YOU THERE...
...NANAMI?

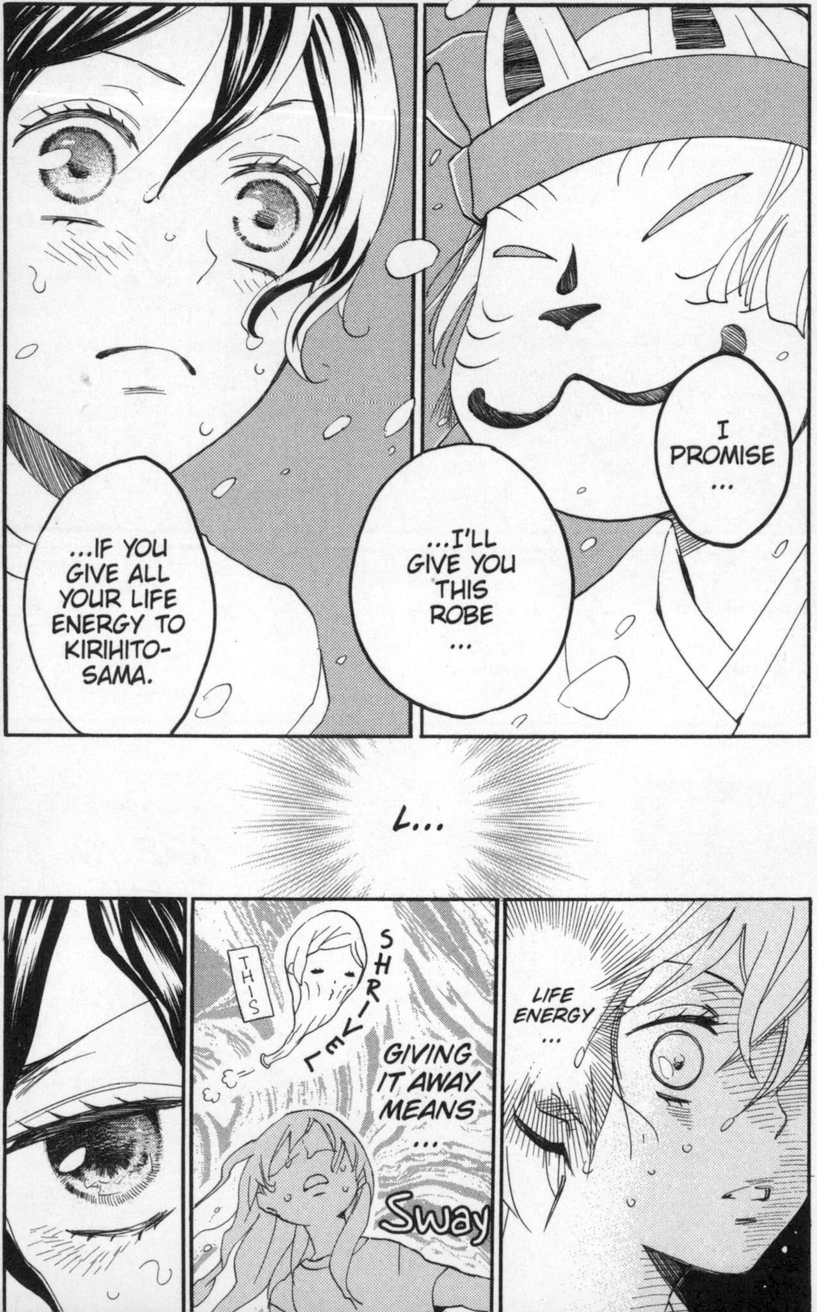
I PROMISE...
...I'LL GIVE YOU THIS ROBE...
...IF YOU GIVE ALL YOUR LIFE ENERGY TO KIRIHITO-SAMA.
I...
LIFE ENERGY...
SHRIVEL
THIS
GIVING IT AWAY MEANS...
Sway

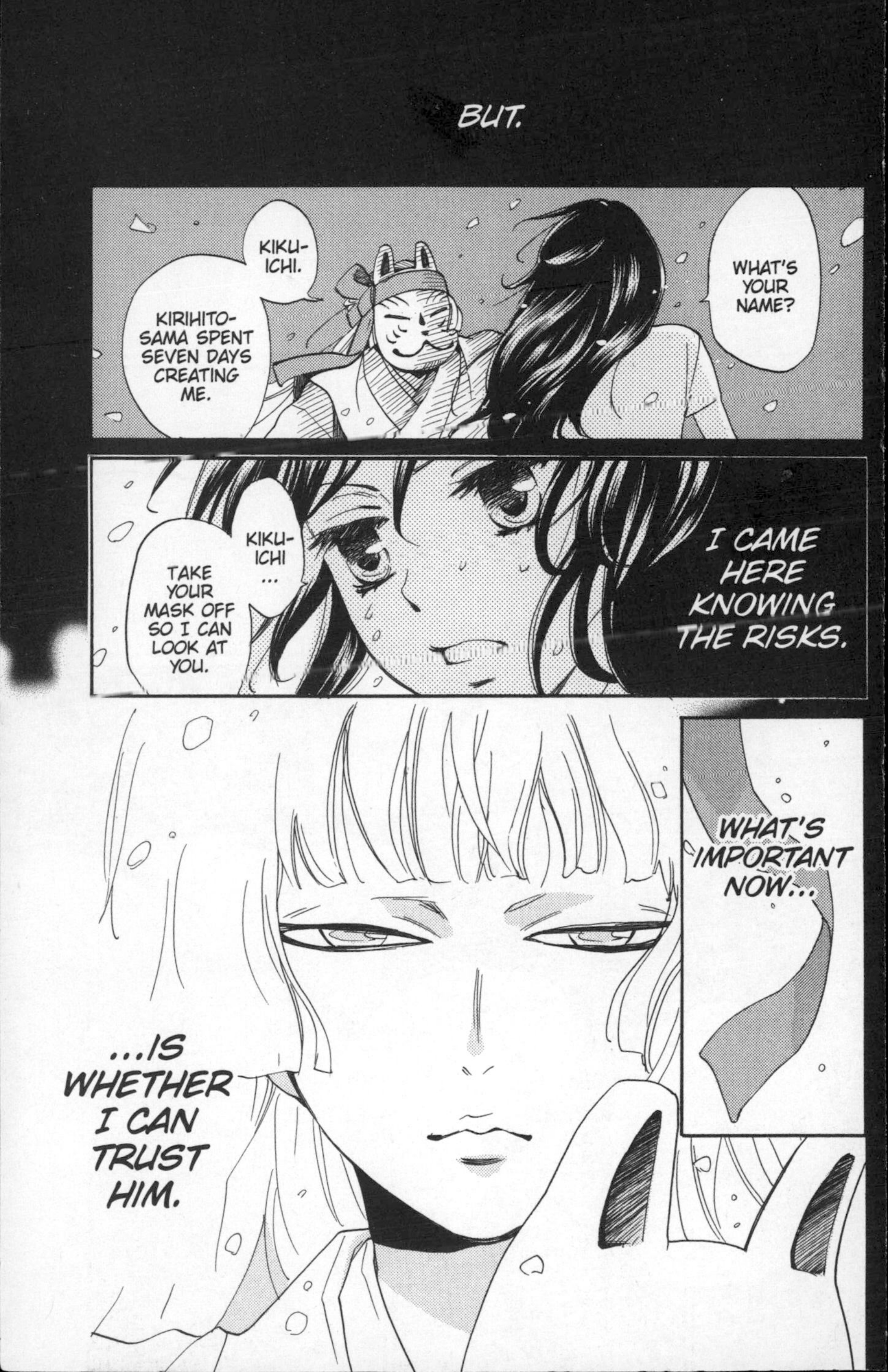
BUT.
WHAT'S YOUR NAME?
KIKU-ICHI.
KIRIHITO-SAMA SPENT SEVEN DAYS CREATING ME.
I CAME HERE KNOWING THE RISKS.
KIKU-ICHI...
TAKE YOUR MASK OFF SO I CAN LOOK AT YOU.
WHAT'S IMPORTANT NOW...
...IS WHETHER I CAN TRUST HIM.

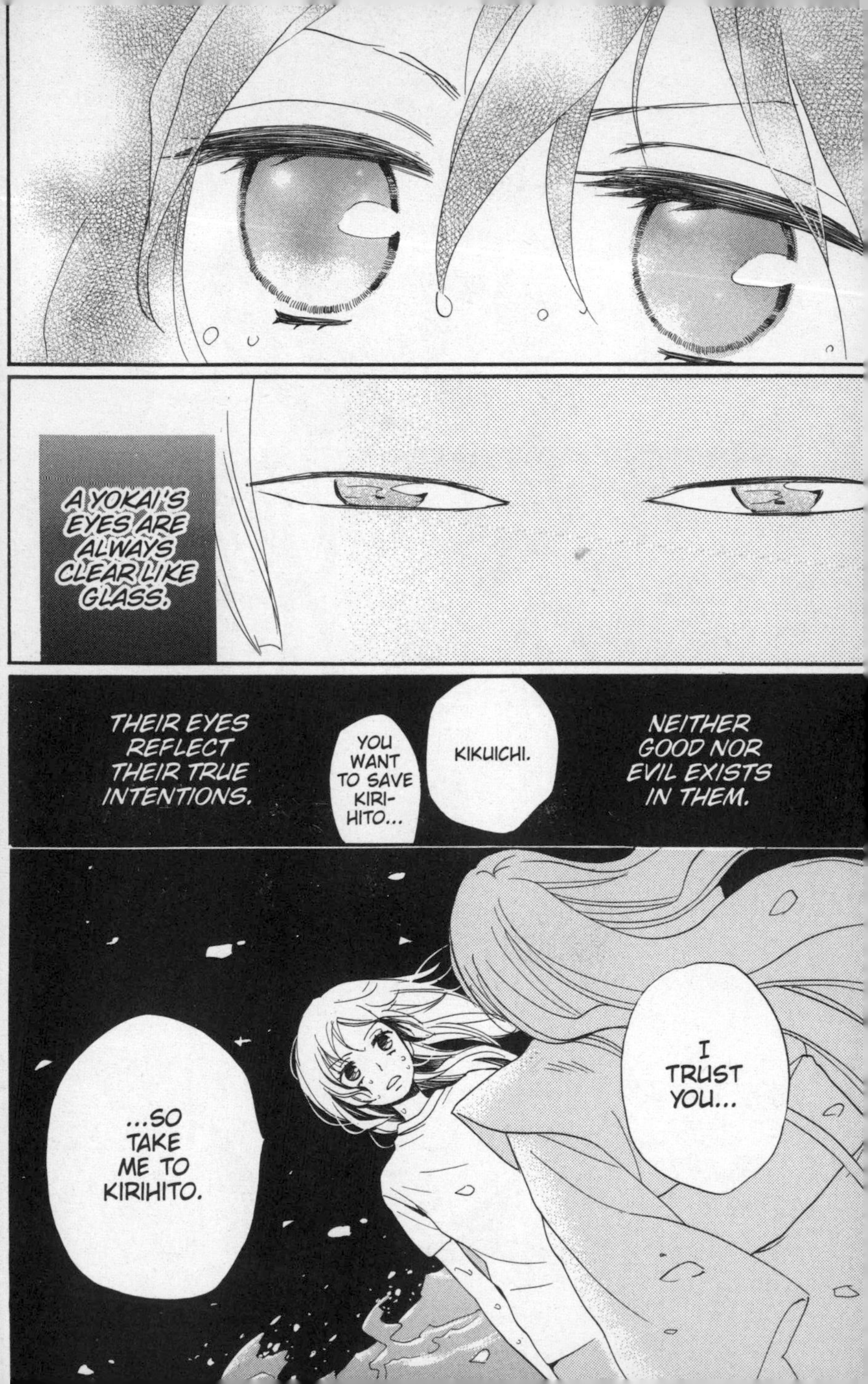
A YOKAI'S EYES ARE ALWAYS CLEAR LIKE GLASS.
NEITHER GOOD NOR EVIL EXISTS IN THEM.
KIKUICHI.
YOU WANT TO SAVE KIRI-HITO...
THEIR EYES REFLECT THEIR TRUE INTENTIONS.
I TRUST YOU...
...SO TAKE ME TO KIRIHITO.

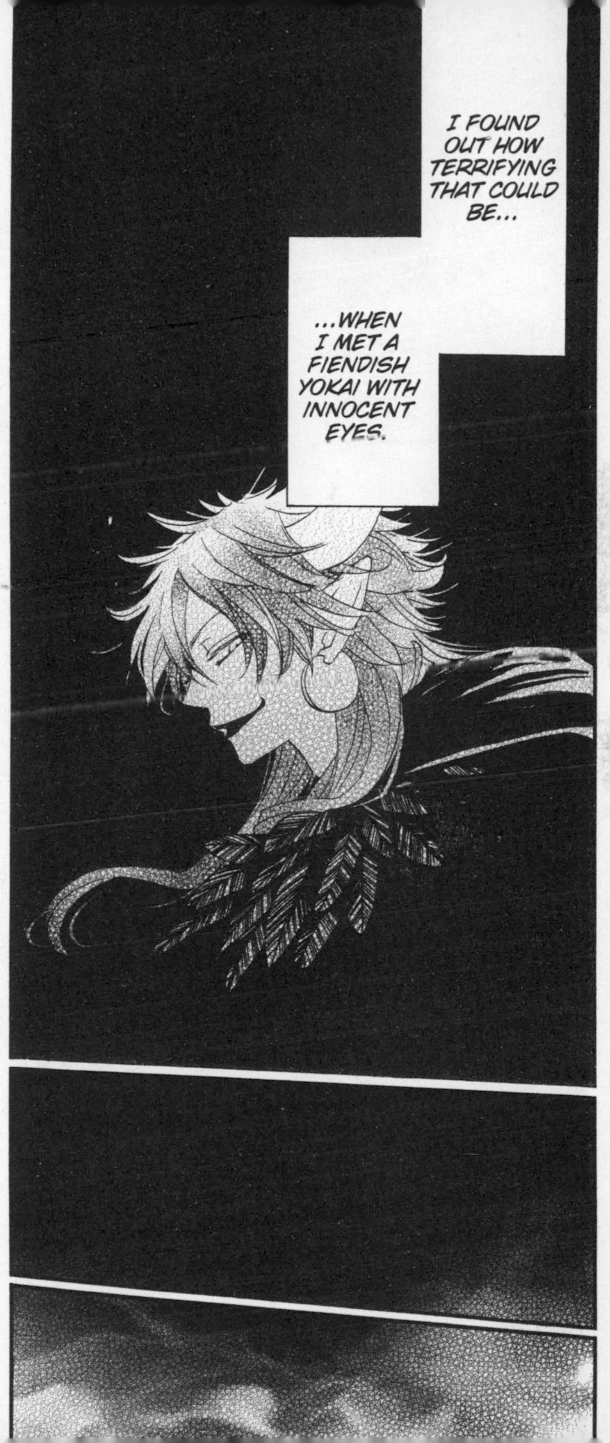
I FOUND OUT HOW TERRIFYING THAT COULD BE...
...WHEN I MET A FIENDISH YOKAI WITH INNOCENT EYES.

Thank you for reading this far!

If you have any comments and thoughts about volume 18, do let me hear from you!

The address is...

Julietta Suzuki
c/o Shojo Beat
VIZ Media, LLC
P.O. Box 77010
San Francisco
CA 94107

I'll be waiting. ☺

Now then.

I hope we'll be able to meet again in the next volume. ♡

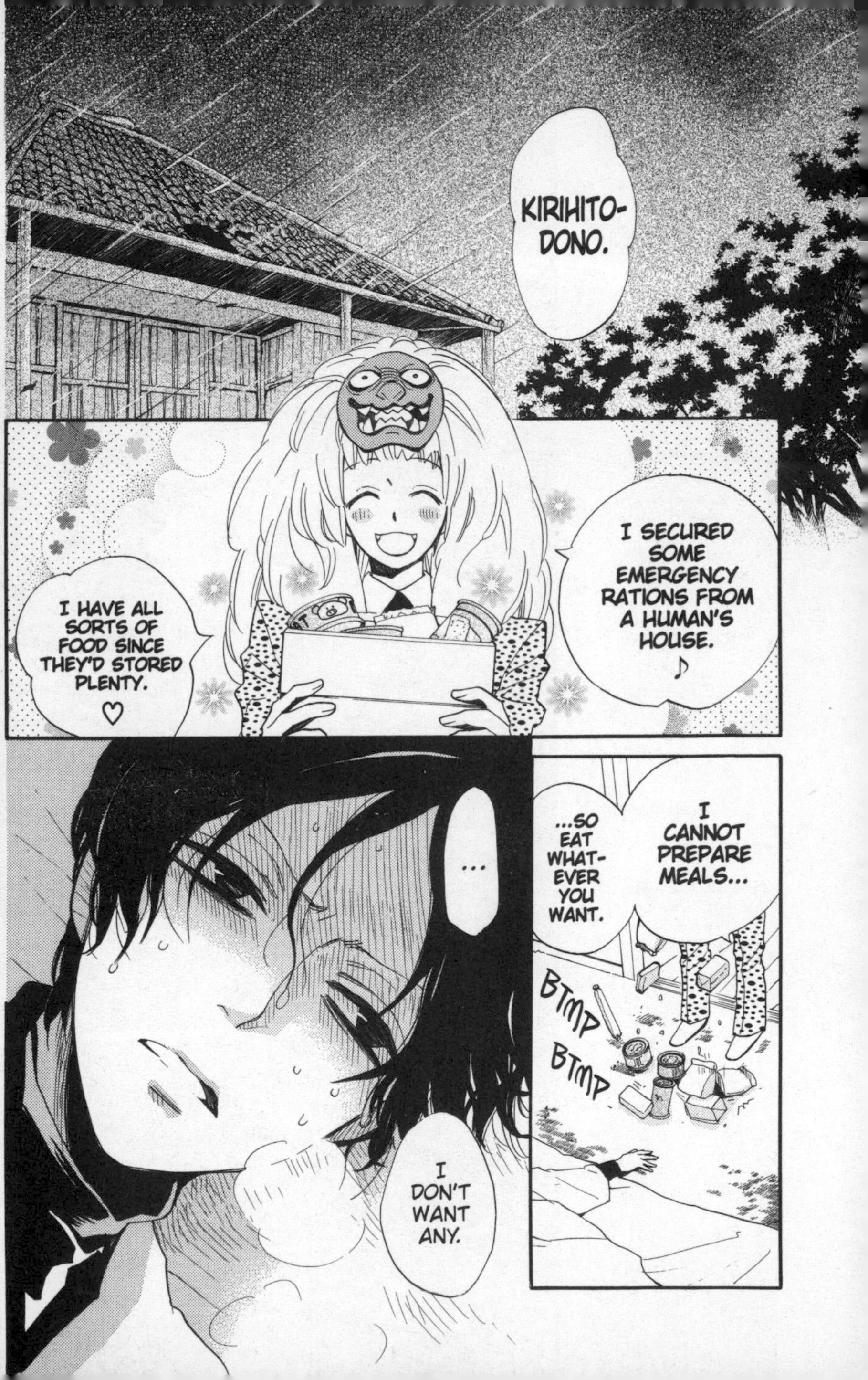
KIRIHITO-DONO.
I SECURED SOME EMERGENCY RATIONS FROM A HUMAN'S HOUSE. ♪
I HAVE ALL SORTS OF FOOD SINCE THEY'D STORED PLENTY. ♡
I CANNOT PREPARE MEALS...
...SO EAT WHAT-EVER YOU WANT.
BTMP
BTMP
...
I DON'T WANT ANY.

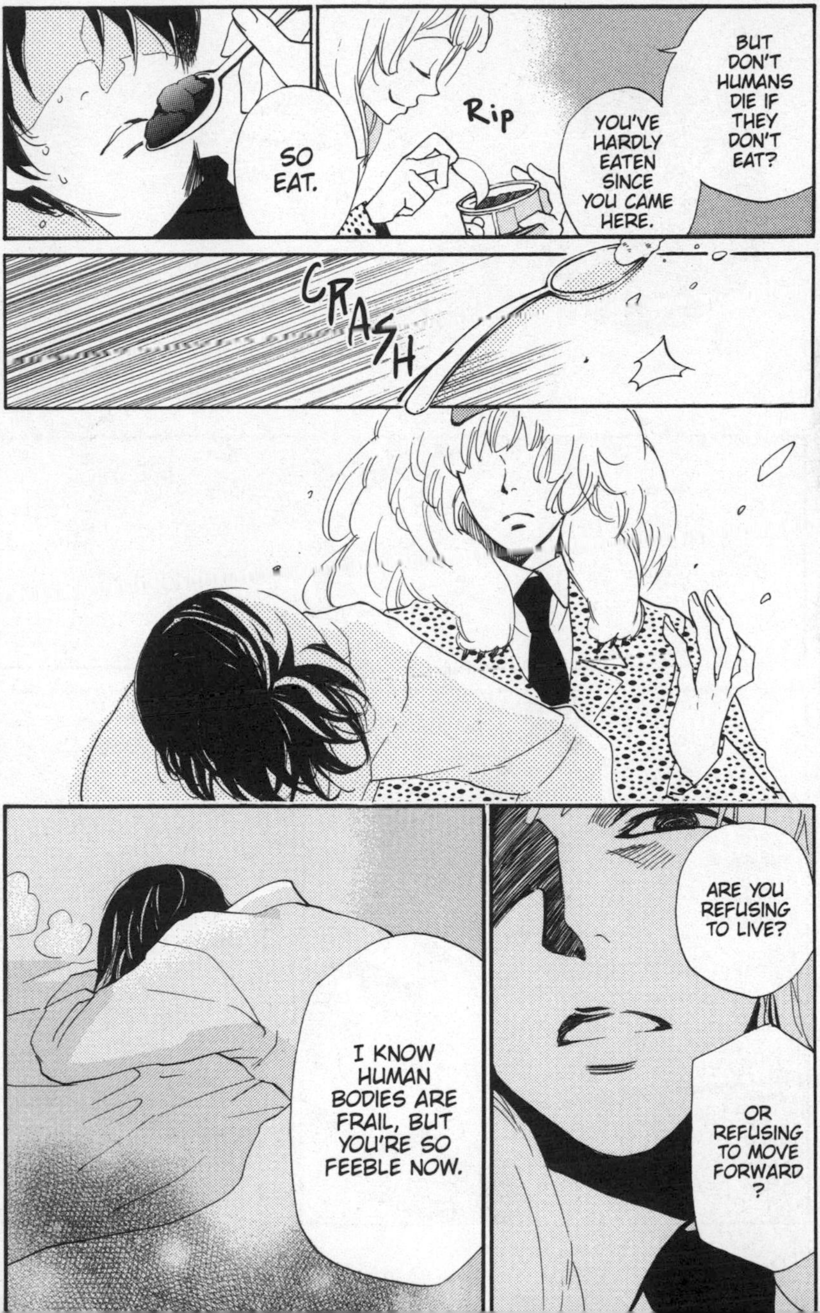
BUT DON'T HUMANS DIE IF THEY DON'T EAT?
YOU'VE HARDLY EATEN SINCE YOU CAME HERE.
Rip
SO EAT.
CRASH
ARE YOU REFUSING TO LIVE?
OR REFUSING TO MOVE FORWARD?
I KNOW HUMAN BODIES ARE FRAIL, BUT YOU'RE SO FEEBLE NOW.

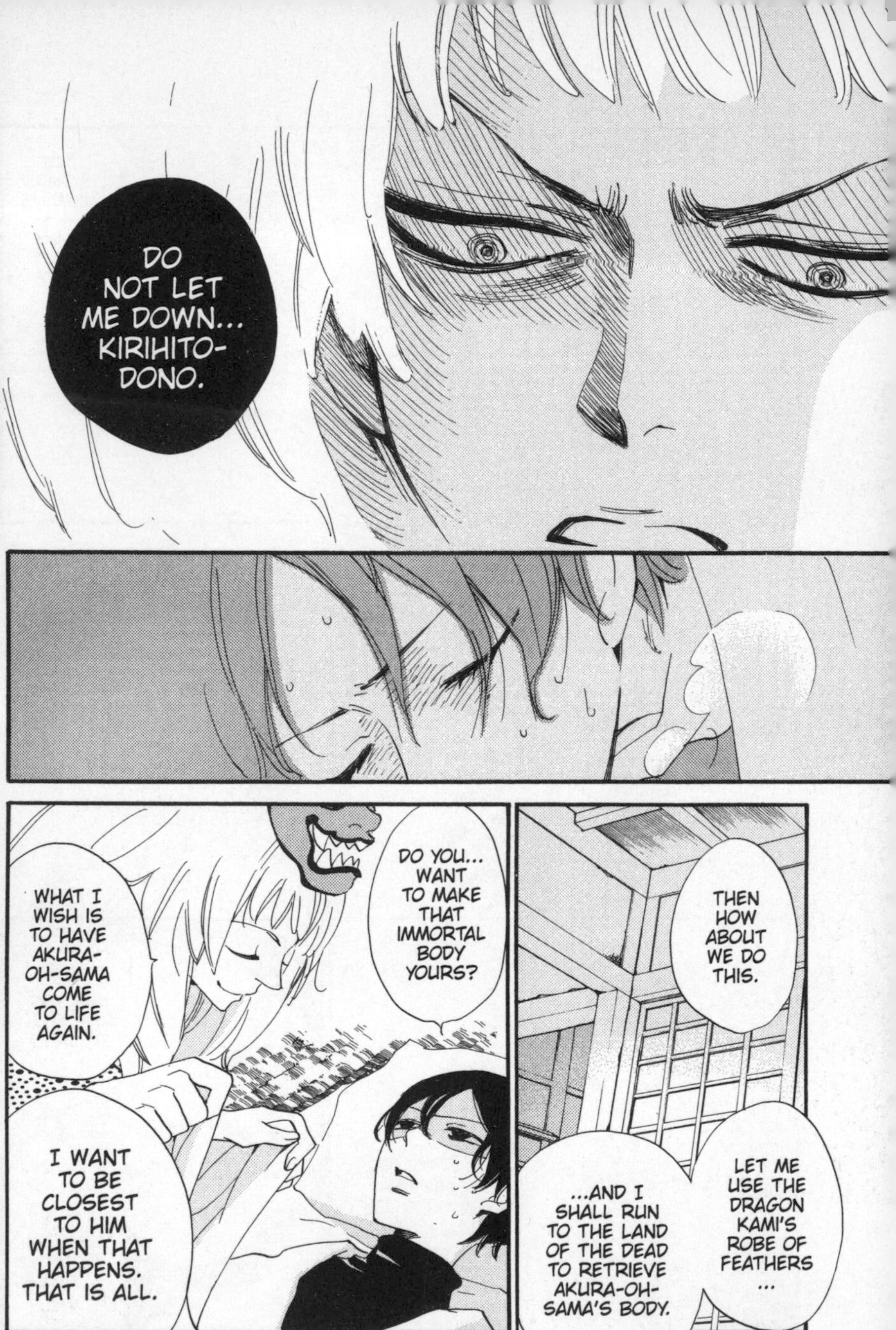
DO NOT LET ME DOWN... KIRIHITO-DONO.
THEN HOW ABOUT WE DO THIS.
LET ME USE THE DRAGON KAMI'S ROBE OF FEATHERS ...
...AND I SHALL RUN TO THE LAND OF THE DEAD TO RETRIEVE AKURA-OH-SAMA'S BODY.
DO YOU... WANT TO MAKE THAT IMMORTAL BODY YOURS?
WHAT I WISH IS TO HAVE AKURA-OH-SAMA COME TO LIFE AGAIN.
I WANT TO BE CLOSEST TO HIM WHEN THAT HAPPENS. THAT IS ALL.

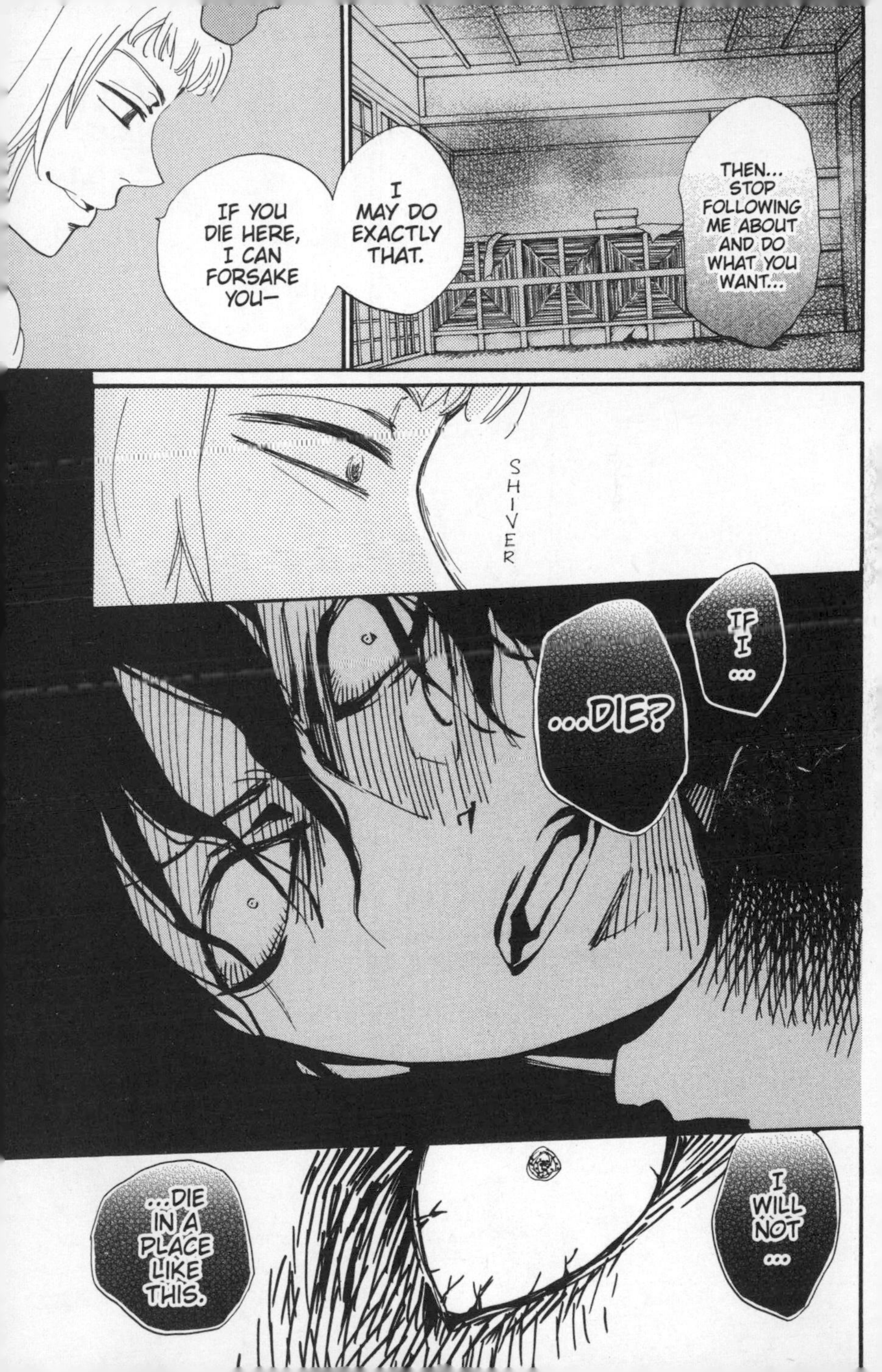
THEN... STOP FOLLOWING ME ABOUT AND DO WHAT YOU WANT...
I MAY DO EXACTLY THAT.
IF YOU DIE HERE, I CAN FORSAKE YOU—
SHIVER
IF I...
...DIE?
I WILL NOT...
...DIE IN A PLACE LIKE THIS.

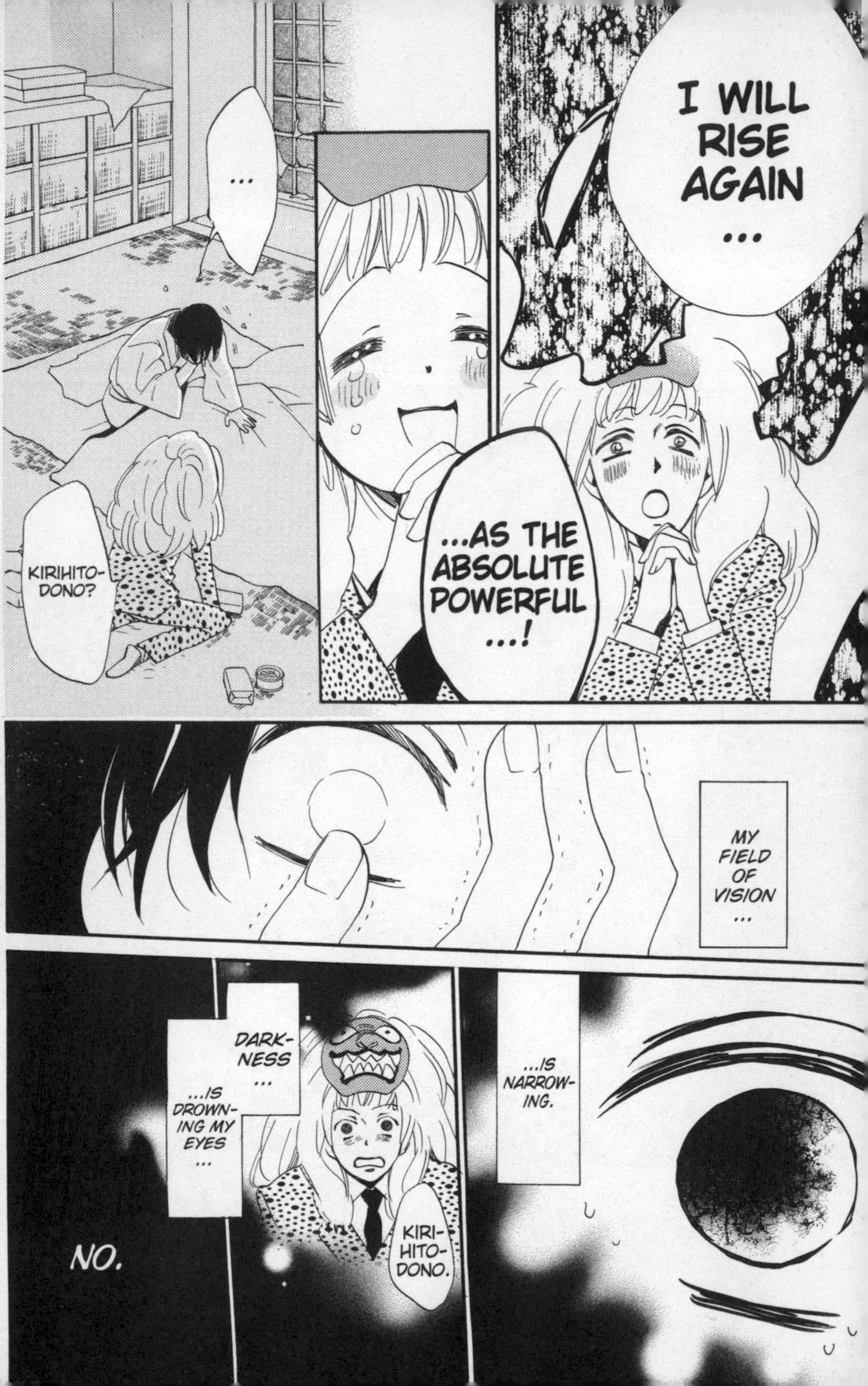
I WILL RISE AGAIN ...
...AS THE ABSOLUTE POWERFUL ...!
...
KIRIHITO-DONO?
MY FIELD OF VISION ...
...IS NARROWING.
DARKNESS ...
...IS DROWNING MY EYES ...
KIRIHITO-DONO.
NO.

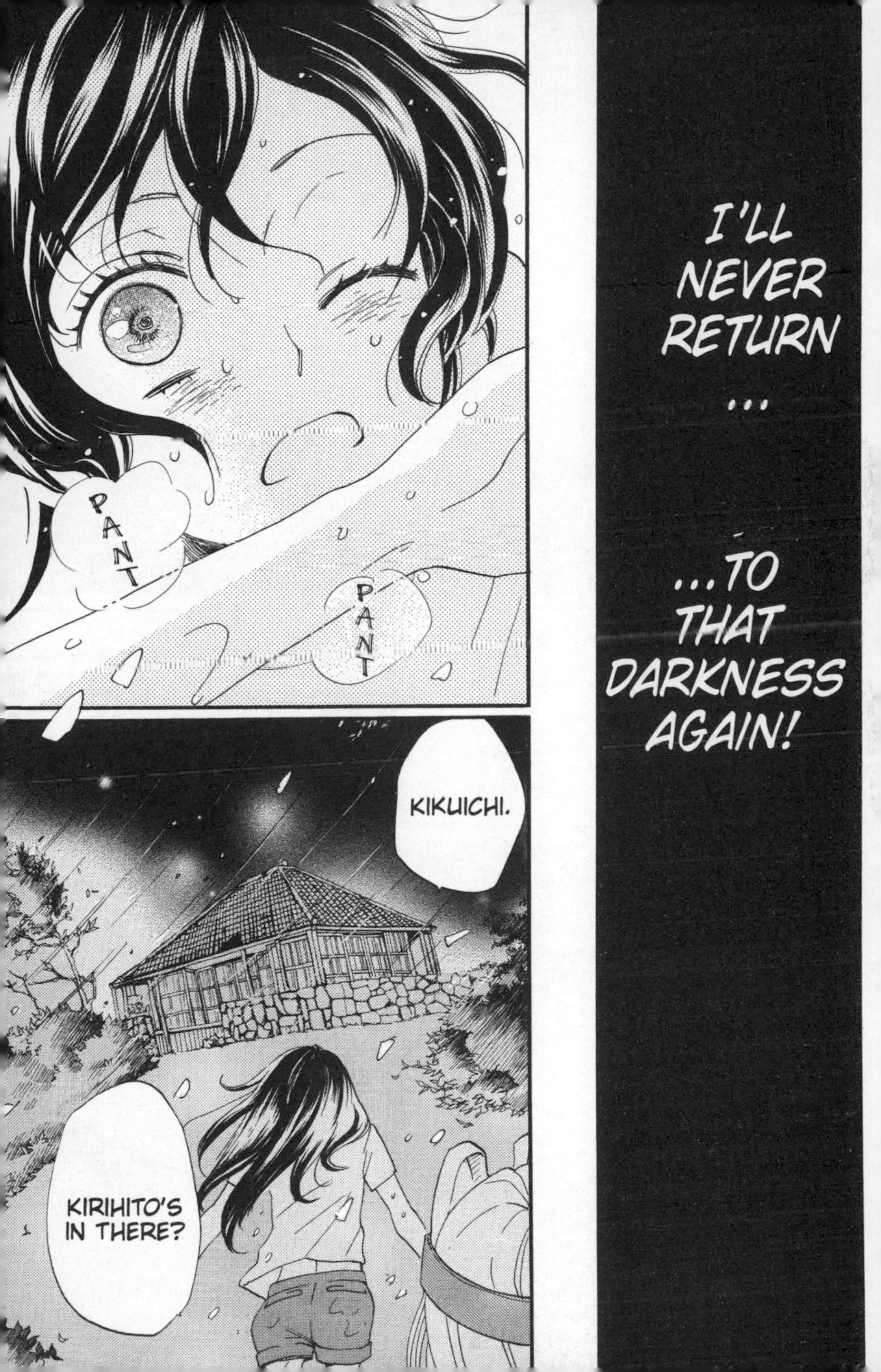
I'LL NEVER RETURN ...
...TO THAT DARKNESS AGAIN!
PANT
PANT
KIKUICHI.
KIRIHITO'S IN THERE?

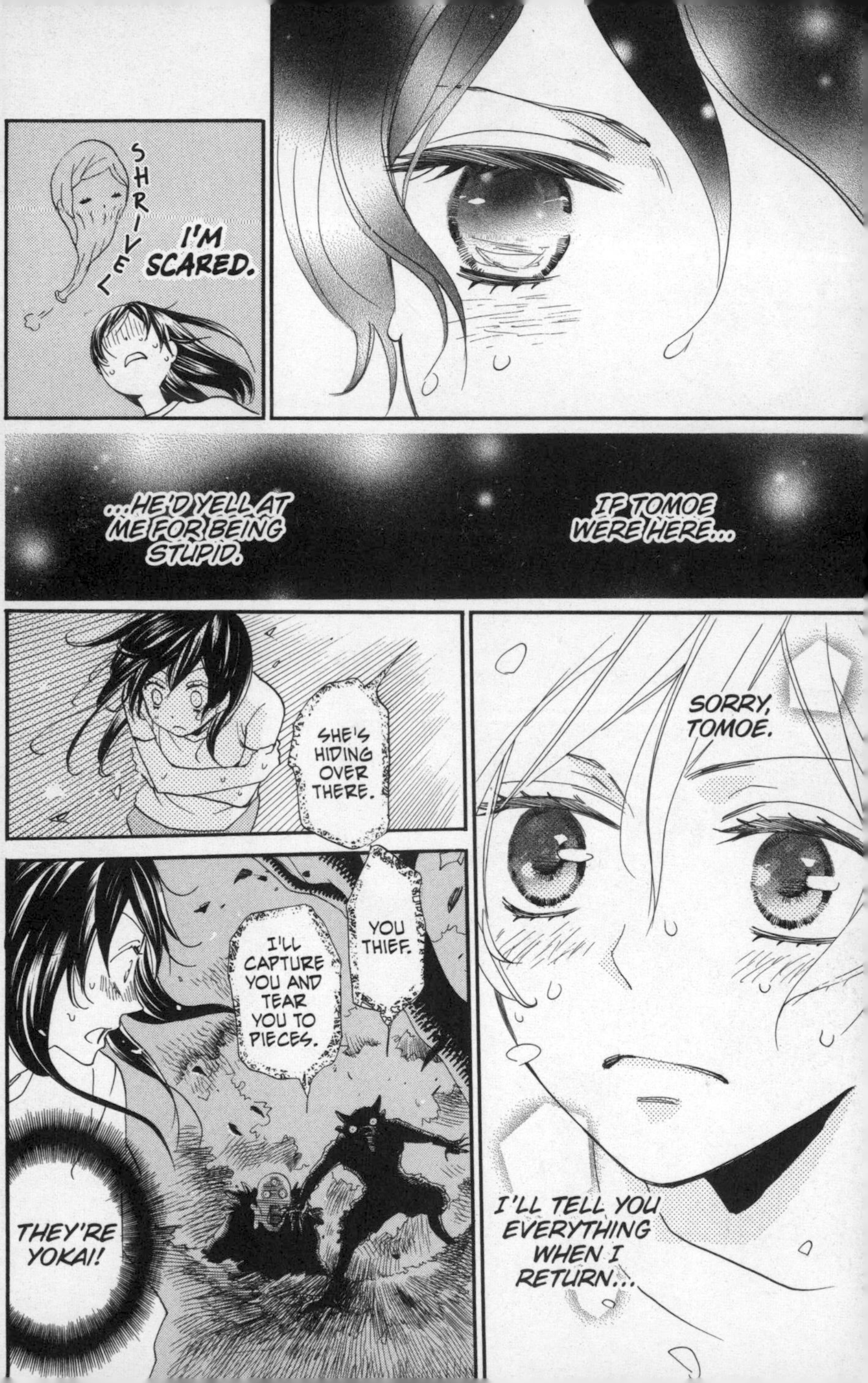
SHRIVEL
I'M SCARED.
IF TOMOE WERE HERE...
...HE'D YELL AT ME FOR BEING STUPID.
SORRY, TOMOE.
I'LL TELL YOU EVERYTHING WHEN I RETURN...
SHE'S HIDING OVER THERE.
YOU THIEF.
I'LL CAPTURE YOU AND TEAR YOU TO PIECES.
THEY'RE YOKAI!

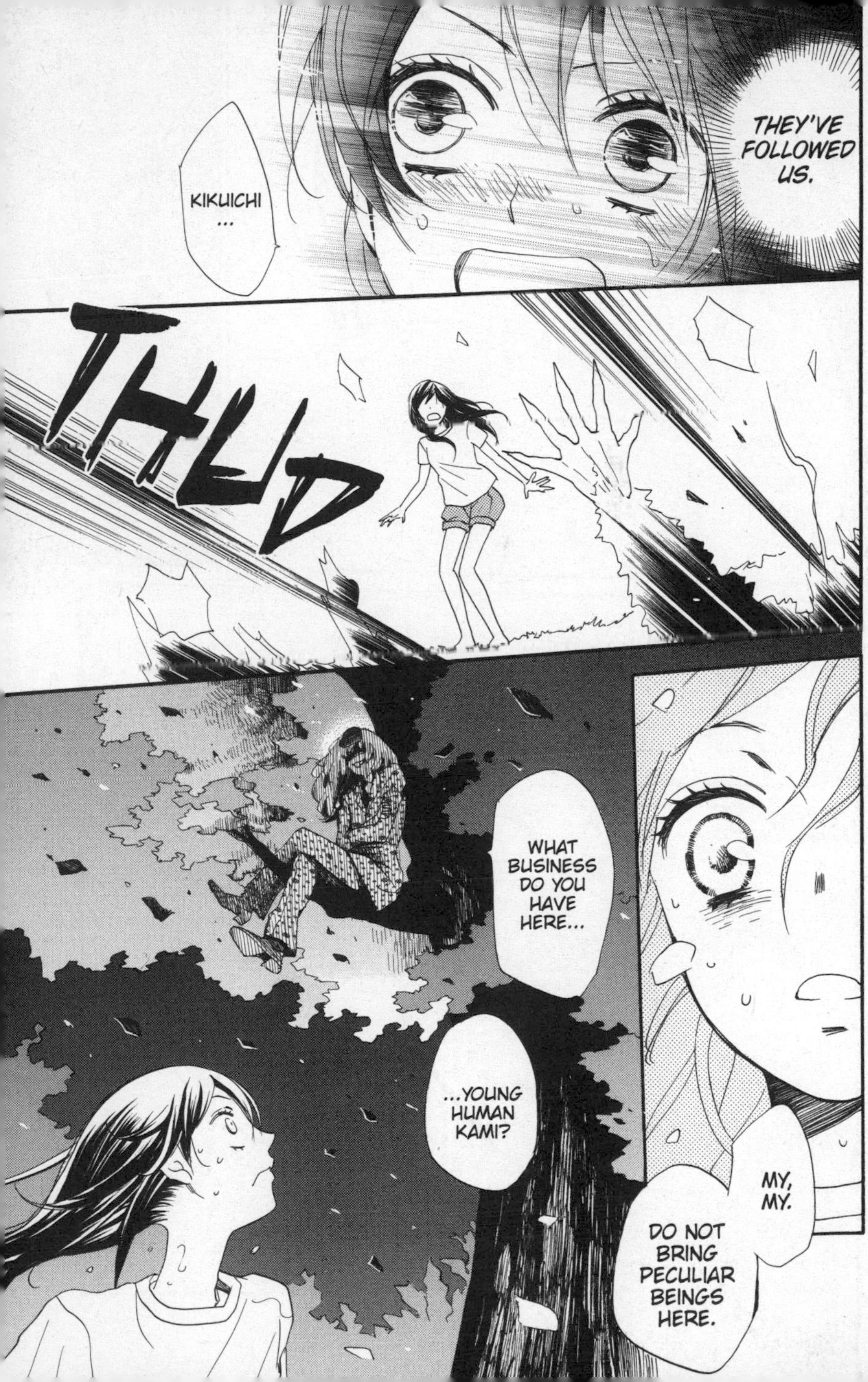
THEY'VE FOLLOWED US.
KIKUICHI ...
THUD
MY, MY.
DO NOT BRING PECULIAR BEINGS HERE.
WHAT BUSINESS DO YOU HAVE HERE...
...YOUNG HUMAN KAMI?

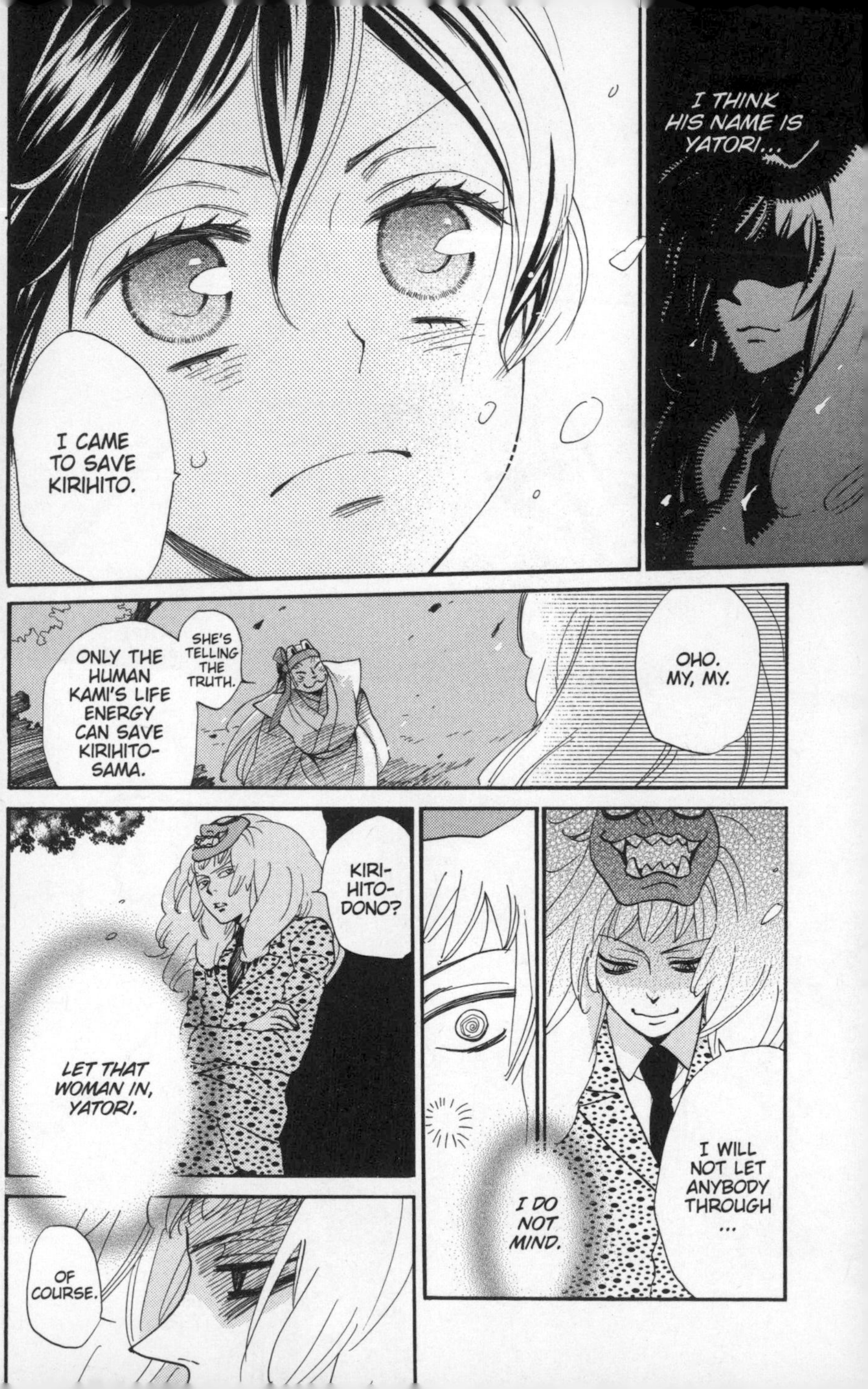
I THINK HIS NAME IS YATORI...
I CAME TO SAVE KIRIHITO.
OHO. MY, MY.
SHE'S TELLING THE TRUTH.
ONLY THE HUMAN KAMI'S LIFE ENERGY CAN SAVE KIRIHITO-SAMA.
I WILL NOT LET ANYBODY THROUGH ...
I DO NOT MIND.
KIRI-HITO-DONO?
LET THAT WOMAN IN, YATORI.
OF COURSE.

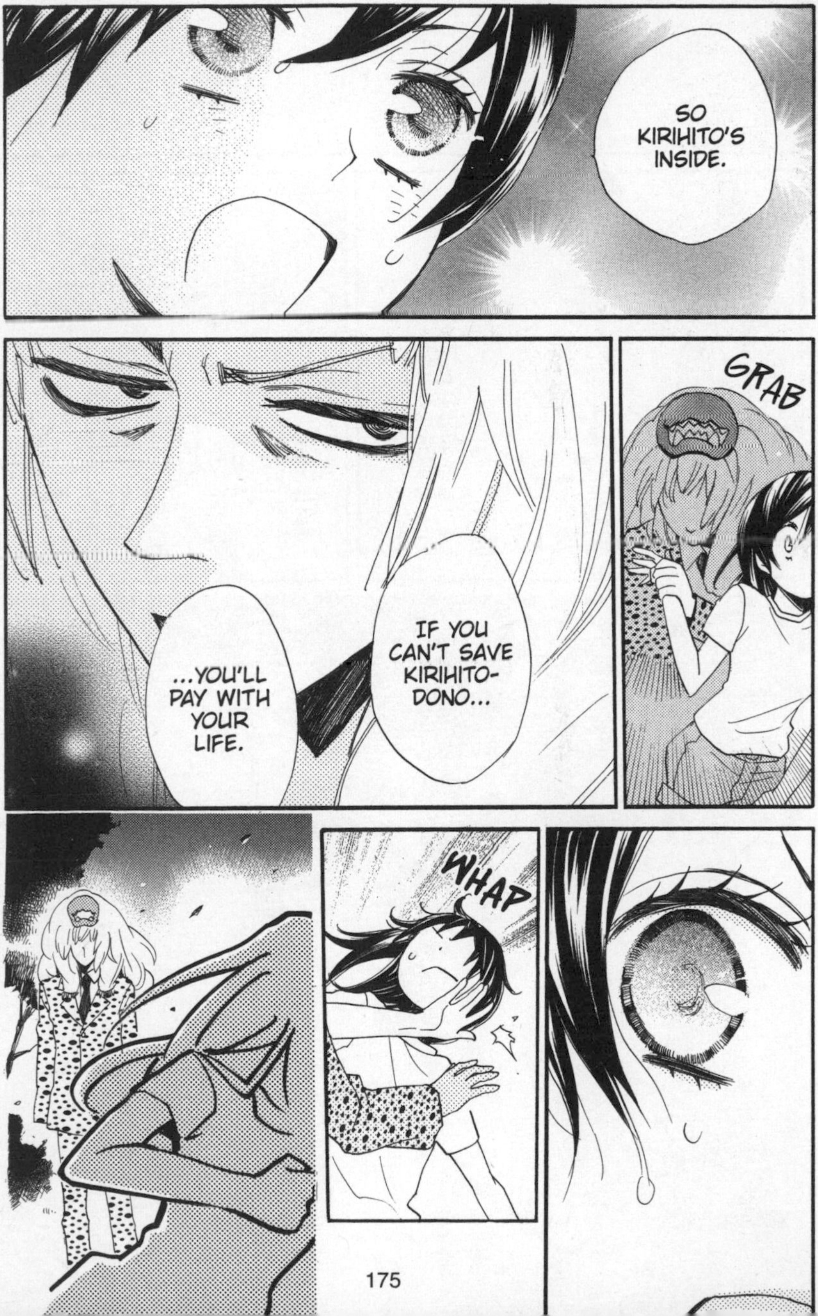
SO KIRIHITO'S INSIDE.
GRAB
IF YOU CAN'T SAVE KIRIHITO-DONO...
...YOU'LL PAY WITH YOUR LIFE.
WHAP

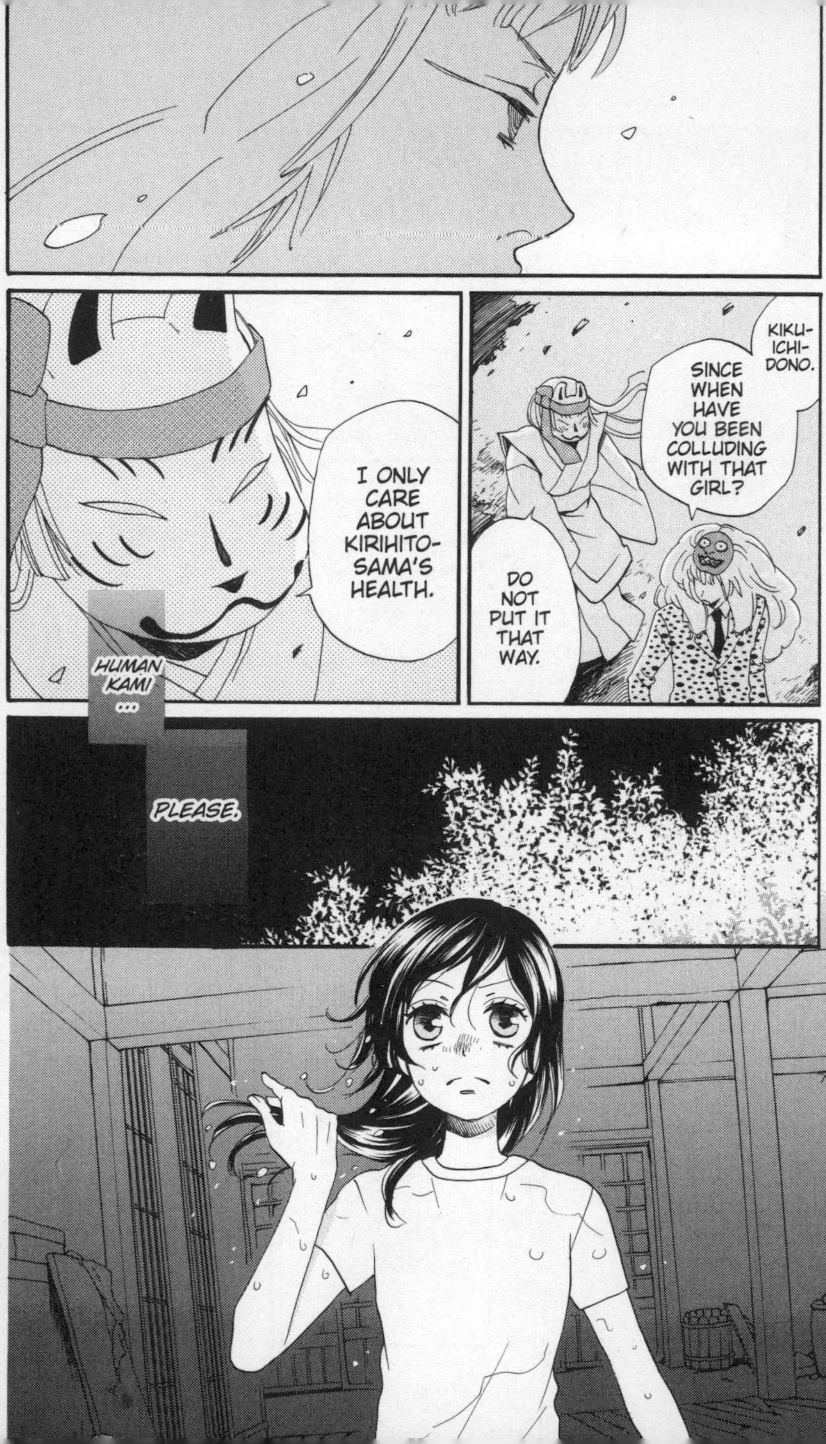
KIKU-ICHI-DONO.
SINCE WHEN HAVE YOU BEEN COLLUDING WITH THAT GIRL?
DO NOT PUT IT THAT WAY.
I ONLY CARE ABOUT KIRIHITO-SAMA'S HEALTH.
HUMAN KAMI...
PLEASE.

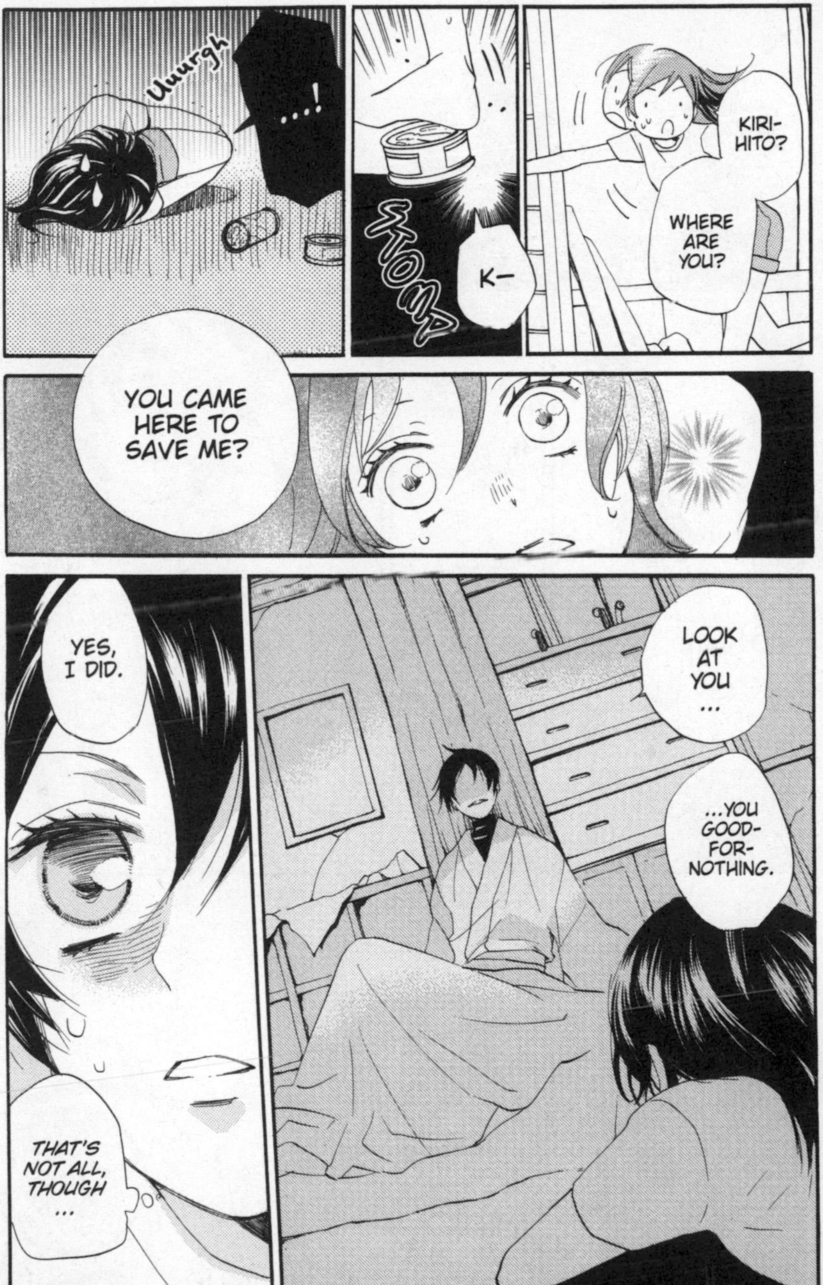
KIRI-HITO?
WHERE ARE YOU?
STOMP
K—
Uuurgh
...!
YOU CAME HERE TO SAVE ME?
LOOK AT YOU ...
...YOU GOOD-FOR-NOTHING.
YES, I DID.
THAT'S NOT ALL, THOUGH ...

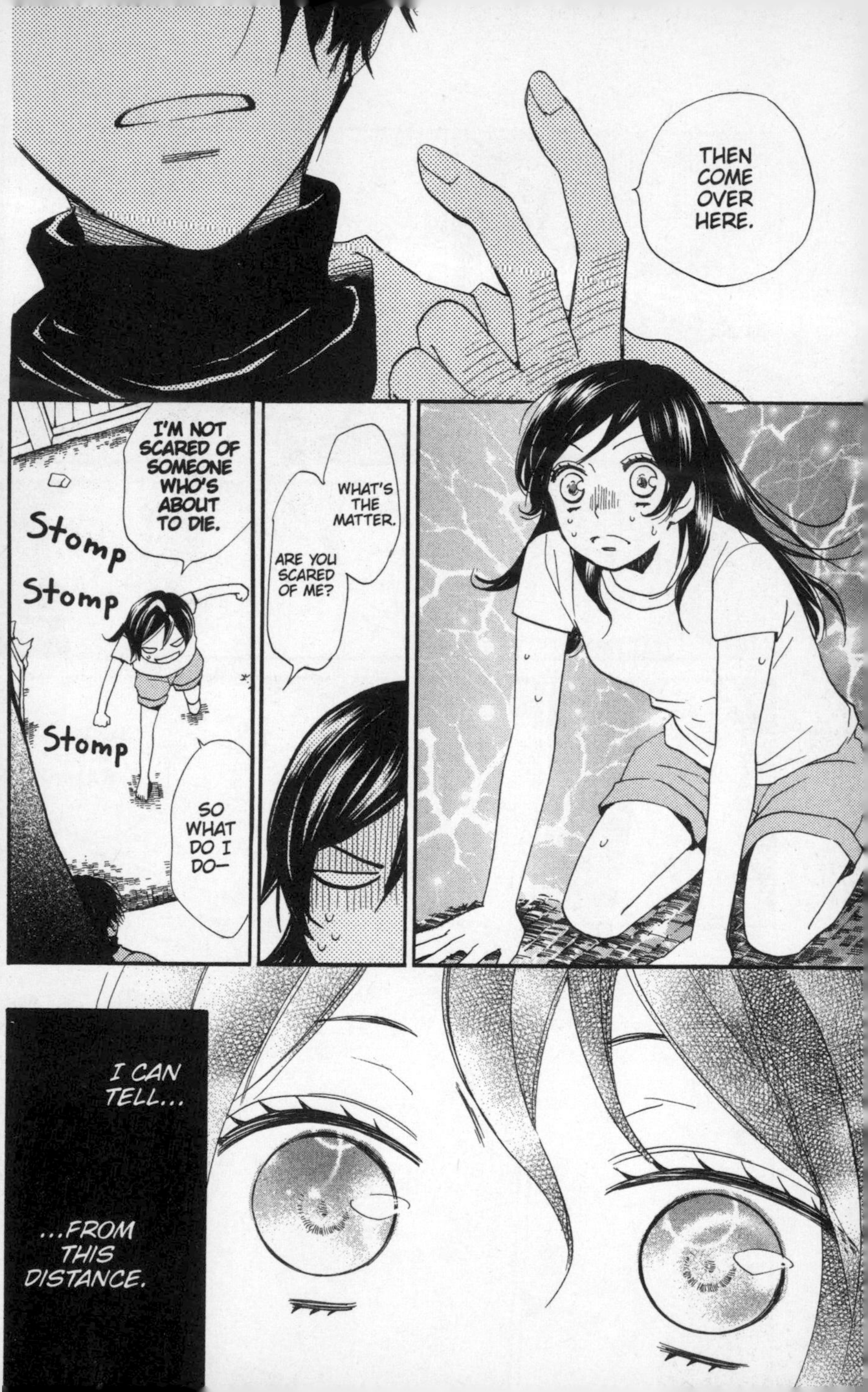
THEN COME OVER HERE.
WHAT'S THE MATTER.
ARE YOU SCARED OF ME?
I'M NOT SCARED OF SOMEONE WHO'S ABOUT TO DIE.
Stomp
Stomp
Stomp
SO WHAT DO I DO—
I CAN TELL...
...FROM THIS DISTANCE.

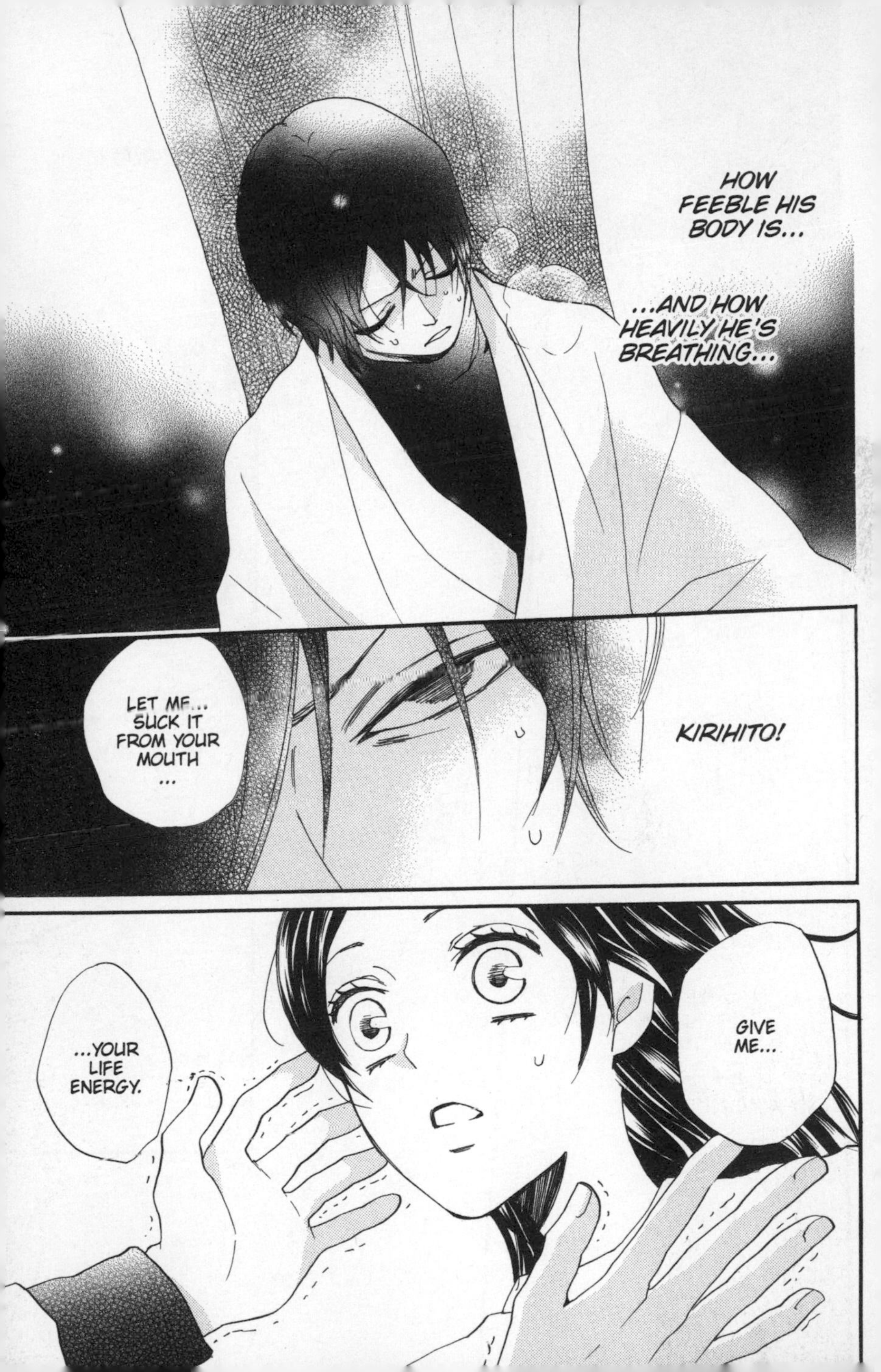
HOW FEEBLE HIS BODY IS...
...AND HOW HEAVILY HE'S BREATHING...
KIRIHITO!
LET ME... SUCK IT FROM YOUR MOUTH ...
GIVE ME...
...YOUR LIFE ENERGY.

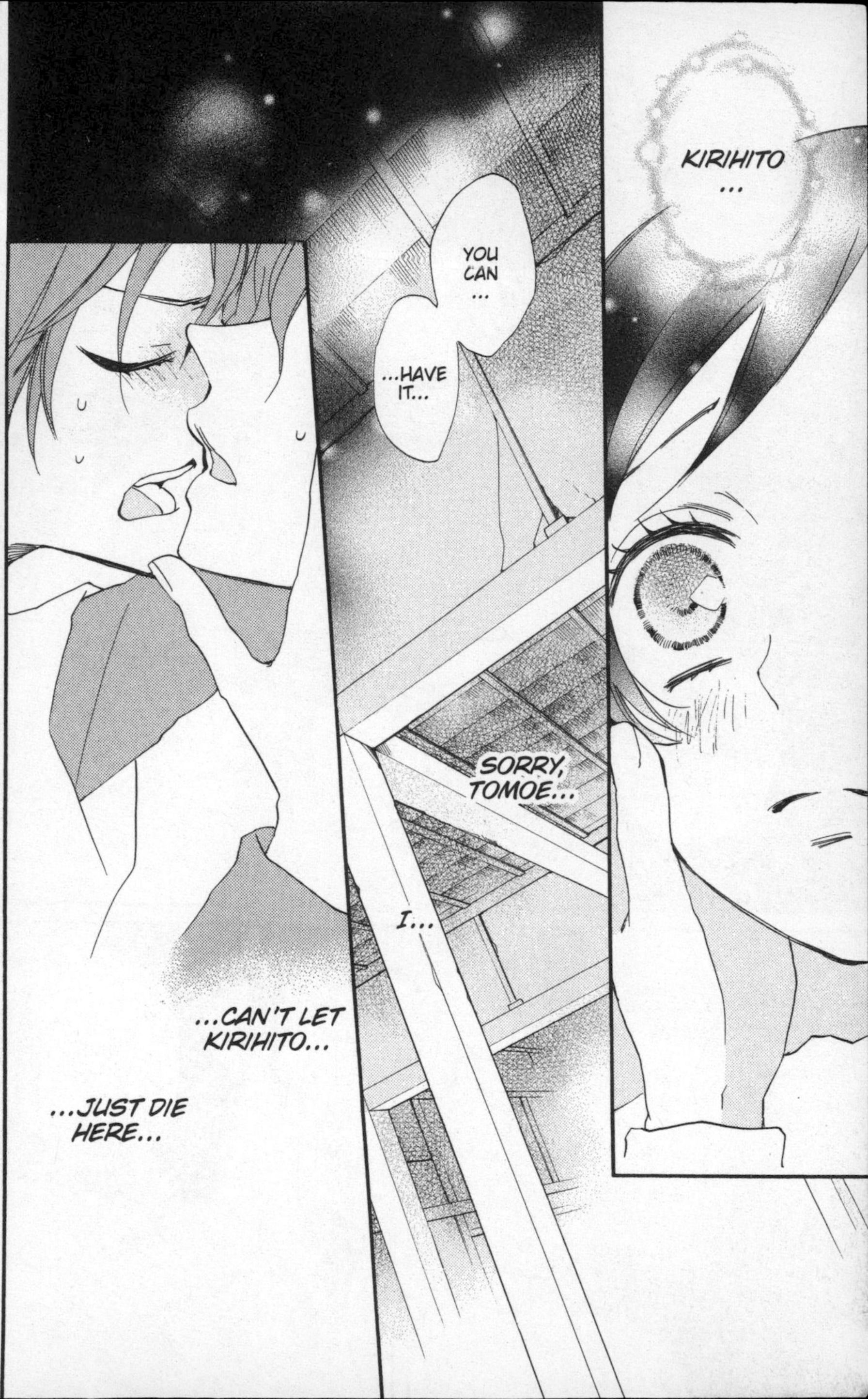
KIRIHITO ...
YOU CAN ...
...HAVE IT...
SORRY, TOMOE...
I...
...CAN'T LET KIRIHITO...
...JUST DIE HERE...

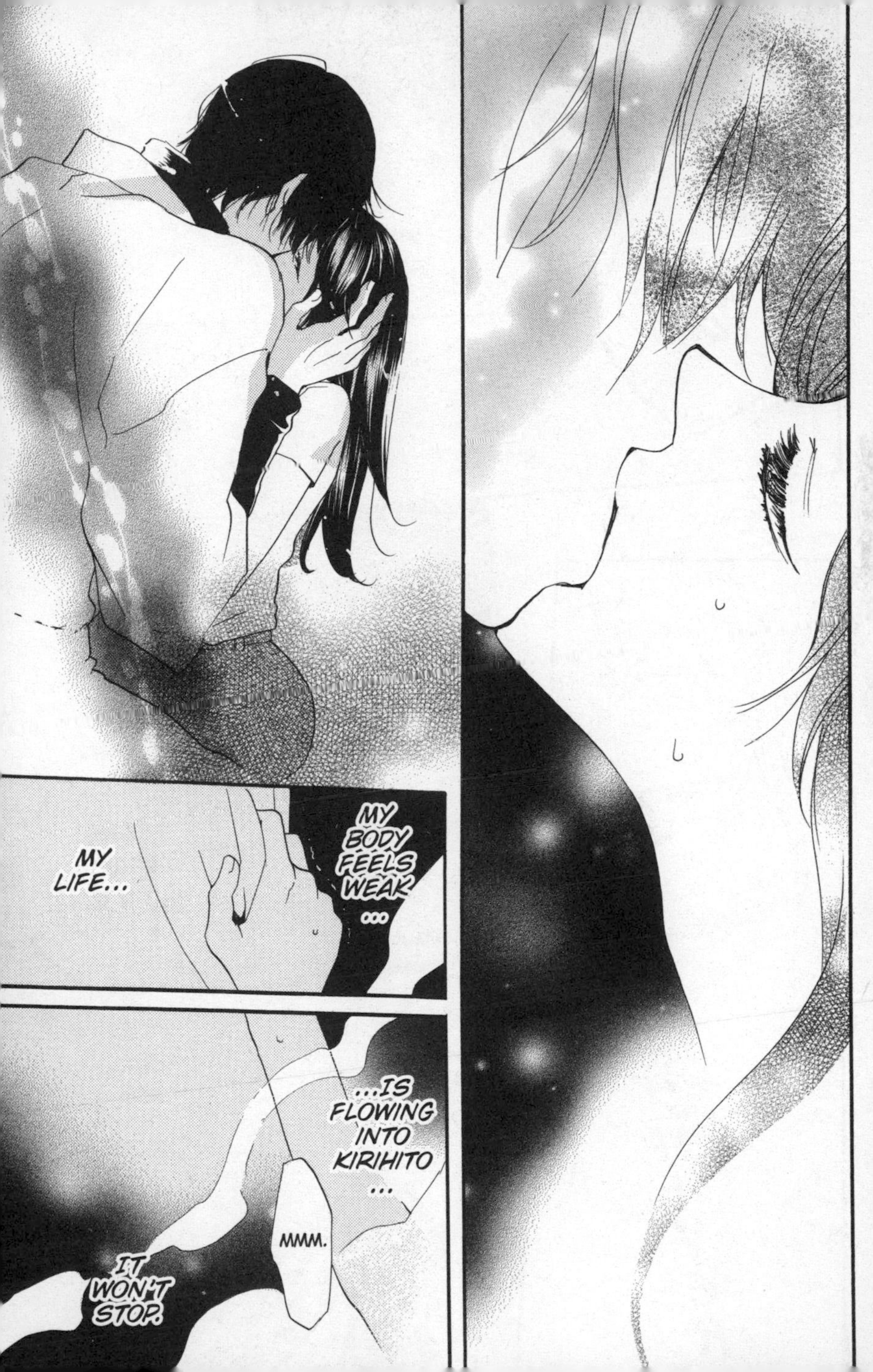
MY BODY FEELS WEAK...
MY LIFE...
...IS FLOWING INTO KIRIHITO...
MMM.
IT WON'T STOP.

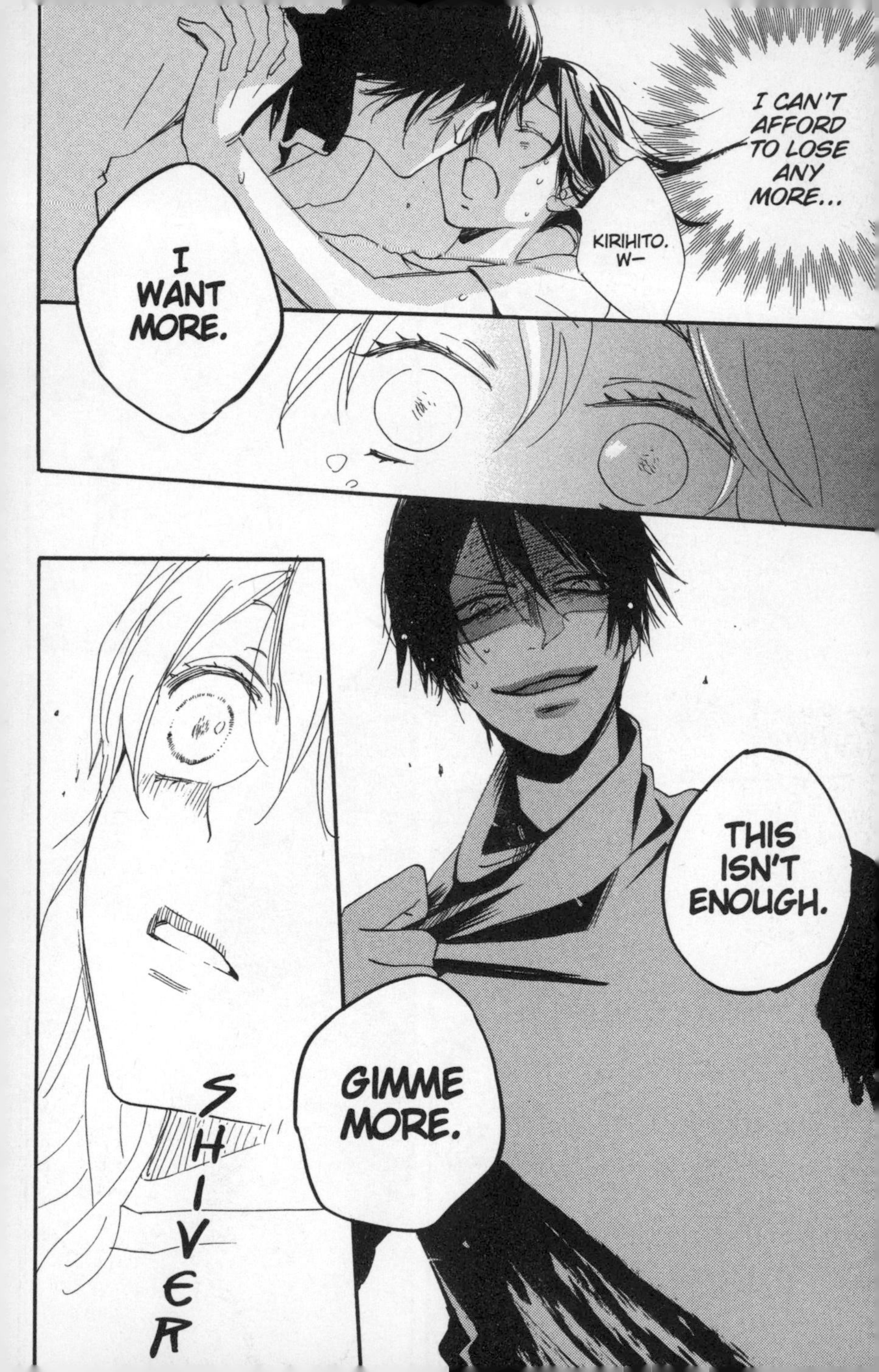
I CAN'T AFFORD TO LOSE ANY MORE...
KIRIHITO. W—
I WANT MORE.
THIS ISN'T ENOUGH.
GIMME MORE.
SHIVER

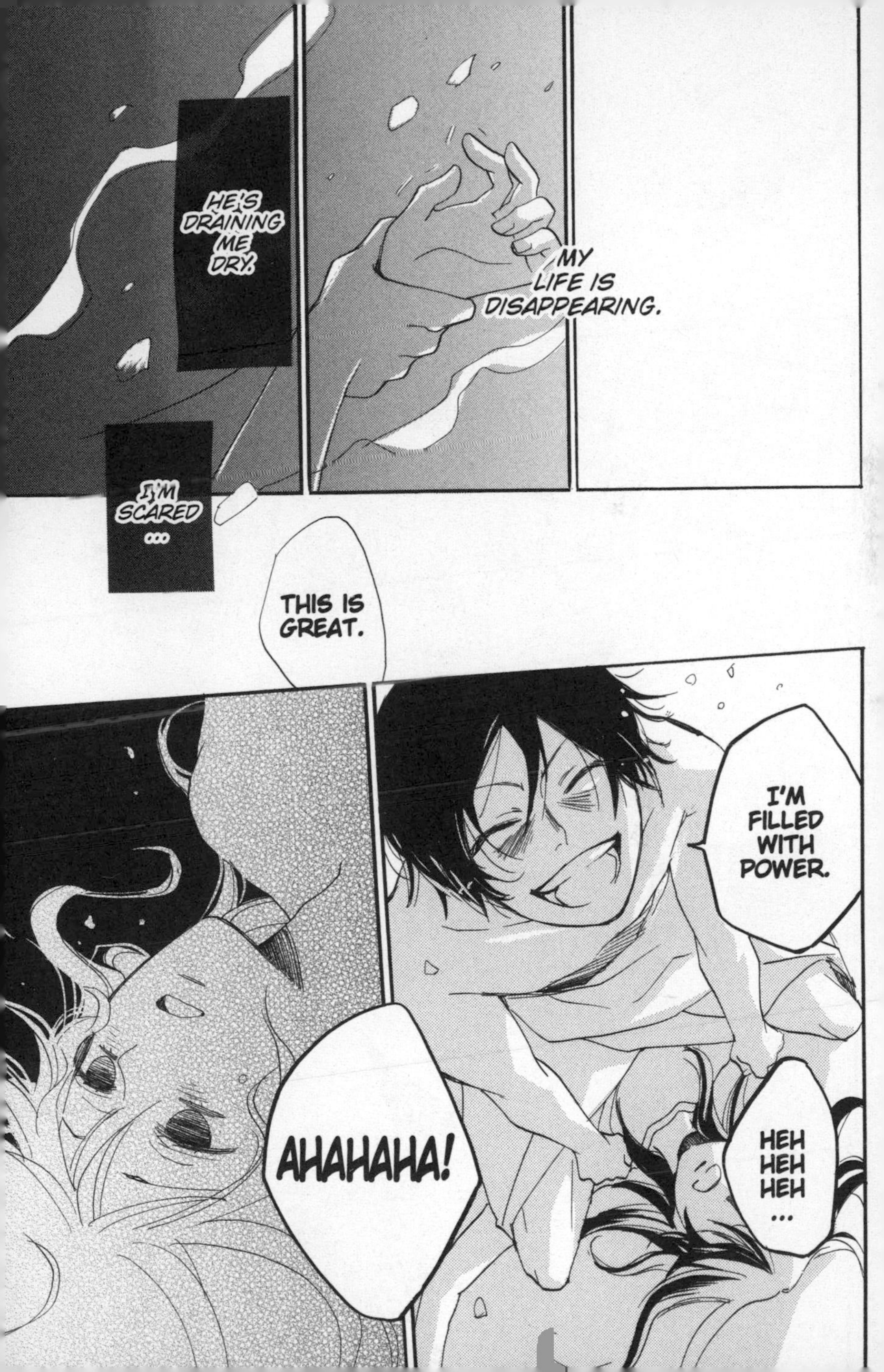
MY LIFE IS DISAPPEARING.
HE'S DRAINING ME DRY.
I'M SCARED...
THIS IS GREAT.
I'M FILLED WITH POWER.
HEH HEH HEH...
AHAHAHA!

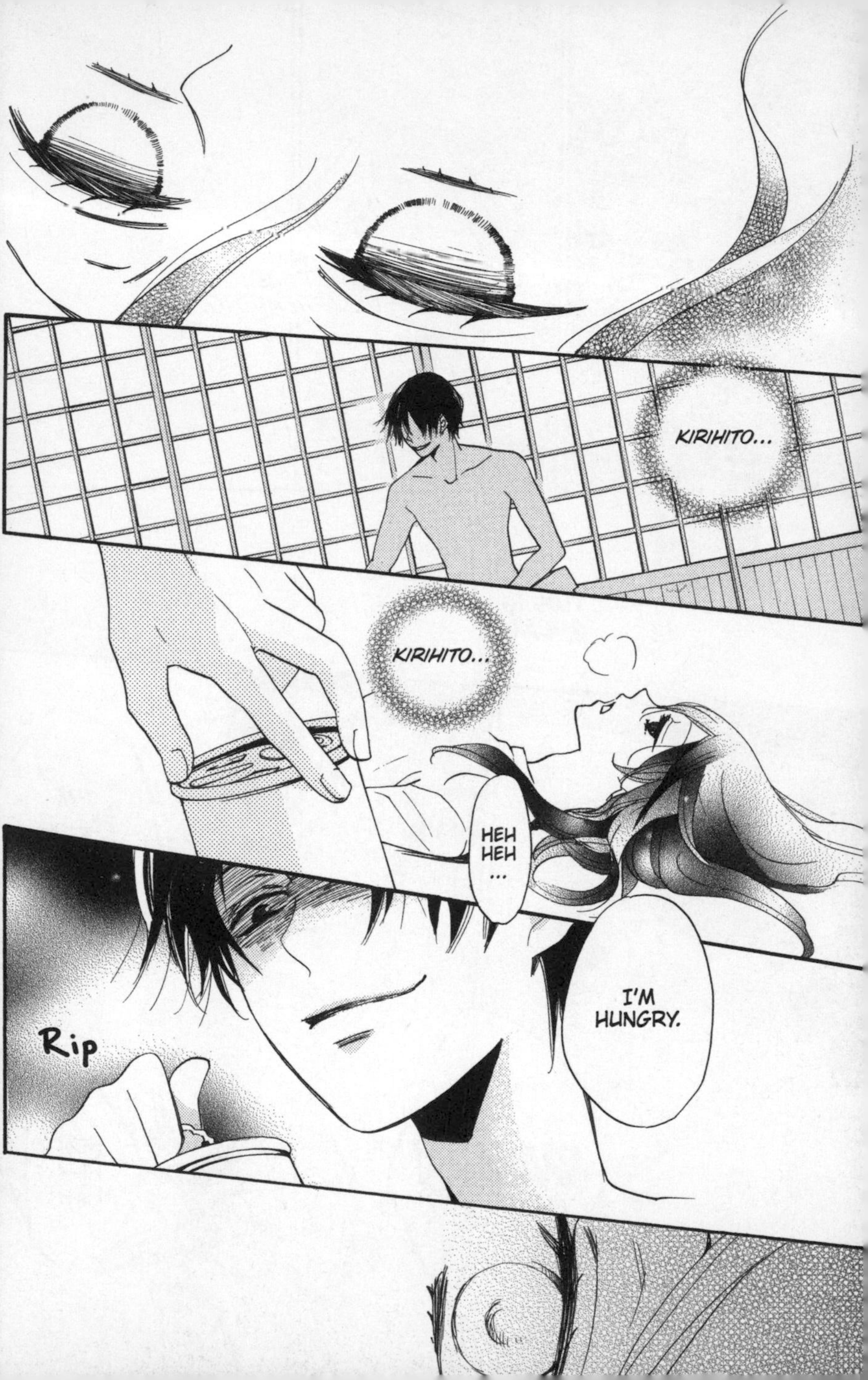
KIRIHITO...
KIRIHITO...
HEH HEH ...
I'M HUNGRY.
Rip

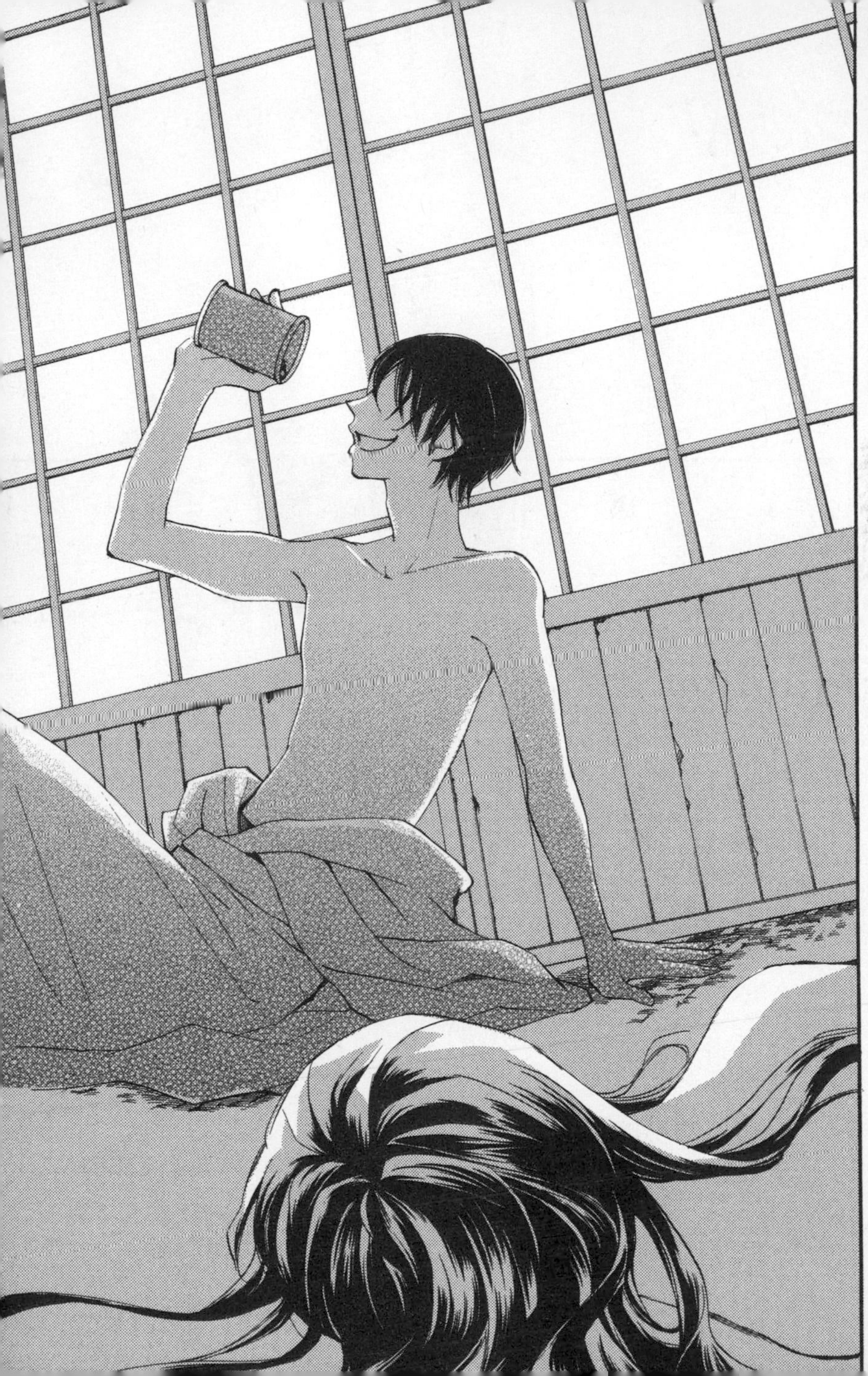

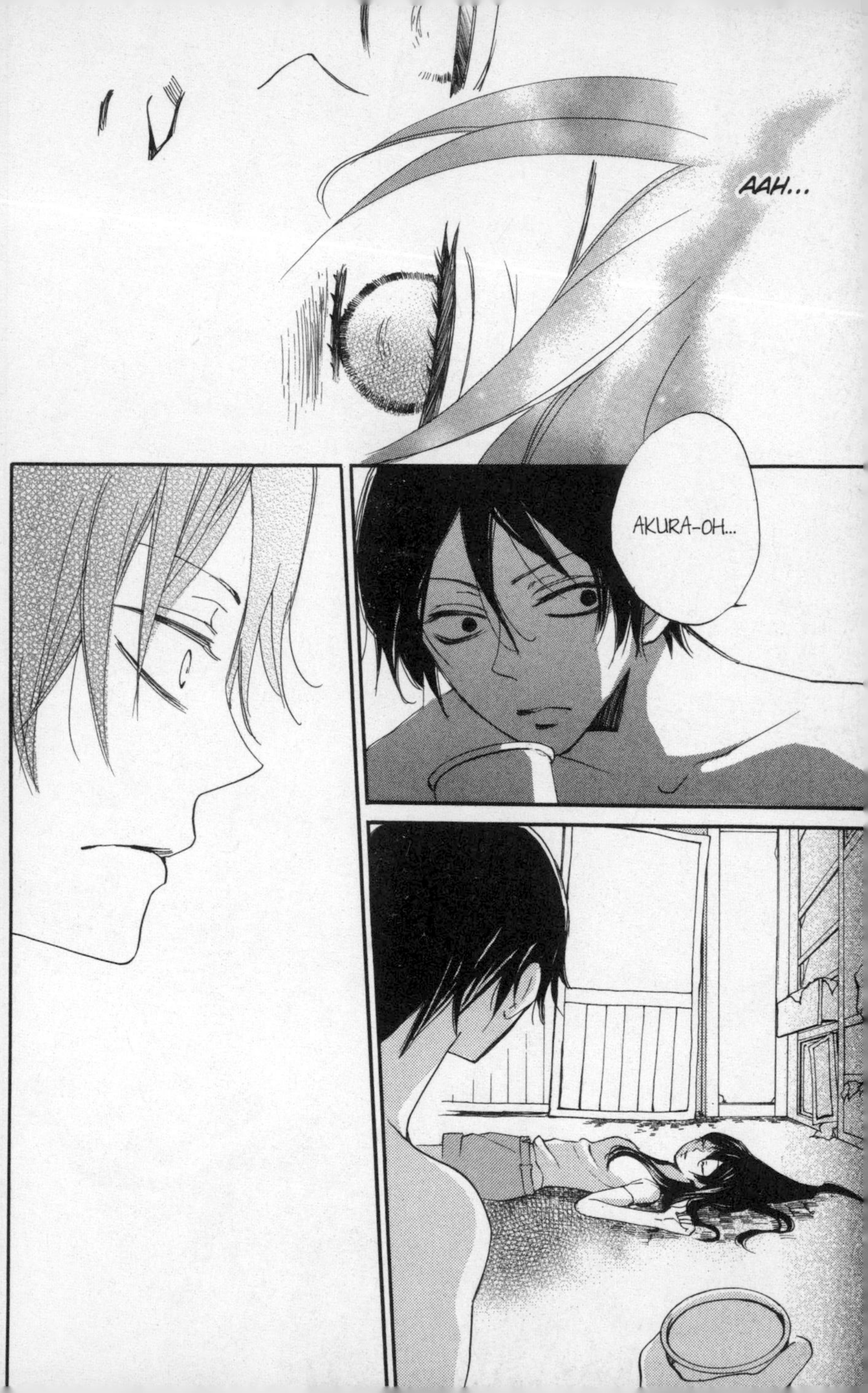
AAH...
AKURA-OH...

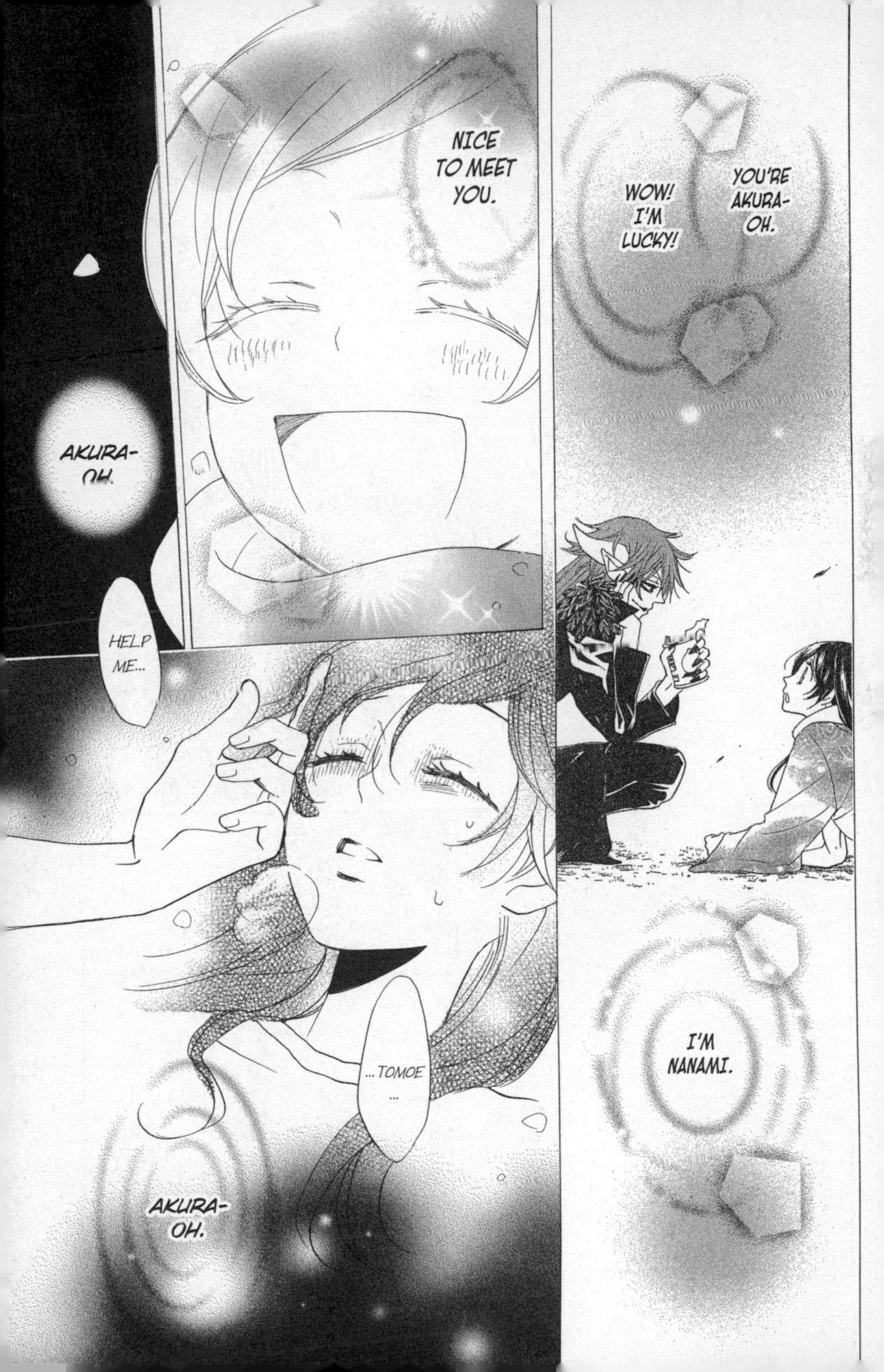
YOU'RE AKURA-OH.
WOW! I'M LUCKY!
I'M NANAMI.
NICE TO MEET YOU.
AKURA-OH.
HELP ME...
...TOMOE ...
AKURA-OH.

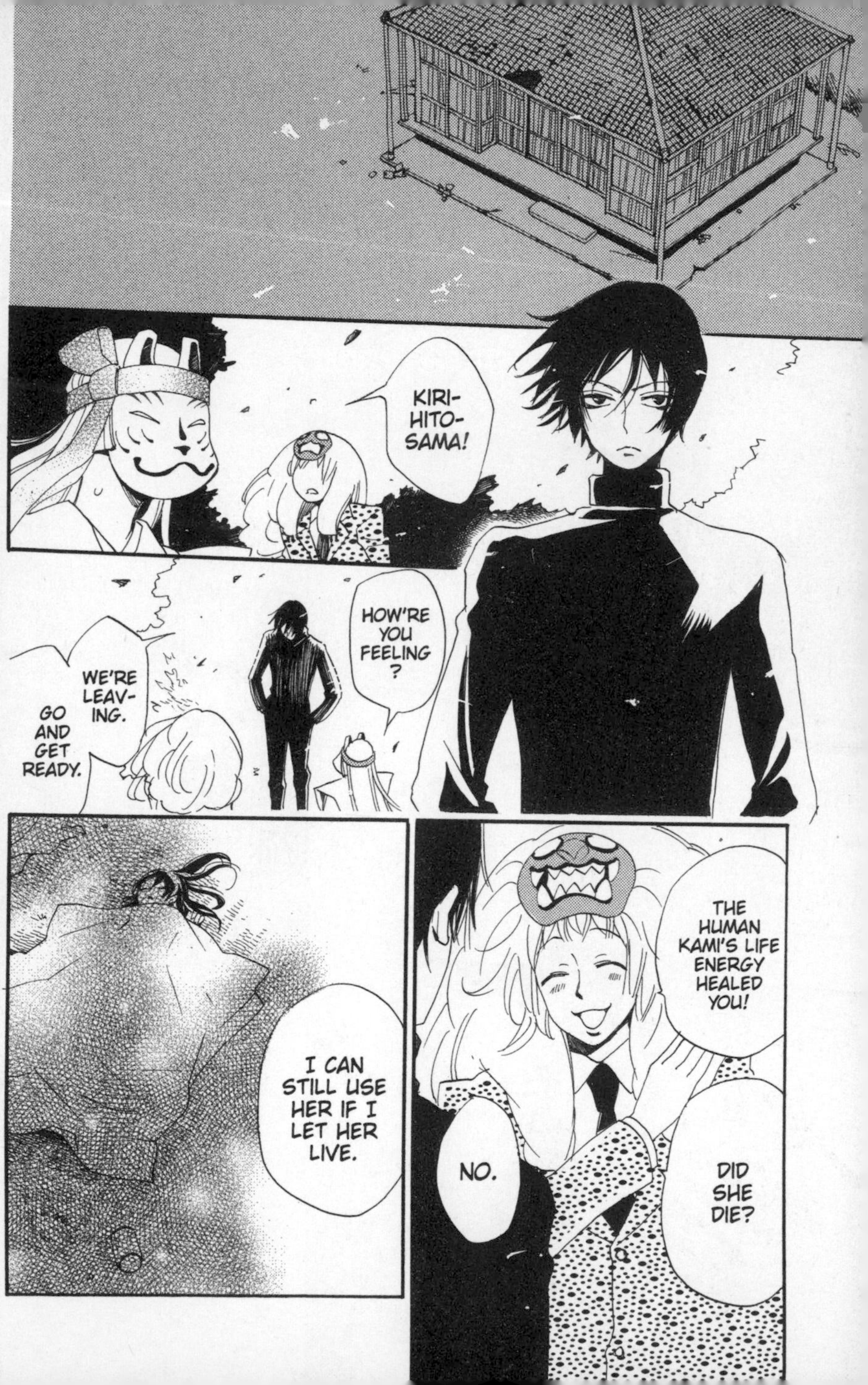
KIRI-HITO-SAMA!
HOW'RE YOU FEELING?
WE'RE LEAVING.
GO AND GET READY.
THE HUMAN KAMI'S LIFE ENERGY HEALED YOU!
DID SHE DIE?
NO.
I CAN STILL USE HER IF I LET HER LIVE.

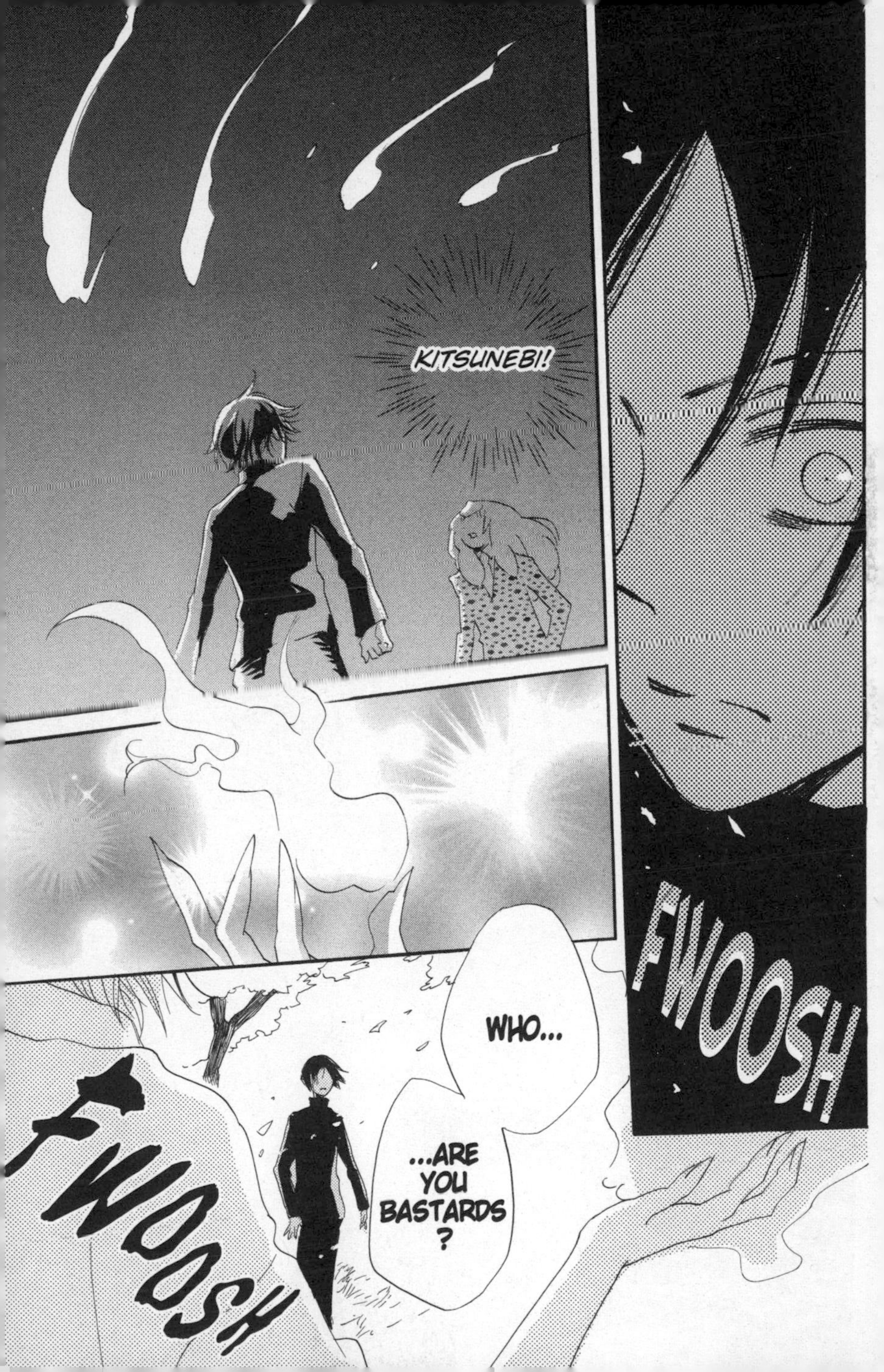
FWOOSH
KITSUNEBI!
WHO...
...ARE YOU BASTARDS?
FWOOSH

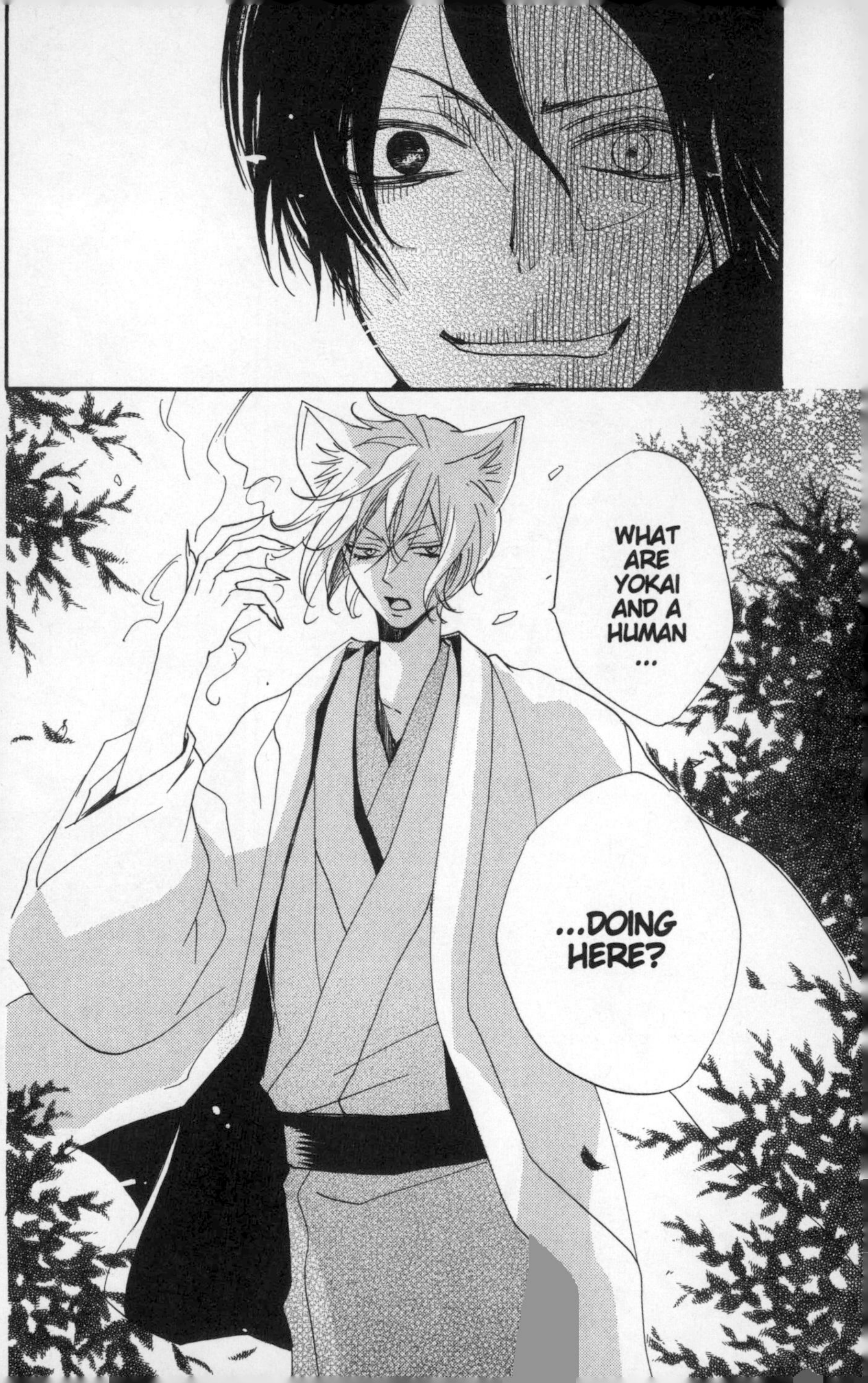
WHAT ARE YOKAI AND A HUMAN ...
...DOING HERE?

The Otherworld

Ayakashi is an archaic term for yokai.

Kami are Shinto deities or spirits. The word can be used for a range of creatures, from nature spirits to strong and dangerous gods.

Komainu are a pair of guardian statues placed at the gate of a shrine, usually carved of stone. Depending on the shrine, they can be lions, foxes, or cows.

Onibi-warashi are like will-o'-the-wisps.

Shinshi are birds, beasts, insects or fish that have a special relationship with a kami.

Tengu are a type of yokai. They are sometimes associated with excess pride.

Tochigami (or *jinushigami*) are deities of a specific area of land.

Yokai are demons, monsters or goblins.

Honorifics

-chan is a diminutive most often used with babies, children or teenage girls.

-dono roughly means "my lord," although not in the aristocratic sense.

-kun is used by persons of superior rank to their juniors. It can sometimes have a familiar connotation.

-san is a standard honorific similar to Mr., Mrs., Miss, or Ms.

-sama is used with people of much higher rank.

Notes

Page 15, panel 4: Valentine chocolates
In Japan on Valentine's Day, women buy chocolates for the men in their lives. Men return the favor on White Day.

Page 16, panel 3: Christmas, festival for lovers
Christmas is considered a romantic date night in Japan.

Page 16, panel 4: Okinawa
Okinawa is the southernmost island in the Japanese chain and has a tropical climate similar to Hawaii.

Page 33, panel 2: Hamburger steak
Japanese hamburgers are closer to Salisbury steak or meatloaf than the hamburgers Americans are used to. The ground meat is mixed with breadcrumbs, egg and sautéed onions and served on a plate rather than a bun. Sometimes the hamburger is topped with a fried egg.

Page 76, panel 2: Shuri castle
The palace capitol of the Ryukyu kingdom (15th to 19th century) and now a popular tourist spot. The castle has been reconstructed after being almost destroyed in the Battle of Okinawa in 1945.

Page 76, panel 2: Taco rice
A local Okinawan food in which taco ingredients are served over rice.

Page 76, panel 2: Naha city
The prefectural capital of Okinawa and the center of Okinawan politics, economy and culture.

Page 80, panel 3: Okinawan lion
Called *shisa* in Japanese, these statues are meant to keep out evil and are usually placed in pairs at entrances, on roofs and on gateposts.

Page 106, panel 6: Zan
Okinawan mermaid yokai. Dugongs, a marine mammal, are also called *zan*.

Page 107, panel 2: Robe of feathers
Myths about a robe of feathers exist all over Japan and are similar to the Swan Maiden fairy tale, where a robe of swan feathers enables the maiden to fly.

Page 119, author note: Shinto home shrine, *Cleyera japonica*
Home shrines are small shrines set up inside homes and offices. It is customary to worship before your home shrine every morning and evening.

Clyera japonica are believed to be holy trees that separate the human world from sacred territory. Fresh branches are placed in front of home shrines and should be replaced before they wilt.

Julietta Suzuki's debut manga *Hoshi ni Naru Hi* (The Day One Becomes a Star) appeared in the 2004 *Hana to Yume Plus*. Her other books include *Akuma to Dolce* (The Devil and Sweets) and *Karakuri Odette*. Born in December in Fukuoka Prefecture, she enjoys having movies play in the background while she works on her manga.

KAMISAMA KISS
VOL. 18
Shojo Beat Edition

STORY AND ART BY
Julietta Suzuki

English Translation & Adaptation/Tomo Kimura
Touch-up Art & Lettering/Joanna Estep
Design/Yukiko Whitley
Editor/Pancha Diaz

KAMISAMA HAJIMEMASHITA by Julietta Suzuki
© Julietta Suzuki 2014
All rights reserved.
First published in Japan in 2014 by HAKUSENSHA, Inc., Tokyo.
English language translation rights arranged with
HAKUSENSHA, Inc., Tokyo.

Printed in the U.S.A.

Published by VIZ Media, LLC
P.O. Box 77010
San Francisco, CA 94107

10 9 8 7 6 5 4 3 2 1
First printing, June 2015

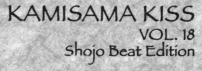

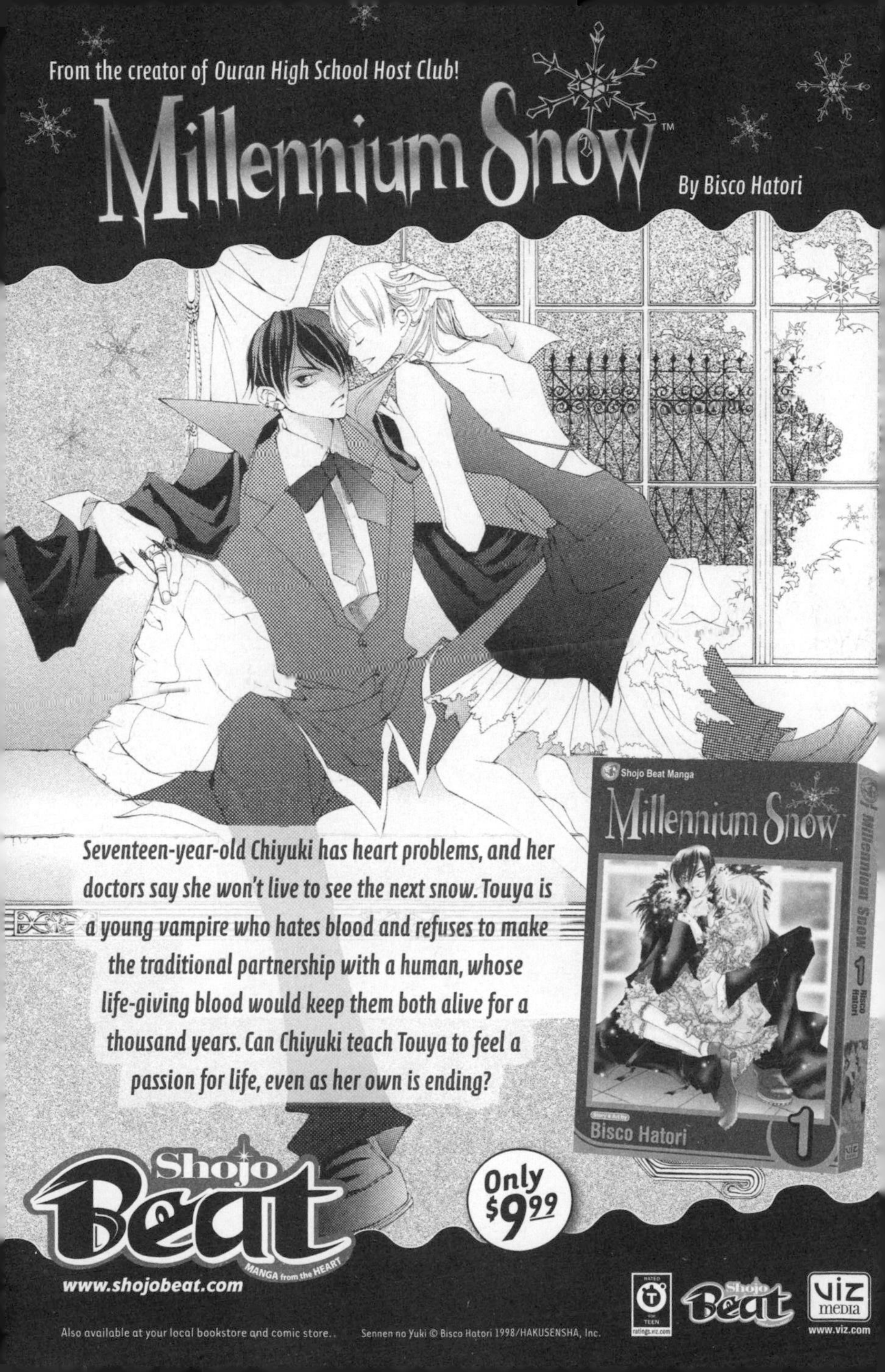
From the creator of Ouran High School Host Club!
Millennium Snow™
By Bisco Hatori
Seventeen-year-old Chiyuki has heart problems, and her doctors say she won't live to see the next snow. Touya is a young vampire who hates blood and refuses to make the traditional partnership with a human, whose life-giving blood would keep them both alive for a thousand years. Can Chiyuki teach Touya to feel a passion for life, even as her own is ending?
Shojo Beat Manga
Millennium Snow
Bisco Hatori
1
Only $9.99
Shojo Beat
MANGA from the HEART
www.shojobeat.com
RATED T TEEN
ratings.viz.com
Shojo Beat
VIZ media
www.viz.com
Also available at your local bookstore and comic store.
Sennen no Yuki © Bisco Hatori 1998/HAKUSENSHA, Inc.

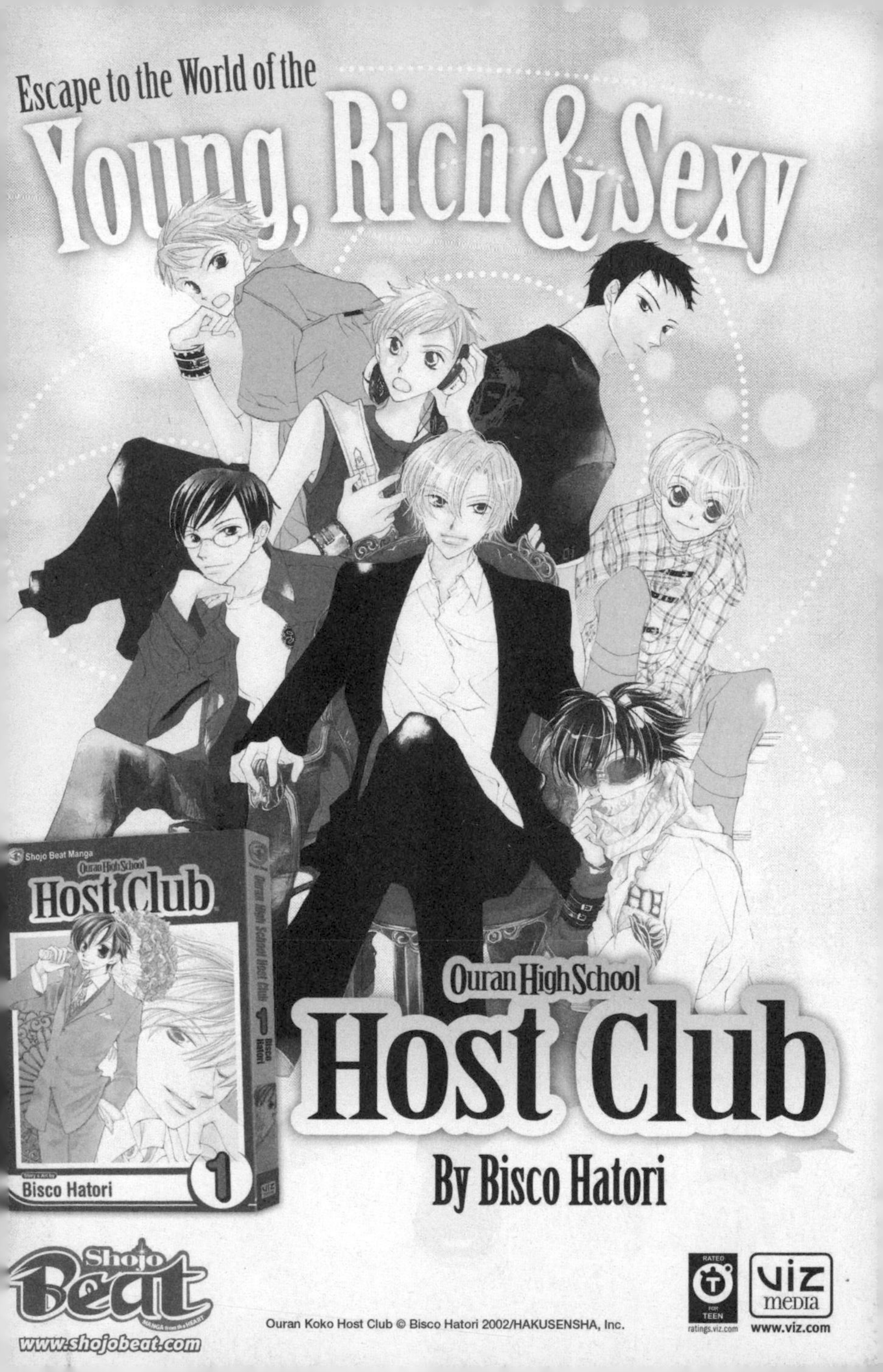
Escape to the World of the
Young, Rich & Sexy
Shojo Beat Manga
Ouran High School
Host Club
Ouran High School Host Club 1 Bisco Hatori
Bisco Hatori
1
Ouran High School
Host Club
By Bisco Hatori
Shojo Beat
www.shojobeat.com
Ouran Koko Host Club © Bisco Hatori 2002/HAKUSENSHA, Inc.
RATED T FOR TEEN
ratings.viz.com
VIZ media
www.viz.com

This is the last page.

In keeping with the original Japanese comic format, this book reads from right to left—so action, sound effects, and word balloons are completely reversed. This preserves the orientation of the original artwork—plus, it's fun! Check out the diagram shown here to get the hang of things, and then turn to the other side of the book to get started!